MW01124779

American Folk Music and Musicians Series

GREENBACK DOLLAR

The Incredible Rise
of The Kingston Trio

WILLIAM J. BUSH

*American Folk Music
and Musicians, No. 17*

THE SCARECROW PRESS, INC.
Lanham • Toronto • Plymouth, UK
2013

Published by Scarecrow Press, Inc.
A wholly owned subsidary of The Rowman & Littlefield Publishing Group, Inc.
4501 Forbes Boulevard, Suite 200, Lanham, Maryland 20706
www.rowman.com

10 Thornbury Road, Plymouth PL6 7PP, United Kingdom

British Library Cataloguing in Publication Information Available

Library of Congress Cataloging-in-Publication Data

Bush, William J., 1946–
  Greenback dollar : the incredible rise of the Kingston Trio / William J. Bush.
    pages cm. — (American folk music and musicians ; no. 17)
  Includes bibliographical references and index.
  ISBN 978-0-8108-8192-1 (pbk. : alk. paper) — ISBN 978-0-8108-8285-0
(ebook) 1. Kingston Trio. 2. Folk singers—United States—Biography.
I. Title.
  ML421.K554B87 2013
  782.421620092'2—dc23   2012031243

∞™ The paper used in this publication meets the minimum requirements of
American National Standard for Information Sciences—Permanence of Paper
for Printed Library Materials, ANSI/NISO Z39.48-1992. Printed in the United
States of America.

For Nick

CONTENTS

FOREWORD

The Kingston Trio was the most popular folk music act from the late 1950s through much of the 1960s. Bill Bush has written the first history of this most important group, using a wide variety of primary and secondary sources, including numerous interviews with all four of the group's members—Bob Shane, Nick Reynolds, Dave Guard, and John Stewart—which give important insights into their personalities, relationships, and experiences. There is much detail on their numerous record albums, public performances, and private lives. The Kingston Trio had an immense influence not only on the direction of popular music at the time, but also on the musical lives of many who led the developing folk music revival, including Joan Baez and Bob Dylan. This volume is a valuable addition to such books in the series as Hank Reineke's biographies *Ramblin' Jack Elliott* and *Arlo Guthrie* and David Dunaway's *A Pete Seeger Discography*, as well as a future study of the blues collector Lawrence Gellert and an edition of the collected writings of Israel G. Young, who owned the Folklore Center in Greenwich Village, which became the heart of folk music in the United States from the late 1950s into the early 1970s.

—Ronald D. Cohen
Series Editor
American Folk Music and Musicians

INTRODUCTION: THE BOOM
HEARD ROUND THE WORLD

In November of 1958, when "Tom Dooley" by The Kingston Trio became the number one song in America, there was nothing like it on the *Billboard* charts.

Certainly, folk music and folk-*like* music was not unknown to the masses. Beginning in the 1940s, such performers as Woody Guthrie, Huddie Ledbetter, Pete Seeger, Burl Ives, Cisco Houston, and many other "folk" had exposed urban audiences to traditional, country, blues, and topical song genres. In the early 1950s, The Weavers again brought folk-oriented music to the pop mainstream with "Goodnight Irene" and "Kisses Sweeter than Wine" only to disappear under the weight of McCarthyism and "Red Scare" blacklisting.

By the mid-1950s, folk music again came to the fore with Harry Belafonte, the King of Calypso; The Easy Riders ("Marianne"); The Folksay Trio, who evolved into The Tarriers ("The Banana Boat Song" and "Cindy, Oh Cindy"); and Lonnie Donegan in England ("Rock Island Line"). And while yet another folk revival may well have been just bubbling under, Dick Weissman—writer, musician, and former member of The Journeymen—pointed out that "the beginning of the real folk-pop boom came with the performances and recordings of the Kingston Trio."[1] It would be the biggest, longest, loudest, and musically earth-shaking boom of all. And it all started with "Tom Dooley."

"That record, *Tom Dooley*, really captured the attention of the industry. It made folk music a household word," said Joe Hickerson, folk performer and co-writer of "Where Have All the Flowers Gone" with Pete Seeger. "It was just amazing. It sent ripples, *tidal waves*, through the folk music industry that lasted for years—and the things that came along after it because of that recording and the Trio's success with subsequent recordings."[2]

The question is, why? Perhaps it was simply a backlash against the raucous rock 'n' roll craze that had surfaced in the mid-1950s, terrifying some clergymen and parents who saw a swivel-hipped Elvis and other teen greasers as a threat to decency, morality, and parental authority.

Or maybe it was just attrition. By late 1958, rock 'n' roll had pretty much done itself in. Elvis's music had gotten progressively tamer and his hair shorter thanks to an Army barber. Jerry Lee Lewis had been hounded off the airwaves in England for marrying his thirteen-year-old cousin, and America didn't like it either. Even Buddy Holly, one of the most inventive of all the '50s rockers, abandoned rock 'n' roll in late 1958 for more "grown up" music, including ballads with lush orchestral arrangements (which, by the way, were played by members of The New York Philharmonic and NBC Symphony). Holly would die in an Iowa plane crash barely three months after his last recording session. The result was a void in popular music just waiting to be filled by something—*anything*—different, and "Tom Dooley" was just quirky enough to be it.

America has always had a warm spot in its heart for the occasional oddball record—from Mrs. Miller to The Chipmunks (who also had a hit in late 1958). Viewed within the context of Top 40 radio, "Tom Dooley" was definitely different—an old song based on the real-life saga of a jealous Confederate Civil War veteran who stabbed his lover to death in 1866 and was caught, tried (twice), and hanged.

Still, "Dooley" didn't just accidentally wind up in the Top 40. It had help from two disc jockeys in Salt Lake City who, after discovering "Tom Dooley" on the Trio's first album, played the song continuously, making it a number one hit in Salt Lake City. They then called their fellow disc jockeys at key stations around the country urging them to play "Tom Dooley." This, in turn, caught the eye of *Billboard* and *Cash Box* trade magazines that published regional disc jockey playlists in each issue—and thus a national hit was born. The old Top 40 maxim "If you play it enough, they will buy it" was certainly true. It is *incredible* that something so simple as "Tom Dooley" could be the prime mover in the evolution of popular music. But it wasn't just *any* three guys playing two chords that made it happen.

The Kingston Trio was formed by three very intelligent, exceptionally talented, and motivated *friends* who loved to sing with each other. Long before The Kingston Trio appealed to the world, the guys appealed to *themselves*. Their personal energy, that oh-so-private alchemy honed through years of hanging out and playing together, gave rise to an American phenomenon the effects of which are still felt today.

The world was filled with talented vocal trios in 1957, far more accomplished and polished than The Kingston version, but none of them had that unique X factor. "It was totally natural," said John Stewart, "and that was a great part of the magic of the Trio; it was that *thing*, that inborn energy that connected with millions of people. It was a force that some groups have and some don't, but it is as real as electricity or running water and it translates to anybody, anywhere in the world."[3]

Indeed, the Trio's impact extended far beyond America and far beyond music. They were as culturally influential as they were musically, not unlike The Beatles (who were Trio fans themselves, by the way) who later appealed to many people on many levels. The Kingston Trio were an ideal role model for the late 1950s: clean-cut, well-behaved (at least publicly), and literate. Parents breathed a sigh of relief. Pink pegged pants were out; striped button-down shirts were in.

The Kingston Trio's persona was friendly, witty, and irresistibly appealing with their collegiate good looks, self-deprecating humor, and let's-have-a-good-time attitude. They were approachable, too. Whether you knew them personally or not, you felt as if you did. They were international stars, but never aloof or above mixing with their fans, especially college students. "It kept us in touch," as Dave Guard put it.[4]

This easy connect extended directly to their music. Virtually any Kingston Trio song could be mastered with two or three simple chords and a capo. They made it look so effortless—and so much fun. This wasn't Mitch Miller and the Gang with their cornball, old-fashioned sing-along chorus. Nor was it The Weavers with their dangerous political overtones. This was The Kingston Trio, three guys from down the block who turned America on to folk music like never before. There had been other urban folk revivals, but it was The Kingston Trio that set the wildfire, single-handedly ushering in the *really* big "folk boom" of the late 1950s and early '60s.

The Kingston Trio placed fourteen albums in the *Billboard* Top 10—with their first five studio albums all reaching number one (a feat unmatched by any other act—before or since) and seven receiving RIAA Gold Album award status—some of which remained on the charts for years.

There were thirty-two original domestic 45 rpm singles releases from the Guard and Stewart Trios, some of which were certified monster hits on their own. Most of these singles were culled from albums, either pushing or pulling album sales along with them—"Tom Dooley," " M.T.A," "The

Tijuana Jail," "A Worried Man," "El Matador," "Bad Man Blunder," "Everglades," "Where Have All The Flowers Gone," "Jane Jane Jane," "Greenback Dollar," "Reverend Mr. Black," and "Desert Pete."

The Kingston Trio were nominated for nine Grammys and won three, the last being in February of 2011 when they received the highly prestigious Lifetime Achievement Award from the National Academy of Recording Arts and Sciences (The Grammys). The award is given "for performers who have made creative contributions of outstanding artistic significance to the recording field." Bob Shane accepted the award for the Trio, with Gretchen Guard, Leslie Reynolds, and Buffy Stewart receiving individual Grammy statuettes for their late husbands. The Kingston Trio were big—and very influential.

Almost immediately after the Trio appeared on the scene, amateur folk groups began sprouting up on college campuses all over the country. Eager to cash in on the craze, major record labels rushed to invent and present their own versions of The Kingston Trio—The Brothers Four; The Limeliters; The Clancy Brothers; Peter, Paul and Mary; The Chad Mitchell Trio; The New Christy Minstrels; The Smothers Brothers; The Serendipity Singers; Bud and Travis; The Journeymen; Ian and Sylvia; The Wayfarers; and scores of others. This was more than a craze. It was a *movement* that affected every facet of American life, from music to fashion to social consciousness.

Everybody in the music business benefited from The Kingston Trio's success—performers, songwriters, agents, concert promoters, record companies, publishers, musical instrument manufacturers. Acoustic guitar and banjo sales, in particular, soared, prompting one guitar manufacturer, C.F. Martin & Co., to build a new factory just to meet a three-year backlog in orders.

In July of 1960, less than two years after the release of "Tom Dooley," *Time* magazine commented on the continued enormous success of the Trio with a vaguely surprised tone:

"The Kingston Trio's *Sold Out* was anything but. With fond backward glances at Billboard's bestseller chart, where *Sold Out* last week led all the rest. Capitol Records was keeping all music shops well supplied with the hottest album cut so far by the hottest group in U.S. popular music. Rock-less, roll-less and rich, the Kingston Trio now bring in 12 percent of Capitol's annual sales, having surpassed Capitol's onetime Top Pop Banana Frank Sinatra. Scarcely out of college, Kingston's Nick Reynolds, Dave Guard and Bob Shane are making some $10,000 a week, can pick-up a six-day fee of $25,000 any time they can conquer their dislike for Las Vegas—'we prefer a less Sodom and Gomorrah-type scene.' Hoisted to these heights by the noose that hung Tom Dooley—the ballad was sleeping in an album they cut in early 1958—the Kingston Trio have added to the burgeoning U.S. folk music boom a slick combination of near-perfect harmony and light blue humor. To help their predominantly collegiate and post-collegiate audiences identify with them, the three do their best to festoon themselves in Ivy wear button-down shirts. They even chose the name Kingston because it had a ring of Princeton about it as well as a suggestion of calypso. Sporting close-cropped hair and a deceptive Social Studies 1-A look, they strum guitars and banjos, foam like dentifrice, tumble onto nightclub stages as if the M.C. had caught them in the middle of their own private party."[5]

As the folk revival gathered momentum, many folk performers used their music as a forum for social change, ushering in the protest music era of the 1960s. While seeds of this genre grew directly from Woody Guthrie's 1930s Dust Bowl ballads, The Kingston Trio's popular acceptance made protest music commercially viable in the '60s. In that context, it might legitimately be argued that without a Bob Shane there never would have been a Bob Dylan. The Kingston Trio may not have delivered the message, but they definitely delivered the medium. They were the perfect musical Whitman Sampler, paving the way for a renaissance of interest in bluegrass, blues, country, and other traditional American music, even modern jazz.

From the outset, it was fashionable among many critics, performers, and folk scholars to diminish The Kingston Trio's legitimacy and influence. Even in recent years popular films such as *A Mighty Wind*, while hilarious on the surface, belittle the importance of many folk era performers, including, tacitly, The Kingston Trio.

The rub? Maybe the Trio made it look *too* easy. Seemingly overnight, three unknown college kids arrived on the scene and changed everything. Who did they think they were, preempting "authentic" performers and getting rich off "our" music? What right did they have? What dues had they paid?

While much of the Trio's appeal lay in the music's apparent simplicity, there was nothing simple or overnight about their success. Every aspect of their career was shrewdly calculated and meticulously planned. Nothing was left to chance. Even before The Kingston Trio recorded their first album, they were exhaustively groomed by a tough, astute San Francisco publicist/manager. They were already seasoned performers, favorites of the North Beach club crowd and Bohemian community.

Prior to forming as a trio, Reynolds, Guard, and Shane had been in several groups during their college years, playing mostly student beer joints

and fraternity luaus around Palo Alto. Shane had also played professionally in Honolulu as "Hawaii's Elvis Presley." After going professional as a
group, their reputation grew along the club circuit, with the Trio playing
major clubs and jazz rooms across the country, starting with San Francisco's
Purple Onion, then on to the Holiday Hotel in Reno, Mr. Kelly's in Chicago, and the Blue Angel and Village Vanguard in New York City, with a
triumphant homecoming at the hungry i in San Francisco. All of this before
they became national "overnight sensations."

Still, on a primary level, The Kingston Trio were based on perhaps
the purest, most natural of foundations— their friendship. Sure, they were
groomed and polished. But most of their "act" was no act at all. It was a
spontaneous extension of who they were as people. If the public found it
enjoyable and was willing to pay to be entertained by it, so much the better.
If The Kingston Trio had never made it big in show business, they would
have been singing together somewhere for the sheer fun of it.

Their critics notwithstanding, the Trio's enormous popularity was
ultimately grounded in their enormous talent, both individually and as
a group. Bobby Shane possessed one of the great baritone voices in the
business, a voice so distinctive that even Frank Sinatra declined to cover
Shane's trademark "Scotch and Soda," candidly admitting that nobody
could possibly top Shane's version. Shane would also prove to be one of
the best acoustic rhythm guitarists to come out of the folk era, a player
of exceptional power and inventiveness whose "lean into it" style is still
copied today. Shane was the group's musical anchor, both vocally and
instrumentally, steady as a rock and always on the note. Together, he and
Nick Reynolds defined the trademark Kingston Trio sound, with Shane's
distinctive lead voice and Reynolds singing harmony a third above it.

Dave Guard, a Stanford graduate student, was a brilliant arranger,
excellent guitar and banjo instrumentalist, and a highly versatile vocalist,
"the man with a thousand voices" as Reynolds once described him. Intellectual and driven, Guard would pore over arcane folk tune collections to
build the Trio's eclectic repertoire. Much of the sophistication and polish
of the early Kingston Trio reflected Guard's influence, particularly his arrangements, the result of an obsessive attention to musical detail. He was
also a master of the long-winded comedy patter learned from Lou Gottlieb
that characterized the Trio's stage act. Guard would later devote himself to
teaching music, authoring books on Celtic mythology, Hawaiian slack-key
guitar, and "Colour Guitar," a guitar teaching methodology he invented.[6]

Nick Reynolds was perhaps the most versatile talent in the group and
unquestionably the most popular with fans. Bob Shane and John Stewart

both point to Reynolds's extraordinary natural abilities as a vocalist and a personality as critical factors in the group's success. "He was clearly the best entertainer in the Trio," said Stewart, "and one of the best natural musicians I have ever worked with." Shane said, "Nobody could nail a harmony part like Nick. He could hit it immediately, exactly where it needed to be, absolutely note perfect—all on the natch, pure genius."[7]

In 1961, Reynolds and Shane recruited John Stewart to take Guard's place, giving the Trio another excellent arranger, instrumentalist, and vocalist, as well as someone to serve as their own in-house source of original material. Stewart would later go on to enjoy a successful solo career that included writing such hits as "Daydream Believer" for The Monkees, as well as writing and recording his own top five hit, "Gold."

Individually, any of the Trio members could have succeeded in the music business. Together, they became the biggest musical group in America, selling tens of millions of records. Over the next decade the Trio played to sold-out audiences worldwide, including virtually every major university, nightclub, and concert venue in the continental United States, Hawaii, Britain, Japan, Australia, and New Zealand.

Over five decades after the release of the Trio's first album, their recordings are as fresh and as vital as the day they were made, remarkable for their energy and exceptional technical quality. They were pioneers who elevated recorded acoustic music to a new level. When the Trio signed with Capitol Records in 1958, Voyle Gilmore, their producer, knew virtually nothing about recording acoustic music. There were no precise limiters or ways of controlling and directing sound. No special acoustic miking techniques. Stereo and multi-tracking were still largely experimental. Together with engineer Bill "Pete" Abbott, Gilmore went on to develop a complex "double voicing" recording technique for the Trio that gave each track a spatial six-voice (or more) choral effect. Today, of course, "stacking tracks" and "fattening vocals" is common practice. But the Trio were one of the first to do it—and do it masterfully.

There were many other innovative dimensions to The Kingston Trio, from structuring "free" college concerts to nondiscriminatory seating clauses to highly focused, single-artist management and booking.

But above all, The Kingston Trio's lasting impact on American life was proving that folk music is, indeed, made for you and me. That truth, and the Trio's success in spreading it, changed the course of popular music and personal tastes in music along with it—including mine.

I first heard The Kingston Trio when my sister came home from college with the . . . *from the "Hungry i"* album. I couldn't understand what the fuss was all about. It would take several years and a copy of *Close-Up* to make me a lifetime Kingston Trio fan. As a music journalist, I came to know all of the members of The Kingston Trio, past and present, especially Nick Reynolds who became a close friend of mine for many years. He was one of the most decent, insightful, and talented people I've ever known. This book is dedicated to him with enormous gratitude, respect, and affection.

I am indebted to the many people who have given their help, time, memories, insight, suggestions, encouragement, inspiration, and friendship. They're listed here alphabetically, but they're all number one to me: Pete Bentley, Ben Blake, Dick Boak, Jesse Bravo, Colleen Broomall, Cathy Bush, Christina Bush, Kathleen Bush, Ron Cohen, Henry Diltz, Joe Gannon, Mike Gore, Bennett Graff, Archie Green, Dave Guard, Gretchen Guard, Tom Guard, Fred Hellerman, Joe Hickerson, Steve Johnson, George and Elias Karras, Chris Kelly, Kitty Kelly, Tom Lamb, Don Mac-Arthur, Roger McGuinn, Don McLean, Jane Meade, Pike Meade, Bob Norberg, Peter Overly, Bob Pomerene, Jay Ranelluci, Dean Reilly, Joan Reynolds, Josh Reynolds, Leslie Reynolds, Nick Reynolds, Jack Rubeck, Timothy B. Schmit, Bud Schoen, Pete Seeger, Bob Shane, Bobbi Shane, Allan Shaw, Pete Sterner, Buffy Stewart, John Stewart, Paul Surratt, Jean Ward, Frank Werber, and George Yanok.

I am especially grateful to Ronald D. Cohen, my editor and associate, for encouraging me to write this book and for including it in his American Folk Music and Musicians series at Scarecrow Press. Many thanks to Bob Shane for his candor and friendship all these years. Above all, thanks to my good friend Allan Shaw, who has worked tirelessly to correct my spelling, grammar, accuracy, and thinking throughout the entire book-writing process.

As kids in New Orleans, we'd sit on the levee after dinner playing our guitars and singing Kingston Trio songs. Two of our favorites were "Mark Twain" and "Low Bridge." They were like a soundtrack to the ships passing back and forth in front of our eyes. We could never quite master Bobby Shane's highly moving donkey imitation, "I ain't-a-goin till I eat my hay! Eee-aww!" But there's always hope.

NOTES

1. Dick Weissman, *Which Side Are You On? An Inside History of the Folk Music Revival in America* (New York: Continuum, 2005), 74.

2. Joe Hickerson, interview with the author, Baltimore, MD, September 28, 2003.

3. John Stewart, interview with the author, San Francisco, CA, December 3, 1983.

4. Dave Guard, interview with the author, Los Altos, CA, November 29, 1983.

5. "Tin Pan Alley: Like from Halls of Ivy," *Time*, July 11, 1960, 56–57.

6. Nick Reynolds, interview with the author, Port Orford, OR, November 11, 1983.

7. Stewart, interview with the author; Bob Shane, interview with the author, Phoenix, AZ, July 20, 2001.

1

CORONADO, 1951

Coronado, California, sits like an emerald crown jewel in the middle of San Diego Bay. Thus its Spanish-derived name, "the crowned one."

The island is small, less than two miles long, with one end occupied by the navy's massive Naval Amphibious Base and Naval Air Station North Island, the official "birthplace of naval aviation." The historic Hotel del Coronado, famed for its old-world luxury and highbrow decorum, takes up the other end. In between are narrow streets lined with small, neat bungalows, 1950s-style apartments, and Victorian mansions, all framed in fichus and bougainvillea.

Secure, insulated, and zealously zoned, Coronado has long been an elite enclave for navy brass, San Diego professionals, and wealthy seasonal visitors.

Legions of Kingston Trio fans, however, know it best as Nick Reynolds's hometown, just across the bay from where he was born in San Diego's Mercy Hospital on July 27, 1933. To truly appreciate the Kingston Trio is to understand from where the members came. Certainly Bob Shane had the voice; Dave Guard and John Stewart had the musicianship. But Nick Reynolds embodied the Trio's *spirit*. Every facet of his talent and personality found its way into the Trio's music and persona—and Reynolds, in turn, was a product of the people and the place that shaped him.

Some may find it ironic that a child born of privilege and wealth would become a springboard for the popular rebirth of an agrarian-based, leftist-linked musical movement of the common "folk." The Reynolds family was anything but common or folksy. Nick's mother, Jane, was a Keck, an affluent and socially prominent family from Orange, New Jersey, and East Hampton, New York. His father, U.S. Navy Captain Stewart Shirley Reynolds, was a Yale graduate from a wealthy Wilkes-Barre, Pennsylvania, family. Ziba Welles Reynolds, Nick's adopted paternal grandfather, was also a high-ranking naval officer. And Aunt Eleanor Ring, Captain Reynolds's sister, was a powerful Republican state delegate and one of Governor Ronald Reagan's major campaign contributors. Nick said that the Keck side of the family were all semi-market robber barons in New York during the Depression, and that his grandmother drove the limousine almost till the day she died. His grandfather on his mother's side, James Madison Seymour, was known as the Lone Wolf of Wall Street. But neither money nor politics, at least in the incubator stage, entered into Nick Reynolds's worldview or career aspirations. It was music that pulled him, yet he never harbored a thought of becoming an entertainer.

As early as he could remember, there was constant music in the Reynolds's home. As children, he and his sisters recalled sitting at the top of the stairs of their Palo Alto house (where they lived briefly) listening to their father play guitar with friends in the living room below. Captain Reynolds headed the navy recruiting office in San Francisco just before World War II, and in his leisure time formed a small string group called The New Friends of Rhythm with several Stanford professors and San Francisco Symphony members.

"They would come over to the house two or three times a week," Nick remembered. "He had a violin player, a viola player, a cello player, maybe a piano player, and he played guitar; they would play and sing '30s jazz things. Beautiful things. My father played six-string, very heavy on the bass strings, did very nice bass runs." From all accounts, the group was quite good, making several recordings and giving a number of concerts throughout the Bay Area. "It was the first time that music entered our *souls*," Reynolds said. "So we were always brought up around music. We all learned how to play ukulele, you know basic chords. Martin was *the* ukulele. In my family, it was the epitome, and they were pretty serious ukulele players. My father had Martin guitars, old ones including a New York Martin that I have."[1]

Later, when the family moved back to Coronado, Captain Reynolds would lead a capella sing-alongs at the dinner table—and not the casual, ok-kids-lets-all-join-in variety either. Grandpa (as he was called by his children) was *very* strict about harmony, and he could be a taskmaster—which Nick said explained why he wasn't allowed to sing with the family very often! Nick was the baby of the family and the shyest of the Reynolds children. "If you sang the wrong note, you were in deep shit," Reynolds said. "Dad didn't get mad, but he'd sit you down and correct you. 'Okay *that's* the wrong note . . . you should be singing *this*.'"[2]

It was similar to barbershop harmony, very simple singing, but very important to young ears that are just learning. Captain Reynolds was very critical about getting it *right*—anybody singing the wrong part would be reminded: "You want to sing in the group, do it right or forget it." Both of Nick's sisters—Barbara, who was the eldest, four years older than Nick, and Jane, who was two years older—had beautiful voices and would sing with their father: duets with Jane and trio harmony with Barbara. Sometimes their mother, Jane, would sing, and there would be four-part harmony. Occasionally, they'd let Nick sing with them, so it would be five-part harmony. "My father had a perfect ear and could pick out the harmonies," Nick remembered. "My sisters had perfect ears, too, Janie especially." Although a little regimented, it was always fun, and sometimes totally spontaneous. "We'd be sitting there having dinner and just break out singing for no apparent reason," adds Jane.[3]

Nick said his dad "knew every old song in the world," including Hawaiian things he'd pick up on his navy travels. Coronado was home base to the Pacific fleet, with a large influx of sailors and tourists coming and going, and Hawaiian and other types of island music were hugely popular there. Records too were big in the Reynolds house, especially Burl Ives, who Nick said was one of his earliest influences; Nick learned every one of Burl Ives's songs from his albums. Hearing "The Blue Tail Fly" for the first time hit Reynolds "like a rock," he said.

But the lasting influence, the one Nick drew upon all of his life and career, came from home. "When you grow up learning real close harmony from masters like my father and sisters, it becomes ingrained in you," Nick said. "Man, you never lose it. You may lose your voice, you might lose your mind, but you never lose your ear, especially if you have a fairly natural ear and continual input from age four—or younger. It's gotta sink in. Singing was the high point of our social life in the family and the closest we ever got at one time. *That's* where my musical training for The Kingston Trio really came from—my father and my sisters, at home, singing at the dinner table and in the living room."[4]

Even as adults, Nick and his sisters would work up intricate harmony arrangements culled from The Andrew Sisters, The Ink Spots, and other pop vocal groups. When The Kingston Trio became superstars, Nick's sisters couldn't believe it. "Janie got so pissed off at me because I made something of it with half the voice, half the ear! She had perfect pitch, a perfect ear, a perfect voice. I mean she was one of the greats. And here I go out and make singing a career! [laughing] She'd say, 'God! *He's* no good!' *We're* the good singers!'" When a Trio fan asked Nick if his harmonies were intuitive or learned, he paused for a moment and responded, "The harmonies are in my head, but they come from my heart." And part of that heart was filled by Jane, Barbara, and his father.[5]

Coronado itself was a wonderfully diverse musical crossroads. Big band jazz, pop, and Mexican music thrived. Stan Kenton, Benny Goodman, and all the legendary show bands played up and down the coast—the Pacific Square Ballroom in San Diego, the Balboa Pavillion in Newport, and the Palladium in Los Angeles. Tijuana, with its Mariachi bands and raucous Mexican bar music, lay just across the border from San Diego.

Music was literally in the Coronado air. "The most beautiful girl in our high school, Mary Ann McKeckney, would bring a ukulele to the beach and sing," Nick recalled. "She was like a pied piper. We'd just sit on the sand and chime right in. There'd be a hundred kids at a beach party at night, all singing along—Hawaiian tunes, Burl Ives, Hank Williams, pop stuff. It sounds square, but it was really great. There was no TV back then; it's what we did for entertainment, and we loved it."[6]

Nick would also sing with friend Billy Pickford, working out elaborate harmony parts, usually buoyed by beer and tequila. Billy was Nick's closest friend, and one of his biggest influences in partying. He was three years older than Nick and into cars, singing, and carousing. The two would get drunk and sing Hawaiian songs for *hours*, working out the parts—"Ok, Billy you sing this, I'll come in over here"—thinking they were singing close harmony, but Nick said they were awful. It was a lot less structured than singing with the family, and while Nick and Billy were learning and trying hard to get it perfect, they were also singing for fun. "We decided that if we were going to do it, we were going to do it right," Nick said. "I think singing with Billy had a lot to do with my input to the Trio—that kind of loose fun quality that Bobby and Dave were used to singing with their Hawaiian songs."[7]

Even after a long evening shift at their part-time jobs, Nick, Billy, and Pike Meade would head to Tijuana to finish off the night singing and carousing, a pastime that would leave a lasting—and later highly useful—impression on Nick. While infamous for its brothels, tourist shakedowns, and anything-goes atmosphere, Tijuana is an incredibly rich source of authentic Mexican music and culture, and Reynolds spent a considerable portion of his youth soaking it all up. There was no curfew and no legal age, and every bar and nightclub had its own Mariachi band blasting background music for boozing, fighting, and all flavors of debauchery. Rooted in traditional Mexican folk tunes, just about anything is game in Mariachi—pop tunes, social and political commentary, bawdy comedy. The music is infectious, with complex vocal and instrumental harmonies and intricate rhythms all peppered with yelps, squeals, and growls. Instrumentally, Mariachi bands typically include trumpet, guitar, vihuela (unique to mariachi), violin, and a massive pot-bellied acoustic bass guitar called a guitarron. Congas and bongos are often thrown in for good measure.

Much of what Nick Reynolds absorbed from Mariachi bands and from listening to records by Augie Goupil and His Royal Tahitians found its way into The Kingston Trio sound and repertoire. "I was into Mexican and Hawaiian and Tahitian music *long* before meeting Bobby and Dave," he pointed out. "Mariachi and Polynesian music are a lot alike, especially harmonies, they both use a lot of fifths and sevenths, so I was able to jump right into a lot of the Hawaiian and Tahitian stuff they were doing."[8]

Reynolds was also an excellent conga and bongo player, skills picked up from Tijuana club drummer Jaime Moran, who would let him sit in on late-night sets. "Nick would take his bongos with him wherever he went," said Pike Meade, "mostly because all the bars in town in those days had piano bars, and he could sit there at the bar playing bongos with the piano music, but he'd always carry his bongos in whenever he went into bars in Coronado and in Tijuana."[9] Later exposure to such drummers as Mongo Santamaria and Willy Bobo, who played on the Trio's avant-garde "Coo Coo U" single, further sharpened Nick's chops.

Rhythmically, one of the basic underpinnings of the Kingston Trio's instrumental sound was Reynolds's higher-pitched Martin 0–18T tenor guitar, which he strummed in double and triple time to Shane's loping, open chord pace on a Martin D-28. He also had a 1929 Martin 2–18 tenor that Harmon Satterlee converted to an eight-string that gave it a Mariachi sound.

John Stewart explained the rhythm structure of the Trio's trademark sound and Nick's role in it: "Well, what it really was if you have a drum set, Bobby's doing the kick drum, and the banjo's doing kind of the snare, but Nick was the high hat! And all of these bands who made fun of Nick for playing the four-string—*that* was the driver!! That drove the band!! You get rid of Nick on that tenor guitar, on those songs, those drivers, you've lost it!"[10]

The result was a decidedly Mariachi-flavored instrumental sound the Trio frequently utilized on fast-paced tunes. Although he never played tenor guitar before joining the Trio, Nick, along with his sisters, learned numerous hula strums on a variety of expensive baritone and soprano Martin ukes supplied by Captain Reynolds.

Vocally, too, the Trio wove Mariachi-inspired harmonies and comedic touches through their material. Nick tuned his ear to harmonies in all kinds of music and was expert at discerning them. Mariachi has multiple layers of vocal harmony, and the Trio employed many of them, including the Mariachi barks, trills, and howls they gleefully interjected into "En El Aqua," "Coplas," "I Bawled," "Tijuana Jail," and "La Bamba."

The Kingston Trio's music, of course, was much more than harmony, technique, or ethnic repertoire. Their X factor was emotional energy, an intensity of feeling and *living* what they were singing that gave their music its power and credibility. "Music with balls," Nick called it. And discovering that distinction at cousin Henry Scott's house was an epiphany.

Henry Scott was a New Yorker, the son of Mary Keck Scott, one of Mrs. Reynolds's sisters. Six years older than Nick, Henry was the source of all wisdom to the young Reynolds—arbiter of taste, ivy-league fashion consultant, adviser on all social matters, sage political observer, and eclectic music collector. He was the big brother Nick never had, the one who gave him his first cigarette and first drink (at age seven), and they would remain extremely close all of their lives. Contrary to recent revisions in Trio mythology, however, it really was Captain Reynolds, not Henry Scott, who was the source of "The Tattooed Lady," the Trio's semi-bawdy gem on *String Along*.

Henry had a tape recorder, and the two would sit in a little apartment behind his mother's house in Coronado and listen to black market tapes of The Almanac Singers and The Weavers singing at union rallies. These were *live* tapes, not made to be records. "That's when I discovered the power of The Weavers; the incredible force of their group singing," Reynolds said. "Hearing them sing 'The banks are made of marble with a guard at every door . . .' Whoa! It was instantaneous! I remember thinking 'what-in-the-hell has just hit me over the head??!!' Nothing ever impressed me like that. *Ever*." It was that same power that Reynolds said the Trio had for a long time—singing with the passion of youth and the passion of fun and the passion of whatever they were doing. "It wasn't *what* The Weavers were singing, it was *how* they were singing it," he said. "The harmony and the intensity of their political passion or whatever it was. It just raised hackles on the back of my neck."[11]

Reynolds would experience the same rush watching Stan Kenton's band as a kid. He described how Kenton would just nod to the horn section—players like Shorty Rogers and Maynard Ferguson—who would stand up and blast a horn ride. To Nick, it was more than a show; it was a central nervous system change. He became intrigued with the dynamics of Kenton's arrangements and stage choreography, with the band standing up and shifting the music an octave higher and turning the song around.

It made a lasting impression on Nick and a definite influence on the Trio's arrangements, with chord inversions and key shifts at the end of songs.

Even years after the Trio ended, Nick Reynolds would still exhibit the same delight in discovery and joie de vivre that first opened his ears to The Weavers, Stan Kenton, jazz, and the Philharmonic and would later articulate the spirit of The Kingston Trio. And while he would not escape some of the pitfalls of celebrity, including alcoholism and two failed marriages, his love of music, enthusiasm, strength of character, and independent spirit never dissipated.

John Stewart would later marvel at how comfortable Reynolds was in his own skin, due in large measure to the security he enjoyed growing up in a loving family. By all accounts, the Reynolds household at 532 Marina Street was a happy one, extremely tight, where self-initiative was valued, personal responsibility was expected, but nothing was mandated.

"Our parents let us do just about anything we wanted to do," said Jane Meade, Nick's sister. "I can remember us taking the ferry over to San Diego by ourselves when we were little kids. They didn't worry, because they knew we were responsible and we'd be okay. We were brought up that way. We had so much fun when we were growing up. It was really just a loving household and lots and lots of music and a lot of affection and love. We had a great upbringing. We really did. And I think this has helped us all through things."[12]

Nick's teenage years were just what you'd expect for somebody growing up on a protected, little island that catered to wealthy families. He attended Coronado High School from the seventh through twelfth grade, with a two-semester disciplinary detour to the Menlo (High) School for his junior year. It seems he started going skin diving every day instead of going to school, got caught, and was promptly shipped up to Palo Alto by his parents to straighten him out.

Pike Meade was also one of his closest friends. The two met in grade school and graduated together at Coronado High School. "I spent 90 percent of my time at his house and the other 10 percent was at my house usually," said Meade. "From sports to cars to skeet shooting to the whole shot. We just did everything together. We were pretty much inseparable through school. Although Nick seemed to be the outgoing, gregarious type in The Kingston Trio, Meade said he really wasn't that way growing up. "We were both kind of shy, and he wasn't at all like you saw him on stage. We both played on the tennis team, played basketball and softball. We even organized our own softball league; this was before little league." The two also shared a passion for skin diving, mostly in Baja California—Tijuana,

Rosarita Beach, and Ensenada. "We hung together night and day and we'd go out and drink beer in high school and party." Pike later married Jane Reynolds, Nick's sister.[13]

Don MacArthur also grew up in Coronado and later became the Trio's road manager from 1959 through 1965. Don remembers he and Nick doing "all the things kids do—playing tennis, softball, hanging out at the beach. I remember when we were maybe 10 or 11 we used to sneak down to the del Coronado hotel very early in the morning and swipe cinnamon buns fresh out of the oven cooling by the kitchen door which was on ground level below the first floor. We'd sneak in and grab a handful and run for it to the beach and eat them."[14]

Pike Mead laughs saying, "Oh God, we got into trouble all the time. But Nick, that little shit, he always escaped. *I* was the one that got caught! He could con you into anything. He was supposed to mow the yard, and his mother would say, 'You've got to pull your own weight around here and that includes mowing the yard.' Well, Nick and I loved to play pinball machines, and of course Nick could always get the nickels to play the pinball machines from a nickel slot machine the Reynolds's had at their house. You weren't supposed to keep the money from the slot machine unless you hit the jackpot, but he knew how to get into the slot machine. Well I didn't have any nickels, so if I wanted to play the pinball machine I had to mow his yard for him. He always conned me into doing his work for him—and I didn't care."[15]

Because Coronado was small, everybody knew each other. It was the 1950s, and while Coronado teens were not exactly prudish, casual sex was not the norm either. Nearby Tijuana whorehouses were a popular and affordable outlet for Coronado males in the throes of puberty. And Nick, too, would learn more than Mariachi south of the border. "Tijuana was our hangout. And it was fantastic," said Pike Meade. "We'd go down there at night and we'd roll in back home at three o'clock in the morning—and then we'd have to go to school. We decided we were going to see how many straight nights we could make it to Tijuana. It was up to about forty times in a row—every night. This was when we were seniors in high school, and even after that."[16]

Music and sports were just two of many interests that occupied Nick's time growing up. He also worked on racing cars and shot skeet, a skill honed while bird hunting as a boy in the woods and fields around Alpine, California. Memories of Alpine were especially precious to Reynolds, who counted the years he spent there from age seven to eleven among the happiest—and most formative—of his life. Located thirty miles northeast of Coronado in the foothills of the Cuyamaca Mountains, Alpine remains rural and relatively underdeveloped. The Reynolds's "ranch," a thirty-acre tract abutting an Indian reservation, was really more of a vacation retreat with four cottages owned by individual families who shared a swimming pool, Victory Garden, peach orchard, orange grove, clean air, spectacular mountain scenery, and the security of being miles away from a major naval port, always a likely wartime target.

Nick loved it up in Alpine, with lots of kids to play with, including the Indian children who were his classmates in a one-room schoolhouse called the Alpine School. He had total freedom at the ranch to do just about anything he wanted to—ride horses, hunt, fish, go birding, have picnics. The weather was good for his asthma, too, which is why his parents bought the ranch in 1939. He said he never felt so completely carefree, and that he always planned to get back the country someday, to do things with his hands and to live a simpler life. After the Trio ended in 1967, he did just that by moving to Port Orford, Oregon, first living in a small cabin, then building a home on the Elk River and opening an antique store. He later bought and operated the local movie house, the Star Theatre.

In Alpine, with Captain Reynolds away at war commanding a troop transport in the North Atlantic, Nick's mother became the head of the ranch household, supported by assorted Keck and Reynolds aunts and cousins. In essence, the ranch became a commune with several other families having their own houses and sharing the communal duties—growing vegetables, milking their own cow, pooling ration coupons to buy butter and meat, which they shared, as well as collecting metal for the war effort. It was just women and children. And while it may have been tough on Mrs. Reynolds with three children to look after, everyone agrees the arrangement worked beautifully and all were well and safe and happy.

Nick especially enjoyed the companionship of cousin Henry Scott, who introduced him to bird watching (or birding, as he called it). Henry was an amateur ornithologist, and the two used to go out birding. They started at three in the morning looking for hoot owls, and by the end of the day, they'd have a list of two hundred birds, going from the backcountry down to the seashore.

But what Nick really savored was the solitude and long hours spent hunting and exploring alone. "I remember loving to do things by myself; it gave me a lot time for thinking," he said, hinting at the very private side of a complex personality. While hardly a loner, Reynolds was naturally introspective, affable yet private, sociable but quite content to be by himself. "There was a part of Nick that was very private," said Don MacArthur.

"Even when we were kids he had his own space that he'd go to." He was also confident in his own assessments and resolute in keeping them—all traits that would later serve him well when he assumed leadership of the Trio upon Dave Guard's departure.[17]

Of all the Trio members, and there have been many over the years, Nick Reynolds was the steadiest and most even tempered, an extremely intelligent, savvy man who *always* knew the score—and usually called it. "He was the straw boss," said Dean Reilly, the group's bassist from 1962 to 1967. "Friendly, easygoing, but he definitely called the shots." Former road manager George Yanok added, "*Nothing* happened without Nick's approval. If they were offered a gig somewhere, and he didn't like it or he thought it cut into their family time, they wouldn't do it—no matter how much money was to be made."[18]

"He's a very complex person, an enigma wrapped in a riddle," John Stewart once observed. "It's so hard to describe him. He's my alter ego, he's a brother, and in the early days of the Trio he was like my dad. He's hysterically funny, he's terminally serious. He's arrogant, he's charming. He's extremely musical, he doesn't like to play music without the Trio, never plays guitar. As people who have been in a big group, you never are out of that group; it's still there no matter how hard you try, at the core of who you are. And yet if you walked into his house, you wouldn't know he was one of the Kingston Trio until you went up the hall to the guest room where he has posters. And yet he's acutely aware of being one of the Trio; if he goes anywhere, he calls it 'going to the petting zoo.' And he has no illusions of who he is now; he knows what he does and who he is, and yet if an offer came along, he would be right back asking for ridiculous money and perks. He can be extremely sensitive and giving, and can at the same time be totally about himself and not care what other people think. He is as gregarious as anyone I've ever met and at the same time as guarded as anyone I've ever met. He's a very complex person." When asked about Reynolds the entertainer, Stewart smiled and said, "He's a white Sammy Davis. He's the greatest natural musician and entertainer—a magic, irresistible performer. When Nick was in his heyday, who could beat him, you know? It's very much hereditary. His whole family is very gregarious and irresistible in a way because they're so up and positive. Nick and I are like siblings because we would both do anything for each other and we both can drive each other crazy better than anybody in the world, like brothers. There's nothing you wouldn't do for him. If somebody else says anything bad about him, oh man, not around me you don't."[19]

There was also a side of Nick Reynolds that reflected a clear sense of right and wrong, and he never hesitated to express it when he saw something he didn't like. It started with his early exposure to prejudice against Native American and Mexican cultures in Alpine and Tijuana. "I knew that these people were regarded as second-class citizens, and I hated it, and I've fought it all my life," he once said. "Even show business, with all its supposed diversity, was filled with discrimination back when we started the Trio. Some black performers had to use the back door of certain hotels when they played in Vegas, even if they were the headliners! We were appalled and did something about it in our own way."[20] The Kingston Trio's performance contract was among the first to include a nondiscriminatory seating clause that prohibited racial or other audience discrimination of any sort at their concerts. They also sang about it. "Deportee," Woody Guthrie's ballad that assailed the treatment of Mexican migrant workers, was one of a collection of socially pointed tunes picked by Nick for the Trio's *Time to Think* album in 1963.

In 1951, Reynolds graduated from Coronado High School, and like a lot of young people who've spent their lives close to home and under the watchful eyes of parents, he was anxious to assert his independence by going away to college. The University of Arizona seemed like the perfect choice. His sister Jane had spent a year there and enjoyed it thoroughly. Located four hundred miles from Coronado in Tucson, the campus afforded a comfortable balance of distance and proximity. What's more, he'd been recruited by University of Arizona's tennis coach (who was also head of admissions) and awarded a tennis scholarship, though Nick would do little to earn it.

Reynolds soon discovered that while Tucson was just a state away, it was light years from Coronado. The city sprawls across the Sonoran Desert, and although slightly higher and cooler than Phoenix, temperatures frequently break 100-plus degrees in the summer, a far cry from the balmy breezes of San Diego Bay. It's also isolated: a hundred miles southeast of Phoenix, situated in a desert bowl surrounded by the Santa Catalina Mountains. If you're used to San Diego, it's like being in the middle of nowhere.

As a result, for students at the University of Arizona the school was pretty much its own world. Despite an image of itself as academically superior to rival Arizona State University, the *Princeton Review* often ranked it among the Top Party Schools in America, based on alcohol and drug use, minimal daily study hours, and popularity of a riotous Greek system. With the exception of drug use, it's probably not much different today from how Nick found it in the fall of 1951. New and nervous in a big, impersonal school and wanting to fit in, he pledged Phi Delta Theta fraternity, an experience so distasteful it never stopped rankling him.

"It was that typical fraternity, rah-rah, macho bullshit routine," he said. "I went through Hell Week, which was really degrading, and after that I didn't really want to have anything to do with fraternities. The only fun part of it for me was being Phi Delt's choral leader. When somebody got pinned we'd go out and serenade the lucky girl at her dorm or sorority house. Sometimes the whole house would go out and sing. That was great fun."[21]

The brightest spot was meeting fellow students Travis Edmondson and Roger Smith, native Californians themselves, although Travis had grown up in nearby Nogales. They were singing as a duo and immediately recognized Nick as a kindred spirit. "I met Travis and Roger my first night at Arizona. Oh god, they were rebels! They were the bad boys! Here are these two guys singing Mexican songs. Unbelievable! We go out and get drunk and almost got arrested because we're out late serenading all the girls hanging out of their dorm windows. Roger and Travis were the most beautiful two singers you'd ever want to hear, and the most beautiful guitar players, too. They were students but they had a little professional duo. I hired them every time my fraternity had a party, and they were just great!" The three would sing as a trio at any place that would have them, and they remained life-long friends.[22]

By his second year at University of Arizona, with poor grades and an even poorer attitude, Reynolds ceased going to class, rented an apartment with a friend from Coronado who was also a Fuller Brush rep, drank beer, chased girls, attempted to hold down two jobs to pay for his new MG TD (including working for the Fuller Brush rep hustling soap and furniture polish to housewives), and soon found himself packing for Coronado. In a letter dated February 11, 1953, University of Arizona registrar and director of admissions C. Zaner Lesher delivered the coup de grace: "The Scholarship Committee of your College has considered carefully the circumstances surrounding your scholarship difficulties and has recommended to the Advisory Council that you be disqualified from the University at this time." While hardly a surprise, it hit hard. "That was a really bad time in my life. I didn't like going to school. I loved having fun and I loved singing. I'd let my folks down, I'd blown college and my parents' money, and finally I had to come slinking back to Coronado."[23]

With the Korean War in full swing, and the draft a certainty, Nick attempted to enlist in the navy to avoid the army but flunked the physical due to his asthma. In deference to his parents and to build his grades back up, he enrolled at both San Diego City College and San Diego State University.

Despite the setback, Coronado was still home and a welcome haven in which to sort things out and get his life back in order. All of Nick's buddies—Donnie MacArthur, Pike Meade, Billy Pickford, Mort Martinez—were still there and jobs were plentiful. He worked as a soda jerk at Oscar's Drive-in (where Pike was the short order cook and Mort the waiter), clothing store clerk, and hotel night manager. None paid more than minimum wage, and to pay off his MG, Nick had to work several jobs at one time. But he could live at home, go to Tijuana after work with his pals, and, best of all, indulge what had become a very serious hobby—racing sports cars with Billy Pickford.

Pickford had inherited a fortune and lived in a huge mansion down on the beach with his recluse father. It had a cavernous garage where he and Reynolds worked on their cars—Billy on a Jaguar and Nick on a Crosley Special—which they'd race as a team at various tracks around Southern California.

Although Pickford had lots of money, traveling the circuit with him was anything but cushy. "Billy was a very wealthy person who wouldn't spend a dime except on himself," Reynolds recalled. "We'd go to the races in Palm Springs, and he'd get a single motel room for he and his wife Patty and me; they'd sleep in the bed and I'd sleep on the floor! Then we'd get dressed up and go to the Shadow Hills Tennis Club where we'd crash these fancy buffets they put on for the big racing people from LA and San Francisco. We'd act like we belonged there, walk right into the reception, load up on food and take it back to the room for the whole weekend."[24]

While Nick's parents allowed him a great deal of freedom because they considered him trustworthy, and because he was always open with them, he made an exception when it came to discussing racing cars, casually minimizing the danger. "They would really have put the kibosh on it," Reynolds said. "My mother was super protective; she was scared to death if anything would happen to any of us kids. I'd lie to them about racing cars, but I'm sure they knew what I was doing," he said. "But they never said much about it."[25]

"Oh, they knew all about it, we all did," said Jane Meade. "And we were worried sick the whole time." Nick and Billy would continue to race for several years, with Nick finally selling his race car after close friend Ernie MacAvey was killed during a race at Pebble Beach. "I drove right by the wreck and saw Ernie laying there. It scared me—and racing in those days was *very* scary. You didn't have big circuits, just airports, and we were racing right through the trees at Pebble Beach."[26]

There were plans, too, for Nick to join Billy and his brother after college in running the Pickford Hotel in Coronado—an establishment the Pickfords had inherited. "I was going to manage the hotel's bar and restaurant," Nick explained, "and that would have been a nice little career for Nicky. But it made me nervous—it was too pat. I'd seen the pattern in Coronado happen with friends of mine who'd gotten married right out of college. If you're raised there, Coronado is a real easy place to get along without having to do a lot. You can go into real estate, you know; it's an automatic market. For years, I fought moving back there. It was too easy for me, not that I had any great ambition to do anything else. I didn't know what the hell I was going to do. I never would have had to take any chances by going back to Coronado, but I think I would have regretted it."[27]

As he would soon discover, the world held far bigger things for Nick Reynolds than Coronado could ever offer.

And some things that it could never replace.

NOTES

1. Nick Reynolds, interview with the author, Port Orford, OR, November 11, 1983.

2. Nick Reynolds, interview with the author, Seminole, FL, October 3, 1986.

3. Reynolds, interview with the author, October 3, 1986; Jane Meade, interview with the author, Coronado, CA, July 7, 2007.

4. Reynolds, interview with the author, October 3, 1986.

5. Reynolds, interview with the author, October 3, 1986.

6. Reynolds, interview with the author, October 3, 1986.

7. Reynolds, interview with the author, October 3, 1986.

8. Reynolds, interview with the author, October 3, 1986.

9. Pike Meade, interview with the author, Coronado, CA, July 29, 2009.

10. John Stewart, interview with the author, Novato, CA, April 6, 2001.

11. Reynolds, interview with the author, October 3, 1986.

12. J. Meade, interview with the author.

13. P. Meade, interview with the author.

14. Don MacArthur, interview with the author, Novato, CA, February 4, 2010.

15. P. Meade, interview with the author.

16. P. Meade, interview with the author.

17. Reynolds, interview with the author, October 3, 1986; MacArthur, interview with the author.

18. Dean Reilly, interview with the author, San Francisco, CA, September 2, 2007; George Yanok, interview with the author, Nashville, TN, October 26, 2003.

19. John Stewart, interview with the author, Novato, CA, April 4, 2001.

20. Nick Reynolds, interview with the author, Seminole, FL, October 5, 1986.

21. Reynolds, interview with the author, October 5, 1986.

22. Reynolds, interview with the author, October 5, 1986.

23. Letter from C. Zaner Lesher to Nicholas Reynolds, February 11, 1953, from the Dave Guard and Richard Johnston Kingston Trio Papers, University Manuscript Collections, University of Wisconsin, Milwaukee; Reynolds, interview with the author, October 5, 1986.

24. Reynolds, interview with the author, October 5, 1986.

25. Reynolds, interview with the author, October 5, 1986.

26. J. Meade, interview with the author; Reynolds, interview with the author, October 5, 1986.

27. Reynolds, interview with the author, October 5, 1986.

2

HILO, 1934

If Coronado, California, was an unlikely hot spot in the resurgence of urban folk music, Hawaii had to be totally off the radar.

Yet the islands have bred at least two of the folk boom's most influential artists, Bob Shane and Dave Guard. Gabby Pahinui, the legendary slack-key guitarist whose boom-chucka-boom rhythms became a Shane trademark, was also a Hawaiian native.

Shane once mused that "the missionaries came to Hawaii to do good and did well"—and certainly he should know.[1] He's a fourth generation Schoen born in Hawaii. His grandfather, Bertram Frederick Schoen (known as BF to the family), was a highly successful shopkeeper of German descent who settled in Hilo on the big island of Hawaii in the late 1890s. His store, Hilo Hardware, began as a saddlery supplying riding gear and other staples to cowboys on the island's massive Parker Ranch and others. When Arthur Castle Schoen, Bertram's son and Bob's father, joined the family business after graduating from Stanford in 1925, it became Hilo Hardware and Sporting Goods.

The Schoen family can trace its roots in Hawaii to the Hitchcocks and Castles, Congregational missionaries from Boston who settled in the islands in the late 1800s, the Castles on Hawaii and the Hitchcocks (on Shane's grandmother's side) on Molokai.

About the name: Schoen is the family name, which Bob's parents and brother retained. Bob legally changed his name to Shane because although the German pronunciation of Schoen is Shane, he felt it was simpler for the public when the spelling and pronunciation were the same. But he wasn't the first in his family to change the spelling, according to his brother, Bud Schoen. "A long time before Bobby was doing anything with the Kingston Trio, our father started a small business and he called it Shane, Inc.—S-H-A-N-E—because he wanted to avoid the pronunciation problem. And it still exists, but it might have been a little bit of an inspiration for Bobby, too."[2]

Bob said, "I used to tell people I changed my name from Schoen to Shane because I'm not Jewish, and my father rather dryly said, 'That's funny, your grandfather was.' To this day I have no idea whether he was telling the truth or making a joke."[3]

"We've had some 'interesting' characters on both sides of the family," Shane recalled. "My mother Margaret, who is a Schaufelberger from Salt Lake City, also of German descent, used to tell us kids that some of her relatives on her mother's side were outlaws back in the Old West. I researched it, and sure enough, a couple of them—the Latimer Brothers—were very bad boys; one was hanged for murder."[4]

Art Schoen met Margaret Schaufelberger when both were attending Stanford in the 1920s; she was an eighteen-year-old economics major, and he was a business student a couple of years older. Upon graduation they married and immediately moved to Hilo. Their first son, Edward Castle ("Bud"), was born in 1928, followed by Robert Castle ("Bobby"), who was born in Hilo Memorial Hospital on February 1, 1934. While Art Schoen was born and raised in Hilo and had helped expand his father's business into a thriving island enterprise, he realized that Honolulu on nearby Oahu would be a far better market for his own store, especially sporting goods. "Yes, but I'm pretty sure what he was doing was getting away from working for his father," Bud Schoen added with a smile.[5]

Art's instincts to move to Honolulu in 1936 would prove overwhelmingly correct. His company, Athletic Supply of Hawaii, Inc., would grow to become the largest wholesale distributor of toys and athletic equipment in the Pacific before being sold in 1978 when Art retired.

At the outset, the move for little Bobby was traumatic. "My earliest recollection of *anything* was when I was a year and a half old when we were leaving Hilo," said Shane. "My mother had me on her lap in a Sikorsky Flying Boat flying out of Hilo Bay to Honolulu. They called it 'the flying slipper' because it looked like a slipper with the high engines and the pontoons hanging down. As we started to take off, I saw the water coming up over the window and it startled me; I remember grabbing on to my mother, and she just calmed me down. Told me everything would be alright—and it was, because Honolulu was a wonderful place to grow up."[6]

The Schoens settled into a large old house on Keamoku Street in Honolulu's Manoa Valley, not far from one of their wealthy Castle relatives, Harold Castle, who lived in a gigantic mansion. "But I didn't know anything about the Castles at that time," Shane said.[7]

The Schoen boys are six years apart in age, a gap that split their childhood interests and friends, but not their friendship. "We never spent a lot of time together, except when we were younger, we just happened to be there together. Bud was older and had his own agenda and I had mine, but we've always been the very tightest of friends. We ran a small investment company together in Hawaii that was started by family members, for family members. Bud has a genius IQ. His physics teacher at Menlo told me that Bud knew more about physics than he did!"[8]

Bud was the first to graduate from Punahou School, in 1946, and would be the first to attend Menlo College, years before Bob. He returned to Honolulu after his sophomore year, working as an engineer at two radio stations. He would eventually become the chief engineer of Hawaiian Telephone, the company from which he eventually retired.

Two adventures the brothers did share were extended trips to the U.S. mainland in 1939 and 1946. "I have a photo of Bud and me on the road with my mom and my great aunt with a new Buick we had picked up in Chicago that we were driving back to the West Coast, stopping at all the National Parks along the way," said Bob. "My dad would come to the mainland on business, and he found it cheaper to buy a new car over here, use it during his trip, leave it on the West Coast for us to use on our trip, and then ship it—and us—back to Hawaii. So I saw a lot of the country at a very early age."[9]

Many childhood photographs of Bob and Bud were taken against the lush tropical backdrop of the Schoen's backyard. Honolulu in the mid to late 1930s had yet to become the massive tourist and retirement Mecca that the jet age would spawn. In 1940, FDR transferred most of the U.S. Pacific fleet to nearby Pearl Harbor as a check on Japanese aggression, creating a sprawling navy, army, and air corps complex in the process. Yet even then much of Honolulu remained pristine amid its coconut palms and hibiscus hedges. Friendly, laid back, and a favorite port of call for international yachtsmen and moneyed travelers, it had only a handful of hotels—such as the Royal Hawaiian (the Pink Palace of the Pacific); the Moana Hotel (the First Lady of Waikiki), now the Moana Surfrider; and Halekulani (originally "Hau Tree")—lining the then uncrowded beach at Waikiki.

Even the schools had an air of island casualness. Punahou School, Shane's alma mater from kindergarten through high school, was especially relaxed. "You could go *barefoot* at Punahou up through the ninth grade," Shane recalled, "which is what most of us kids did most of the time anyway. After WW II, we moved to another house in the Manoa Valley that was right behind Punahou, so it was real easy to get to school."[10]

"I never wore shoes until I got to the seventh grade—*never*," said Bud Schoen. "I mean, I didn't have any shoes! When we'd make trips to the mainland my mother would bring home a pair of tennis shoes from the store because she was embarrassed to have me go barefoot into the shoe store. And we'd buy a pair of shoes to wear on the mainland and of course the next time I wore them they were too small so we'd have to repeat the whole thing again. And I'm sure Bob was the same situation. Nobody wore shoes."[11]

Punahou School was founded by Congregational missionaries in 1841 to avoid having to send their children to the mainland for schooling, and later it catered primarily to Honolulu's wealthy, including Hawaiian royalty. Punahou has always been viewed as elite and highly progressive, and today it ranks academically among the top three high schools in the United States, boasting such distinguished alumni as President Barack Obama, Steve Case (founder of AOL), and of course, Bob Shane and Dave Guard.

Of his early childhood years in Honolulu, Shane only said, "I lived a good, average little boy's life. It's hard for me to remember my early years because nothing really stood out as bad. Ours was a good family, a nice family. I've always felt that anybody who took the teachings of Christ, Buddha, the Koran—it's all basically the same: if you are a good person, good things will happen. If you're a bad person, bad things will happen. And that's basically the way I've always tried to live. I come from missionaries on both sides of the family. We didn't go to church, but we lived by the word of God."[12]

Bob and brother Bud also lived by the strict word of Art Schoen, even in absentia. At the outbreak of World War II, Art enlisted in the U.S. Navy Reserve as an officer and was gone during most of his sons' formative years. He was at the invasion of Saipan, in charge of laying out the beach—who was going to go where—positioning soldiers and sailors after landing. Later he was the advanced space plans officer for the invasion of Japan, which, of course, never happened. "As a result, he became a father figure in uniform," Shane explained, "and everything about him to me was much stricter than he actually was. It was very important to him that Bud and I know, from him, that Mom was in charge and that no grief was to be given to her—and he was right, you know. I never did give her any grief. I was a pretty nice kid."[13]

"Our dad was more of a disciplinarian than our mother was," said Bud. "And he was especially strict on Bob, because Bob was much more of a cutup and bad boy than I was, I guess. He was always after Bob for not being more serious about life. But when Bob got his first job as a musician and then later was playing at the Lau Yee Chai Restaurant in Waikiki where they had well-known acts playing there, I think my father kind of changed his mind. But of course he kept saying 'you know you've got to save your money' and all—he knew Bobby's weaknesses."[14]

Shane was a natural-born entertainer, and he was excellent at it from the start. Choosing to become a professional, however, was more than a career path. It was an affirmation of his self-worth and a way to show his father that he could be successful at something worthwhile of his *own* choosing.

"Oh, I think everybody feels that way," Shane agreed. "I love being an entertainer for the good reasons. Not only for the ego blast, but I truly enjoy entertaining people and making them feel good." And Shane has done just that practically all of his life. As Dave Guard once observed of Bobby the entertainer, "It's not an obsession; it's a compulsion." Shane said that many years later his father took him aside and said, "When you found your calling, I was so happy you stayed with it all your life because that's what I tried to tell you—to get into a kind of [long-lasting] business like I did."[15]

Well, maybe. One can't help but sense that there was something deeper between Art Schoen and his youngest son. Bobby was born the Golden Boy, which, ironically, may have made him the black sheep of the family in Art's eyes. Even after The Kingston Trio became international stars, Art could hardly believe it, assuming that it was a short-lived fluke and certainly no substitute for a "real" career in business. Did Art think that Bobby had it too easy? After all, Art worked hard all his life, including socializing with clients and customers, and here Bobby was idolized the world over without having to lift a finger. Bobby had it all—the looks, the voice, the personality, and, when the Trio hit it big, all the money, too.

Bobby's relationship with his mother was totally different. "Bobby and his mother were just close as peas in a pod," Nick Reynolds observed. "To see them stand up and sing the 'Hawaiian Wedding Song,' which you've heard other people sing a thousand times, but Bobby and his mom did it a capella, by themselves. It'd bring tears to your eyes." Bud Schoen said that it was their mother who encouraged Bob to become a professional singer in the first place and was delighted when he actually got jobs playing.[16]

Art Schoen was well-liked, fun loving, and diligent. An avid golfer and shrewd businessman, he often played the area's best courses with friends who were, not coincidentally, his clients as well. As Bob would later learn,

Art's business was based largely on his gregarious personality, following the classic "friends do business with friends" principle of salesmanship.

Margaret Schoen handled the office duties and helped keep the business running smoothly, and was equally adept at mixing business and sociability. The couple is still remembered for their great parties and warm hospitality. Though deferential to Art, Margaret had a strong, independent personality, was an excellent businesswoman, and was close to her children, especially Bob. While she professed having no real musical talent, she was an excellent classical pianist who played only when alone. "She was very good looking," Bud recalled. "And she could sing, dance the hula, play the piano; I think it might have been hereditary with Bobby being such a good singer, because she was a good singer."[17]

Despite Bob's sketchy recall of early childhood events, there's a terrifying memory that still remains vivid: "When World War II started, we were staying in a place called Beach Walk Apartments right on the beach at Waikiki; I think I was about seven years old at the time," said Shane. "On the morning of December 7th, 1941, just before Pearl Harbor was bombed, I remember running out on the beach with Bud and seeing a Japanese plane come out from Diamond Head about fifty feet over the water right in front of us—so close you could see the pilot's face. And he dropped incendiary bombs on top of the gun emplacements next door at Fort DeRussy. He did that to mark them so that the wave of the Jap planes behind him wouldn't waste their bombs on these guns. That was his job. Fort DeRussy had sixteen-inch guns all permanently facing out to sea, so they weren't any good for defending Pearl Harbor anyway. About this time we heard on the radio that Pearl Harbor was being bombed, so we got hustled up and taken to the highlands because we didn't know if they were going to invade us by land, too. We watched all day and all night the smoke and fires at Pearl Harbor." Bud Schoen remembers a second explosion, an errant U.S. bomb accidently dropped from an airplane, landing down the block from their apartment later that morning, wounding a number of people in the neighborhood, although no one was killed. Art Schoen had volunteered his store's panel truck for ambulance duty at Pearl Harbor and Hickham Field, leaving Margaret and the boys for the next two days while he drove the truck. Despite the terror all must have felt, Margaret was a strong and reassuring presence. "Mom was very calm," Bob said. "She was very cool. She was *always* very cool."[18]

A more pleasant memory, one that Shane still talks about today, is growing up in Hawaii. The beach is, of course, the focus of island life. "We all spent time as beach people; we became what people call 'beach bums," Shane said. "When you're growing up in Hawaii, the beach is the main thing you've got. That's where the action is, it's where the people are, it's where you socialize." A smiling photo of Bob and his beach boy pals taken in 1952 shows them leaning against a beached catamaran at Waikiki, although Shane said they did little sailing. "We were really into body surfing. The surfer craze with surfboards wasn't really big in Hawaii when I was a kid. It was body surfing and you used fins. As you got older and better at it, you'd start seeking out better places to body surf, and some of them were pretty dangerous. We surfed primarily at Waikiki and Hanauma Bay, which was a nice quiet place to body surf, and Makapu'u Bay, where Dave's ashes are today."[19]

The strongest appeal of the beach was the girls, both native and imported varieties. For white boys, dating Hawaiian girls, or wahines, could come at substantial physical risk. Native boys didn't like their women mingling with *haoile* guys (meaning no blood, no color) and wouldn't hesitate to beat the hell out of any white transgressor. Although Shane downplays any racial tension at Punahou, prejudice—brown-versus-white prejudice—has always existed in the islands, exacerbated in wartime by hordes of U.S. servicemen on the prowl. It's not about a majority holding down a minority, because there is no majority in Hawaii, with a mix of 20 percent white, 20 percent Japanese, 20 percent Chinese, and 20 percent Filipino. Equal opportunity prejudice for all.

White girls were another matter altogether, especially on Waikiki with its steady stream of vacationers and airline stewardesses packing the beach hotels, bars, and nightclubs. And not unlike Coronado, where music served as social currency, Bob too used his good looks and tenor guitar like a pied piper. He and friend Roger Smith, who had come to Hawaii in the naval reserves (and who later married Ann Margret and became a Hollywood star), were quite adept at meeting wealthy tourist women along the beach. The beach was the perfect staging area for fun, romance, and, in Shane's case, a career in music with another Waikiki raconteur and fellow Punahou student, Dave Guard.

Donald David Guard was the first generation of his family born in Hawaii, in Honolulu, on October 19, 1934. His father, Carl, originally from Tampa, Florida, was a colonel in the U.S. Army Reserve and a civil engineer. His mother, Marjorie Elizabeth Kent, was from Birds, Illinois, but grew up in Washington, D.C., the daughter of a naval pharmacist, which ultimately brought her to Honolulu's Ford Island in 1931. Her family had previously lived in Indiana and the Philippines. Her brother, Edward Kent, would become the dean of the Columbia Law School.

A year later Marjorie met and married Carl "Jack" Guard, newly arrived himself from the school of engineering at the University of Florida (where he roomed with dancer and actor Buddy Ebsen). The couple soon settled into base housing at Hickam Field, where they would live with their young son David until Pearl Harbor was bombed in 1941. With both parents working full time—Jack as a civil engineer for the army at nearby Fort Shafter, where he was building walls and roads around Honolulu, and Marjorie as secretary to Lucius D. Clay, Pacific commander in chief of the U.S. Army Air Corps at Hickam—young David would find himself alone for many of his formative years.

"He spent a lot of time going to the movies by himself as a kid," said Dave's son, Tom Guard. "He saw a lot of those Bob Hope and Bing Crosby movies, and Abbott and Costello movies, just watching all the movies run. His folks would leave a dollar on the table every morning for him to take care of himself. They weren't very well to do; they were struggling a lot I guess like most people in the '30s and yeah, it was hard times even out there. He was an only child, so he really subsisted with a strong imagination. He told me that he was a rather hyperactive kid, so I guess he was just really gung ho to take things in at a high speed and very interested and very motivated." Guard was pretty much a loner from the start, and this early separation would have lasting effects. He would feel a sense of isolation and not fitting in for the rest of his life. "When you're the only child, you're always within yourself, you are not strung into other things," he explained. "It's always been quite alone for me, always. Even with a crowd, or a sizable family here, I'm always trying to figure my role in it."[20]

Supposedly, Guard deeply resented being left alone and blamed his mother for not staying home with him as a child. But Gretchen Guard stated that Dave often said things to writers about his parents for effect, and that much of it was an exaggeration. "The only thing I got from David in the way of resentment of his parents was the fact that his mother worked all the time," Gretchen said, "and in those days most mothers didn't work. They stayed home and took care of their children and husbands and their house and all that. But I didn't get the feeling that he really resented his parents any more than most people do at a certain stage. His mother would have to get up early, and she'd be gone by the time David woke up. She always had maids to take care of him when he was really little, but then later on when he was old enough to get up and get off to school himself, he would find a dollar on the dining room table and a note saying 'See you later and go to a movie after school if you'd like.' His parents were wonderful, I thought. They were sweet, generous, fun-loving people. They both worked a lot, and they would go out to eat a lot and take David with them, and they enjoyed going to luaus whenever people were in town. They stayed in one place for a long, long time. They were not affected at all, just very down to earth people. And they absolutely supported David in whatever he wanted to do. You know how parents are with an only child. He was the center of everything. And David was very close to them. His mother was smart and well-read and a big influence in his life, although I don't think he gave her enough credit really. She used to have funny little sayings. She had him baptized in a Methodist church when he was little, even though they were not churchgoers and later on he asked her why she did that and she said, 'Well it can't hurt and it might help!' And then one of her favorite sayings was 'Do right and you'll never go wrong.' And she was kind of earthy that way."[21]

Dave once told an interviewer that his parents didn't push him to be an overachiever, although he was obviously gifted, telling him, "You don't have to be first, just do your best." But in truth, David *did* have to be first. His constant drive to achieve perfection, be it making the honor roll at Punahou or being the "acknowledged leader" of The Kingston Trio, was somehow his hedge against having it all taken away. It was pure self-preservation. "As a kid, I just figured screw it," he once said. "Things are going to be my way and I'll pay whatever dues are necessary to keep it that way."[22]

It is difficult to sift through Guard's earliest school years, because he said little about them to others. Long after he left The Kingston Trio, Guard began a detailed day-by-day journal of his life from an early age, which he re-constructed from memory, in which he documents his attendance at Lincoln School in Honolulu for first grade in 1940, then shifting briefly to nearby Pauoa Elementary for second grade.

Then came the morning of December 7, 1941. Unlike the Shanes who were several miles away from Pearl Harbor, the Guards were literally next door to the bombing (and attendant shrapnel from U.S. anti-aircraft guns) in a new quadraplex home at Hickam Field. Tom Guard shared an entry of his father's personal journal, describing the horror of the bombing through the eyes of a child. "The Japanese bombed Pearl Harbor and I can see the faces of the pilots, bombs and burning planes falling," the seven-year-old boy remembered. "Chaos and panic—mom and I returned to the old landlord at Makiki Street—we slept under the street in drainage tunnels among the sand bags. A dog bites me and I'm taken to the doctor at Pearl Harbor. We go back to Hickam but it just doesn't look safe. Dad comes out the underground post for the first time at that point."[23]

With the ensuing chaos following the bombing, Dave and his mother were shipped stateside to New York and eventually Washington, D.C., where his maternal grandmother lived and where Dave was enrolled in third grade at the Benjamin Stoddert Elementary School. He would also travel to Tampa, Florida, to visit his paternal grandparents, Mr. and Mrs. Carl John Guard Sr. By 1943, after the Battle of Midway when Hawaii seemed safe, Dave and his mother were back in Honolulu, living in a downtown 1930s-style apartment on Launiu Street in Waikiki, close to Lincoln School where Dave would remain through sixth grade. He entered the seventh grade at Punahou School in 1946. Lincoln School would prove an important milestone in Guard's musical development.

"Lincoln School was on the edge of a park called Thomas Square," Guard recalled, "and across the park was the Honolulu Academy of Art. The conductor of the Melbourne Symphony, Fritz Hart, had been stranded there during the war, so once every couple of weeks the whole school would go over there and he would lead us in folk singing—'Shenandoah' and lots of English folk songs in particular because he was very familiar with those. But that's where I got my taste of any kind of folk music other than Hawaiian music that was all over the place. We didn't know we were actually in a folk music environment." Fritz Hart and his concerts in the park would make a deep impression on Guard, as he recalled years later for his personal journal. "I am in love with his music and his lyrics," he wrote in his entry dated August 25, 1943. But it was the Hawaiians that instilled in him a life-long love of native island music and culture.[24]

It is important to distinguish authentic Hawaiian music from music played in Honolulu hotels because the two are not synonymous. What musicologists regard as "Hawaiian music" is borne out of Polynesian island culture and rhythms, borrowing heavily from Tahitian and Andean sources. "Before the missionaries, there really wasn't any 'Hawaiian music,' per se," said Shane. "It was just chants. The missionaries introduced church music to the islands and it all got mixed together. Even Gabby Pahanui's music, which a lot of people equate with 'authentic' Hawaiian music, is really based on stuff he borrowed from Portuguese music." Honolulu hotel music, on the other hand, borrows heavily from Las Vegas lounge acts, mixing in Tin Pan Alley and burlesque comedy. As teenagers, Dave and Bob were drawn to both the authentic Hawaiian and Tahitian genres as well as hotel lounge music and comedy, often hanging around the touristy Lau Yee Chai Chinese restaurant on Waikiki to pick up tunes and jokey routines from the Vegas lounge acts imported from the mainland. "We were too young to go in," Guard recalled, "so we'd sneak up and listen to it at the back door of the club and go down the next day and sing it on the beach for quarters from the tourists. We stole all their material, whoever was coming through town, and everybody thought that was great saying all these one-liners and quips and everything." The two would also haunt the Waikiki Yacht Club at Ala Wai Harbor, picking up Tahitian and other Polynesian tunes from transient yachtsmen. They also listened to Eddy Lund and His Tahitians, a hugely popular band in Tahiti and Hawaii, led by pianist, songwriter, and bandleader Eddy Lund, "the Father of Modern Tahitian Folk Music." It was this mutual interest in music, as well as body surfing, that first brought Shane and Guard together.[25]

Although Guard had been at Punahou since seventh grade, Shane's earliest recollection of him was not until their junior year when both tried out for the Punahou track team. "We were both broad jumpers," said Shane, "and then we started hanging out. We both liked body surfing at Makapu'u Bay, and singing and stuff. We were good friends, but not close friends." Guard remembers their first meeting being not on the track field, but outside the teenage canteen in high school at Punahou looking for girls. "Bobby knew how to play guitar, and he knew this Tahitian song, but he only knew the tune; he didn't know how to sing the words to it. And I knew the words because I'd been picking it off the record, one of these 78 rpm things," he recalled. "You'd stop the record and back it up and try to figure what it was. I learned it that way. So I had the words and he had the guitar thing, and we sat down and put that together to learn the song, and tried to lure the little girls out of the dance unsupervised." Shane said that it's true that he learned some of the early Tahitian tunes from Dave, primarily lyrics, but that George "Tautu" Archer, the popular Tahitian singer and dancer who sold Shane his first tenor guitar, also taught him Tahitian songs as well—including the one that got him and Dave into singing Tahitian music to start with.[26]

Dave took ukulele lessons in eighth grade school at Punahou—and flunked. It was Bob who taught Dave his first chords on tenor guitar, C and G, tuned to the first four strings of standard guitar tuning. "Later, I talked Dave's mother into buying him a guitar," Shane said. "I told her, 'I really know that Dave would like to have a guitar and he even mentioned to me the kind of guitar he thought was a good guitar,' and they bought him a mahogany Martin." Shane, too, had been drawn to the guitar—and girls— at age ten after watching family friend Harold Harvey sing and play at one of the Schoens' parties. "He was an important guy, the General Manager of McKesson and Robbins liquor division in Hawaii, and he'd been around," said Shane. "He'd been in George White's *Scandals*, a Broadway production in the '20s. He played great songs on the guitar and he always had lots of girls around him. *That* impressed me. I'd say that Harold was my first big influence."[27]

Shane said he was always the quiet and shy type in high school, yet his many exploits at Punahou belie any such reticence or shyness. Both he and Guard appeared in school plays, including the *The Mad Woman of Chaillot* as well as the junior variety talent show where they sang "Goodnight Irene" and "On Top of Old Smokey," their first public singing appearance together. Shane was also cast in the musical *The Student Prince*. "I had a good part, that of the aging Count von Mark, the only non-singing part in the entire musical! And I was the only one in that show that ended up becoming a professional singer!" High school plays may have given them a mutual interest, but it was the relentless pursuit of girls that was the real underlying bond of their friendship, and it soon took them to Fort DeRussy in Shane's old Waikiki neighborhood.[28]

While the fort was still an active military installation, it had a beach park that was open to the public, but Shane said not a lot of the public knew about it. "It was right in the middle of Waikiki because the military always grabs the best property," Guard added, "and our fathers had cards because they were in the service, so we got the fifteen-cent beer and stuff like that." The park had a thirty-foot tower on the water, and the area around it had been dredged out so that swimmers could dive from the top of the tower, with the more adventurous hotdoggers doing "suicides," which involved going into a jackknife position mid-dive and not pulling out—making a lot of bubbles in the salt water. It made such a splash, in fact, that it inspired Bob and Dave to start a diving routine as a complement to their singing act.

But the greatest attraction to Fort DeRussy, even greater than the young girls, was music—especially the music of The Weavers.

"They had a fantastic jukebox that all the service people were listening to, and it was the hip stuff that was happening at the time amongst *adults*, not young men or women, but adults—the kind of music they liked," Shane recalled. "And The Weavers were one of the top records on there. That's how we were exposed to The Weavers—and Lefty Frizzell, Hank Williams, Harry Belafonte, and lots of other pop and country singers, and later, Elvis Presley. That jukebox had 'em all." As Nick Reynolds had discovered an ocean away, and almost at the same time, The Weavers were *the* way—the single, most profound musical and performing influence of the yet-to-be-formed Kingston Trio. "I think we were all drawn by the simplicity—and the energy—of it," Guard reflected.[29]

Interestingly, Shane and Guard were invited to Hawaiian parties to play Tahitian music, not folk music or even Hawaiian. "That was our way of being different from the Hawaiians," Guard explained. "The Hawaiians had it worked out with Hawaiian stuff, but they didn't know the Tahitian stuff, which we thought was wild and exciting. And certainly the other people didn't have it covered either, so we took it up and found it was very entertaining. My prime interest had been Tahitian music, actually." But as Guard readily admitted, it was The Weavers and slack-key guitarist Gabby Pahinui that made the biggest impression on him. When asked if there was a direct link between the type of driving rhythm Shane and Guard used in The Kingston Trio and the jangling beat of Gabby Pahinui, Dave said, "Oh absolutely. That's right from a thumb-up-down-up-down strum with your index finger. It's basic, the hula beat, is what it was. And it's more like an oceanic feel than, let's say, a Chuck Berry feel where you've got a machine—you know, right to the eight-to-the bar sort of boogie beat sort of thing."[30]

While Bob and Dave were born in Hawaii, they were not Hawaiians. They were Honolulu natives—Americans, with American parents and American roots. The appeal of the mainland—the motherland—was instinctual and ever present in their lives. As a very young child, Shane had already seen much of the American West, but not the rest of the country. Guard, chafing under the rules at Punahou and a less-than-happy home life, couldn't wait to bolt stateside, enrolling in the Menlo School in Menlo Park, California, for his senior year of high school in 1950, the same school that Nick Reynolds was attending at the same time, although they never met. With Guard hoping to attend Stanford in nearby Palo Alto and with the Menlo School viewed as a Stanford prep school, the move seemed obvious. "I was tired of Hawaii and I was really interested in San Francisco," Guard remembered. "It was really my ambition to live in the San Francisco area. I saved my money and asked my parents if I did half, would they do half. And they didn't really feel like it, but I finagled it out of them and came up here. I just really liked the Bay Area and thought it was really interesting and so that's what I did when I got up to the high school. I started getting into listening to the R & B stations, KDIA was the main one, I think. They didn't want you to go any place when you're in school, but I hitchhiked up to the city which was absolutely forbidden."[31]

But it was more than boredom with Hawaii that brought Dave to the mainland. It was a girl named Shannon whom Dave met at Punahou and said he had been in love with throughout high school. Her father was in the navy and presumably was transferred to the Bay Area, and Dave was determined to follow, which he did. Unfortunately, Shannon was quickly smitten with a Stanford track star whom she eventually married. Ironically, his name was John Stewart (but no relation to John Stewart who later replaced Guard in The Kingston Trio).

Shane had also planned to attend college in California, and entered Menlo School of Business Administration, a newly initiated four-year program, as a freshman. It, too, was considered an intermediate step, an academic boot camp for those not quite ready for the scholastic rigors of Stanford. But Shane said that while he intended to switch to Stanford in his junior rear, he discovered that he preferred the smaller classes and closer teacher contact at Menlo and stayed there instead. It had always been assumed that Bob would follow his father Art into the family sporting goods business, a move that may have been contrary to his own instincts. The choice of Menlo School of Business Administration and planned segue into Stanford (Art and Margaret's alma mater) was clearly in deference to his father's wishes. Bob would later discover, however, that business was not his calling—and never would be—regardless of Art's wishes or even his insistence.

There would be other parallels and mutual magnets—places, shared interests and musical tastes, even karmic happenstance—that would predestine the formation of The Kingston Trio. By the time Shane, Reynolds, and Guard independently reached the same geographic area—Shane and Reynolds at Menlo School of Business Administration in Menlo Park and Guard at Stanford a few miles away in Palo Alto—all of the dynamics were in place, good and bad, for a group of enormous power, creativity, and conflict. Intelligence would be the group's cachet as well as its bane. Although Guard would assume the title as the Trio's acknowledged leader, none of its members could be easily led. They were all *too* intelligent; three highly gifted, strong-willed individuals who sometimes pulled in tandem, sometimes not. Conflict, especially between Shane and Guard, was a foregone conclusion. And though Shane maintains that there was no early rivalry between Dave and him, it was the same competitive tension that arose vying for girls at the Punahou canteen or the I-know-the-chords-but-you-know-the lyrics one-upmanship that gave The Kingston Trio its necessary tension and energy.

"From the beginning, I could sense a strain," Nick Reynolds recalled. "Their whole style in life was different, their motivation, or the reason they played music." Gretchen Guard, too, recognized their competitiveness, but not combativeness. "I was well aware of it, and I think it was because they were from the same hometown and because they had gone to the same school and they both wanted to be musicians. I think it was just a natural competitiveness that might arise between brothers or cousins or twins, even. They were both very capable and both very quick, but very different in their interests in a lot of ways. But they had the music in common, and their backgrounds and sort of regionality in common. But yeah, they were competitive, no doubt about it."³²

When asked if there was any serious rivalry between the two, Shane said, "If there was, I didn't know it. I don't think he did either. I don't think that was it. I used to make fun of the fact that I knew he was smarter as far as 'book learning' was concerned because he was a student and I was a playboy. I wanted to have more fun and he wanted to do that, too, but he made sure that he studied. He was just a good buddy. We ran track together. He was a long jumper, I guess, I was a broad jumper and he was a 440 man, I think. I'm not sure. And we didn't fare that well at it, but we went out for different sports, but didn't do really great in them; we just had fun with them. And then we went to the beach a lot together and hung out at the beach. We had a gang of people that hung out at the beach. And a couple of them are still my best friends."³³

While they had mutual interests, Guard and Shane were radically different personalities. And it was those differences, or opposites, that would first attract and, with over-familiarity, ultimately repel the two.

Dave Guard was the antitheses of Bob Shane. He was intellectually curious, meticulous, controlling, deliberate, and occasionally difficult. His obsession with detail would serve the Trio well, however, giving it an intellectual yin to Shane's yang. While Bob operated on the visceral, Dave left *nothing* to chance, a hard worker (and a clever one) who crossed every *t* and dotted every *i*. "Dave was very bright," Shane acknowledged, "and he was a renegade at heart."³⁴

In Shane's case, the situation was exacerbated by the fact that musically everything came easy for him. He was born with one of the great voices in popular music. He could sing anything, play anything, do anything on demand, without really working at it. He was also blessed with good looks and an easy charm, a combination that could cause resentment among the best of friends, including, possibly, his father.

Were it not for Nick Reynolds, the skilled diplomat, peacemaker, and harmonizer, both literally and figuratively, the Trio would never have prevailed against such long odds. Reynolds would be the glue, strong yet flexible, that would keep it all together. So perfect was this combination of chemistry, so precise and ideal the alignment of people, place, and time, the Trio *had* to have been meant to be.

"There are no accidents," Nick Reynolds would often say, and history would bear him out. But in the fall of 1956, nobody knew it yet.

NOTES

1. Bob Shane, "An Evening with The Kingston Trio," *The Kingston Trio* (concert program, 1966), 11.
2. Bud Schoen, interview with the author, Kailua, Oahu, HI, June 6, 2008.
3. Bob Shane, interview with the author, Phoenix, AZ, August 21, 2007.
4. Bob Shane, phone interview with the author, December 16, 2007.
5. Schoen, interview with the author.
6. Shane, interview with the author, August 21, 2007.
7. Shane, interview with the author, August 21, 2007.
8. Shane, interview with the author, August 21, 2007.
9. Shane, interview with the author, August 21, 2007.
10. Shane, interview with the author, August 21, 2007.
11. Schoen, interview with the author.
12. Shane, interview with the author, August 21, 2007.
13. Shane, interview with the author, August 21, 2007.
14. Schoen, interview with the author.
15. Dave Guard, interview with the author, Los Altos, CA, November 29, 1983; Shane, interview with author, August 21, 2007.
16. Nick Reynolds, interview with the author, Seminole, FL, October 6, 1986.
17. Schoen, interview with the author.
18. Shane, interview with the author, August 21, 2007.
19. Shane, interview with the author, August 21, 2007.
20. Tom Guard, interview with the author, North Attleboro, MA, March 25, 2006; Dave Guard, interview with Richard Johnston, January 3, 1974, from the Dave Guard and Richard Johnston Kingston Trio Papers, University Manuscript Collections, University of Wisconsin, Milwaukee.
21. Gretchen Guard, interview with the author, Santa Fe, NM, January 10, 2010.
22. D. Guard, interview with Johnston.
23. Dave Guard, date unknown, personal journal excerpt per Tom Guard.
24. Dave Guard, phone interview with the author, November 28, 1983.
25. Bob Shane, interview with the author, Phoenix, AZ, July 20, 2001; D. Guard, interview with the author, November 28, 1983.
26. Bob Shane, interview with the author, Phoenix, AZ, January 28, 2008; D. Guard, interview with the author, November 28, 1983.
27. Shane, interview with the author, January 28, 2008; Shane, interview with the author, December 16, 2007.
28. Bob Shane, interview with the author, Phoenix, AZ, January 1, 2010.

29. Shane, interview with the author, December 16, 2007; D. Guard, interview with the author, November 28, 1983.

30. D. Guard, interview with the author, November 28, 1983.

31. D. Guard, interview with the author, November 28, 1983.

32. Nick Reynolds, interview with the author, Seminole, FL, October 4, 1986; Gretchen Guard, interview with the author, April 28, 2006.

33. Shane, interview with the author, August 21, 2007.

34. Shane, interview with the author, August, 21, 2007.

3

MENLO, 1956

"I showed up at Menlo not knowing a soul," Nick Reynolds recalled, describing his first meeting with Bob Shane in 1955, "and the first day I walk into this accounting class and there's this guy slumped over his desk in the last row sleeping! He had a book propped up to hide his face. I thought anybody that's got the balls to do that, I've *got* to meet."[1]

Shane, too, recalled their first meeting with a wry smile. "He probably didn't tell you that I had a half-empty pint of whiskey sticking out of my back pocket! The first thing I asked him was, 'Do you have a car?' He said 'Yes,' and I said 'Well, I've got a guitar' and we immediately went out and got drunk—and we've been brothers ever since."[2]

This "brotherhood" revolved primarily around a shared enthusiasm for chasing girls and drinking beer. Of the two, Nick was the more serious academically, not daring to flunk out of a third and probably last shot at a business degree. Bob, on the other hand, took a more cavalier attitude toward scholastics, elated to be two thousand miles away from Art Schoen's critical eye and free to do as he pleased.

Thus began what would be a pivotal relationship at a pivotal time and place in Nick Reynolds's and Bob Shane's lives. That both would pick Menlo was, as Reynolds would later muse, no accident.

Founded in 1927 as a two-year junior college for men, Menlo was viewed by some as an extended prep school for students aiming for the really higher education at nearby Stanford—or for students not sure what to aim for at all.

For the younger, more ambitious student, Menlo operated its own preparatory high school, the Menlo School, which shared the same campus with the college. It was the same boarding school that Dave Guard and Nick Reynolds had briefly attended, although the two never met, and from which Guard graduated in 1951 on the way to Stanford. In 1949, the school began its distinguished four-year Menlo School of Business Administration that, along with somewhat forgiving admission policies, made it attractive to Reynolds and Shane.

"Not having the greatest grades in the world, I certainly wasn't getting into a school like USC or UCLA," Reynolds correctly observed.[3] Since he hadn't proved himself as a tennis star at Arizona, there weren't going to be any more tennis scholarships either, so Menlo was a good option, if not the only one. Besides, his parents liked the idea of Nick being in a familiar place, the family having lived in nearby Palo Alto and Nick having attended the Menlo School for his junior year of high school

Menlo was a serious business school. Although more informal than Stanford or USC, it was highly regarded academically and professionally, with a faculty that included both distinguished business educators and successful practicing executives. "It was a *great* school—the first school I ever went to where I felt really comfortable," said Reynolds, "not only because I met Bobby Shane the first day, but it was also real laid back. I had a lot of fun at Menlo, but I really learned a lot, too. They knew what the real business world was all about. Like, the people who taught you business law at Menlo were *practicing* business law in Palo Alto."[4] And true to their reputation, the professors knew what it took to get into Stanford and tailored a good part of their curriculum to that end.

Reynolds would make excellent grades at Menlo in part, he said, because he rarely missed class. Shane was just the opposite. "Bobby had a problem having a structured life of any kind, and he had a hard time going to class; he just couldn't get out of bed. We'd be partying all night long, and I'd limp into class, drink some coffee and take a couple of Benzedrine. But not Bobby." Shane was in El Camino Hall, the residence hall where the jocks and "the bad boys" stayed, and Reynolds would stop by in the morning to make sure Shane had gotten out of bed in time to make class. "He'd tell me, 'I'm just gonna take a quick shower and I'll be right there.' He'd show up like ten minutes before class was over with this long, elaborate bullshit story about how he'd slipped in the shower and hit his head and on and on; they were a work of art. It was hilarious."[5]

According to Reynolds, it wasn't laziness on Shane's part. "Bobby's parents had sent him to school and he felt some obligation to do something, but he was way too busy having a good time, and working real hard at not conforming. I was conscientious and he needed somebody like that to look after him. So I sorta became his driver, best friend, and personal assistant."[6] It was the perfect yin and yang, and it defined much of their relationship for the rest of their lives. Reynolds's first impressions of Shane are telling, a classic case of opposites attracting, but with a twist—they were also a lot alike, codependents and comrades in goofing-off: "When I first met Bobby, I thought 'Well, all right! Now *this* is the kind of person I've wanted to meet all of my life! I want to hang out and get some of this energy! Nobody was on the same wavelength as Bobby, but *I* was—and it shocked him. We got to know each other real well real quick."[7]

Shane, for his part, felt an immediate affinity with Reynolds. "Nick Reynolds was the only person I ever met in my life who I immediately, instinctively liked—like I'd known him all my life," Shane said. "I don't know what it was. We used to call it the X factor in the Trio; it's what we had together. Him sitting next to me in accounting class, waking me up and then saying, 'Hi, I'm Nick Reynolds, I saw you sleeping here, I wanted to meet you.' That was obviously my kind of guy, too. He was just a really neat guy. He had a knowledgeable personality to him. He was a little older than I was and I could tell that immediately because he knew a little more stuff than I did. I remember he used to be so funny. They called me 'the sex symbol' in the Trio, but Nick Reynolds got more chicks than I ever thought of getting, you know. John Stewart said that, too! He said, 'Nick was a legend unto us all.'"[8]

Music was a natural and easy bond for Shane and Reynolds, a mutual interest that quickly became part of their daily routine. After classes let out around 2 p.m., the two would start hitting the bars up in the hills behind Stanford and Palo Alto, little country inns and outdoor beer joints like Mama Garcia's La Casa Blanca that catered to the Menlo crowd, or sometimes Rosatti's (now the Alpine Inn), the Stanford hangout. It's beautiful in the hills, with lakes and picnic grounds where Shane and Reynolds would go to swim and meet girls, and great bars where the two would entertain for all the free beer they wanted. They'd then go back and hit the bars on El Camino Real, starting with Greg's, their favorite, directly across the street from Menlo.

In any of these bars, anybody with a little talent could get up and play for free beer and, most importantly, a better shot at the coeds. Shane had a distinct advantage in both regards. By the time he'd arrived at Menlo, he was a skilled entertainer and a skilled ladies' man with raffish good looks, a smooth easy manner, and a magnificent singing voice. He'd already perfected his bar show—Elvis impersonations, Hawaiian songs, a few love songs, bawdy comedy—that had worked so well on vacationing young women in Waikiki bars. "He'd get up there with just a tenor guitar and do his thing," said Nick admiringly. "And you know what kind of a voice he has, in those days especially, my God! The girls would be gushing! Then he'd crack up all the beer-drinking college kids with some raunchy songs. I started to back him up on bongos just so I could get in on some of the action!"[9]

From the outset, Reynolds keyed right into singing with Shane. "I could sing along with him, I could lip sync with him. After a while I learned the words by him saying them, and I was also learning them by enunciation, so in a week I was singing Hawaiian songs. I had no idea what they were saying, and still don't know. 'My Lovely Ginger Lei'—that's one of the songs Billy Pickford and I used to sing. Bobby would sing all the Hawaiian songs that Billy and I knew, so already I knew a lot of them. I'd say, 'Do ya know . . .'' and he'd say, 'Oh yeah!' I never listened to Bobby's influences—*he* was the influence on me. He brought me out of my shell and gave me a little confidence, too."[10]

Friends of Bobby's from Hawaii, like Al Harrington (real name Alvin Ta'a), a Samoan football player at Stanford, and Donnie MacArthur, Nick's friend from Coronado who was attending nearby San Mateo Community College, would sometimes join in the fun. But there was no group at all at this early stage, just Bobby and Nick singing as a duo. If Al Harrington stopped by and wanted to do a few Samoan songs or a Samoan dance, it was a bonus and they'd shift to their Hawaiian and Tahitian material.

"We had our act down so good, we could go anyplace," Nick said. "And our little act was easy for other people to slide in and out of. We'd do the same thing, with or without them. We had a plan. Bobby would set up the deal—he was the leader of that particular regiment. I was the 'shill.' Bobby was the 'star.' And it was fine for me because I had to take seconds, you know [laughing]—and it was a lot better than none! I was fascinated and loved every minute of it."[11]

Their modus operandi was always the same: drive to San Francisco in Shane's Pontiac, park a block away from a bar they'd already cased for secretaries stopping for drinks after work (the Tahitian Hut on California Street was a favorite with the office crowd), go in and order a couple of beers, and then Shane would approach the bartender, "Uh, do you mind if I bring my guitar in and just play a couple of little songs, just at the table. We won't disturb anybody. We're from Menlo." It was all so innocent and polite, clean-cut college boys just wanting to do a little singing. What's the harm? Of course, it's perfectly all right to play!

Shane would then start strumming and singing over in the corner, Reynolds would slide in with a little harmony and the bongos would come out, and pretty soon half the bar would be over at their table. Soon people would be coming in off the street to join in singing. The bartenders *loved* it. People would buy them drinks, and if there weren't enough people, the bartenders would buy. Shane would be doing his "act" and Reynolds would give him center stage, knowing precisely when to join in. It worked every time. "We could just go into a place and terrorize it," said Shane. "We'd even go into the pure folk music places that were just starting to pop up here and there and sing a bunch of risqué songs; people would be cheering for us and we'd leave with a couple of chicks!"[12]

For Shane, singing in bars often took a back seat to another favorite pastime—pinball machines. A legalized form of gambling in California, pinball machines combined the fun of playing with the excitement of winning money by racking up points. Shane was hooked on it, sometimes spending ten hours at a time banging the sides of machines. It was exasperating for Reynolds, who was there to entertain secretaries and drink beer. Sometimes he could coax Shane away from the machines to sing for ten or fifteen minutes, sometimes not. Shane's compulsion for gambling once took the two beyond pinball machines to the real deal in Nevada, driving up to Reno in Reynolds's '55 Ford with a five-gallon gas can to get them back to Menlo; a low, two-day rate at the El Cortez Hotel (including meals); and thirty-five dollars each to gamble. Shane said he won—and lost—forty-two thousand dollars on his original thirty-five dollars.

Many assume that The Kingston Trio came together conceptually when Dave Guard joined Shane and Reynolds; that somehow the blend of these three talents coalesced into a magical musical phenomena. True, but the *foundation* of The Kingston Trio, ground zero, rested primarily on Bobby Shane's bar act—the dynamics, the repertoire, the humor, the *spirit* itself. Reynolds would later say, "Bobby holding court in those bars back then, man, there was just nobody that could come near to him doing that. I mean Bobby had the act down *perfectly*. He had it before I even came to Menlo. The Kingston Trio was just an embellishment; it started by building off of Bobby's act."[13]

Shane, of course, did not divine his act. He was heavily influenced by The Four Jokers, a Las Vegas lounge act that played the Lau Yee Chai, the Waikiki restaurant and bar that he and Guard had haunted and that Shane would later play himself. The Jokers specialized in risqué songs ("How Can I Get Any Sun on My Leg If You Won't Get Off of My Lap"). They'd also "localize" their songs and on-stage comedy banter with local names and references they'd picked reading the *Honolulu Advertiser* and the *Star Bulletin* or by hanging around the beach to pick up local gossip. Nick and Bobby borrowed freely from the Jokers' repertoire, developing such an extensive act that Shane said they could sing two hours' worth of songs, mostly risqué, and never repeat anything.

Shane had been singing at Menlo since his freshman year with numerous drinking buddies, including some black friends that he was hanging out with and he was the only white guy. "They were working at Stanford as stewards in the eating clubs. They had great songs and they were great people. We formed a wonderful togetherness, and I knew them for a lot of years after that. They taught me a lot of the Doo Wop stuff that was popular, like The Crows, and groups like that. And I got into it! And when I'd go back to Hawaii, I would sing some of that stuff with my beach boy buddies—and *they* got into it!"[14]

Shane explained that much of this early training was pure mimicry at which he became very adept, especially his famed Elvis impersonation, which later earned him the ad hoc title Hawaii's Elvis Presley. At Menlo in his freshman and sophomore years, he developed numerous imitations, copying Harry Belafonte and Hank Williams and other singers. Not knowing how to read music, he listened to records, copying each singer exactly as they sang their songs. If he heard a Hank Williams tune, such as "Your Cheatin' Heart," he would sing as much like Williams as he could because he felt that people liked to hear him sing just how they heard the songs on the record. Shane would then go up to Mamma Garcia's on Portola Road and sing country, Hawaiian, and comedy songs for free beer. This was long before meeting Nick Reynolds, whom he later introduced to the same bars.

And then there was Dave Guard.

For Dave Guard, Stanford was basically the route to a career, business or any other, and had been a given between Dave and his family since high school. And while it wasn't the sole reason he attended the Menlo School for his senior year, it was certainly near the top of the list. Guard's parents were not wealthy, but they weren't poor either, and they managed to come up with enough money to send him to Stanford—and more.

"David was their only child," said Gretchen Guard, "and they worked all of their lives—both of them did—and they bought the best education for him that money can buy. He went to Punahou, he went to Menlo School, he went to Stanford, he went to Stanford Business School—and they paid for all of it. I would say they were pretty devoted to him."[15]

To supplement his income, Dave worked several part-time jobs. He was a "hasher," lingo for a food service worker in the campus dining halls such as a dishwasher or waiter, working twenty hours a week. He also had a summer job as a gardener, and he cut a deal with Rudy's for a steak dinner every night that he sang there. In his freshman year, Dave broke his back falling from the second floor of Encina Hall, the freshman dorm. It was an accident waiting to happen. The second floor had a window with a fire escape that exited into a garden area, and another window—with no fire escape—that overlooked a courtyard. Since the floor's bathroom was all the way down the hall, it was commonplace for tipsy—or lazy—students to just walk out on the fire escape at night to urinate. Guard had returned to the dorm after a night of celebrating his birthday and walked out the wrong window. He was put in a body cast and airlifted back to Hawaii to recuperate, and he missed several semesters before returning to Stanford. Dave became an economics major, he said, because economics courses were five credit hours each and involved mostly reading (which he could do while recuperating) with nominal classroom attendance. It also allowed him to catch up more quickly. His natural aptitude for mathematics didn't hurt, either. After graduation from Stanford in 1956 with a degree in economics, Dave enrolled in Stanford's Graduate School of Business, but dropped out after a year.

Before Nick arrived at Menlo, Dave and Bob would occasionally sing as a duo at Rosatti's, Mama Garcia's (also known as La Casa Blanca), Rudy's, the Town Hall, the Pagliaci, and other campus beer joints. But the two were still not especially close, and were individually working some of the same bars for beer, and in Guard's case, meals. Obviously they could draw a crowd on their own. A small ad in a local paper proudly announced, "Calypso with Bob Shane and his guitar Tonite at the Pagliaci." While Stanford and Menlo were only a few miles apart, they were light years away socially. Dave, a Sigma Nu, was heavily involved in the fraternity scene, while Bobby was hanging out with his carousing buddies at Menlo. Eventually, Bob introduced Nick to Dave, although Nick said he did not remember when or how or any first impressions of Dave, except that Dave gradually began appearing with him and Bobby in their haunts around Menlo as well as in San Francisco bars.

If it was on Bob's turf, namely, bars in which he knew the bartenders or owners, Bob would be the main attraction and Dave would just sing along with him as a duo, or sing a few solo tunes that Bobby didn't know. Sometimes Dave would give Bob a rest and sing with Nick while Bobby played the pinball machine. Dave would sometimes round out the group as a trio, but usually it was just Bob and Nick.

"Nick and I were at Menlo, so we primarily sang together as a duo, even professionally," Shane explained. "We had a little card made up that said, 'We sing anywhere for money.' Dave was at Stanford, which is a couple of miles away. And he was much more studied in what he sang. But he would get together with us once in a while out at Rosatti's or Mama Garcia's and he'd do some risqué stuff with us, but mostly he was into the intellectual thing and singing more serious stuff. Nick and I just were having fun and Dave was learning to be straight, learning to be serious."[16]

Dave's fraternity connection did, however, result in frat house gigs for the three, mostly luaus or pool parties, where they'd don Hawaiian shirts and sing Hawaiian and Tahitian songs. Bobby and Dave also reprised their old comedy diving act from their Fort DeRussy days. At one such outing Dave was injured and required stitches. Al Harrington would occasionally join the group, thrilling the crowd with elaborate Samoan knife and flame dances that involved juggling and throwing long knives. It was quite a package, netting the boys as much as fifty dollars a night, good money back then.

Musically, the three were listening to what most of the country was listening to at the time—Belafonte, The Platters, Fats Domino, Bill Haley & The Comets, pop crooners, and, of course, a brand new voice, Elvis Presley. Yet at this point, the focus was still collegiate and decidedly home-grown. One local venue, in particular, would become especially important.

The Cracked Pot was located on U.S. Route 101 between Menlo Park and Redwood City on the El Camino Real. Owned by San Francisco boxing legend Ray "the Pride of the Mission" Lunny, and his partner, Johnny Johnston, the little bar was brand new when Reynolds, Shane, and Guard attended its grand opening in 1955. Any new watering hole in a college town is a welcome addition, and the place was packed with students from Menlo, Stanford, and nearby San Mateo College. Soon, Nick, Bob, and Dave auditioned for Lunny and his partner, who loved what they saw and heard, and immediately hired the three to drum up business on Wednesday night, the slowest night of the week. Reynolds was also hired to tend bar in the afternoons until Lunny and Johnston got in. The Pot would only seat about seventy-five people, but the owners built the boys a small stage and the Cracked Pot became their little club, "our place" as Nick would refer to it.

Everything seemed to be moving along so nicely until Shane flunked out of Menlo. While not totally a surprise, Bob's being "asked to not return" for his senior year was still a shock to him, throwing an unexpected wrench in both his education and any musical career plans he might have considered with Nick and Dave.

"At the end of the year, I didn't have enough credits," he explained, "because I just never could make eight o'clock classes and Nick could. I was staying up all night playing in bars. After meeting Nick, I went from a B average to a D average. I don't know to this day how Nick got his degree. I waited years before they gave me my degree." Perhaps more unsettling to him was the prospect of returning to Hawaii and the I-told-you-so attitude of Art Schoen. "My dad had always wanted me to work in the family business, so I went back and began working with him. It only lasted for a few weeks because I realized that the business was based on his personality—and my personality is not the same. That was kind of weird. So then I went to work at Sears to learn retailing what my father was wholesaling."[17] But while Shane had resigned himself to returning to Honolulu, he had no intention of giving up music, telling Reynolds that he would continue to sing in Hawaii and enroll in night school. He quickly got an unexpected break.

"I was playing on the beach and a guy said, 'Hey, I heard that Pearl City Tavern is doing a thing where if you go in on Tuesday night—the second Tuesday of the month—they do auditions.' So I went over there, had eight shots of tequila before I went on, and don't have any idea what I did. I was drinking with the owner! He called me the next day and offered me a two-week job." The Pearl City Tavern in Oahu City was just one of several clubs and restaurants Shane would play over the next six months, including the Waikiki Lau Yee Chai in Honolulu ("Bob Shane with a Little Bit of Everything from Folk Songs to Rock 'n' Roll"), the Ocean View Club at the Hotel Palm Terrace ("Rock 'n' Roll with Mr. Shane—Rocks Like Elvis and Also Sings Like Harry Belafonte !!"), the Marigold Club in Waipahu, Oahu, and Club Jetty's in Nawiliwili, Kaui. It wasn't big money—$155.84 less deductions per week union scale—but it was good money and, more importantly, Shane was doing what he loved to do most.[18]

One of the highlights of Shane's solo club career was meeting one of his heroes, blues legend Josh White, who was appearing in Honolulu. "We all used to get together at a late night restaurant in Waikiki called Captain D's," Shane recalled. "Josh saw my four-string tenor guitar at the restaurant and said, 'Why don't you play a six-string guitar? It will make a fuller sound and make you sound better.' I told him I was self-taught and I thought it was really hard. He handed me his Martin and showed me how to overlap the chords I played on my tenor. Within forty-five minutes I was playing quite well. Josh White actually taught me how to play three chords in four keys in forty-five minutes. What a fantastic man. He later became a very dear friend and taught me a lot about working and show business in general. Right after Josh White showed me how to play the chords on a six-string as opposed to the tenor, I went out and bought my first Martin D-28 at Bergstrom Music in Honolulu, and I was hooked."[19]

At first Shane's departure from Menlo had created a void in Reynolds's life, but it also opened up his relationship with Dave Guard. The two started singing as a duo, and sometimes as a trio with Willie Gage, one of Dave's Sigma Nu brothers. Joe Gannon, a friend of Nick's and Bobby's from Menlo, was also asked to play bass because, according to Nick, it looked better with someone standing back there even if nobody could hear him.

Gannon admits that he had bluffed his way into the group by telling Guard and Reynolds that he played bass, which was a stretch. "I actually didn't play anything very well," he admitted. "I started out playing a washtub kind of thing. See, the guys were all going out and having fun and getting drunk every night and I told them I could play bass, which is not really true. So I got a real bass and we played at the Cracked Pot."[20]

This ad hoc group was totally fluid, playing as a trio with Willie Gage one night and as a quartet or quintet or whatever size group showed up the next, with Joe Gannon or Curley Carswell or Al Harrington or Donnie MacArthur or whoever. Donnie, Nick's close friend from Coronado, would sometimes play bongos in synch with Nick on conga drum or trading off rhythms. Sometimes people in the audience would join in, including a girl in the audience at the Pagliaci down the block from the Cracked Pot who actually became a full-fledged member of the group. "One night we were playing and all of a sudden a young lady jumped up onstage and started to sing with us," Joe Gannon recalled. "It was Barb Bogue, and she was one sweet young thing."[21]

Barbara Bogue was a schoolteacher from Portland, Oregon, who had recently gotten her degree from Oregon State and moved to Menlo Park for a teaching job. She was a pretty strawberry blonde, full of energy, with an amazing contralto singing voice. Although she had no formal vocal training, she sang in the choir in college and developed a unique kind of vocalization. "She had a voice that could really jump up so many octaves," said Joe Gannon, who later married Bogue. "She used to do these like flute-sounding vocal parts over the top of the guys singing harmony . . . and I'd just go 'boom, boom, boom, doo, doo, doo' upping volume on the bass."[22]

"She had a real high voice, sort of an Yma Sumac type contralto," Reynolds recalled. "And she and Dave would improvise stuff. They would just scare you to death—they'd be going on for ten or fifteen minutes . . . 'ah oo ah oo' . . . 'ah oo ah oo' . . . you know, this very ethereal stuff. And I'd play the bongos, Joe would be playing bass fiddle, Dave would be playing the guitar, and Barbara would just be sitting in a chair doing this improvisational, sort of jungle music. It was really far out. This would take

up half the show sometimes. But it was great 'cause it had a Latin beat.
They weren't saying anything; they were just going off on this very far out
tangent. But people didn't care. Then we'd sing our regular stuff."[23]

Guard was determined to kick it up a notch as a group, hopefully
breaking into the legit San Francisco club scene. With Shane gone, he was
now the undisputed leader of this amorphous group that was now billed
as Dave Guard and The Calypsonians and included Guard, Reynolds, Joe
Gannon, and Barbara Bogue. The group bought identical striped shirts
from the College Shop in Palo Alto (setting the paradigm for Kingston
Trio stage outfits), had professional photos taken including some with
coats and ties, and recorded a series of demos at the Music House Studio
in San Mateo and, according to Nick Reynolds, at Sound Recorders in
San Francisco. At the same time, the group actively auditioned for gigs
in North Beach, including Facs II and a promising audition at the Purple
Onion on November 24, 1956, as Nick enthusiastically recounts in a letter
to his parents:[24]

Dec. 10—1956

Dear Momma & Dads,

Sorry it took so long to get info on purple onion etc., finally have it
so here goes. We auditioned the Saturday after I returned from Thanks-
giving, at 3:00 in the afternoon. Also auditioning at the same time were
six other singers, comedians, etc.

I was a smashing success. They didn't even talk to the other people.

We talked about money & unions, etc. and they said that we should
have one more "live" audition (in front of an audience) before really
talking business. They called us Tuesday and we went up that night. It
was a packed house, we sang three songs & the crowd brought us back
for two encores. More damn fun. They wanted to sign us to a contract
right then to take the place of Pat Roco who was leaving this Sat. (article enclosed from Chronicle). This is where the bubble burst.

Dave has not seen his parents in 3 years & has to go home for Christmas, needless to say the same for me & Barbara. As they have to have
someone to fill in the spot they are going to hire someone else for this
period of three wks. We are still on good terms with them (they love
us). What will happen after the first of the year no one knows. It was
all very exciting & no one is disappointed more than the purple onion.
It's really a tremendous boost for our ego and a real feather in our cap.

Love & Kisses to all—

Love,

Nacker

Earlier they had joined the musicians union, the American Federation of Musicians, San Mateo Local 6, where Reynolds laughingly remembered he had to play the bongos for about thirty seconds to "prove" he was a musician. Barbara Bogue had a connection to a San Francisco talent agent, Dick Reinhart, with whom they signed and got their first real San Francisco booking, a weekend engagement at the Italian Village located at Columbus and Lombard. The Village was a large supper club that catered primarily to tourists and family events such as weddings and bar mitzvahs. It also booked a variety of talent, big name stars such as Sophie Tucker and local favorites such as Turk Murphy's Jazz Band in the main room, and piano players, cabaret singers, and tryouts downstairs in the lounge. Dave Guard and The Calypsonians were booked into the lounge.

Joe Gannon said that prior to the Italian Village engagement, he had arranged for the group to play in the lounge at Bimbo's 365 Club, a North Beach supper club famous for its "girl in a fishbowl" attraction.

At the time of the booking, Nick had already left the group and returned home to Coronado to investigate opening a restaurant and bar with the Pickfords, with Nick's parents as potential co-investors. In his absence, Don MacArthur joined Dave Guard and The Calypsonians (or The Kingston Quartet as it was briefly called after Nick left the group).

"I was not really committed totally yet," Reynolds recalled, "and Dave called me and said, 'I wish you could come up this weekend. We're playing at the Italian Village and it'd be really great because it's a really great opportunity.' My folks gave me the bread, I flew to San Francisco and we played in the Italian Village. Donnie MacArthur had replaced me in the group, playing bongos, and was kind of heartbroken that he didn't get to play in the big game. But Dave told him what the deal was: 'It's fine when Nick's not around. If Nick's around, he sings with me.' Donnie didn't really do any singing. It was just a lounge type of a crowd; it was really a bomb. But it was pretty big time. It was one of those huge, old-timey nightclubs where they had the main room where Sophie Tucker was packing them in. Everybody had their wedding there, all the Italians. It was a big Italian contingency."[25]

It may have been a "bomb," as Nick put it, but among the few who took in Dave Guard and The Calypsonians' Saturday night show downstairs in the lounge was a customer who saw a potential super group waiting to happen.

NOTES

1. Nick Reynolds, interview with the author, Port Orford, OR, November 11, 1983.

2. Bob Shane, interview with the author, Phoenix, AZ, November 23, 1983.

3. Nick Reynolds, interview with the author, Seminole, FL, October 3, 1986.

4. Reynolds, interview with the author, October 3, 1986.

5. Reynolds, interview with the author, October 3, 1986.

6. Reynolds, interview with the author, October 3, 1986.

7. Reynolds, interview with the author, October 3, 1986.

8. Bob Shane, interview with the author, Phoenix, AZ, April 6, 2009.

9. Reynolds, interview with the author, October 3, 1986.

10. Reynolds, interview with the author, October 3, 1986.

11. Reynolds, interview with the author, October 3, 1986.

12. Shane, interview with the author, April 6, 2009.

13. Reynolds, interview with author, October 3, 1986.

14. Bob Shane, interview with author, Phoenix, AZ, August 21, 2007.

15. Gretchen Guard, interview with the author, Santa Fe, NM, January 10, 2010.

16. Bob Shane, interview with the author, Phoenix, AZ, July 20, 2001; Shane, interview with the author, August 21, 2007.

17. Shane, interview with the author, April 6, 2009.

18. Bob Shane, interview with author, Phoenix, AZ, August 22, 2007.

19. Shane, interview with author, August 21, 2007.

20. Joe Gannon, interview with the author, Maui, HI, March 21, 2010.

21. Gannon, interview with the author.

22. Gannon, interview with the author.

23. Reynolds, interview with the author, October 3, 1986.

24. Letter from Nick Reynolds to Mr. and Mrs. Stuart Reynolds, December 10, 1956.

25. Reynolds, interview with the author, October 3, 1986.

4

FRANK

Frank Werber was only thirty-one years old when he first laid eyes on the group of fledgling "entertainers" that would become The Kingston Trio. Yet he had already lived a hundred lifetimes, each filled with an abundance of drama, intrigue, and complexity that few ever experience.

Frank Nicholas Werber was born in Cologne, Germany, on March 27, 1929. His father was Jewish; his mother, a Christian, died in childbirth five years after Frank was born, leaving Frank and his father, Edwin, to face an increasingly terrifying world.

With the rise of Adolf Hitler and his pathological persecution of the Jews, Frank and his father fled, first to Poland and then to Belgium in 1933, and from there to southern France, where they were captured by the Nazis during the war. The two were imprisoned in a Nazi concentration camp in Vichy France for a year, barely missing execution.

With the help of the French underground, Edwin and young Frank escaped and made their way through Casablanca and Dakar in North Africa and ultimately on to Martinique, a French island in the eastern Caribbean, finally arriving in New York in 1941.

While America was a haven from the murderous Nazis, it did not shield young Frank from anti-Semitism or the stigma of being a destitute immigrant who barely spoke English.

Nor did it alleviate their incessant search for work that, over the next decade, saw Frank and his father living in New York City, Jacksonville (Florida), New Orleans, and Denver, with Frank ultimately leaving his father and moving on to Dallas, Las Vegas (New Mexico), and finally, San Francisco. Frank's formal education consisted of high school, a year at the University of Colorado, and a couple of semesters at The Art Institute of Chicago. His *real* education, the one that would sustain him throughout his life, came from real-world experience amplified by his innate high intelligence, inquisitiveness, and need to survive.

Frank was urbane, shrewd, sensitive, and eclectic, a hustler and worldly beyond his years, having seen and traveled much of it with his father and, later, as a midshipmen in the U.S. Navy in his early twenties.

While Werber would acknowledge that the traumatic experiences of his childhood did have an effect on him, he was philosophical, even sanguine, of its lasting relevance. "I didn't think of myself as a starving kid in a concentration camp, but I was in that space at that time," he reflected. "If you really looked at my life, hey, I never thought of saying 'I had a horrible life.' In fact, I've had a *great* life, a fucking charming, great life. But [I] don't deny the experiences. It all came down."[1] And while he rarely mentioned the atrocities he had witnessed as a child, he never forgot even the smallest detail of his childhood. Don MacArthur, the Trio's first road manager, recalls a side trip he and Frank took to Brussels in 1964 when the Trio was playing at the opening of the London Hilton.

"We rented a car in Brussels and Frank was looking for the camera shop his father worked at after they fled Germany and the Nazis. Brussels is a big city. We were driving all over while Frank tried to figure out where the camera shop was. All of a sudden there was a huge, like, twenty-story building in front of us that was kind of diamond shaped, and Frank said, 'If we go around the back of this building there should be a school and then right past the school there's some shops and one of them is a little camera store.' So we cruised around the corner and sure enough there was the school, and we went around the next corner and there was the camera shop. When we got out of the car, I'm telling you it was really emotional. He just broke down. It really brought back some heavy-duty memories for him. He started crying. I started crying. It was really very touching."[2]

More than anything, such experiences gave Werber the resoluteness to not just survive, but to *succeed*. Over the course of his life, he was a Holocaust survivor, refugee, ditchdigger, cabdriver, ski lift operator, sailor, construction worker, itinerant drifter, baby photographer, golf caddy, UPI (United Press International) photo stringer, night club manager, artist manager, restaurant owner, and PR flack, to name a few of many occupations—all of which he did with determination.

"At 12, I was working—working ever since—never having a day off; never a vacation. There was never a time I wasn't made to feel like I should be in some bucks; it was laid out to me that I should cover my own scene. I was made to understand that I should take care of myself. My dad loved me; that was covered. But I never liked what things were available in my

life. There weren't any options." San Francisco provided him with those
options. "I never felt a part of society. I was a stranger in the strange land.
San Francisco was the first place that felt good," he said, "where I could
communicate with somebody"—referring to the city's large artist, poet,
musician, and writer population.[3]

North Beach had long been a Mecca for free spirits of all kinds.
Located northeast of downtown, bordering Chinatown and Fisherman's
Wharf, to the south and north, respectively, and Russian Hill to the west,
the neighborhood was long known as Little Italy due to its large Italian
American population, including baseball great Joe DiMaggio. It was also
the epicenter of the 1950s' beat literary culture with Jack Kerouac, Neal
Cassady, Allen Ginsberg, Alan Watts, and Lawrence Ferlinghetti (founder
of City Lights Bookstore on the corner of Columbus and Broadway). It
was also the city's nightclub district, bordering the red light zone, where
striptease joints lived in perfect harmony with bars, jazz clubs, cafes, bistros,
and restaurants.

That Frank would gravitate to North Beach and ultimately meet
and come to know Enrico Banducci, the owner and impresario of the
neighborhood's legendary hungry i nightclub and restaurant, was a cosmic
certainty.

Everybody in the San Francisco entertainment and restaurant scene
knew Enrico, the colorful, sometimes eccentric, businessman, chef, brawler,
star maker, tastemaker, trendsetter, guru, folk hero, court holder, friend of
politicos and celebrities, and champion of artists, comics, musicians, and
singers, both well-known and unknown. Enrico was the "heart and soul"
of the North Beach entertainment scene, as one writer would describe him
on the occasion of his death years later. "Crazier than a fucking hoot owl"
is how Werber described Banducci and their often volatile relationship.[4]

Born Harry Charles Banducci in Bakersfield, California, in 1922,
he ran away to San Francisco at age thirteen to study violin with several
distinguished violinists. He eventually changed his name to Enrico, supposedly in honor of Enrico Caruso (although his daughter says he just
liked Enrico better). In 1949, Banducci borrowed eight hundred dollars
and bought the original hungry i located in the basement of the Columbus
Tower at 149 Columbus Avenue (the corner of Columbus and Kearney)
from its founder, Eric "Big Daddy" Nord, a beat poet, actor and nightclub
owner. Under Banducci, the i was initially little more than a neighborhood gathering spot for actors, poets, beats, and assorted other bohemians,
with informal "shows" on Sunday that included readings, rantings, music,
and whatever. By 1952, Enrico was staging nightly entertainment starting

with Stan Wilson, a black folksinger from Oakland and one of the first revival "folk" to frequent San Francisco. Two years later Banducci moved the hungry i around the corner to 599 Jackson Street, a much bigger "cellar club" venue, with the lounge upstairs and the main show room in the basement, increasing seating from eighty-two to over four hundred. With a newly acquired liquor license, the hungry i quickly became one of San Francisco's leading nightclubs featuring new jazz, folk, and stand-up comedy talent showcases.

Over the years, Enrico helped launch the careers of numerous singers, musicians, comedians, folk groups, and jazz artists, including Mort Sahl, Lenny Bruce, Professor Irwin Corey, Shelley Berman, Bill Cosby, Tom Lehrer, Mike Nichols and Elaine May, Dick Gregory, Woody Allen, Jonathan Winters, Dick Cavett, Bob Newhart, The Smothers Brothers, Maya Angelou, Vince Guaraldi, Barbra Streisand, The Gateway Singers, The Kingston Trio, The Limeliters, Josh White, Miriam Makeba, and literally dozens more. Alvah Bessie, the blacklisted Hollywood screenwriter, was the announcer and worked the lights. And Frank Werber helped Banducci do it all.

As a UPI photographer, Frank had his own camera, access to the UPI photo lab, and free film, which allowed him to freelance baby pictures as well as visit the North Beach night spots on the "celeb beat." The hungry i was one of those spots, and soon Frank was working part time for Enrico taking couple-at-the-bar photos. Because he was theatrically oriented, Werber worked the stage lights and the sound, arranged the set order, auditioned the talent, and passed along his impressions and recommendations to Enrico, who did the talent buying.

Like Enrico, Frank was an advocate for the artists who would appear at the hungry i and later at the Purple Onion, especially comedians, giving them both personal and professional advice as he saw it. He literally scored every performance, without fail. If he saw ways to sharpen the acts or improve repertoire and delivery, he'd tell the artists. He became an astute judge of what worked and what didn't. "I spent every night in the club—a minimum of three, sometimes four shows—and I evaluated it to myself or for any acts that were interested in what this young punk had to say. I paid close attention to what the audiences did or didn't like. For background, that was my schooling."[5] Werber could be tough, but he was never destructive. He would use this combination of candor and sensitivity to better focus the artist, be it Bob Newhart or Bob Shane.

Werber remained with Banducci for four or five years, depending on how you count the many times he quit or was fired. He and Enrico both loved and hated each other and often traded roles of teacher and student to their mutual benefit. Frank said that working for Enrico sometimes made him think he was going insane, but that he actually liked it. "I suddenly found myself in a world where I no longer felt like a 'schlub' on the outside," he said.[6] For that alone, Werber was grateful, but he still moved on—even if it was only around the block.

Frank's tenure at the hungry i made him well-known to artists, agents, journalists, and club owners throughout the Bay Area. Having been a UPI photographer on the San Francisco–New York beat, he was well trained and connected to local and national media. Publicity and artist management seemed a natural career progression, even if it meant having Enrico as a client. His friendship with artists like Mort Sahl and close contact with San Francisco columnist Herb Caen didn't hurt either.

Before long, Werber opened the Frank Werber Agency at 140 Columbus Street in a tiny loft office above a barbershop next to the Purple Onion. Clients included the Purple Onion (in which Banducci had an ownership stake), the hungry i, Ann's 440 on Broadway, Romanoff's restaurant, and the Papagayo Room at the Fairmont Hotel. It was a move that would soon have a momentous impact on Werber's life and fortunes.

Legend has it that wannabe agent/manager Frank Werber, acting on a tip from a waiter at the Purple Onion, took a ride down to the Cracked Pot in Redwood City to check out the Trio. And that Werber was so impressed he signed Bob Shane, Nick Reynolds, and Dave Guard to a management contract on the spot, writing out the terms on a cocktail napkin. Not so.

"Frank was on the lookout for Enrico Banducci who was now a client," Reynolds explained, "and he had also handled the publicity for the Purple Onion and wanted to branch out. He'd never managed anybody before, but he'd seen a lot. He was a frustrated performer himself. So yeah, he came down to the Cracked Pot. The romantic thing of writing a contract on a napkin on the spot is bullshit, you know. There might have been some notes and some phone numbers exchanged, but that was about it."[7]

What's more, by the time Werber showed up at the Cracked Pot, Shane had already left California and was back in Honolulu working for his father and playing in clubs at night. And while the waiter, Chuck Marcoux, may have seen a pre–Kingston Trio audition at the Old Spaghetti House where Marcoux worked before the Purple Onion, that's not who Frank saw at the Cracked Pot.

"The guys I first saw were Dave Guard and The Calypsonians, which was Dave, Nick, and three or four dudes—and they didn't do too much," Werber recalled. "The group was fairly loose when I met them. One time it would be four, and one time it would be two or six, it was sort of a college conglomerate. But I felt their *energy*. My background had been in nightclubs, and I just got a feeling for what worked and reached the people. They projected an energy that was very vibrant, very catching. It was to those straight times what punk rock was to its time. They weren't doing 'Boney Maroni,' but they were moving and shouting, and that's energy released and that's what I went on."[8]

Even though nothing panned out with Werber on the first visit, the Cracked Pot was very important to the future formation of The Kingston Trio, providing critical experience in playing to club audiences, the more raucous and beery the better, and would serve them well in the year ahead. As it turned out, it put Nick and Dave—and later Bobby—on Frank's radar.

The group that Frank had seen at the Cracked Pot, while popular with the college crowd, was nowhere near ready for the urbane San Francisco club scene, and while Frank clearly saw some potential, he could hardly make any real promises at that point. It was a later Dave Guard and The Calypsonians' appearance, the one-night gig at the Italian Village in San Francisco, that actually got Werber's attention. By that time, the lineup had been culled down to a more "serious" group that included Dave Guard, Nick Reynolds, Barbara Bogue, and Joe Gannon. Frank was invited by Dave and Nick to attend *that* show, and while he was more enthusiastic about what he saw and heard, there were still problems.

"It was tough to get work for four people in those days," Werber explained. "I felt the bass player [Joe Gannon] was not an asset, though his wife [Barbara Bogue] was. And, as a matter of fact, I told Dave that. But they felt they couldn't fire Joe because Barbara would leave. I told Dave and Nick, 'If you can fire him, come back and see me.' They did that, and that's when Bobby joined. So the thing started from scratch at that point. And it was raw energy, it was their feeling and it was their time. We were all part of an experience, and we met at the right conjecture of space and time."[9]

Dave Guard, however, did not wish to share that space with Bob Shane. "He thought Bobby was too much of a fuck-up, too much responsibility," Reynolds said. "He didn't want his life ruled by someone who was going to aggravate the shit out of him; someone who was not going to take orders. I can remember going round and round with Dave about it, and him saying 'God, I don't need the pressure of Bobby not showing up or being lazy. I can't ever work with Bobby Shane.' I said, 'yeah, but it's not going to happen without Bobby and it's not going to happen without me. You'll have Barbara Bogue and that's all you're going to have, Dave—and yourself.' And David basically knew that, but he hated to have to commit himself to something that he would lose control of entirely. He had complete control over The Calypsonians even if it wasn't much fun and it wasn't very good musically—interesting sometimes—but definitely not a pop act."[10] Bob wasn't anxious to work with Dave, either, knowing Dave's penchant for bossiness and rigidity to ideas other than his own. What Guard viewed as being a "fuck-up" was precisely at the core of Shane's genius for performing "on the natch." Both elements—Guard's intellectual precision and Shane's shoot-from-the hip-and-heart instincts—were major components of what would make The Kingston Trio so unique and, ultimately, so successful.

Reynolds, at the time, still wouldn't fully commit to either Guard or Shane because, as he put it, his family was conservative and he was planning a career in line with his upbringing and his family's expectations. But there was something else, too, that no one but Nick knew.

With Shane in Hawaii and Guard preoccupied with graduate school, Nick would occasionally hit the hungry i by himself where one night he discovered that Travis Edmondson, his singing buddy from the University of Arizona, had joined The Gateway Singers and was playing with them at the club. (Travis would leave The Gateway Singers in 1958 to form Bud and Travis with Bud Dashiell.)

"He got a hold of me one of the nights I was sitting in the audience," Reynolds remembered, and he said, "'I'm thinking about getting out of The Gateway Singers. I don't see any major success for myself in this thing. Would you like to sing together?" I said, 'God Travis! What a compliment!' Here's this big star, man, making three hundred bucks a week. If *I* could make three hundred bucks a week I'd be wealthy! So he said, 'Come on over to the house.' I was sort of sneaking away from Dave to go do this. Travis lived in a funny little apartment up in a strange section of south San Francisco where we started wood shedding, just Travis and I, singing some songs we both knew. He was also going to teach me how to play the electric bass guitar. And then he said, 'What do you think if I get Jerry Walter [The Gateway Singers' main arranger and banjo player], 'cause Jerry would like to do this, too.' I said, my God! Two of The Gateway Singers want me to play with them?!!! So Jerry came over, and he was a little suspect of me, this damn college kid [laughing], you know, who didn't know how to play an instrument. But we rehearsed two or three times with Jerry, and then everything sort of blew up."[11]

It was hardly a surprise to Nick. "Travis was another one like Bobby, who had the perfect magnetism and the perfect voice, and he was not happy doing anything but singing and playing. But The Gateway Singers as a whole was entirely different than the singular parts. Jerry Walter was very political in the East Bay, as was Lou Gottleib to an extent. Any group that Travis was with there was always a little dissension because he was like Peck's bad boy, you know?" There was also a racial matter. Elmer-lee Thomas, the beautiful and powerful black singer who many feel was the key voice in the group, became an issue with Travis, especially when segregation hit them in the face at a gig in Lake Tahoe where Elmerlee was denied entry into the casino where they were headlining. "Travis had grandiose ideas, you know," Nick said. "We'll have our own trio, sing our own songs, make a lot of money. . . . We don't need the problem of having a black person in the group; let's go someplace where we can play." While Reynolds was flattered to be asked to join, and briefly considered it, the allure of playing with Shane and Guard, no matter how contentious it was at times, was too powerful to resist. "Bobby had come back and I just said, 'Well, I've made a commitment to these other guys so I'm going to follow up on that.'"[12]

Frank had laid it out very clearly. They needed to be a trio and it needed to be Dave Guard, Nick Reynolds, and Bob Shane. "There's a future for you," Werber told the three. "But you've got to be more structured than you are now—and none of this bullshit about running off to Hawaii if you get pissed off. Commit yourself for a year, or forget it."[13]

"Everything was kind of lining up for us," Reynolds explained, "Dave finally said, 'Okay, I'll try it for a year,' and I finally made the commitment to come back from Coronado because Bobby made the commitment to come back and work with Dave."[14] It was decided that Frank Werber would be their manager, and San Francisco would be their base. Frank got them out of their contract with agent Dick Reinhart, and a verbal deal was made between the four of them.

Guard, Reynolds, and Shane couldn't have been in better hands.

With Werber they were getting more than a manager. They were getting a managing *partner*. And although Frank had never managed an artist before ("We were all amateurs," he once laughingly confided), he knew exactly what it took to be successful in show business—and *stay* successful.

Focus was critical. He had observed what had happened between many artists and their managers, the negative energies and distractions that ultimately sapped their talent and spirit and destroyed their careers. He had initially been attracted by the energy of the Trio, the personal contact they made with each other and with their audiences. *That* was their cachet—their X factor—that would distinguish and elevate The Kingston Trio from all other folk groups past and future, and ultimately make them an international phenomenon. That essence had to be protected and nurtured, Werber reasoned—"keeping it pure" he called it—and he would "take care of everything else," so that Guard, Reynolds, and Shane could focus solely on their act without distractions.

Business—or more pointedly, money—has always been a lethal distraction in any artistic relationship. Typically, managers take a percentage of their artists' gross revenue—before expenses—assuming little or no liability for anything. Werber was different. He viewed The Kingston Trio as a partnership, with the four of them having an equal share of Kingston Trio, Inc., as their corporation would later be named. They would share equally in the wealth as well as the expenses; their corporation would cover personal liability. It would remove any specter of unwarranted financial gain by any individual member. Most importantly, they would all share one goal—to be a successful show business act. And while each would have a voice in corporate and artistic decisions, Werber demanded their total commitment to work hard and follow *his* direction in the shaping of the act. He was to be the boss. Period.

"I've joked about being a benevolent dictator," Werber once reflected, "but I've gotta feel I can do what I think is right within the limitations of the game. But in order for me to do that—if you'll accept me on those terms—then, for me to do the things that are right, I've got to have your input involved. Otherwise, I violate the first understanding of how to move somebody. So, that's a prerequisite, but I wanna be left with 'give *me* the decision-making space.' I want the bridge, but you've got to give me the input. Then I'll decide how that input is to be translated."[15]

It was all about building the act. There would be fines for anything that negatively affected the group—being late, missing a rehearsal, excessive drinking, foul language on stage, and inappropriate behavior of any sort. Even cigarette smoking was frowned upon, although tolerated in moderation. "It was almost like, 'Jesus will take care of you if pay attention,'" said Bob Shane. "A church teaches you to do the right thing. Well this was the Church of Werber. You pay attention to what I say and do the right thing, and we'll all be happy together. And some of the direction he gave us in the beginning was *very* definitely what we needed."[16] For his part, Frank focused his managerial efforts solely on the Trio; he was a "one-act manager," and would remain so for years.

Although no one knew it at the time, Werber's shrewd instincts would help make The Kingston Trio not only a wealthy phenomenon in music, but a case study in astute single client management.

"Frank Werber's style of centralized management has guided The Kingston Trio to fame and riches—and caused the entertainment world to sit up and take notice," *Business Week* observed in early 1963. "Without so much as plucking a guitar, Werber is already leaving his mark in show business. The bewhiskered San Franciscan is one of a breed of 'strong' managers—men who devote all their time and energy to one client and assume a variety of management functions that ordinarily require a pack of percentage-grabbing managers and agents."[17]

The group rarely ventured far beyond North Beach in 1957. Dave and Nick moved into an old Victorian house at 2009 Vallejo Street, three blocks from Frank's office—Nick in a small, one window basement studio and Dave, who had married the year before, in a large top-floor apartment with his wife Gretchen. Bobby lived in a boarding house a few doors down the block. To save money, the three would eat at the Green Valley restaurant where a full meal cost only $1.25—including wine. The Humble Bagel, on the corner of Green and Grant, was another favorite eatery and hangout. Nick bought a Volkswagen cargo van to shuttle the group and their instruments back and forth between Frank's office, and later, to occasional gigs up and down the coast to sharpen their chops and try out new songs and comedy bits. Initially, the three began to rehearse in Dave's living room, but Frank had a different plan.

The boys would meet in *his* office next door to the Purple Onion. And for the next year, it would become the group's rehearsal hall, war room, and sanctuary—all under Frank's watchful eye. As the Trio's manager and partner, Werber had the responsibility to find them work. But first they needed to build an act that was sellable to tough club owners. As the publicist for the Purple Onion, Frank had the ear of the club's owners, Bud and Virginia "Ginnie" Steinhoff, as well as club manager Barry Drew, who selected the talent. But Werber held back on auditioning the group for the Purple Onion—or any other club—until he felt the act was presentable.

The stories of this self-imposed "wood shedding" are many, and though rehearsals were rigorous, they were never drudgery. Frank knew the business and what audiences would like, and he could be a taskmaster, but he too was learning as they went along, so there was a lot of give-and-take between the four of them. But just having the benefit of his objectivity and the discipline of scheduled rehearsals was invaluable. With no money coming in, other than personal savings and what parents would chip in monthly, everybody felt the pinch. A lot was riding on this gamble. With Dave having quit graduate school, Nick turning down a ready-made career, and Bobby further straining his relationship with his father, failure was not an option.

As a result, *everything* was carefully thought out, planned, worked over, and perfected—the songs, harmonies, jokes, timing, pacing, lighting, stage presence, wardrobe. Nothing was improvised. Rehearsals ran from 2 to 6 p.m. every day in a little diamond-shaped garret room off of Frank's office. Each song was recorded on Werber's *Wollensak* tape recorder, played back and dissected, and taped again. Later, when they actually began working at the Purple Onion, they'd rehearse right up to show time, go down and play their show, and go right back up to Frank's office to review the show—and rehearse even more if necessary. Sometimes they'd rehearse downstairs in the off hours on the Purple Onion's stage.

"We tried to organize our shows from the beginning," Dave Guard remembered. "Nick was sort of the impresario that way. He would write down the tunes in order and said, 'Okay we've got to structure this so that the first tune is funny and then we do something straighter and then we can do a ballad and then we can do something sort of serious and then we've got to bring it up right after that.' So, I mean, it had sort of a pace. He was always the guy that was structuring stuff. From the very beginning, he insisted on writing out all the lyrics instead of just playing them—we've got first chorus here, second chorus there, and all that. So he was very conscious of putting those on paper. Later on I got to putting them on paper myself, but he was the guy that originally insisted on it and was conscious of structuring those things. So I think that's what it came out of, that we had to have a certain number of tunes like this and a certain number like that, and so it balanced out at the real performance."[18]

The meetings in Frank's office also focused on hard issues that needed to be addressed right away, the first being what they were going to name the group. Bob and Nick as a duo were never really called anything other than Bob and Nick—if they were called anything at all. "The Calypsonians" was floated as a possibility, but they all thought it "tied them down too much in a narrow musical vein." When Dave suggested "The Dave Guard Trio," it was immediately and soundly rejected by the others. "Why not?!!!" Dave stammered. "That's what I thought it was going to be!" Nick said it was one of the first really strained moments in the new trio. Dave Guard and The Calypsonians had called themselves The Kingston Quartet when Nick had briefly left the group after graduation and Don MacArthur had taken his place. But Bob said that he, Nick, and Dave thought of The Kingston Trio as a group name at the Cracked Pot because of Harry Belafonte's "met a little girl in Kingston town" lyric in "Jamaica Farewell." Ultimately, they settled on The Kingston Trio because, as Reynolds reasoned, "it sounds kind of Ivy League"—Kingston, Rhode Island, back East-y, kind of preppy, but it also had kind of a Jamaican or Caribbean flavor.

An even harder issue, and one that would have lasting consequences, was the decision to avoid anything political or even remotely controversial in the act. "Dave just didn't want to make any waves," said Reynolds, a point that Guard denied, saying that it was *Werber* who insisted that the group do no political or controversial material. They talked about The Weavers, The Gateway Singers, Belafonte—who was doing what and how committed should they be. In truth, none of them really had any political statements they wanted to make. "But we *did* have our own personal feelings about it," Reynolds emphasized. While many of the songs they were starting to sing had political overtones, it was the *musicality* and emotion of the song, not the hard content, that moved them. "We wanted to sing songs we *all* liked without going too far one way or the other—middle of the road," Reynolds said. To do otherwise, he reasoned, would "not to be true of us." This conservative approach carried over to their visual image. Dave Guard and The Calypsonians had initiated the striped shirts motif; Werber and the Trio added gray flannel pants, black loafers, and white socks. Clean cut. *That* was going to be their trademark.[19]

The Kingston Trio would be forever criticized for their apolitical stance, a strategic decision that would later overshadow and even preclude acknowledgment of the enormous, and profound, influence the group had on popular music in general, and folk music—*including* protest music—in particular. The training they were receiving at Werber's second-floor loft was by no means their only source of inspiration. Most of their free time was spent carefully studying established acts at the hungry i, Purple Onion, and other area clubs. It was a learning method that would continue well into their musical careers. Lou Gottlieb of The Gateway Singers, and later The Limeliters, would provide the inspiration for Guard's long-winded banter used as between-song filler. Gottlieb and fellow Gateway member Jerry Walter would also have a profound effect on the group's song arranging and harmony building. Bobby was especially drawn to Stan Wilson who provided a good deal of material for Shane as well as the Trio. Josh White was also helpful in transitioning Shane from tenor guitar to six-string guitar.

The entire North Beach milieu, in fact, galvanized the Trio to the possibility of becoming professional entertainers. Watching jazz greats Chico Hamilton and Stan Getz at the Black Hawk, hip comedians Mort Sahl and Lenny Bruce at the hungry i, Phyllis Diller at the Purple Onion *all* made an indelible impression. In time, they began hanging out with the San Francisco folk elite, going out with them after their last shows, eating and talking and listening to them as to what was going on around the North Beach circuit. Barbara Dane, Melvina Reynolds, Maya Angelou, Stan Wilson, Lou Gottlieb, Rod McKuen, and others were all friends; blues legends

Sonny Terry and Brownie McGhee even played in Dave's apartment. "I was sent out for the Jack Daniels—which was a requirement!" Reynolds fondly recalled, "and we sat until daylight listening to those guys play."[20]

While they were still hitting the bars nightly, they were also discovering a side of San Francisco they'd never known. "Getting a taste of the San Francisco culture was just thrilling in those days," Reynolds reminisced. "We'd go to these jazz and poetry readings where there'd be a piano player and horn player, and Alan Watts would stand up and recite a whole bunch of stuff I didn't even understand, but I knew something was happening because the places were packed! We were getting in on the end of the beatnik period. Frank Werber had a houseboat in Sausalito, and we discovered Sausalito and just fell in love with it. That's where all the bohemians and artists were—down on the waterfront in houseboats. Alan Watts and Allen Ginsberg, everybody was around there. We'd see them all in the park."[21]

Folk music, especially the urban Greenwich Village coffee house variety, seemed to naturally attract a bohemian element including "beat" poets, writers, philosophers, artists, singers, and other unconventional thinkers. And while Guard, Reynolds, Shane, and Werber were hardly members of the "beat generation," there was definitely an affinity in spirit. Reynolds would often say, "There are no accidents," and it's not surprising that San Francisco, and more particularly North Beach, would become the epicenter of the beat counterculture. As the folk revival of the late 1940s migrated west, it flourished in the Bay Area—North Beach, Sausalito, and especially Berkeley. The Berkley Little Theatre staged numerous concerts in the mid-1950s featuring such folk luminaries as Pete Seeger, Theodore Bikel, Billy Faier, Sonny Terry and Brownie McGhee, Barbara Dane, Odetta, and other national folk and blues acts. The Kingston Trio too would later play the Berkeley Little Theatre shortly after the release of "Tom Dooley" in early September of 1958 to a less-than-full house.

But the defining moment, the one that set The Kingston Trio on an irreversible track, was seeing The Weavers in person at the Opera House in San Francisco.

"It was the *big* experience of our lives, the most thrilling experience ever," Nick Reynolds recalled, still emotional at the memory. "Holy Christ! We were all in tears from the first note they sang to the last note they sang—I could not believe it, I just couldn't believe it, it was the most magical evening I've ever spent in my life. It was the first time and last time I'd ever see The Weavers—Pete, Lee, Fred, and Ronnie. Oh my God! The dynamics, and this *thing* I'd heard through their records. Put them in with a couple thousand people that have got a cause, watch out man, it was so fantastic. And they were just singing their regular show—'Wimoweh,'

'Buddy, Can You Spare a Dime?'—all the great stuff that was on their Carnegie Hall concert album. Dave, Bobby, and I were just kids, so we didn't go backstage. They were our idols and seeing them was just a dream. We left there and didn't know what the hell was going on. But *that's* when our whole effort was meshed in with that type of music."[22]

And what better stage to launch their "whole effort" than downstairs at the Purple Onion.

NOTES

1. Frank Werber, interview with Richard Johnston, Sausalito, CA, April 2, 1975, from the Dave Guard and Richard Johnston Kingston Trio collection of materials, 1956–1986, University Manuscript Collections, University of Wisconsin, Milwaukee.

2. Don MacArthur, interview with the author, Novato, CA, February 12, 2010.

3. Werber, interview with Johnston, April 2, 1975.

4. Werber, interview with Johnston, April 2, 1975.

5. Frank Werber, interview with Paul Surratt, "The Frank Werber Interview," in *The Kingston Trio on Record*, by Benjamin Blake, Jack Rubec, and Allan Shaw (Naperville, IL: Kingston Corner, Inc., 1986), 17.

6. Werber, interview with Johnston, April 2, 1975.

7. Nick Reynolds, interview with the author, Seminole, FL, October 3, 1986.

8. Frank Werber, interview with the author, Silver City, NM, April 17, 1984.

9. Frank Werber, interview with the author, Silver City, NM, February 12, 1984.

10. Reynolds, interview with the author.

11. Reynolds, interview with the author.

12. Reynolds, interview with the author.

13. Werber, interview with the author, October 3, 1986.

14. Reynolds, interview with the author.

15. Frank Werber, interview with Richard Johnston, January 1974, from the Dave Guard and Richard Johnston Kingston Trio collection of materials, 1956–1986, University Manuscript Collections, University of Wisconsin, Milwaukee.

16. Bob Shane, interview with the author, Phoenix, AZ, April 6, 2009.

17. "Fourth Man Makes the Trio Tick," *Business Week*, February 23, 1963.

18. Dave Guard, interview with the author, Los Altos, CA, November 30, 1983.

19. Reynolds, interview with the author.

20. Reynolds, interview with the author.

21. Reynolds, interview with the author.

22. Reynolds, interview with the author.

5

THE PURPLE
ONION . . . AND CHUCKLES

Legend has it that success came quickly for The Kingston Trio, and that it was a short sprint from Frank Werber's loft to the Purple Onion and all points east. But it wasn't that simple.

The management of the Purple Onion was no easy sell. The Kingston Trio and both of its earlier permutations—Dave Guard and The Calypsonians and The Kingston Quartet—all had auditioned at the Purple Onion before the Trio were booked there. Bob Shane had even auditioned there as a solo act with the help of Travis Edmondson, who knew the owners, but Shane never got a gig there until he was a member of The Kingston Trio. The Purple Onion had a good nose for talent and they were *very* particular.

Opened in 1952 by Irving "Bud" Steinhoff, his wife Virginia ("Ginnie"), and her brother Keith Rockwell, who was also the club's first manager, the Purple Onion was one of North Beach's original—and later world-renowned—cellar clubs. The name was suggested by Enrico Banducci, who, when Bud Steinhoff mentioned that he was thinking of calling his new club the Song Cellar, supposedly opined, "That's a terrible name! Anything would be better—even the Purple Onion."[1]

Located at 140 Columbus across the street from Columbus Tower, the Purple Onion in the 1950s was an intimate eighty-seat club, an ideal venue for stand-up comedians, jazz trios, and solo singers. Like its counterpart, the hungry i, the Purple Onion would play numerous unknown acts who would go on to the big time—The Smothers Brothers, Maya Angelou, Phyllis Diller, Vikki Carr, Ketty Lester, Jim Nabors, Bob Newhart, Lenny Bruce, and, of course, The Kingston Trio, who "broke out" at the Onion.

By all accounts, the Steinhoffs and manager Barry Drew welcomed unknown talent and held open auditions the last Saturday of the month.

They were generous with their time, happy to lend artistic advice, and according to an April 4, 1957, letter from Nick Reynolds to his mother, their generosity extended to letting Dave Guard and The Calypsonians use their cellar stage to record demos to "get a better record to send to L.A." The group had recently cut demos at Sound Recorders, and although their agent at the time, Dick Reinhart, had been pleased with their efforts and was ready to send dubs to several labels in Los Angeles, the group felt they could do better. Nick's letter goes on to say, "While we were singing, the advertising agent for the 'Hungry I' (Gateway Singers' club across the street) came in. . . . He immediately left and returned five minutes later with the owner of the 'H.I.' [hungry i]. Needless to say we have an appointment with him tonight to 'just talk.' Never can tell what will happen."[2]

The "advertising agent," presumably, was Frank Werber, who apparently was working *both* sides of the street, pitching a potential new act to the hungry i—the Purple Onion's *competition*—from within the Purple Onion itself. Reynolds said that Frank brought Enrico over to just "hear us doing our thing." Enrico was very cool. He wasn't terribly excited, but Frank wanted to get his opinion. He probably told Frank, "Well they need a lot of work in order to play a serious show," which was true at the time. And that's when Frank put the three to work—rehearsing in the Onion's showroom in the afternoon when it was empty to get used to a club atmosphere, recording demos and practice tapes, using their microphones.

The question is whether the group Enrico saw recording demos at the Purple Onion was Dave Guard and The Calypsonians, who previously auditioned at the Purple Onion several months before and were now in their final throes, or whether it was a newly formed Kingston Trio with Bobby Shane, recording demos to give to Jimmy Saphier. Time has blurred memories of specific dates and individuals, and according to one source, Shane did not return from Hawaii to join up with Guard and Reynolds until May 1, 1957, nearly a month after Reynolds's April 4 letter to his mother. Another source says that Shane returned in early March. What *is* known for certain is that The Kingston Trio's first official engagement at the Purple Onion was from May 27 to June 1, 1957, as a temporary replacement for Onion regular and popular North Beach comedienne, Phyllis Diller. To ensure a big crowd—and hopefully a return engagement—Werber and the Trio sent out over five hundred postcards to friends, frat brothers, and anyone else they could think of at Stanford and Menlo to load up the audience. The card read, "Harken! We're At The PURPLE ONION May 27th to June 1st KINGSTON TRIO Dave Guard Bob Shane Nick Reynolds P.S. The Rest Of The Show Is Great Too!!"

The cards worked beautifully, and the gig was extended for a month. "All these college kids came up from the peninsula, and it was wild! We could do no wrong!" Reynolds recalled. "We opened on a Monday and the place was packed for like two weeks, which then went on for month because Phyllis was held over for her next job. Absolute ecstasy! Here I am playing nothing but the conga drum and singing and we were just getting great audiences. It was scary as hell 'cause here we're in the second biggest club in San Francisco as far as the avant-garde. We were in heaven, and we were really entertaining. All the kids were telling their parents about us and the *parents* were coming down for the late show, and all of a sudden we're the toast of San Francisco!" By July 1, The Kingston Trio were the Purple Onion's new headliners and would remain at the club for seven more months.[3]

Through it all, Frank stood in the back of the club every night observing the audience reactions, gauging the audience age, and who was digging what. "We'd see his profile, the nose," said Reynolds, laughing. "We called him 'the ferret,' but he was sort of like a weasel observing everything."[4] They also nicknamed him "Sid Falco," the fictitious PR man played by Tony Curtis in the 1957 movie *The Sweet Smell of Success*. The name was apropos because it was Werber's tenaciousness that landed the Purple Onion gig. "He was quite instrumental," Dave Guard felt. "He was the PR man for the hungry i and the Purple Onion and several other clubs, so that right there he was always in a bargaining position with those owners really. He was always putting the bug in their ear to do it."[5] He had known well in advance of Diller's upcoming engagement at the Millionaire Club in Dallas, urging Barry Drew to "give the kids a break" while Phyllis would be away for two weeks.

Phyllis had been the Purple Onion's resident headliner, the Alameda County housewife with five kids who had literally taken San Francisco by storm with her wisecracking, self-deprecating humor and she never looked back. She was always gracious to the Trio, and she and Reynolds would become close, lifelong friends. Years later, when Bob Shane ran into her at a party he said, "Phyllis, I don't know if you remember this or not but I asked you how old you were when we were first playing at Purple Onion and you told me. So I know every year you lied! [laughs]. She said, 'Damn, somebody's gonna find out how old I really am!' So I said, 'Well then are you finally gonna go to bed with me?' And she said, 'You *would* too, wouldn't you!'"[6]

Phyllis returned from Dallas, but decided to take a break from the Purple Onion, leaving The Kingston Trio the club's top attraction. While initially paid only about eighty dollars a week each, the gig would be worth millions to the group in exposure, because the Purple Onion would be the catalyst for their success. It was obvious that they had found a loving home with the Steinhoffs, as a note from Nick to "friends" in Coronado reveals:[7]

July 31—1957

Dear Friends,

I had the most lovely birthday possible. I loved all the presents & the cake arrived in fine shape. I can't thank you enough for everything. Right in the middle of the second show on Sat. night, the manager of the P.O. brought out another cake, candles & all, and everyone in the audience sang "Happy Birthday" (too embarrassing). Everything was perfect & still is up here. Am happy & healthy & fat.

Much love to all
Nacker

Meanwhile, Frank, ever the promoter, secured numerous promotional jobs for the group—modeling Genter sweaters and swimsuits, doing commercials for Hublein cocktails and Rye Crisp ("the Light Rye Cracker"), an appearance at the Emporium Teenage Fashion Show (where they sang for fifteen minutes), singing for the Peninsula Chapter Executive Secretaries, Inc., annual Bosses Night at the Peninsula Golf and Country Club, even a gig at the ultra-exclusive (and ultra-conservative) Bohemian Grove on the Russian River ninety miles north of San Francisco, arranged by Nick's father who was a member. "It was the full thing," Guard said, "whatever the business would take, we were going to do it. We even tried to take dancing lessons for a while, you know, anything that would make it."[8]

But the only thing that would really ensure success was an asset they already possessed, yet took for granted on a nightly basis—their voices. After the first three nightly shows at the Purple Onion—three 45-minute sets of ten to twelve songs per show—the three began losing their voices. Werber was determined to protect and enhance that asset in the surest way, so he sent them to Judy Davis across the bay in Oakland.

Judy (Adelaide) Davis was a highly respected vocal coach, "the Stars' Vocal Coach," whose students included Frank Sinatra, Judy Garland, Mary Martin, Barbra Streisand, Grace Slick, Vikki Carr, Jerry Garcia, and later, not coincidentally, Peter, Paul and Mary. Born in Red Bluff, California, and raised in Oakland, Davis attended the University of California at Berkeley where she graduated with bachelor's and master's degrees in music. She also worked as an assistant choreographer at Warner Brothers in

Los Angeles with her husband, choreographer Hal Davis. The two would later open a dance studio in Oakland.

While Judy Davis was a celebrated vocal coach, she was never a professional singer, the result of a bad tonsillectomy in her late teens that damaged her vocal cords. The injury prompted her to study the anatomy of speech and singing to learn how vocal cords produce sound and, more specifically, musical notes—both the right way and the wrong way.

Voice control, proper breathing, enunciation and projection, strengthening and protecting vocal cords were all part of her teaching method. She could be a tough taskmaster, but her students loved her and nobody argued with her results. "I'm just a vocal plumber," she once remarked, "I fix pipes."[9]

Dave Guard explained her methodology and how it helped the Trio. "She wanted to make musicians out of us basically," Guard said. "So she gave us musicianship lessons and dictated keys and scales and what have you. She taught us vocal exercises, stretching your voice, teaching us to sing differently. Most people sing like they speak and that's with a thing [epiglottis] in your throat that stops when you're speaking. When you speak you're stuttering basically. Your throat's closing all the time, whereas singing is an open thing. So Judy taught us how to open up; you sort of just plump up like a bagpipe and then you just blow past the formation in your mouth. So you form your mouth into certain shapes and then just blow air past that rather than thinking that you're generating it out of your throat. So that took a bunch of re-education, and the way you form your vowels and stuff. We had to completely re-perceive the English language."[10]

"What she did is she taught you how to make the most of your breathing and your voice to make it last and to make it sing out," said Bob Shane. "And she taught us . . . how to maintain that power on a road trip of six weeks in a row and be able to do the same kind of thing every night and feel good about doing it. I think it made us more melodic, and it definitely gave us stronger voices."[11]

Working with Davis was one of several critical moves that continued to pay off for the Trio throughout their careers. Years later Davis's "vocal eases" were still religiously used to limber up their voices before every recording session, including those with John Stewart, who was also sent to Davis after being picked as Guard's replacement.

Their fully planned schedule, as Guard described it, allowed little room for deviation. "I was getting up at seven o'clock to take a sunbath up on the roof, and then at eight o'clock go eat breakfast, at nine o'clock we had vocal lessons over in Oakland, and that'd take just about all morning, eat lunch and then rehearse all afternoon, eat dinner and then go play all night sort of thing. So it was living on almost no sleep and all rehearsal."[12]

Nick Reynolds did, however, find time to fall in love with Frank's part-time secretary and nightclub comedienne, Joan Harriss. At the time she was married to comedian Pat Paulsen, answering the phone and filing papers for Werber by day and performing at Ann's 440 by night. Because Frank handled the PR for both clubs, as well as the hungry i, there was plenty of interplay between the three clubs' various performers.

Unlike the Trio, who were new to show business, Joan Harriss had grown up in North Beach and Russian Hill and had been around the club scene since she was a kid. She met Pat Paulsen through his brother, for whom she auditioned for a theatrical review, and eventually the three put a comedy act together. With Pat's encouragement, Harriss got a union card and soon was doing stand-up comedy at FACS II, the Black Hawk, and Ann's 440, where Nick first saw her perform. "He was just shy, warm, and friendly," says Joan of her first impression of Nick.[13] But it wasn't until later at the Purple Onion that she saw the Trio perform—and she wasn't overly impressed.

"I didn't think they were amateurs," she recalled. "They were college kids in little striped shirts singing folk songs. They were just kind of cute. I wasn't knocked out. Folk music wasn't that big a deal to me. I liked The Weavers. So I wasn't against them, but I wasn't a fan. I really liked jazz and swing and things like that."[14] Reynolds, too, was an ardent jazz fan, with trumpeter Chet Baker and big band leader Stan Kenton among his favorites, so the two had music in common. The link with Werber and the Purple Onion also facilitated the couple's growing friendship.

"On your nights off you'd go around and see the other club's shows cause you were a working entertainer and you could get in free," Joan explained. "And then sometimes we'd eat in Chinatown at two in the morning. I didn't have a car so when we went out to eat, Nick started giving me a ride home 'cause I was on his way. He had a little one-room apartment in Pacific Heights and a little red Austin Healey. That's how it kind of started there."[15] Before long the two were "madly in love," eventually being caught "in flagrante delicto" by Paulsen who maintained his deadpan comedic delivery, exclaiming, "Not in front of the cat?!" For the next year and a half, Nick and Joan would be together, go their separate ways, get back together, briefly share a friend's apartment in New York, get a houseboat in Sausalito, get an annulment from Pat Paulsen, and then finally tie the knot on September 13, 1958.

A year earlier, Dave Guard had married Gretchen Ballard, a Stanford coed and fine arts major he met in his senior year when she was a freshman. Gretchen was born in Chicago but grew up in San Marino, California, with the exception of three years in New Orleans during World War II where her father was a navy lieutenant in the supply corps. Her parents were originally from Seattle, migrating to Southern California in the late 1930s. Her father, Eaton (or EB, as he was called), was an executive in the Broadway-Hale Stores chain; her mother, Beverly, was a housewife. Gretchen's love of art was instilled and encouraged by her parents, both of whom were active in the Los Angeles arts and music community, with Beverly serving as a docent at the Los Angeles County Museum for twenty years.

Gretchen was introduced to Dave by a girl she knew from high school who was then at Stanford and was pinned to Dave, and it was not until her friend broke up with him that the two began dating. She was impressed from the start. "He was very smart and very funny and very articulate and kind of dazzling, you know," she recalled. "I'm sure you heard him onstage making announcements; he was so funny and so offbeat. He was always very curious about everything. I never thought of him as an intellectual but I thought he had a very lively mind and kind of an authentic and fresh way of looking at life. Those are the things I remember most about him."[16]

While they frequented all of the Stanford hangouts, the Cracked Pot was the couple's favorite, and where she was introduced to Nick and Bobby. Of the Trio wives, Gretchen was the only one who was there from the very start, watching them evolve from sitting on the edge of the Cracked Pot stage swilling beer and shouting out funny songs, to singing to sophisticated club audiences in North Beach and ultimately around the world.

"Nobody ever expected them to do anything except play at parties and play for friends," she said. "The dynamic of the group was one of their greatest assets and it was there from the very beginning. You know their personalities were so different and yet as a group they just worked beautifully and played off each other in a very appealing way. They were never false; they were kind of straight up about what they said and what they sang and what they joked about. And they were never sentimental or ever seemed to be selling out or anything. They played what they enjoyed playing and singing, and they were really irreverent. To college kids, that's really appealing and that appealed to me, too. I guess I'm saying that I liked David and the group for the same reasons that everybody else did."[17]

The view of the world from the top of 2009 Vallejo was clear and sunny for the Guards in 1957. A baby was on the way, the act was getting rave reviews, and Dave began studying the banjo, taking one short—but very inspiring—lesson from local folk luminary and virtuoso banjo player Billy Faier. A native of Brooklyn, New York, Faier drifted into San Francisco in the early 1950s by way of Oregon and became a key mover and shaker in the Bay Area folk scene. He performed in the first Berkeley Little Theatre folk concert and began his own weekly folk music program, *The Story of American Folk Music*, on KPFA. He was also well connected with the city's folk elite, including Barbara Dane, Stan Wilson, and folk concert organizer Barry Olivier. Faier gave numerous concerts throughout the Bay Area. His *Art of the Five-String Banjo* recording on Riverside, like Pete Seeger's *How to Play the 5-String Banjo* (which Guard also studied), became essential for every serious banjo student, including Dave Guard.

"Dave practiced constantly and we were living in a one-room apartment—so I'm *very* aware of how much he practiced," Gretchen Guard said with a laugh. "It was a challenge but he picked it up and he got really good at it. I've listened to Billy Faier's recordings since then and I realize how much he got from Billy—and from Pete Seeger. It was that style of really clean picking and frailing, too. He started from knowing nothing about the banjo and really mastered it."[18]

Pete Seeger remembered getting a letter from Guard ordering his banjo book, followed by a second letter telling him of his progress. "I think it was the first edition, I got a letter from this student at Stanford University who sent me $1.59 and a year later another letter where he said to me 'Pete, I've been putting that book to hard use. I and two others have a Trio we call The Kingston Trio,' and this was Dave Guard. I've forgotten the dates exactly when his letter was sent to me, but he was still at Stanford and he had two other students in the group, I suppose Nick and whoever else it was."[19]

Guard would remain friendly with Seeger throughout his time in the Trio and well after. Seeger became an important source of material for the group, supplying such tunes as "Bonnie Hielan' Laddie" and "Where Have All the Flowers Gone," the latter penned by Seeger with verses by Joe Hickerson added later. Seeger was also a founding member of The Weavers from whose repertoire the early Trio also drew heavily—"Wimoweh," "Bay of Mexico," and "When the Saints Go Marching In" being a few of many.

The inclusion of a banjo in the Trio's instrumentation was yet another critical move in the group's musical development. Initially, Guard's banjo work consisted of elementary frailing and hunt-and-peck picking played on an old S.S. Stewart banjo belonging to Nick's father. Such old-timey banjos have an inherent "plunkety-plunk" tone, producing a far less melodic and polished sound that later distinguished Guard's playing. As he became more proficient, Dave progressed to a Vega Pete Seeger Long Neck five-string model with its crisp, loud timbre that became central to The Kingston Trio sound. Guard was a highly inventive player, adapting the banjo to a variety of musically diverse songs ranging from the Mexican flavored "Farewell Adelita," to the bluegrassy "Blue Eyed Gal," to the delicate precision of "Old John Webb."

Many just assumed it was Guard or later Stewart playing banjo on the Trio's records, but it was often Shane. In fact, Shane was the first in the group to play banjo, also using Captain Reynolds's old banjo with the fifth string removed, as well as his own Bacon and Day four-string plectrum. He would later play a Vega four-string plectrum model. "Tom Dooley," "Three Jolly Coachmen," "When the Saints Go Marching In," "Little Maggie," "New York Girls," "A Worried Man" (with Guard), and "Coming from the Mountains" were among the tunes on which Shane played the banjo. "If it was strumming, it was likely me," Shane said.[20]

Nick Reynolds, too, would contribute to the Trio's instrumental mix beyond bongos and conga, albeit subtly at first. Reynolds had played ukulele since he was a kid, saying that he was too lazy to learn to play a six-string guitar. When the Trio first formed, he played only bongos and a conga drum, more as a way to hang out with Shane and Guard than to further any musical ambitions. Shane also played ukulele as well as four-string tenor guitar and would not advance to a full-size six-string guitar until returning to Hawaii a year later. It was not until the group began playing professionally at the Purple Onion that Reynolds transitioned to tenor guitar, more as a visual prop—something to put between himself and the audience—than adding any real musical texture. The move was prompted by Guard who informed Reynolds that he looked like a geek standing empty-handed on stage when he wasn't playing the drums. Since tenor guitar was similar to ukulele tuning (often tuned like the first four strings of a guitar), the transition was relatively easy. It also gave Reynolds more versatility. Later, Reynolds's tenor guitar playing would add greatly to The Kingston Trio overall instrumental sound.

On the early Trio albums, Reynolds's tenor guitar is sometimes barely audible, perhaps the result of sharing his instrumental track with the bass, or simply being overpowered by Shane's big Martin D-28 and Guard's loud banjo. Reynolds played with a felt ukulele pick which also muted the volume. In 1960 Reynolds had his 2-18 tenor converted to an 8-string to gain more volume and to add a "different color" to the mix. He also added a larger Martin 0-18T tenor to his instrument mix that increased the volume as well. During the Stewart years Nick's tenor playing became much more prominent, especially with his 8-string that drove many of the faster paced tunes. The Trio also selectively double-voiced their instruments on some of their recordings. What's more, Reynolds switched to a plastic flat pick that not only increased the volume but wore holes in the tops of his guitars!

The popularity of The Kingston Trio in North Beach had grown so rapidly by the end of 1957 that Gray Line tour busses were dropping off loads of tourists at the Purple Onion. They were indeed the darlings of San Francisco, playing to sold-out crowds every night. Famed New York photographer Maynard Frank Wolfe photographed the three on the Purple Onion's cellar steps for a *Playboy* article on San Francisco nightlife that would give them national exposure. A record contract was in sight. Things were happening quickly. And while the Purple Onion would forever be in their hearts, it was evident that the time had come to move on to bigger things.

Werber suggested they take a month off, rest up, and get ready to hit the road. He knew that the warm and fuzzy reception of North Beach audiences, while genuine, was not necessarily indicative of what they would face elsewhere. They needed toughing up away from the safe and familiar. The lounge at Newt Crumley's Holiday Hotel in downtown Reno would be good for starters, followed by dates at Mr. Kelly's in Chicago and the Village Vanguard in New York City. Nick Reynolds's letter to his parents in early February 1958 details their rude awakening after only four days of a three-week engagement at the Holiday Hotel:

> After our first show on Thursday they asked us to stay an additional week for $1000; we still don't know whether we will do it or not as it will only give us about three days before we have to be in Chicago. Also I don't know if we can last that long physically and mentally. Both Dave and Bob are terribly hoarse and this is only the fourth day. We have to sing an average of 65 songs a night over a six-hour period and this is a little different than the average 25 at the Onion. We also have to fight the gambling noise and the general attitude of the people that come to Reno. They are not there to be entertained but to gamble period. This is a terrible blow to the ego but one everybody faces when they play these jobs. If you get one or two people clapping per show you're considered not only by the hotel but other entertainers a huge success. So far we have been a tremendous success."[21]

At the Holiday Hotel the Trio alternated on stage with ventriloquist Wayne Roland's puppet Chuckles, and The Bon Vivant Strollers, but there were very few chuckles or good times to be had. "We learned humility there," Shane said. "The lounge only seated forty people, and we were standing up behind the bar. If you played too loud they told us to 'shut up.' If we played too soft, they told us to 'play louder.'"[22] Reynolds said "it was the hardest gig we ever had, playing the lounge in a big hotel," and added, "but we were on the marquee! Except for the painted wall at the Purple Onion, we were never on a marquee before. And that impressed the hell out of me! 'The Kingston Trio' up on the lighted marquee out front. Playing in the lounge was a real awakening. We had to do 5 or 6 shows a night, and they turned the sound off because we were too damn loud for the casino!"[23] It would be the first real rude awakening the group would experience making it in "the big time."

And it certainly wouldn't be their last.

NOTES

1. Enrico Banducci to Bud Steinhoff.

2. Nick Reynolds to Mrs. Stewart Reynolds, April 4, 1957.

3. Nick Reynolds, interview with the author, Port Orford, OR, July 10, 1986.

4. Nick Reynolds, interview with the author, Seminole, FL, October 3, 1986.

5. Dave Guard, interview with the author, Los Altos, CA, November 28, 1983.

6. Bob Shane, interview with the author, Phoenix, AZ, April 6, 2009.

7. Nick Reynolds to "Friends," July 31, 1957.

8. D. Guard, interview with the author, November 28, 1983.

9. Jesse Hamlin, "Judy Davis of Oakland—Vocal Coach to Stars," *San Francisco Chronicle*, January 31, 2001.

10. Dave Guard, interview with the author, Los Altos, CA, November 29, 1983.

11. Bob Shane, interview with the author, Phoenix, AZ, August 22, 2007.

12. D. Guard, interview with the author, November 28, 1983.

13. Joan Reynolds, interview with the author, Sausalito, CA, August 16, 2010.

14. J. Reynolds, interview with the author.

15. J. Reynolds, interview with the author.

16. Gretchen Guard, interview with the author, Santa Fe, NM, April 28, 2006.

17. G. Guard, interview with the author, April 28, 2006.

18. Gretchen Guard, interview with the author, Santa Fe, NM, September 3, 2006.

19. Pete Seeger, interview with the author, Beacon, NY, August 31, 2008.

20. Shane, interview with the author, August 22, 2007.

21. Nick Reynolds to Mr. and Mrs. Stuart Reynolds, February 1958.

22. Bob Shane, *The Kingston Trio Story: Wherever We May Go*, DVD (Shout! Factory, 2006).

23. N. Reynolds, interview with the author, October 3, 1986.

6

THE ROAD TO SUCCESS

"They pay you to travel. You do the shows for free."

—Bob Shane

That Frank Werber had booked the Trio into a Reno hotel/casino lounge, a Chicago steak house, and two revered New York City jazz clubs was an inspired move. He reasoned, correctly, that each audience would be different—geographically, demographically, and psychologically. For four months they would be out of their comfort zone, working harder and longer, and playing to far more demanding audiences. This was the reality of making it in the big time. Securing a recording contract was key to the plan as well.

From the outset, Werber actively sought a record deal, having the Trio periodically record demos that were sent to several labels, including Liberty, Dot, and Capitol in Los Angeles. Dot wanted to do a singles-only contract, which Werber rejected, and he held out for an album deal with Capitol that eventually came through. The Capitol contract, however, came about largely through word of mouth, via James L. "Jimmy" Saphier, Bob Hope's and Andy Williams's agent, who first saw the Trio at the Purple Onion the previous summer. It was Saphier who gave demo tapes of the Trio to Glenn Wallach, Capitol's president, who in turn gave them to Voyle Gilmore, one of the company's top producers and, later, head of Artist & Repertoire (A&R). Lee Gillette, one of Capitol's staff producers who primarily recorded groups for the label, was interested in the Trio, so Gilmore sent him to the Purple Onion to investigate. Gillette came back ambivalent about the group (Gilmore once privately wondered whether Gillette had actually even gone to see the Trio), so Gilmore himself went up to take a closer look. He was not ambivalent. "They just knocked me out," he said. "They were stars, no question about it."[1]

The recording sessions for *The Kingston Trio* (or T996 as it's known among Trio buffs) took place over three days—February 5, 6, and 7, 1958—in Capitol's Studio B in Hollywood, with Gilmore producing and Curly Walter assisting. The Trio were literally recording their club act, minus the audience, doing the same songs they had been singing three times a night for months, so the sessions went smoothly and quickly. Gilmore was a highly respected, old-school producer, having recorded Frank Sinatra, The Four Freshman, The Four Preps, Louis Prima and Keely Smith, Dick Dale, and Al Martino, as well as putting together compilations for Dean Martin and Judy Garland. He'd been a big band drummer in San Francisco in the 1930s and married a big band singer, and had one son, John Gilmore. In the late 1940s, he joined Capital Records, working six and a half years in sales before joining the creative department as a producer and arranger. In 1963, he became head of A&R from which he retired in the early 1970s. In his twenty-plus years with Capitol, Gilmore produced dozens of important albums and singles, including all of The Kingston Trio and Frank Sinatra output. He was allegedly one of the few people who ever kept Sinatra waiting, which may have resulted in Frank's heated departure from the label to start his own record company, Reprise, in 1960.

Voyle Gilmore was an extremely knowledgeable producer, both musically and technically, with a quiet demeanor and gentlemanly manner that belied his substantial acumen and resolve. He appreciated consensus and solicited many opinions, which some took as being indecisive, but he ultimately acted on his own instincts. Unlike some producers who overly impose their own creative sensibilities on an artist's performance, Gilmore rarely interfered, letting the artists do what they thought best. And while he never hesitated to voice his opinion, he saw his role as providing whatever support the artists needed to deliver their best effort—be it session musicians, technical assistance, artistic advice, or constructive/instructive critiquing. Much of what Gilmore provided took place in post-production, selecting the optimal takes, mixing and enhancing, and adding as much production value as possible and appropriate. His highly successful results speak for themselves.

At the time of the first session with the Trio, Gilmore and Curly Walter had little or no experience recording pure acoustic music, such as bluegrass or folk music, although Walter would later move up to an A&R position at Capitol, signing The Dillards for two singles and working with new acts to the label. Both Nick Reynolds and Bob Shane recalled that the three gathered around a single hanging mike, "sort of an omni approach" Reynolds called it, with a floor mike used for the acoustic bass played by Elmer Lynn "Buzz" Wheeler, the resident bass player at the Purple Onion.

Adding a bass player came on the advice of Jackie Cain and Roy Kral of Jackie and Roy, the jazz vocal duo who were also in Reno when the Trio played the Holiday Hotel. "They came to see us in the lounge—and they loved us!" Reynolds recalled. "The first thing Roy Kral said was, 'You gotta get a bass player! There's a part missing. Round it out. You don't want to add another voice, because what you guys are doing is great, but you gotta get a bass player.' And so we did."[2] Dave Guard said that when they got to New York, Joe Benjamin from Stan Getz's group offered to sit in with them, so they'd had some experience with bass. "It always seemed to sound better when we had a bass player along," said Guard, "so we said 'Hey, let's take a chance.' So it really added a lot, I think, and gave it a classical counterpoint thing."[3]

The first session for *The Kingston Trio* almost didn't happen. In the excitement of getting to the studio, Reynolds pulled out of his motel onto Sunset Boulevard in his new Austin Healey and was hit head-on. No one was hurt, but Reynolds's car was demolished. "My mind was on the recording session and all the money coming from it. I damn near didn't get to the recording session," he said. "I didn't have wheels for a year because I didn't have the money to fix it. No insurance."[4]

There was another surprise waiting for Reynolds in Studio B. When the single vocal mike was set up, it was positioned at mouth level for Shane and Guard, both men being over six feet tall. Reynolds at five feet six was nearly a foot short of the mike. "They couldn't get me high enough to get close to the mike, so this guy brought in a wooden box and said, 'We used this for Edith Piaf—this is Edith Piaf's box. It's now *your* box, Nick.' And there I am, standing on about a two-foot box—in heaven!"[5]

There were no technical tricks or embellishments on the session. Gilmore would later credit himself with helping to perfect double voicing, an overdubbing technique of fattening vocals by re-recording and overlaying the same vocal tracks and running them through Capitol's echo chambers in the mix-down. Gilmore used this technique with The Four Preps' *26 Miles* in 1957, and although the technology and equipment were in place at the time of the Trio's first recording sessions, the technique was not to be used on a Trio album until *At Large*. The echo chambers, however, were used to help sweeten T996 to excellent effect.

Throughout the session Gilmore hardly said a word. "He was very quiet," Nick remembered. "None of us really knew what was happening.

Gilmore wasn't saying anything; he was just kind of fascinated by what was coming down."[6] The songs had been so well rehearsed that once the vocal mike and a bass floor mike had been placed and adjusted, the three just started singing. There was no "punching in." If a mistake was made with the lyrics or someone hit a bad note, the track had to be done over from the beginning. Nor did they have any monitors to hear themselves sing, so the three stood close to each other around one vocal mike to hear each other as they recorded. It was their natural blend, and it sounded great to everybody when they listened to the playbacks on the studio's big speakers.

Shane was impressed with Gilmore's quiet approach saying, "He was perfect for us. He did everything. Every gold record we got, Gilmore was the producer. I don't think we realized how much he contributed to The Kingston Trio sound until much later. He was really a very groovy guy. He never pumped his own thing. He was just a quiet easygoing guy who had great ideas and he made them happen. He never tried to take credit for it. You see, those people had their job, we had our job. Our job was to go ahead and make the record. Theirs was just to make it sound better in the studio."[7]

The rivalry between Guard and Shane surfaced briefly during the first session as "Scotch and Soda" was about to be recorded. While the two had learned the tune together, and it was already in their club set list sung by Shane, Guard had his own—and much different—version that was rarely played on stage. Reynolds said it was *always* a bone of contention between the two. To avoid any arguments during the session, Frank suggested they "let Bobby try Scotch and Soda first." Knowing how Guard was feeling, Nick took Dave aside saying, "Maybe you and I ought to go out and get a beer and they can just do it with the bass player." It ended up that Shane was left alone with Buzz Wheeler to record the song. Reynolds and Guard went around the corner to a bar and when they returned Frank said, "We got it, you wanna hear it?"[8] Nothing further was said. The just-recorded track, however, timed out too short for airplay, so the chorus was copied and added to the end of the song to lengthen it. A photo session with Capitol's staff photographer, Ken Veeder, was also completed during these three days, shot in Capitol's own Tower photo studio on the ninth floor with enough photos for *The Kingston Trio* and . . . *from the "Hungry i,"* their yet-to-be-recorded follow-up album.

With the first album in the bag, the group returned briefly to the Purple Onion, then headed to Reno and the start of their three-week engagement from hell at the Holiday Hotel. On March 24, 1958, the Trio travelled to Chicago and a much-abbreviated engagement at Mr. Kelly's with chanteuse Faye DeWitt and Marks and Freego. Only three nights of a two-week contract were fulfilled due to having to pretape their national television debut, "Rumors of Evening," in Los Angeles. But the short Chicago gig introduced them to some *very* influential people, starting with the owners of the club, the Marienthal brothers. Later, when the Trio came back to honor their return engagement contract with Mr. Kelly's, the Marienthal brothers were so impressed with the group's personal integrity that they ran a full-page ad in *Variety* praising the Trio with the headline "Hats Off To The Kingston Trio" over a line drawing of Nick, Bob, and Dave with halos above their heads, and copy that read:

> AN HONOR TO SHOW BUSINESS—The brothers Marienthal, owners of Chicago's London House and Mr. Kelly's, take off their hats to The Kingston Trio and their manager, Frank Werber. Despite the tremendous demand for their services since first appearing at Mr. Kelly's, this exciting young trio complied with their contract for a return engagement, went on with the show graciously and with such enthusiasm that they broke all attendance records at Mister Kelly's. In fact, the Andy Frain organization had to be called to handle the unprecedented crowds. Such professional integrity, especially in a group so young, is to be commended and is an honor to show business. We are eagerly looking forward to their next appearance at Mister Kelly's.[9]

Mr. Kelly's opened in 1953 as the London House, a combination steak house and jazz club, owned by Oscar and George Marienthal, who later renamed it Mr. Kelly's. The Rush Street club/restaurant would become one of the country's premier jazz, folk, and comedy showcases, and a classy "break-in club" for exceptional new talent, until closing in 1975. The Trio had gotten the gig at Mr. Kelly's through Chicago-based photographer Maynard Frank Wolfe, who had recently done the photo shoot with the Trio in San Francisco for *Playboy* magazine and who put in a good word to the Marienthal brothers. After the shellacking at the Holiday Hotel lounge in Reno, Mr. Kelly's was a welcome surprise. The Trio's three nightly shows were sold out, with audiences and fellow performers enthusiastic and helpful. Johnny Freego, one half of Marks and Freego, sat in with the Trio playing bass, which greatly boosted their overall sound. According to Guard, their great reception at Mr. Kelly's led to their getting the gig at the Village Vanguard. The Trio would discover that Chicago was a *great* town for folk music, with a friendly and well-established folk community.

The city had numerous folk and jazz venues including the Gate of Horn, Mr. Kelly's, Navy Pier, Orchestra Hall, the Civic Opera House,

Aragon Ballroom, McCormick Place, Old Town School of Folk Music, and all south-side Chicago blues clubs. What's more, Chicago was a great en-route gig for folkies working both coasts such as Odetta, Josh White, Theo Bikel, The Gateway Singers, Barbara Dane, Bud and Travis, Stan Wilson, Pete Seeger, Oscar Brand, Jean Ritchie, and The Kingston Trio. Large or small, Chicago had the venue and the audience to fit any folk act.

Chicago would become The Kingston Trio's favorite city throughout their career, an enjoyable respite from the road, with a favorite hotel, the infamous Maryland Hotel on Rush Street ("a dump" Reynolds called it but *the* meeting place for all the show people), and later an apartment just off Rush Street, friendly bars, and a huge cadre of friends. They loved Chicago and Chicago loved them back. Reynolds recalled an impromptu Kingston Trio "homecoming" in 1962 led by a Chicago Fire Department ladder truck with lights flashing and horns honking pulling up to their apartment building with The Clancy Brothers and an inebriated Jesuit priest hanging off the back rail.

On March 30, 1958, the Trio reported to Studio 31 at CBS Television City in Los Angeles to pretape CBS Playhouse 90's *Rumors of Evening*. The three played American pilots in wartime Britain, singing "Scarlet Ribbons" over the phone to Barbara Bel Geddes on a rainy night. Later in the show they lip-synched "Three Jolly Coachmen." While "Scarlet Ribbons" had been previously recorded in Denver for a single and "Three Jolly Coach-men" had been recorded at Capitol for the Trio's first album, CBS wanted both tunes re-recorded for timing and interplay purposes, which Reynolds says they did at Capitol. There is a session sheet for "Scarlet Ribbons" and "When the Saints Go Marching In" dated April 4, 1958, but none for "Three Jolly Coachmen," unless it was incorrectly entered as "When the Saints Go Marching In." The "Rumors" cast also included Billie Burke (the good Witch of the West in *The Wizard of Oz*) and character actor Robert Loggia. This gig, too, came through Jimmy Saphier, who by this time had been enlisted as the Trio's agent for television, radio, and mov-ies. The script was written by Bill Durkee at whose insistence the Trio were added to the cast. Durkee had seen the group at the Purple Onion, probably on the advice of Saphier. He introduced himself as a writer for television and that he had just written a script for a Playhouse 90 drama and would love to have the Trio appear in it. *Rumors of Evening* aired on May 1, 1958.

The Trio's arrival in New York City on April 1, 1958, for a three-week stand at the Village Vanguard signaled, in their minds, that they had finally *arrived*. "It was the feeling that New York was the big time, you know?" Guard said. "I figured that New York was a place that you really did your best music."[10] According to the reviews, they did. Even as relative unknowns at the Village Vanguard and later at the posh Blue Angel in May, they were greeted warmly and treated with respect. At their first show, the audience included Freddy Hellerman of The Weavers, with Mary Travers on his arm, who had come specifically to see them. At the time, Mary was singing in a Broadway show that starred Mort Sahl. Bobby Shane was immediately smitten, and reportedly so was Mary. "Bobby takes off with Mary, not to be seen for several days," Reynolds recalled laughingly. "They couldn't help themselves. They were like those two miniature magnet dogs that kiss."[11] Shane, of course, remembered it differently, but with the same ending, saying, "The first time we went to the Village Vanguard, we asked about where the scene was for folk singing and they said, 'Oh you go to Washington Square. You'll meet a lot of great people there.' And I saw Mary Travers there singing with somebody. So you know, it was a summer day and I just liked her voice and liked the way she was singing with some guy. So I introduced myself and we went out with each other for several days, had a great time."[12]

Several years later, in 1961, when Peter, Paul and Mary were just starting out, they were booked into Storyville in Boston, one of George Wein's two jazz/folk clubs of the same name. Wein immediately called the Trio, who were playing at the Donnelly Theater. "I got this group, they're just coming up from New York, and they've never played outside of New York and they heard you were playing here. They'd like to meet you." So Shane, Reynolds, and Stewart went over to Wein's club to see Peter, Paul and Mary and afterward were introduced to the newcomers. "Have you ever met these people?" George asked the Trio. "One of them," Shane replied with a sly smile. "Hi Bobby!" Mary giggled back. The two would remain close friends for the rest of her life.[13]

Theodore Bikel, the popular folk singer and actor, was also among the Trio's acquaintances in New York, spreading the word about the Trio and helping to establish their legitimacy within the cliquish New York folk community. Bikel hosted a Saturday afternoon radio show broadcast from the Village Gate that attracted all the folkies from the Village, and he invited the Trio to be on the show. Reynolds was terrified that they'd be skewered by the locals and asked Fred Hellerman of The Weavers to come with them to the interview. "They won't put *you* down!" Reynolds told Hellerman. "But *I'm* scared shitless. These people have teeth!" So Hellerman went with the Trio, sitting in on the interview, dryly adding tongue-in-cheek banter. "These boys are really okay. I don't care for their comic routines. I tried to steal some of their songs. Actually, we've got them under lawsuit and we're going to win! There's no problem! The money's all mine! I may get lots of money!"[14]

While it seems incongruent that the Trio would be booked into jazz clubs, it was a perfectly natural fit. Jazz and urban folk performers in the 1950s were considered avant-garde, hip, and esoteric. The Village Vanguard and the Blue Angel booked many of the same jazz and folk acts as Mr. Kelly's, the hungry i, and the Purple Onion, which were primarily jazz rooms to begin with. Over the next decade, The Kingston Trio would form strong personal and professional bonds with many jazz people, including Stan Getz, Gerry Mulligan (who actually got up onstage to "jam" with the Trio), George Shearing, Dave Brubeck, Keely Smith, Bill Holman, Jackie and Roy, Shelly Mann, Lambert, Hendricks and Ross, Thelonious Monk, Mose Allison, Bill Evans, and lots more. Later, many of these artists would tour with the Trio, and The Kingston Trio would appear at the Newport Jazz Festival and headline the first Newport Folk Festival. But perhaps the best jazz testament of all was The Kingston Trio being featured on the cover of the June 11, 1959, issue of *DownBeat* magazine, the jazz bible. The accompanying article by Richard Hadlock noted that the Trio's crowded summer itinerary would include at least two jazz festivals, French Lick, Indiana, and Newport. "However, the Kingstons do not pretend to offer jazz in any form though. But all three are avid modern jazz fans. They are particularly enthusiastic about the Lambert-Ross-Hendricks group," he assured readers. Guard was quick point out their affinity for other jazz artists as well, saying, "I like good rhythm-and-blues as well as The Modern Jazz Quartet and Thelonious Monk. We played opposite Monk at the Vanguard, and at first he seemed too far out. But his music grows on you. When we left, we were all boosters for Monk." Nick Reynolds added even more jazzers to their list of jazz favorites, "I just love music—Chico Hamilton, Annie Ross, Jackie and Roy—anybody who's good."[15] Truth was, the Trio really did love jazz, particularly Reynolds, as did their resident jazz bassist David Wheat.

On their first trip to New York, Werber, Shane, and Guard stayed at the Albert Hotel on East 11th Street. Reynolds and Joan Harriss preferred staying at a friend's apartment on West 11th Street, and later, after the two were married, at the Hotel Earle on Washington Square in the Village. Dave, Gretchen, and their baby, Catherine, would also move to a hotel near Central Park and then into an apartment off Times Square. As the Trio became established, with block bookings on the East Coast, the families found it more convenient to rent apartments or houses in New York or

Cape Cod to serve as a base away from home. Gretchen Guard recalls that while it was often fun, it was not always ideal.

"We thought it would be a good idea to kind of set up house on the East Coast, so we lived in New York for two or three months. I was pretty much taking care of Catherine, but it was kind of nice that we could be near their work. We decided it would be too extravagant to go on living in a hotel, so somebody in the business offered us their apartment on 48th Street near Broadway. As soon as we moved in, this was in January, the Trio suddenly got a lot of college jobs in Montana and Wyoming—which is a long way away. So I was trying to move into this apartment with a little baby. I really wasn't dealing with The Kingston Trio at all; I was just dealing with the logistics of having a baby in a strange city while living in a three-floor walk-up, getting a telephone and baby buggy and everything else. After a few weeks of this business of living on 48th Street and the baby and I being woken up all night long with sirens and fights and everything, I just decided we'll go back West and David can come visit us whenever he can. So that's what we did. We went back to California."[16]

Joe Glaser's Associated Booking Corporation, the jazz and big band agency, booked all Trio-related jazz dates, including the first gigs at Mr. Kelly's, the Village Vanguard, and the Blue Angel. Impresarios such as Max Gordon, the founder and owner of the Village Vanguard, and Herbert Jacoby, who co-owned and ran the Blue Angel with Gordon, were also very influential people in the New York club scene. If they thought well enough of an act to book it into their clubs, it was viewed as an implicit seal of approval. Gordon and Jacobi also listened to Joe Glaser and Bert Block, Glaser's second-in-command, who would pitch talent they felt appropriate to their clubs. The Trio had also gotten a good recommendation from the Marienthal brothers at Mr. Kelly's, which also impressed Max Gordon. Reynolds felt that Gordon and Jacoby helped create a buzz for the Trio in New York even before their first album or they had a hit.

"We had become kind of little cult figures in New York," said Reynolds. "The people who were uptown went downtown to the Village Vanguard to see us. The club only sat about 100 people but news travels fast. New York is a very small town in the entertainment business, and they had picked up on us down in the Village. Then we came uptown to the Blue Angel and everybody said, 'Well, we gotta go see this little phenomenon.' The clubs had their own publicists and they placed articles with Walter Winchell and others saying, 'Hey, this is what's going on!' and the hype started. I mean, you couldn't get near the Blue Angel when we were playing there when our first album came out—and *before* it came out."[17]

The Blue Angel truly fit its "uptown" designation, both figuratively and literally. Opened in 1943 on East 55th Street on the tony Upper East Side, the supper club was the epitome of decorum, with a strict dress code that even required all male performers to wear tuxedoes. The Trio, of course, declined, saying that their striped, half-sleeved shirts reflected the fun, spontaneity, and spirited nature of their music. It was part of their professional persona. The Angel's management wisely acquiesced, a surprise to many who knew the exacting nature of the club's owners. Over the course of its twenty-three years, the Blue Angel's plush Back Room featured some of the country's top jazz, pop, folk, and comedy entertainers—Harry Belafonte, Miles Davis, Thelonious Monk, Charlie Mingus, Pearl Bailey, Eartha Kitt, Johnny Mathis, Barbra Streisand, Nichols and May, Woody Allen, and Carol Burnett, as well as The Kingston Trio. Gordon had broken in many of these acts at the Village Vanguard and then sent them up to the Blue Angel—or vice versa. It was a prestigious gig for any performer, established or not, and an important appellation of quality—*and* approval—by Max Gordon.

As Nat Hentoff pointed out in his introduction to *Live at the Village Vanguard*, Gordon's reminiscences of his beloved club and the legends who played there, nightclub owners wield enormous power to make or break performers, most of it predicated on, "What can you do for me?" And while Gordon was a shrewd businessman who kept the doors open at the Village Vanguard for many more decades, he was also an astute judge of talent.

Gordon genuinely liked The Kingston Trio, both personally and as an act. The Trio made numerous friends at the Village Vanguard and the Blue Angel, especially jazz musicians whom they would later include on their tours, as well as celebrities, such as Paul Newman and Joanne Woodward. Even New York City mayor Robert F. Wagner was appreciative of the Trio as his May 8, 1958, telegram to the group demonstrated: "May I extend my thanks to you for your generous offer to appear in the Citizenship Day Ceremonies marking 'I Am An American Day' on Sunday afternoon May 18th on the Mall in Central Park. I shall look forward to greeting you then in person."[18]

What was remarkable is that barely two years earlier the Trio were playing pinball machines and slamming down beers at the Cracked Pot between free-for-all sets with anybody who wanted to sing. Now they were hanging out with Paul Newman and Fred Hellerman of The Weavers and getting rave reviews in the *New York Times*. But it wasn't all fun and games. With their first album about to be released on June 1, 1958, the pressure was already on from Capitol for another album. "While you're hot, you put out the product and capitalize on it," the contract implicitly read between the lines. So they rehearsed constantly in New York, honing the act and looking for new material. Werber's rehearsal regimen was put back into effect with the group rehearsing from one o'clock in the afternoon till six or seven every night, usually at the club so they wouldn't have to move their instruments. And while their gigs at the Village Vanguard and the Blue Angel were only two 45-minute shows a night, at 9:30 p.m. and another at midnight, New York audiences were very sophisticated and *every* show had to be their best. Much of the Trio's second studio album, *At Large,* was planned and rehearsed in an upstairs room at the Blue Angel and recorded at Capitol's New York studios on West 46th Street.

The Trio's triumphant return to San Francisco in June 1958 for an extended engagement at the hungry i would be a disappointment for some. The Trio had become a legitimate show business act at the Purple Onion thanks in part to the Steinhoffs and manager Barry Drew, who were willing to give an unknown group a chance as well as their friendship. Drew even rented one of his houseboats in Sausalito to Nick, where he and Shane, and later Joan Harriss, would live for a year. Werber made the decision to play the hungry i instead of the Purple Onion, knowing that it would be disloyal to the club, but felt they had no choice based on the enormous success the Trio had experienced in New York and Chicago. The hungry i was larger, had more prestige (being the main nightclub attraction in San Francisco), and paid four times more than the Purple Onion. Playing any club with less stature—or less money—would be viewed as a step backward.

Both Shane and Reynolds felt badly. "It was very embarrassing—and there was animosity," said Reynolds. "They felt very much betrayed. And I felt guilty all the time. I went over and said hi, and I could tell their rancor was up, so I just didn't bother hanging out over there anymore. I said, 'Well, that's the way it is if you're going to progress,' and our career certainly wouldn't have progressed as much going back there. It would have been a real down move on our career with the roll we were on, to go back to the Purple Onion. They'll even admit that."[19]

"I would have loved to do it at the Purple Onion," Shane added. "But it wasn't big enough. I mean you come down a set of stairs from the street, open the door, walk in, and the stage is directly on the right. It was not raised. It was just right on the floor. The Onion only seated ninety people! It took us a year and a trip to New York to get across the street to the hungry i from the Purple Onion."[20]

Enrico Banducci was ecstatic. The Kingston Trio's first show at the hungry i sold out immediately and every night thereafter, with lines around the block and a three-hour wait to get in. They were indeed the "toast of the town," hometown boys made *really* good, drawing even bigger crowds than Mort Sahl, the hungry i's all-time attendance record setter. Enrico was used to polished acts like The Gateway Singers and the sophisticated audiences who came to see them. And now here were three young ex-college boys, barely out of school, packing his club like he'd never seen before. They were the same three boys Frank had shown him a year or so earlier rehearsing at the Purple Onion one afternoon and whom Enrico had dismissed as needing "more polish." During the hungry i engagement Dave Guard caught the flu, and Nick and Bob debated whether they'd have to cancel for at least two nights, or go out as a duo and do their old barroom act with Hawaiian songs mixed in with songs from the new album. Nick Reynolds laughed at Enrico's desperate plea: "Look at those people standing around the block!!!! Oh my God!!!! Nick, Nick, please! Goddamn, I'll feed you the rest of your life, and your babies, Jesus! Please! Do the show! We're looking at a thousand dollars in my pocket!"[21] Enrico literally meant the feeding part. He was a superb chef, one of the best in San Francisco according to Shane, and every night after hours he'd personally cook gourmet Italian dinners for the Trio as an added bonus.

Capitol Records was equally pleased with the venue. The hungry i drew tens of thousands of tourists a year from all over the country and the world. And every one of them was a potential record buyer and spreader of The Kingston Trio gospel in their respective hometowns. Their first album had been out only a short time when the Trio opened at the hungry i in the summer of 1958, but by the end of their month-long engagement, many people in their audiences knew the words to every song on their album and were singing along en masse. The boys themselves were taking advantage of the word of mouth, setting up a card table in the lobby and selling albums with assistance from Joanne Edmondson, Travis's wife who helped run the concession. "We bought a whole bunch of our albums wholesale for seventy-five cents a copy," Guard remembered. "After our set we'd go get dressed, lock the front door of the club so people couldn't get out after the show, and sit at a little card table. People asked what we were doing. We said, 'Oh, we're just personalizing albums—you want one?' We sold upwards of seventy-five records a night."[22]

According to the Capitol production logs, The Kingston Trio recorded . . . *from the "Hungry i"* (T1107) over two nights, August 15 and 16, 1958, although others said it was recorded over the course of the entire week. Capitol rented the pool hall above the club where Voyle Gilmore and the engineers set up the recording equipment, running wires down to the showroom in the building's basement. The decision to do a live record-ing was based, in part, on economics. With the Trio's first album beginning to pick up action, Capitol decided that a second album should be ready to sell if the first one broke loose. At the outset, Capital never viewed The Kingston Trio as a major act with long-term potential. Jimmy Saphier and Voyle Gilmore liked them, and Frank Werber had been persuasive in nego-tiating a basic one album contract with a generous royalty accelerator clause should the group become a hit by some fluke. So the company was mildly surprised with the sales of T996, largely due to word of mouth from people who had seen the Trio in person or heard about them from those who had. "Tom Dooley" had yet to be released as a single, although a Salt Lake City disc jockey and his friend, a local hi-fi equipment/record store owner, had already zeroed-in on "Tom Dooley" from the album as the Pick of the Week. A second studio album, however, would have required the Trio to travel to Los Angeles, interrupting their income flow (and Enrico's) and the enormous momentum they had created at the hungry i. Capitol wanted all new material, so the group had been rehearsing fresh songs and mixing them into their stage sets. What's more, a live album would showcase their off-beat humor and bright personalities, one of the group's major appeals.

The Trio just played their regular show, with Capitol carefully edit-ing and balancing the various taped segments to make it as seamless overall as possible. Gilmore didn't want it perfect. He wanted it *realistic*, leaving in the mistakes, the jokes (including the weak ones), the stage patter, and audience reactions; just what you'd hear in a live show setting. The album was not *entirely* live, however, with "Gue Gue" being edited in from an August 11, 1958, mini-recording session at Capitol in Hollywood. The song was so beautiful that the Trio would say, with a straight face, that it left the audience speechless, in reference to the lack of audience ambience surrounding the album cut.

Common belief has it that David "Buck" Wheat played bass on . . . *from the "Hungry i,"* and both Capitol's production log and Dave Guard substantiated it. Yet Nick Reynolds and Buck Wheat himself denied it, with Wheat saying that the bass player was actually John Mosher, a con-temporary and friend of both Wheat and Dean Reilly. According to Reilly, Mosher was a jazz and legit orchestral bass player from Sioux City, Iowa, who became one of San Francisco's "first call" musicians and a mainstay player at the Fairmont Hotel's Venetian Room and the San Francisco Play-boy Club. Wheat did come into The Kingston Trio circle during the hun-gry i period, however, visiting the club one night and introducing himself to the Trio, although Guard recalled that they had met at the Purple Onion a year or so before. Wheat did not become the group's bassist until the Trio's first gig at Salt Lake City's enormous Rainbow Randevu Ballroom (known later as The Terrace) on September 5 and 6, 1958. Enlisting Wheat as a fourth touring and recording member of the group was a monumental musical and intellectual plus for The Kingston Trio.

Born in San Antonio, Texas, on March 19, 1922, "Bucky" was an accomplished stand-up acoustic jazz bassist, jazz guitarist, songwriter, and arranger. He had recorded with The Chet Baker Trio, The Playboy Jazz All Stars, The Jerome Richardson Quartet, and numerous other jazz artists. His composition, "Better than Anything," co-written with Bill Loughborough, would become a jazz standard, recorded by Al Jarreau and Lena Horne among others. He and Loughborough also founded the Boobam Bamboo Drum Company, which produced handmade, tuned acrylic tubes of various lengths that produced a variety of drum sounds. Nick Reynolds's drum solo on "O Ken Karanga" from the Trio's *Close-Up* and *College Concert* albums was played on BooBams.

Wheat provided superb accompaniment, sometimes subtle, sometimes driving, always exactly right, on eleven Kingston albums, from *Here We Go Again* through *College Concert*, as well as hundreds of live concerts worldwide. He was highly intelligent, a gifted, versatile musician of impeccable taste, and oh-so-hip; he knew the score on everything, both figuratively and literally. While Nick and Bobby had each other, Dave had Bucky as a mentor, teacher, and father figure. It was Bucky who turned Dave on to George Russell's "Lydian Chromatic Concept of Tonal Organization for Improvisation." He also turned the Trio on to the purest, strongest marijuana on the planet, at the time known only to discerning jazz musicians and other avant-garde spirits.

"The first time I ever got *really* loaded," Nick Reynolds said, "was when we were playing at the Blue Angel. These four very tall black guys, with black leather coats walked in one night and said, 'Buck Wheat around, man?' Bucky was famous throughout the whole jazz world, and all the musicians came to see him. So I said, 'Yeah, he's upstairs in the dressing room,' and they all came in and went up to the dressing room, and Bucky introduced them to us—it was The Modern Jazz Quartet—*all* of them, the originals. We just shucked and jived up there, you know, Bucky might have lit up one, and they said, 'Come on, Nick, would you like a ride back down to the Village?' Bucky was going to take them to his hotel down there. They had a Volkswagen van and we got in that, and it was the middle of winter. All the windows were closed, and here are these guys, with Buckwheat, in a closed van—you couldn't see out the window, it looked like fog inside. By the time I got out of the van way down in the Village, I was so loaded. I didn't even have any hits in the van, I didn't need them. These guys were being little piggies, and it was so cute. And here I was again, sitting with the elite of the elite, man. Hanging out, and laughing and giggling and just having a great time. It was a thrill just to be in the presence of this kind of company, you know. I felt very honored. Bucky was held in great reverence as a musician, and as a friend, and as a real trustworthy person—and someone who always had the best. He would bring presents to people all around the country! He would make it a point. He had friends throughout the jazz world, and he'd bring them little care packages and things." Nick Reynolds also recalled landing on a deserted Greeley, Colorado, airstrip late at night, deplaning the Trio's leased Beechcraft after smoking Bucky-rolled joints in the back of the plane during the flight. "I remember getting off the plane and just sort of walking off into the distance. I don't even remember there being an airport. I've never been so loaded in my life! Buckwheat was the sweetest, most beautiful, most gentle cat. No problem with Bucky. A constant joy to be around. He was like a Papa Bear, you know, and we were really close to Bucky too."[23]

Joan Reynolds remembered how important Bucky was to the Trio, musically and intellectually. "It wasn't until they got Bucky that something happened to tighten it up because he was a bass guy," says Joan, "and he had a hipness that they didn't have in their little circle. His 'traveling companion' was his bass, and it always had a ticket and a seat on the plane. We called it 'Mr. Bass' and of course we'd say to the stewardesses, 'This is Mr. Bass and he's got the tickets.' You loved Bucky. You had to. He was loaded all the time, but very seldom was he over the top."[24]

Salt Lake City would be a pivotal point in the emergence of The Kingston Trio. In 1958, Top 40 radio was the ruling media, which meant playing the same songs over and over, with every major city having its own "kingmaker" disc jockey who had a lot of latitude to interject personal favorites beyond a prescribed playlist based on record popularity. In Salt Lake City, Paul Coburn was the undisputed top jock, one of KLUB's "Fabulous Five" DJs as they were called, which also included Bill Terry, who was a huge proponent of the Trio and who joined Coburn in playing cuts from their first album. Broadcast six hours a day, six days a week, Paul Coburn's "Coburn Caravan" ("It's a colorful, cool, crazy, colossal, caravan of records") had the ear of listeners in five western states. Both Coburn and Bill Terry were smitten with The Kingston Trio's first album, singling out "Tom Dooley" for nonstop airplay. They were joined by Ron Zenger and his sister Barbara, owners of the House of Music, a custom hi-fi components store with a massive retail record department, in picking "Tom Dooley" and the album as their picks of the week as well. For years, Coburn would be a powerful bellwether disc jockey, along with other key jocks around the country, reporting weekly to *Billboard* with his picks and opinions. Coburn was extremely proactive in promoting the Trio, spreading the word to other national jocks, even talking with hotel managers in Las Vegas, pushing the Trio whenever possible. It was mutually beneficial, of course, helping to reinforce Coburn as Salt Lake's leading radio personality, a role greatly enhanced by his friendship with the Trio. He was also an accomplished guitar, ukulele, and banjo player, which may explain his enthusiasm for the Trio in the first place.

So well had Paul Coburn and Bill Terry worked their magic that by the time the Trio arrived in Salt Lake City on September 5, 1958, for a two-day visit, The Kingston Trio held five of the Top 10 most requested songs in Salt Lake City. That automatically makes the artist a superstar in that town, and that was exactly how The Kingston Trio were received. They were met at the airport by Eugene Jeleznik, the concert promoter and classical violinist who paid them a whopping one thousand dollars for a two-day visit, huge money for a relatively unknown act. Paul Coburn, Bill Terry, and several of the other "Fabulous Five" were there too, joining the Trio for a motorcycle-escorted parade through downtown Salt Lake City.

It was strictly red carpet treatment for the Trio, including being put up in the Hotel Utah, the city's best hotel, giving numerous interviews to the media, and attending a packed autograph party after playing to a sold-out crowd at Rainbow Randevu, a massive enclosed dance hall. They were all over the radio, chatting with Salt Lake City's top disc jockeys, who, in turn, called their disc jockey friends in Miami, Seattle, El Paso, and other big cities around the country touting "Tom Dooley" and The Kingston Trio. The jocks also put pressure on Voyle Gilmore to release "Tom Dooley" as a single, which he resisted, until he could no longer ignore the clamor and growing momentum.

Flush with a thousand dollars in cash from the Salt Lake City concert promoter, Werber decided that the Trio and he deserved a little break before heading back to the hungry i. "We're going to treat ourselves to a little of this," Werber said gleefully, holding up the cash. "We're going to spend the thousand bucks, right now! We're just going to blow it, treat ourselves. We're all going to L.A. and hang out at the Garden of Allah."[25] The old Garden of Allah on Sunset Boulevard and Crescent in West Hollywood was one of the city's most famous (some say infamous) hotels, comprised of twenty-five Spanish-style villas with a large swimming pool, restaurant, and plenty of privacy. Rudolph Valentino, Charlie Chaplin, Humphrey Bogart and Lauren Bacall, Greta Garbo, Errol Flynn, and Marlene Dietrich were among the many Hollywood stars who frequented the Garden of Allah from 1927 to 1959, when it closed. Werber and the Trio members each checked into separate suites at the hotel, essential for Shane and Reynolds, who had two special "guests" arriving later from Salt Lake City. It would create real friction within the group when the two girls showed up poolside, surprising—and infuriating—Dave Guard. Shane and Reynolds held their ground; this wasn't business, it was their fun and too bad if the "acknowledged leader" didn't like it. Reynolds and Shane were still single, although that would soon change for Reynolds on September 22, 1958.

Much has been said about the divisiveness within the Trio, with Guard's absence at Reynolds's wedding given as proof that he had become odd man out, with Shane and Reynolds the buddies. While it's true that Guard was not invited, neither was Frank, though Reynolds had been Guard's best man a couple of years earlier. Reynolds pointed to the Garden of Allah incident as the beginning of the alienation between Guard and his two Trio mates. "My siding with Bobby was the start of it," he reflected.[26] Physical separation didn't help, either. The Guards lived in Palo Alto, and they had a baby at the time. Shane and Reynolds, and later Joan Harriss, lived together on a houseboat in Sausalito. It wasn't that easy for all of them to connect. What's more, Shane and Reynolds were bachelors, and took full advantage of their growing celebrity, partying all night—every night—with wealthy Nob Hill socialites, often including outrageous and very drunken scenarios. Guard knew none of it; he was at home every night with his wife and child. When Nick and Joan decided to marry, they agreed it would be low-key, a small wedding party of just four people at a little church in Sausalito, with Bobby Shane serving as best man, and Susie Pierce, a friend of Joan's, as maid of honor. Afterward, the four drove back to the houseboat for drinks and later visited with Frank and his girlfriend at his house just up the hill from the docks in Sausalito. While Reynolds said that there were no ill feelings, that it wasn't important that the Guards weren't invited because a big party was planned for the next night at the hungry i to announce the wedding to the public, it nonetheless stung Guard. Frank had arranged for a champagne toast on stage, and a wedding cake was set up out front after the show. It was a party for all the employees at the hungry i—and all the Trio's friends from the Purple Onion, including waiter Chuck Marcoux and manager Barry Drew, who still lived in the houseboat next to Reynolds. Drew never had any animosity towards the Trio, even though he was the manager of the Purple Onion; it was the owners who were angry. The Guards were in attendance, too, and a year later they were invited to Bobby's wedding to Louise Brandon in Washington, D.C.

After finishing up the last few days of their hungry i engagement and a short honeymoon trip to Lake Elsinore for the Reynolds, Werber and the Trio flew to Honolulu on October 1, 1958, to start a seven-week engagement at the Royal Hawaiian Hotel's Surf Room. Joan Reynolds was still working for Frank and stayed behind to take care of some business, leaving Nick and Bobby to party in Honolulu, visiting Bobby's old haunts and hanging out with his beach boy friends. The gig had been booked directly by the Royal Hawaiian, who already knew Bobby and Dave, reaching Frank Werber through the boys' families and bypassing Joe Glaser's Associated Booking Corporation agency in the process. It was like Salt Lake City all over again; they were the pets of the island, Reynolds reflected. They would pay for nothing—with *everything* on the house. Each of the four had their own luxury suite. All meals, all drinks—even their plane tickets over and back from the mainland—were taken care of by the Royal Hawaiian. But the Trio more than earned it, packing the Surf Room every night. And sitting right up front at a ringside table were Margaret and Art Schoen and their friends, along with Marjorie and Jack Guard and their friends, plus a legion of Bobby's old beach boy buddies.

On October 23, 1958, barely midway through their seven-week engagement at the Royal Hawaiian Hotel, the Trio received a telegram from Voyle Gilmore informing them that "Tom Dooley" had just passed the half million mark in sales, and that album sales were nearing one hundred thousand and climbing. It closed with an understated, "See you October 29. Best of Luck."

Frank called everyone into his room in the afternoon and said, "I want you to read something. Don't get scared!" He then handed the envelope with Gilmore's telegram to the boys. They were mystified, wondering aloud, "What the hell's going on!!??" The telegram said, in effect, "Get your ass back here! We gotta jump on it right now!" "Then the shit hit the fan," said Nick.[27]

Indeed. On November 22, 1958, "Tom Dooley" hit number one on *Billboard*'s Hot 100, ultimately spending twenty-one weeks on the charts. The Kingston Trio was on its way to becoming one of the most popular, financially successful, and influential musical groups in the history of American popular music. They would be both revered and pilloried. Loved and despised. Things would never be the same after "Tom Dooley." It changed everything—and everybody.

⨎

Hawaii was especially alluring to the Trio. Not only was it beautiful and fun and hospitable, it was easy on their vocal cords. Unlike playing cold, drafty amphitheaters in the wintery Midwest that were always harsh and dry on their throats, the air in Hawaii was always warm and moist. Reynolds said that you could literally sing all day long if you had the chops because the air was like an elixir pouring down your throat. But it was also hot in Hawaii and at the time the Royal Hawaiian was not air-conditioned. As a result, the Trio rarely rehearsed in Hawaii, singing only on stage at night. Hawaii would become a frequent venue for the Trio, including the Royal Hawaiian Hotel (both the Surf and Monarch Rooms), Hawaii's 50th State Fair, the Honolulu International Center, the Waikiki Shell, and the Conroy Bowl at Schofield Barracks.

Hawaii was also one of Elvis Presley's favorite haunts, and inevitably the Trio ran into the King, literally. "We were playing at the Waikiki Shell, and Elvis just stepped out of the elevator as we were going in," Reynolds recalled. "He went 'Ohhh, God!!!!' He gave Bobby a big hug and said, 'I've really wanted to meet you boys,' but he was kind of a little groggy, and he had two or three big guys with him and they didn't want him to talk to us *at all.* They wanted to get him someplace for whatever appointment he had, and Elvis said, 'I'd do anything to just sit around and pick with you guys, you know. Maybe later on we could get together.' And, we said, 'Oh, yeah!' He was the biggest star in the world! And we never saw him again."[28]

Actually, Shane did see Elvis a few years later in Honolulu and told him that he actually got his start impersonating him in 1956, to which Elvis replied, "What would you wanna do *that* for?" And that was it. The Trio did get a Christmas card from Elvis and the colonel when Presley was just coming back from his army stint in Germany. Shane also got one sent to him personally, but unsigned.

John Stewart, too, would later meet up with Elvis in a Las Vegas hotel coffee shop at two in the morning. The Trio had played their last show, and Stewart was having breakfast by himself when Elvis walked in with two beautiful showgirls on each arm. "Heh, heh, Stewart, I see you're by yourself again," Presley said with a lopsided grin as he walked past Stewart's booth.[29] Ironically, Elvis had agreed to record Stewart's "Runaway Fool of Love," which was written about and for Presley, but died before they could set up the session.

NOTES

1. Voyle Gilmore, interview with Richard Johnston, January 1, 1973, from the Dave Guard and Richard Johnston Kingston Trio collection of materials, 1956–1986, University Manuscript Collections, University of Wisconsin, Milwaukee.

2. Nick Reynolds, interview with the author, Seminole, FL, October 4, 1986.

3. Dave Guard, interview with the author, Los Altos, CA, November 28, 1983.

4. N. Reynolds, interview with the author, October 4, 1986.

5. N. Reynolds, interview with the author, October 4, 1986.

6. N. Reynolds, interview with the author, October 4, 1986.

7. Bob Shane, interview with the author, Phoenix, AZ, April 7, 2009.

8. N. Reynolds, interview with the author, October 4, 1986.

9. Oscar and George Marienthal, "Hats Off to The Kingston Trio," *Variety*, March 16, 1960, 60.

10. D. Guard, interview with the author.

11. N. Reynolds, interview with the author, October 4, 1986.

12. Bob Shane, interview with the author, Phoenix, AZ, April 6, 2009.

13. Shane, interview with the author, April, 6, 2009.

14. N. Reynolds, interview with the author, October 4, 1986.

15. Richard Hadlock, "The Kingston Trio Story, 'Tom Dooley—Tom Dooley!'" *Downbeat*, June 11, 1959.

16. Gretchen Guard, interview with the author, Santa Fe, NM, September 9, 2006.

17. N. Reynolds, interview with the author, October 4, 1986.

18. Hon. Robert F. Wagner, Western Union Telegram to The Kingston Trio, Albert Hotel, 23 East 10th Street, New York City, May 8, 1958.

19. N. Reynolds, interview with the author, October 4, 1986.

20. Bob Shane, interview with the author, Phoenix, AZ, March 6, 2009.

21. Enrico Banducci to Nick Reynolds, 1958; Nick Reynolds, interview with the author, Seminole, FL, October 5, 1986.

22. Bruce Pollock, "Dave Guard: The Kingston Trio," in *When Rock Was Young* (New York: Holt, Rinehart and Winston, 1981), 134.

23. Nick Reynolds, interview with the author, Seminole, FL, October 6, 1986.

24. Joan Reynolds, interview with the author, Sausalito, CA, August 16, 2011.

25. Frank Werber to Dave Guard, Bob Shane, and Nick Reynolds, September 7, 1958; N. Reynolds, interview with author, October 6, 1986.

26. N. Reynolds, interview with the author, October 6, 1986.

27. Frank Werber to Dave Guard, Bob Shane, and Nick Reynolds, October 23, 1958; N. Reynolds, interview with author, October 6, 1986.

28. N. Reynolds, interview with the author, October 6, 1986.

29. John Stewart, conversation with the author, Malibu, CA, 1985.

7

TOM DOOLEY GOES TO COLLEGE

"Tom Dooley" was a fluke. That it would even be recorded by The Kingston Trio, let alone become the anthem of a national urban folk revival, was pure happenstance. The Trio heard the tune from an older, white-haired gentleman, a retired doctor they were told, who wandered into the Purple Onion while they were rehearsing in the showroom one afternoon. It was one of the Purple Onion's bimonthly audition days, where local talent vied for a spot at the club.

Supposedly, the man had been singing the tune all over the world. The boys asked if he would write down the lyrics, which they rehearsed that night between shows, and built their own arrangement using his lyrics. They made only one change, to the bridge in the middle with a shift in octave—"Hang down your head and cry, hang down your head and cry." The man told them that the song was public domain, but Nick Reynolds admitted that they didn't even know what public domain meant in those days. They were very naive, and Capitol wasn't much more enlightened. The company used a screening system that purportedly distinguished music that was with Capitol's publishers from that which was public domain. When "Tom Dooley" was run through the system, it immediately brought up a list of titles, and Capitol said, "That brings up public domain in our book."

But the lyrics were *not* public domain. Reynolds later estimated that at least 150 people claimed ownership of the arrangement of "Tom Dooley," and that it took years to find the true authors. A copyright infringement suit filed against the Trio in 1963 was settled out of court, and writer and publishing royalties were paid to the plaintiff. In truth, no one expected to sell any records or have any publisher's or writer's royalties anyway. It was something they never even considered. And while Capitol thought "Tom

Dooley" was a sure hit, the Trio thought of it as only an interesting ballad that would fit nicely with the other tunes on the album.

Surprisingly, the song had been recorded at least as early as 1929, based on the real life and death of Tom Dula, a confederate veteran who allegedly stabbed his cheating lover, Laura Foster, out of jealousy (and for giving him syphilis as a result of her numerous dalliances) in Wilkes County, North Carolina. He was convicted twice and hanged in Statesville, North Carolina, on May 1, 1868. The song has been passed down—and around—it seems forever. It's credited to Frank Proffitt Sr., a traditional singer and fretless banjo player who heard the song from his father—who in turn heard it from *his* grandmother, Adeline Pardue, who actually knew Tom Dula and Laura Foster. Singer and folklorist Frank Warner collected the song from Proffitt in 1938 and taught it to fellow folklorist Alan Lomax, who published it in his *Folksong U.S.A.* in 1947. Frank Warner released his own version of the song on his 1952 album *American Folk Songs and Ballads*. Subsequently, the song was covered by The Folksay Trio (Erik Darling, Bob Carey, and Roger Sprung), followed by Paul Clayton (Worthington) in 1956, and The Tarriers (Erik Darling, Bob Carey, and Alan Arkin) in 1957. The Kingston Trio recorded it a year later in 1958.

In his in-depth study of "Tom Dooley," Peter J. Curry questioned Nick Reynolds's assertion that the Trio learned "Tom Dooley" from an unknown singer who auditioned at the Purple Onion one afternoon. "This story is improbable given that it would be difficult to learn all the words to 'Tom Dooley' or any song of more than a few lines in one hearing," Curry wrote. "It is possible, however, that they learned the basic melody and some of the words of the song from the 'unknown singer' and looked elsewhere for a complete text of the song."[1] The point is reasonably taken, with Curry citing Charles Wolfe's article in the Bear Family's *The Guard Years* anthology, including the following excerpt: "According to most sources, The Kingston Trio learned Tom Dooley in August 1957 from a now-forgotten singer auditioning at San Francisco's Purple Onion, where the group appeared as the club's featured act. However, trio leader Dave Guard candidly admitted to others that he took the song (and presumably *Bay of Mexico* as well) from the Stinson 'Folksay Trio' album. Guard rearranged the piece for dramatic effects, cutting the tempo and adding a narrative prolog. The results set the old ballad spinning on yet another cycle of fame."[2] At the same time, Curry quoted Bob Shane's remarks from a 1993 radio interview concerning how the Trio got "Tom Dooley": "I heard it originally on a Tarriers album, a speeded up version," Shane recalled, "and the other fellows heard the version of the guy who is given credit for collecting it, Warner, something like that. . . . They saw him audition at the Purple Onion and they heard him do it. So we took the backgrounds we had on that and we eventually rewrote it just enough to claim it for our own and signed our name to it, got sued, and lost because it was in Lomax's collection before that."[3]

A persistent rumor floated around for years that The Kingston Trio drove to Ferguson, North Carolina, after a concert at Davidson College in Statesville on April 9, 1959, and absconded with Tom Dula's tombstone, which Reynolds said was pure nonsense.

"We didn't steal the marker! They'd taken the old one out at the gravesite, and they'd constructed a rather large, shrine-type monument as a replacement. The old marker just said T. D., but I don't think it was the original one because it looked brand new but it had some old concrete at the bottom. It was only like a foot square, max. And they *gave* that to us based on the popularity of the record. They said, 'We'd like to present this tombstone, where would you like us to send it?' We couldn't take it on the road—it weighed fifty or sixty pounds—so it was shipped back to Frank. They couldn't have been sweeter in Statesville. It was the first time we'd ever seen the Deep South and the political structures involved. Everybody was one big happy family down there. We'd did a benefit there later on, for the homeless, or something." They also became personal friends with some of the townspeople and would visit Statesville whenever they were in the vicinity. "It sort of became a second home to us," Reynolds said.[4]

Even with early indications that "Tom Dooley" was going be a hit, it's not surprising that Capitol sat on it for as long as it did. The Trio were not considered a top act yet and perhaps would never be one. Less than one thousand dollars had been spent on production of T996, and only one thousand copies were initially pressed. Despite impassioned entreaties from Paul Coburn to Capitol to start moving on "Tom Dooley," that "something big" was already happening in Salt Lake City, and that they had a hit on their hands, Capitol did virtually nothing to accelerate or capitalize on the single or the album from which it came. Voyle Gilmore was not oblivious to what was happening, but he could be indecisive, overly thoughtful, and painstakingly careful not to make any "quick" assumptions. Although "Tom Dooley" had been issued as a single on August 1, 1958, Capitol did no real promotion until big sales figures started rolling in October of 1958, when sales passed the half million copies mark. It would eventually sell 3 million copies (although recent estimates put the figure at double that amount).

Frank Werber had no say in Capitol's marketing decisions, but he certainly controlled where the group played, for how much, and for how long. With growing popularity comes an incremental increase in the asking price for any successful act, especially one riding a number one national hit record. Part of paying dues on the way up is to play for exposure first and money second. Even with sellout crowds at the hungry i the Trio were virtually playing for scale, and according to Reynolds the Royal Hawaiian gig was probably no more than $1,500 a week. By this time, the group had signed with Associated Booking Corporation, who priced the Trio at $10,500 for a ten-day engagement at the La Fiesta nightclub in Juarez, Mexico. To do so, however, the Trio had to negotiate leaving the Royal Hawaiian to go to Mexico, which meant that they'd have to sign a return contract to fulfill the engagement at a later date at the same rate as the original contract—*plus* sign another contract to come back when they had hit it big. Over the years, the Trio cut short engagements at Mr. Kelly's, the Blue Angel, the hungry i, and the Royal Hawaiian to play bigger venues for bigger money, but returned to play for much lower rates—sometimes as much as three times lower than what they were commanding with their newfound celebrity. They were still playing one club for $750 a week when "Tom Dooley" hit, when they could easily command $3,200 a night—and higher—elsewhere.

Yet it still made sense. Gilmore's entreaty to get back to the mainland, to hit it hard while the record was hot, albeit late in coming, was critical. La Fiesta, "the most beautiful showplace in all the Americas," was an important and highly visible venue for young entertainers on the rise as well as established stars—and fading ones, too. Frank Sinatra, Wayne Newton, Sammy Davis Jr., Steve Lawrence, Al Martino, Marty Robbins, Sophie Tucker, The Four Freshman, Frankie Avalon, and Fabian played in the lavish showroom.

Located across the river from El Paso, La Fiesta would become one of the Trio's favorite early venues and the Trio would become one of La Fiesta's favorite acts. The Trio were enormously popular in Juarez and nearby El Paso, and both cities turned out en masse to greet them. Their shows quickly sold out, which attracted a great deal of business to nearby restaurants and shops in the process. On one visit a Mexican waiter whom the Trio got to know at La Fiesta invited the boys to be his family's guest at a traditional dinner to celebrate his daughter's baptism. They gladly accepted, bringing the family presents and hiring a mariachi band to play at the dinner, with the Trio singing "Coplas" and "La Bamba" as a special treat. Soon the dinner turned into a block party with the whole neighborhood joining in the fun. "The men were drinking wine from a goatskin bag and passing around a bowl of chilies," Reynolds recounted, "so Bobby reached for a big yellow chili in the middle of the bowl, and the men yelled, 'No, Mr. Shane! No, Mr. Shane!' Bobby said, 'Aw, give me that, nothing's too hot for me!' He gobbled this thing down and his eyes got huge—he looked like Felix the cat, you know, eyes spinning around. His teeth almost fell out of his mouth. He went to his knees. I thought he was going to have a heart attack. They were all real worried about him. They tried to warn him, 'Don't do this, Mr. Shane. It's not a smart thing.' But he survived, you know, Bobby."[5] Later, the boys attended a bullfight and were thrilled to see "The Kingston Trio in La Fiesta" beautifully chalked out on the arena floor.

The Trio would appear at La Fiesta only once more, in October of 1961, shortly after John Stewart joined the group. It, too, would be a memorable engagement—even before it started. The three were staying in El Paso and decided to take a ride over to Juarez to check out the club and wound up in a street bar. Stewart, who rarely drank, started shooting back tequila for the first time while Shane was attempting to squirt wine into his mouth from a goatskin wine bag, a favorite local tradition. Instead, Shane squirted wine all over himself—and Stewart's white shirt. Fists flew, and the two went over a table trying to punch each other "like a John Wayne movie." Then Stewart took a swing at Shane's stomach but instead hit his big silver belt buckle. "I just started jumping around the room holding my fist going 'Oh! Oh! Oh!' Nobody ever landed a blow. We ended up struggling on the ground in the snow. We were pissed off, half pissed off and half laughing. But we had wine all over us! And they drove us back to the border where our station wagon was, and threw us out. You know, being kicked out of Juarez is really hard to do!"[6]

With "Tom Dooley" the number one record in the nation and the album close behind, Werber and the Trio were faced with the question of how to handle it all; how to plan the tours and maximize the offers that were suddenly flooding in, including national TV shows such as *The Dinah Shore Chevy Show*, *Kraft Music Hall* with Milton Berle, *The Perry Como Show*, *The Jimmie Rodgers Show*, *The Jack Benny Program*, *The Garry Moore Show*, and *The George Burns Show*. The Frank Werber Agency was too small and too inexperienced to handle a superstar act, opening the door to Joe Glaser and Bert Block at Glaser's Associated Booking Corporation, whose staff of bookers cobbled together many of the Trio's early big tours. Individual promoters, too, would play a big role in The Kingston Trio's ability to cover the country. Irving Granz, Lou Robbins, Al Kingsley, Eddie Sarkesian, George Wein, Jerry Perenchio, Don Cange—and Frank Werber—all did their part in their respective geographic areas and venue specialties.

Throughout their career, The Kingston Trio played mainly three types of performance venues or formats—concerts, clubs, and private parties. Concerts were typically two hours in length (with intermission), clubs were forty-five minutes to one hour, and private parties were same as club dates but sometimes longer or shorter depending on circumstances. On occasion they would play special events such as the President's Scholars Reception, charity balls, store openings, rallies, and fund-raisers. "Just bring the money. The boys will show up!"

Of all Trio fans, college students were the biggest and most enthusiastic audience, with on-campus concerts their most popular performance venue. From the beginning, the Trio courted the college market—and vice versa. The Trio were one of their own, three young guys barely out of college themselves. Their stage simply shifted from the Cracked Pot to college gymnasiums and field houses. The affinity between the Trio and the college students was palpable and equally enjoyed by both.

"We were getting as much out of them as they were out of us," Dave Guard explained. "We were really staying in contact with college kids because we were just out of college at the time. So we'd go to all these parties after the show, see what was happening, see if there's any profit to be made there. And so we stayed very close. I think we were sort of role models. Like, when somebody's a freshman they think the seniors are real hot stuff. Well, who do the seniors look up to? It was that sort of thing. They want to see somebody that's just over the wall, somebody who knew what to do after you get pushed into the cold world. We were one of the few groups that invented their own thing to do. I mean we wanted to do something that was natural to us and we just couldn't face putting on suits at all, so out of sheer panic we kind of clung together in that respect and I think it showed that musicians could go out and carve their own territory if possible."[7]

In the late 1950s, the average college student was white, middle-upper class, usually from a Republican family, "emerging adults" whose musical tastes included some of the new rock and roll, but was more "grown up" in their aesthetics. Calypso, modern jazz, folk (Weavers style), and big band (Stan Kenton style) were all doing well on college campuses in the late '50s. "Hip" *was* hip, but nothing radical, thanks. "Tom Dooley" was just different enough to light their fire and set the stage for a massive paradigm shift. "If they [the Trio] hadn't made the personal appearances they did in those early years, it wouldn't have happened the way it did," Werber surmised. "Their super saturation of colleges is what made them. 'Tom Dooley' was the key that opened the door, and the college stage was the place to go through that door." Werber not only recognized the potential power of a college market, he made sure that every college and university, big or small, could afford to bring The Kingston Trio to their campus. "There wasn't such a thing as a 'concert tour' at the college level or the city level," Werber said. "Oh, there was Alan Freed's Caravan, or Segovia at the Opera House, but nobody did what we did. The Trio was the birth of the college concert market. We created it. And I tried to make them [the Trio] attainable, not out of reach, to break down the footlights. Above all, that it should never be a rip off."[8] Thus, the "free" Kingston Trio College Concert was born. The idea came to Werber from two young manager/promoters from Los Angeles, Alan Kingsley and Lou Robbins.

At the time, the entire cost of a college concert was borne by the college itself, usually paid out of a student body fund for special events at different times of the year. The standard terms for a Kingston Trio concert included a guaranteed minimum versus a percentage of the gate, whichever was larger. Half the guarantee was due up front, and the balance was due at intermission. If it was a package show, say, The Kingston Trio, Dave Brubeck Quartet, and a comedian, which they sometimes did in bigger cities, the guarantee could be hefty since it covered all three acts' expenses including equipment rental (Brubeck didn't play just *any* piano), special lighting, security, and whatever else was in the contract rider. Not only did a big guarantee preclude most small colleges with limited student body funds, it was tough for the act itself to get solid bookings all over the country in any given period of time.

The solution was simple: do the concert for free—and take the entire admission revenue in lieu of standard fee. For a group as big as The Kingston Trio, appearing by itself, filling any college venue, big or small, was not a problem. In some instances, the Trio might ask for a small guarantee say, $1,500 versus 80 percent of the gate. So for as little as a $750 down payment, a small college could get The Kingston Trio for next to nothing—*and* make 20 percent of the total admission. There was very little out-of-pocket expense for the college—concert staffing was usually student volunteers, the gym or field house was rent free to the college and usually had its own sound and lighting equipment already in place, local and student newspaper advertising was nominal, and the Trio sold their own concert program. The Trio got its $1,500 guarantee, 100 percent of the proceeds from the programs, and 80 percent of the gate. Everybody was happy. And with this kind of flexible pricing, the Trio made themselves available to everybody, the biggest colleges and the smallest. What's more, college students were the biggest record-buying segment in the country. So not only were the Trio selling a concert performance, they were reinforcing their biggest, most loyal and enthusiastic record customer and sometimes selling albums to those loyal customers in the lobby, as well.

Remarkably, the Trio found that no matter where they played, from a small southern or New England college to a huge Big 10 university in the Midwest, the reception of the Trio was always the same. Every school appreciated the same humor, cheered the same songs, lined up for the same autographs. It proved that despite regional and ideological differences, America is one country at heart. If they laughed at Daytona Beach Community College, they laughed just as hard at UCLA. Reynolds was always enthusiastic about the college market saying, "We'd be silly to get off the college circuit. It's an instant market; the best audience for us. The students are very responsive, and they're old enough to know what's going on. The kids today are aware; they bother to listen to the lyrics and don't take anything at face value. Collegians won't get stampeded into fads."[9]

Like the Purple Onion and the hungry i audiences in San Francisco, college students took The Kingston Trio home with them via their albums, spreading the gospel to family and friends around the country. Decades later, the same college students who attended Kingston Trio concerts in their college years would form the core of the Trio's enormous, worldwide fan base. The Trio not only created the college market, they *kept* it and, according to Shane, expanded it. "At any of The Kingston Trio shows today you see a sea of white hair," he pointed out. "But you also see *their kids* who are now in their forties and fifties—and you see their *grandkids*, too, who are now in their twenties And they all come up to see us after the show, all different ages."[10]

This personal accessibility has always been one of the Trio's most endearing qualities. They truly liked fans, but were also cautious, though they never let it get in the way of fans who wanted to meet them. "We were the first act to ever be like that," Shane added. "When we finished the show and packed up our instruments, we'd walk right out into the audience area to meet people and sign autographs. There were never any problems. Nobody pawed us or started anything. Everybody was very respectful and we made a lot of friends and created lots of good feelings. People said The Kingston Trio is one of us, which we were. And we showed them that we weren't the usual show business people that were inaccessible. We tried to stay that way pretty much all of our careers. I remember we were playing at the University of Alabama in '66," Shane continued, "and after the show I'd gone out to drink with the guys at the KA house. And in a short amount of time, I had them singing along with me on certain songs. So I called Stewart at the hotel and woke him up and said, 'John you should come over here and hear this group sing one of your songs.' And he came over and I had them sing 'Lock All the Windows,' the chorus. It was beautiful."[11]

Dave Guard said that playing to large college audiences indirectly influenced how the Trio sang. "What really changed our style was playing at the University of Oregon one night. We'd been playing at small places and suddenly it was like 7,000 people in this field house. It was the biggest thing we'd played; earlier it was about 4,500. It was completely full, and we realized we had to slow down the whole act by maybe 25 percent. All the tempos and all the jokes had to be big and round because no one could hear because of the echo. So that was very instrumental in making the thing far more musical. Before it was a lot of nervous energy, but we had to really take it away from the way *we* were hearing it and putting it into a form that could be heard and understood by anybody. The timing extended and the rhythm changed to how the fat lady could dance rather than the mosquito jumping around. If you hear the first album, there's a lot of accelerando and it got really hectic in the end. Later on it was much slower, so it completely changed the concept and made it musical."[12]

The Trio discovered that the ideal sized audience was in the three to four thousand range with a good sound system. Anything bigger lost the intimacy, that all-important personal connection that was a key factor in the Trio's success. They were close to their audiences, especially college kids with their keen intelligence and enthusiasm. They got it—without even trying. "It was fun to play any of the big college gigs because the audience was just pre-sold; they were so appreciative," Nick Reynolds added. "Even at the end of the road really, when rock and roll started taking over. I remember sometimes college kids were stunned at how good our act was. They were prepared to hate us. We played Kent State in the middle of a snowstorm and we hung out with these kids afterwards and they just loved us. They said, 'Oh you guys are great!' because they were like the new hippies—they helped us push our car out of the snow. We helped them push a car out of the snow. And they really thought we were terrific guys. They changed their whole tune about us. They thought we were going to be old mossbacks."[13]

In their first big year of solid touring, beginning in late 1958 through 1959, the Trio crisscrossed the country, from west to east, top to bottom, interspersed with jumps to Hawaii. The preponderance of those dates were colleges. "I think we were 328 days on the road in 1959 or something like that," Guard estimated. "It was very exciting. You'd be tired all the time, but you know it's a great way to see America. That's why we were in The Kingston Trio. It was kind of like a patriotic thing almost, from two guys who were from Hawaii and the other guy was really from Coronado, which is what, six miles 'way from the Mexican border stuck way out in the corner there, so we really wanted to see what the country was and it's a real beautiful place."[14]

Ideally, tour dates are based on efficient logistics, with venues within reasonable proximity of each other, allowing plenty of time for travel, set up, and break down in between dates. Typically, the Trio, their bass player, and the road manager would fly to the first city on the tour. If subsequent gigs were clustered within easy driving distance of each other, they would rent two cars—a sedan for the three Trio members and a station wagon for the road manager, the bassist, and the instruments. As their popularity grew and dates rapidly filled in back-to-back, their concerts were often several states apart, making driving impractical or impossible. It was decided that they would charter their own plane, so Werber leased a six-passenger, twin-engine Beechcraft D18, piloted by John Rich, a highly decorated World War II veteran and former B-29 pilot from Salt Lake City.

Beech Model D18s were workhorses, having seen military service as trainers, as well as numerous civilian uses—from corporate travel to carrying freight to skydiving. It carried a crew of two pilots and six passengers a distance of 1,200 miles at a cruising speed of 195 miles an hour. It carried The Kingston Trio tens of thousands of miles throughout the United States during 1959, including an unscheduled stop in Clarence Yoder's frozen Goshen, Indiana, farm field on March 13th.

According to the *South Bend Tribune*, the Trio's plane came to a halt at 5:45 p.m. in a field just off Elkhart County Road 38, one mile south of Goshen and twenty-five miles from Notre Dame. "Skid marks on the mud indicated the plane wasn't braked until the final ten feet of the landing," the paper detailed, saying that pilot John Rich was a veteran of twenty years flying and was accustomed to forced landings including one on Iwo Jima in a B-29 with seven feet of wing shot off and with inoperable controls. That experience probably saved their lives.[15]

It had been a smooth, mostly sunny flight from Nashville where the Trio had appeared the night before at Vanderbilt University, en route to Notre Dame in South Bend, Indiana. As the plane nosed into northern Indiana, it was hit by one of the area's infamous "lake snow" blizzards coming off Lake Michigan. Almost simultaneously, the plane's generator and electrical system went out—including radios and twin ignition system—followed by the loud bang of an exploding fire extinguisher under Dave

Guard's seat. Pete Sterner, Frank Werber's stepbrother from Mill Valley
and the Trio's first road manager, was riding up front with the pilot. "John
Rich immediately started looking for a place to land because we were running out of gas," said Sterner, "and it was snowing so hard you could hardly
see anything out the window. We were real low to the ground, barely
missing the phone lines. So John says to me, 'Tell them to buckle up back
there, we're going in.' Then he said, 'Hang on to the wheel and keep it
level while I look out the window.'"[16]

Dave Guard was terrified. "We thought, Oh Christ! Something bad's
happening," Guard remembered. "This was just about the time Buddy Holly
got killed, and we were flying in a little plane of our own around the Midwest in the worst of weather. There was a blizzard starting up and some air-
planes were lost in the area and every airplane had to maintain radio silence.
We got totally lost and then the electricity went out on the plane—there
were no lights or anything like that. So we had to swoop down and read road
signs to find out where the heck we were. We finally landed in a farmer's
field with all these frozen turkeys wrapped in plastic in it and then skidded to
a stop like about three feet away from the fence. Pretty exciting stuff. When
we were hitting the ground, I said 'Here's to the Big Bopper!'"[17]

The Buddy Holly crash similarity wasn't lost on Nick Reynolds, either. The Trio had been regularly cheating fate in much the same way that
cost Holly, Richie Valens, and The Big Bopper their lives six weeks earlier.
Regardless of the weather, the Trio were determined to make it to every
performance. If TWA or American wouldn't chance it, they'd find somebody who would. "I remember someplace up in Idaho or way up in the
North Plains, and the commercial airlines wouldn't fly," said Nick, "and it
was like 150 miles to the gig and we couldn't make it by car in time for the
show. So we chartered some damn daredevils in a couple of small Pipers to
fly us up there in this weather. And that was hairy, my dear. I mean *nobody*
else would fly. We would just sneak off the end of the runway, man. And
we would get there. And it was real scary and *real* dangerous, you know.
During this time after Buddy Holly had died, we just blocked that out of
our minds saying, you know, that can't happen to us. But it happened to
Buddy Holly while we were touring. I remember reading about it, and
saying 'Holy Christ! We're doing exactly the same stupid kind of thing.'"[18]

Ironically, it was Friday the 13th, yet miraculously nobody was hurt
in the forced landing. Sterner said dozens of people came on to the field
from out of nowhere to see if the passengers were okay only to be greeted
by Bob Shane, who held his right hand up and said, "How!" Indian style.
A cab was called to take the Trio, Bucky, and Pete Sterner to Notre Dame,

stopping at a liquor store on the way where they each bought—and slammed down—two six-packs of beer in celebration of their survival. John Rich stayed with the plane until repairs could be made and flew it out of the field the next day.

The performance at Notre Dame in South Bend was one of the most memorable and emotionally charged in the Trio's history. By this time, the news of the crash landing had reached the university and the crowd was waiting for them. "Notre Dame is famous for the noise they make at the football games, their spirit," Guard said. "So we went into the field house, and it sounded like a jet plane just about was taking off in the hangar there. I think it was the second or third Friday of Lent, and they were all raging maniacs. I never heard so much noise."[19]

Just prior to going on stage the Trio were met by one of the priests in the administration who advised them to *not* do their full nightclub act or to use any profane or vulgar language, pointing out that this was the "University of Our Lady," and that any such behavior would be highly inappropriate. Addressing the audience after their first number, Guard said that it was great to be alive and that they were sure it was only because they were playing Notre Dame on a Friday night. The crowd, of course, erupted in wild cheering once again. "If it wasn't for you guys, we wouldn't be here, so we're gonna do a really good show," he promised. "But we've been told that we can't do our full nightclub act because it would ruin the school's reputation." In response, a voice yelled out from the back of the audience, "AW, HORSE SHIT!" The crowd reaction was thunderous. "The noise was the loudest I've ever heard," Guard recalled, "and it was just one continuous roar all night long. So it's like a combination of coming from the darkest moments of your life to the brightest on the same night."[20]

Shane, too, never forgot the terror and euphoria of Friday the 13th, 1959, and the sobering reminder it left them. With success in show business there is no turning back, and the road does, indeed, go on forever, as Shane noted: "We went *right* back on the road the next day. We were getting into the swing of the tours. It was as easy as you could get. We were playing for big money and making converts and all that—we were playing the part. We were doing it well and it was very smooth. But if you had bad weather or if you had a flight that was going through bad weather or something—those things would make you learn some humility. And we learned *a lot* of humility. Because we had planes that had near misses and all kinds of stuff, you know. So it really taught you a lot about being out there on the road."[21]

After a concert the next night at the University of Michigan, the three took a commercial flight to Washington, D.C., for Bob Shane and Louise

Brandon's wedding. The two had met in Honolulu during the Trio's first engagement at the Royal Hawaiian Hotel. They were introduced by Art Schoen via his sister Evelyn Schoen, Bob's aunt, who had shared a stateroom with Louise on the SS *Lurline*. In those days, the ship's policy was that young women traveling alone were automatically paired with another single woman passenger. As fate would have it, Evelyn Schoen was traveling to Honolulu to visit Bob's family and was assigned to the same stateroom as Louise. Louise, in turn, was bound for the Royal Hawaiian Hotel where she had been offered a job to manage an expensive women's gift and fashions boutique in the hotel. She was the daughter of Inman Brandon, a prominent Atlanta attorney and businessman, and one of the founders of the Atlanta Transit Company that eventually became the Metropolitan Atlanta Transit Authority, or MARTA. The Brandons were "old money," Atlanta aristocracy, and their daughter was raised in the city's highest social circles. She was poised, intelligent, beautiful, and Shane fell head over heels. "Bobby fell in love with Louise and Louise fell in love with him, and boy it was just beautiful," said Reynolds. "Oh, she was very nice! You know, a sweetheart. Great. She could see Bobby's bullshit. But he was really in love, man. I mean, immediate. Love at first sight. And so they kept on, you know, corresponding and seeing each other whenever they could 'cause we were on the road the whole time."[22]

The wedding was scheduled for Sunday, March 15, 1959, at the National Presbyterian Church in Washington, D.C., where the Brandons were also socially prominent. The wedding party and their guests stayed at The Jefferson, one the city's most elite and historic hotels, located four blocks from the White House. It was owned by Louise's grandfather, A. R. Glancy, who had developed the Pontiac automobile and was the executive vice president of General Motors and the president of Pontiac. Their elegant wedding itinerary booklet was titled, "Louise and Bob's Wedding Weekend," and enumerated elegant dinners, cocktails, dancing, limousines, and theater reservations for "Bells Are Ringing" starring Judy Holliday at the National Theatre.

Dave Guard and Nick Reynolds were in attendance, with Nick serving as Bob's best man. "The wedding was gorgeous," Reynolds recalled. "I bought a casual suit instead of getting a formal type, like a dark gray suit or something, and Bobby got pissed off!"[23] Shane still remembers it vividly: "He was my best man, and he wore a brown corduroy suit with black loafers and white socks! I told him, 'You look like a dork!'"[24] Reynolds turned red with embarrassment. He *did* look like a dork! Short "high water" pants coming up around the knees and Bass Weejuns. Nonetheless, everyone had a great time. The new Mr. and Mrs. Robert C. Schoen would have to wait till January for a honeymoon cruise to Hawaii. The Trio were booked back to back in March and April, and they were off to Minnesota for a college concert the day after the wedding.

By the following night, the euphoria of Notre Dame and the fun of Shane's wedding partying would be replaced with something decidedly more sobering—and ugly. On the afternoon of March 17, 1959, the Trio drove onto the campus of Grinnell College in Grinnell, Iowa, and were met with a sign hanging from the gym exclaiming, "Down with Phony Folksingers." It was the first time that the Trio had been openly faced with such criticism. They'd heard whispers and a few snipes from the folk establishment, but nothing from the public at large. Although it was only a few students from the local folk club who started the trouble, it deeply offended the Trio and left a bad taste in their mouth for many years. In 1987, Reynolds visited an orthopedic surgeon in Eugene, Oregon, who was to perform his hip replacement. "Oh, by the way," the doctor said casually, "I'm a big fan of yours. As a matter of fact, I handed you your check at Grinnell, Iowa." The doctor had been the president or the treasurer of the student body. Reynolds said it immediately brought back memories of one of the lowest points of their early college tours. "We did the show, but our heart wasn't quite in it after seeing this banner," he recalled. "It was kinda like they were saying, 'Oh, fuck you guys,' you know. I thought, if you want to be rude, fine, because 99 percent of the students *didn't* feel that way, because they loved us. And that was the one and only time that ever happened." While the Trio never claimed to be folksingers—and never wanted to be—they *were* in fact folksingers, singing classic and modern folk songs that nobody would have ever heard if it had not been for The Kingston Trio.[25]

If Grinell was one of the lowest points in their career, *Life* magazine would soon provide one of the highest—featuring The Kingston Trio on the cover of their August 3, 1959, edition. Shot by legendary photographer/ photojournalist Alfred Eisenstaedt, "the Father of 35mm Photojournalism," on a rooftop in New York City, it gave the group a professional legitimacy and prestige like no other magazine or medium could. In those days, anyone featured on the cover of *Life* was a bona fide celebrity. The Trio had been contacted in Juarez as to the possibility of a cover, and had appeared in an earlier *Life* article on "Tom Dooley" in December of 1958. When the cover issue was proposed, Eisenstaedt took shots of the Trio at Chautauqua Lake Amphitheatre in upstate New York as well as at the Newport Jazz Festival and in Harwich, Massachusetts, on Cape Cod with their wives. The article, entitled "A Trio in Tune Makes the Top," was largely fluff, essentially a photo story featuring the Trio on tour with their wives and light commentary and banter. The cover was the real story. Some say the cover photo was actually shot in Boston, but the Trio remembered it as shot on a rooftop in New York City. The day after the magazine hit the stands, the Trio were at the airport in Newark where numerous people approached them saying, "You must be one of The Kingston Trio!" or "We saw you in *Life* magazine! You looked great!" The Trio almost didn't make the cover. On a diplomatic trip to South America in the spring of 1959, Vice President Nixon was spat upon and stoned by anti-American protestors in Caracas, Venezuela, and Lima, Peru. This news event would have preempted The Kingston Trio cover and article had news photos of the melee been received by *Life* in time. Luckily, the photos missed the plane, so the magazine proceeded with the Trio story as planned.[26]

Despite the highs, one of the greatest challenges of touring was dealing with fatigue and boredom. John Stewart once observed, "The road is not real. After a while every town and every gig looks the same. You wake up in the morning not knowing where the hell you are. Just the boredom can drive you absolutely crazy." The reward, of course—beyond money—is the incredible rush of recognition and adulation that reaffirms why some entertainers continually put themselves through such stress. "For the most part, I enjoyed it immensely," Stewart said. "I was young enough to enjoy it, and there is a big difference when every town you go to you are the major event and everyone is going crazy to see you that night before you even play a note, you walk out to that kind of ovation. It is a real upper. You just can't wait to get to the next town. It's an experience that you just are never the same after something like that, and the people you meet and the experiences of life in America and the world that you get to see coming out of Pomona. But the adulation is the dangerous thing. You go from all that cheering and people thinking you're a god, to a hotel room where it's just you and a TV set. So you say to yourself, 'I've gotta feel like that again, except that I'm in my room! Looking back, I didn't think it was a mental grind at all. No way could I do it today. I was twenty-one years old."[27]

The routine was always the same: fly in, rent two cars, locate the gig, check into the motel, grab dinner (or not), rehearse in the room or in the car if necessary, do the concert (usually at 8 p.m.), hang with the locals (or not), fly out the next morning. Repeat over and over, year in and year out. Other than beer and Terpin Hydrate cough syrup that contained codeine, drugs were not a part of the Trio scene. Cocaine was virtually unheard of at the time. Pot was around, and the Trio would "do our share, but it was no big deal." And Debutol—"diet pills"—were available to anybody in the music business through a doctor and part-time promoter in Tulsa who specialized in keeping truckers and entertainers wide awake for days. Not that the Trio were saints. While there were plenty of high jinks and distractions to fight boredom, the Trio's travel years were remarkably tame. Shane in fact became so bored once that he took to shooting fish with a .22 caliber pistol from his Edgewater hotel window overlooking Puget Sound. If the group had several dates in one area that were easily driveable, they would use one city as their base camp. In the northeast, that was usually New York City. "The minute we'd hit New York, John and Nick would head for the Village and Bobby would head for 21," George Yanok recalled. "He invited me to come along for lunch one time, and it was great. Bobby was impeccably dressed, including a diamond stick pin, and they all knew him there. He was a celebrity."[28]

The Kingston Trio touring entourage consisted of Reynolds, Shane, Guard, and later Stewart; bassist David Wheat (who was replaced by Dean Reilly in 1962); and their road manager. Frank Werber would join the troupe for important gigs, such as national TV dates or a presidential concert at the White House. Over the course of both the Guard and Stewart Trios there were five road managers, starting with Pete Sterner, who left the job shortly after the plane crash, followed by Don MacArthur, Mickey Paradise, Joe Gannon, and George Yanok.

Don MacArthur was with the Trio longest, from 1959 to 1965, having been recruited from a Coronado sports shop by Joan Reynolds on behalf of Werber. He was a natural choice, having grown up in Coronado and being a close friend of Nick since grade school. In high school, they joined the naval reserves together, attending meetings to make a few bucks each month and to avoid being drafted into the army. Eventually MacArthur was drafted and quickly joined the navy. "Nick got lucky," MacArthur said with a laugh, "because he had some problem with asthma as a kid and so he got out of going into the service. And *he* was the one who had talked me into joining the naval reserves to begin with!"[29]

MacArthur's first official outing with the Trio was running lights and sound at a concert at the Santa Monica Civic Auditorium. "Frank handed me a list of the songs they were going to sing, showed me the light board backstage and said, 'Here you go; you'll figure it out.' Joan Reynolds was standing right next to me, and she knew a little bit about how the songs were going to go and how to sort of change the lighting, so I just followed her lead for a while and then all of a sudden I was an expert—I thought. On one of the songs I blacked the stage out before the song was over! I remember I was fading to black and there was like half a verse still left, and when I brought the lights back on I remember Dave Guard was looking over at me like, 'What are you doing!?' I just shook my head and said, 'I don't know. What am I doing?' So that's how I learned how to do lights and sound—by the seat of my pants."[30]

Lights were important because the Trio *itself* was the act, so dramatic lighting was a key ingredient, setting and changing the mood according to the pace and subject matter of the songs. The other critical component was the single vocal microphone, which drew the three of them together. There was also a short floor mike for the bass. Just lights and mikes. "We were a 'lean-mean-working-machine,'" Reynolds would say. Keep it simple, as their contract rider detailed:

> In order to give a satisfactory performance, the Kingston Trio requires certain staging
> a. The employer agrees to furnish two super trooper arc spotlights and two operators
> b. Foot Lights, red and blue. Overhead border lights, red and blue
> c. Color gels for spot lights
>   1. Medium pink
>   2. Flesh pink
>   3. Special lavender
>   4. Red
>   5. Medium light blue
>   6. Dark blue
>   7. Dark lavender
> d. Communication between both spot lights and back stage (must be headsets)
> e. One upright voice microphone—non-directional (360 degree pattern)
> f. One upright microphone for bass player, 2 1/2' stand for mic (non-directional)
> g. One table 7' x 4' (approximately)
> h. Three glasses, one pitcher (for water)
> i. One chair (armless)
> j. Dressing room—toilet facilities
> Employer to supply high-grade bass violin (instrument)
>   NOTE The aforementioned requirements are a *definite* necessity. Any omission will be considered a direct breach of this contract.

As MacArthur would learn, the road manager was a vital player in virtually every facet of the Trio's concert tours, including buying and transporting their "uniforms" as they called their trademark striped shirts, flannel slacks, and black "show shoes." Most of these shirts were right off the rack, usually Gants or similar quality Ivy League brands bought at department stores or from local men's shops such as Johnson and Gray in Sausalito. When the Trio first began, a seamstress in Hawaii handmade a number of colorful custom striped shirts for the group. Years after leaving the group, Nick intimated, "If I ever see another striped shirt, I'm gonna puke!"—and he meant it.[31]

"My responsibilities were to take care of them *first*," MacArthur explained. "I booked all the flights, carried all the tickets, booked all the hotel reservations, made sure that all the instruments and all their luggage got from point A to point B. Each of the guys carried their own instruments. When we got to the hotel, I'd run down to the concert place and check out the sound, check out the lights, make sure everything was ready to go. I made sure that we had program books on hand, found people to sell the books, and collected the program book money. Then I would settle up with the concert promoters because it was usually a flat fee that the Trio was getting plus a percentage, whichever was higher. Frank already had the upfront guaranteed money and we usually always went into the percentages, so these concert guys would just cut us a check and I'd stick it in my wallet and send it back to Frank or hang on to it until we got home."[32]

George Yanok, the Trio's road manager from 1966 to the end in 1967, did the math: "It was four people and fifteen pieces of luggage. Four people with four suitcases; that leaves eleven. The conga drum traveled in its own case; that left ten. John's five-string banjo, John's six-string guitar and sometimes a twelve-string that he would sometimes carry. I'm not counting now—Nick's tenor guitar and Bobby had a guitar. And what we called the Trio bag, which was a bag full of shirts and pants and shoes and belts and socks. And, oh yeah, I had a suitcase, too." George said that when he took over as road manager from Joe Gannon, he was given a how-to-go-on-tour-with-The-Kingston-Trio manual that Gannon and Werber had written as a handy reference. "It was a lot of practical things—how to tip on the road, how to handle promoters, how to handle the stage crew, basic stuff," said Yanok. "But as far as handling the guys on the road, Frank always said, 'Keep in touch, call the office every day—and *get the money*.' Get the money by intermission, get the check by intermission. And sometimes when we played places like Virginia Military Institute, they gave me five thousand dollars in twenty-dollar bills. Carrying that around for three days in a suitcase, I swore to God I was going to lose it somewhere!"[33]

Rarely was collecting the night's receipts a problem. While short in height, MacArthur was no pushover; he was strong and fast with his fists, "a tough little Irishman," Reynolds called him. Guard, too, was vigilant in calculating percentages and would often confer with MacArthur on how much revenue a concert really produced versus a promoter's claims of having "lost his shirt." In the six years that MacArthur toured with the Trio there was only one instance of a promoter stiffing the group. Not bad odds considering the hundreds of concerts the group gave during that period.

At their absolute peak, The Kingston Trio routinely made from $15,000 to $20,000 per concert, and often *a lot* more depending on the size of the venue and the percentages. According to *Variety*, the major entertainment trade paper, The Kingston Trio pulled in more than $380,000 in a two-month tour of just *weekend* dates and an occasional college weekday concert in the fall of 1960. "[The] Group realized 60% to 70% of the gross, depending on the seating capacity. The smaller concert halls paid them 70% privilege, and in many of the larger ones, 60% was accepted,"[34] the paper detailed. On a two-night Hollywood Bowl booking earlier the same year, which included The Kingston Trio, Peggy Lee, Henry Mancini, and the George Shearing Quintet, $110,000 was grossed from 34,838 ticket holders. In late 1950s and early '60s dollars, it was an *enormous* amount of money. By 1966 and 1967, as the Trio were winding down, they were still making good money but nowhere near the vast sums of the past. They would book Saturday night performances for between $5,000 to $7,500, plus a healthy percentage of the gate, and shoulder nights incrementally less. Over the years, the Trio gradually began to saturate major markets and surrounding areas. It wasn't that people didn't want to see The Kingston Trio; they just didn't want to see them as often. How many times can one group play Chicago or New York or Washington or Vegas and still put on a fresh show. Once a year? Twice a year? Every other year? As their popularity waned and frequency increased out of financial necessity, good bookings that would pay top dollar for the act became harder to find. Small wonder. It was essentially the same old act—same songs, same jokes; they were doing it by rote.

With the completion of *Time to Think* in December of 1963, the Trio began what would be an almost two-month hiatus from the road and the studio. It was *their* time to think. "They were tired, they weren't having any fun, they were doing lousy shows," said George Yanok. "And they just wanted to go to ground for a while and try to bring it back around. So they rehearsed for two months. I think they realized that they couldn't do it on automatic pilot." There was a decided agreement—let's get off the road for a while, let's not go out and let's get our chops back. "And the odd thing was that the first gig that they did after that, I opened for them in Fresno and I got a good review and they got a bad review! They never let me forget that I was the guy that got the good review in Fresno! That was always the joke."[35]

While MacArthur made the road manager job sound fairly cut-and-dried, he had to deal with four very different personalities. Guard saw himself as the boss and couldn't be controlled, yet MacArthur said he never had to worry about Dave being late or missing a plane or being irresponsible. He was always on time, did his job, didn't drink, and didn't womanize. "Bob and Nick both liked to party a bit, so did I, and we had some hangovers but certainly we had a lot of fun and we were always able to get where we had to go. As far as temperament was concerned, Shane was the easiest guy in the world to get along with. Nothing ever seemed to bother him. Nick was always the worrier. If the plane was at seven, he'd be up at five; he was always up and ready to go no matter what. Nick was always responsible, always worried that things weren't gonna be just right so he just made sure. A lot of the little side stuff was my job, but he always had my back, you know? Don't forget this, don't forget that—in case I missed anything. And of course when it came to he and Bobby, Nick was always looking after Bobby. And Shane was always the other way around. Man, I had to drag him out of bed! He wasn't easy to get up, but you know what? We always made it somehow. The next morning we were up at the crack of dawn and on a plane to the next gig and that was it, day after day."[36]

Reynolds' fear of flying was legendary, exacerbated no doubt by the crash landing on the way to Notre Dame. "Well, he was always just a white knuckler," said MacArthur. "He didn't like taking off and landing. I remember one time we got into this super storm and we were just puddle jumping from one little town to the next, and man, that plane was just bouncing all over the place! Nick was scared to death, and I didn't know what to say to him. So finally I said, 'You know what? I honestly believe in my soul that I will never die in an airplane crash.' And he said, 'That's probably right, but this plane's gonna go down and crash, *I'm* gonna get killed, and *you're* gonna live!' It was really a pretty spooky storm, and we were going to make two or three stops before we got to where we were going, and after the first stop, he got off and rented a car and drove the rest of the way."[37]

Over the course of ten years, the Trio would log over a million miles, through good weather and bad, playing to millions of people in every type of venue and medium, from high school gyms to the White House. If you asked any one of the Trio members what their favorite gig was, each of them would tell you—"all of them." But dig a little deeper, and they'd share their favorites.

"You know, there were so many gigs I liked over the years," said Bob Shane. "But the big concerts—the Hollywood Bowl, the other big outdoor places in LA and the Carter Barron Amphitheatre in Washington, D.C., where our opening acts were people like Bill Cosby and Roger Miller, people that were really hot at the time, but not as hot as we were, so they were our opening act. And Barbra Streisand opening for us at the Masonic Auditorium in San Francisco just as she was hitting it big. Stuff like that was really groovy."[38]

"Always Notre Dame," said John Stewart. "They went crazy—we'd go out, the applause was so deafening it hurt. The Hollywood Bowl. Vegas—two shows a night to *that* crowd really honed my comedy chops. Sahara Tahoe. Mr. Kelly's. The hungry i—my God you can't beat that. And playing at the White House for Johnson. I've always been a history buff. I mean, I've always been Captain America. For me, to go to the White House—and I'd met Kennedy at the White House—so very much the ghost of Kennedy was there. And Leonard Bernstein was there and Sidney Poitier, and it was outside on the White House lawn and you could look over and see the ellipse. And to sing "Where Have All the Flowers Gone" to Johnson during the Vietnamese war and to see the White House and the Washington monument while we were singing it was one of the most rewarding experiences I've ever had."[39]

Nick was especially proud of playing Carnegie Hall *twice* on consecutive nights in 1960 and the wonderful reception they received from urbane New York audiences. By all accounts, their second appearance in particular was on par with those of The Weavers at their best in terms of audience reaction. "We just *killed* them," said Nick, as one reviewer confirmed: "Carnegie Hall (New York) went collegiate last Wednesday night when the Kingston Trio presented two sellout concerts for a wildly enthusiastic young audience. The 'Boola-Boola' spirit prevailed onstage as well as off. Performing with their usual air of artful spontaneity, the Trio—at the midnight show—exuberantly warbled a flock of folk sagas—whacking guitars, banjos and bongos—and generally behaving as if the huge Carnegie stage were one big frat house. The boys generated considerable vocal excitement on 'Bimini,' 'They Call the Wind Mariah,' 'Bad Man Blunder' and other familiar items. Dave Guard's poignant solo, 'Mauela' ('Sonora') was particularly effective. The Trio closed with a sock rendition of 'When the Saints Go Marching In' for maximum audience impact."[40]

Through it all, every Kingston Trio road manager learned that simple was better. George Yanok was given perhaps the simplest, most sage advice of all about how to manage the Trio on the road from Frank Werber:[41]

1. Never lie to Nick, because he'll know.
2. Always bring shoes and socks in the Trio bag because Bobby's liable to show up barefoot.
3. John will tune the banjo before a show until you tell him to stop.

NOTES

1. Peter J. Curry, "Tom Dooley: The Ballad That Started the Folk Boom," *The Kingston Trio Place*, 1998, www.kingstontrioplace.com.

2. Charles Wolfe, "Tom Dooley: Legend and Song," *The Kingston Trio: The Guard Years*, Bear Family Records, BCD 16160 KK, 1997, 6-CD box set book, 28–36.

3. From 1983 Bob Shane radio interview, New York City, station unidentified, cited in Curry, "Tom Dooley."

4. Nick Reynolds, interview with the author, Seminole, FL, October 3, 1986.

5. Nick Reynolds, interview with the author, Seminole, FL, October 5, 1986.

6. John Stewart, interview with the author, Novato, CA, April 6, 2001.

7. Dave Guard, interview with the author, Los Altos, CA, November 29, 1983.

8. Frank Werber, interview with Richard Johnston, San Francisco, CA, January 16, 1974, from the Dave Guard and Richard Johnston Kingston Trio collection of materials, 1956–1986, University Manuscript Collections, University of Wisconsin, Milwaukee.

9. Quoted in Eliot Tiegel, "Kingston Trio 3 Hails Campus Dates," *Billboard*, September 9, 1966.

10. Bob Shane, interview with the author, Phoenix, AZ, August 21, 2007.

11. Shane, interview with the author, August 21, 2007.

12. Guard, interview with the author, November 29, 1983.

13. Nick Reynolds, interview with the author, Seminole, FL, October 6, 1986.

14. Guard, interview with the author, November 29, 1983.

15. *The South Bend Tribune*, March 14, 1959, 1.

16. Pete Sterner, interview with the author, Sausalito, CA, August 23, 2011.

17. Dave Guard, interview with the author, Los Altos, CA, November 28, 1983.

18. Reynolds, interview with the author, October 5, 1986.

19. Guard, interview with the author, November 29, 1983.

20. Guard, interview with the author, November 29, 1983.

21. Bob Shane, interview with the author, Phoenix, AZ, April 6, 2009.

22. Nick Reynolds, interview with the author, Seminole, FL, October 4, 1986.

23. Reynolds, interview with the author, October 4, 1986.

24. Bob Shane, interview with the author, Phoenix, AZ, April 6, 2009.

25. Reynolds, interview with the author, October 4, 1986.

26. "A Trio in Tune Makes the Top," *Life*, August 3, 1959, 61–64.

27. Stewart, interview with the author.

28. George Yanok, 2003, interview with the author, Nashville, TN, October 26, 2003.

29. Don MacArthur, interview with the author, Novato, CA, February 4, 2010.

30. MacArthur, interview with the author, February 4, 2010.

31. Nick Reynolds, interview with the author, conversation with author, Scottsdale, AZ, August 14, 2006.

32. MacArthur, interview, February 4, 2010.

33. George Yanok, interview with the author, Nashville, TN, February 16, 2010.

34. "Kingston 3 Tour Pulls $380,000," *Variety*, December 7, 1960.

35. Yanok, interview with the author, February 16, 2010.

36. Don MacArthur, interview with the author, Novato, CA, February 12, 2010.

37. MacArthur, interview with the author, February 12, 2010.

38. Bob Shane, interview with the author, Phoenix, AZ, April 7, 2009.

39. Stewart, interview with the author.

40. June Brady, "Kingston Click in Carnegie Stint," *Billboard*, November 28, 1960.

41. Yanok, interview with the author, February 16, 2010.

The Kingston Trio, 1967. *Copyright Henry Diltz*

Nick Reynolds. *Copyright Henry Diltz*

Bob Shane. *Copyright Henry Diltz*

John Stewart. *Copyright Henry Diltz*

Dave Guard, age 2–3. *Guard Family Collection*

Dave Guard. *Copyright Henry Diltz*

Lake Chautauqua, NY, July 11, 1959. *Paul Surratt/Archives of Music Preservation*

Bob and Louise Shane Wedding, March 15, 1959. *Bob Shane Collection*

Early Bob Shane Promotion, Honolulu, 1956. *Bob Shane Collection*

In the studio with Lou Gottlieb. *Allan Shaw Collection*

John Stewart, age 4. *Stewart Family Collection*

"While we were down there watching the bull fights . . ." *Bob Shane Collection*

Honolulu, 1956. *Bob Shane Collection*

West Orange, New Jersey, February 17, 1963. *William J. Bush Collection*

Circle Star Theatre, San Carlos. *Copyright Jesse Bravo*

Nick Reynolds, age 11, Alpine, California. *Reynolds Family Collection*

Stars and their cars. *Bob Shane Collection*

Harken!
WE'RE AT THE

PURPLE ONION

MAY 27TH TO JUNE 1ST

KINGSTON TRIO

DAVE
GUARD

BOB
SHANE

NICK
REYNOLDS

P. S. THE REST OF THE SHOW IS GREAT TOO ! !

The start of it all, 1957. *Bush Collection*

Recording . . . *from the "Hungry i,"* August 15/16, 1958. *Allan Shaw Collection*

The Reynolds family, 1948, Coronado, California. *Reynolds Family Collection*

Bob, Roger Smith and friends, Waikiki, 1956. *Bob Shane Collection*

"Rumors of Evening," Los Angeles, 1958. *Bob Shane Collection*

Salt Lake City, Utah, September 5, 1958. *Bob Shane Collection*

The Shane family, Honolulu, 1938. *Bob Shane Collection*

Bob and Dave, studio B. *Allan Shaw Collection*

Bob, Nick and TD, Ferguson, NC. *Bob Shane Collection*

Trio and Voyle Gilmore hit gold, Hollywood, 1959. *Allan Shaw Collection*

The Blue Angel, New York City, June 1958. *Bob Shane Collection*

The tour that never was, Laguna, California, 1991. *Copyright Henry Diltz*

The Trio and George Wein, Newport, 1959. *Bob Shane Collection*

College Concert sound check, UCLA, December 6, 1961. *Allan Shaw Collection*

Fred Hellerman, Dave, and Bob, New York City, May 1958. *Bob Shane Collection*

Waikiki Shell, June 7, 1960. *Bob Shane Collection*

Washington, D.C., circa 1964. *Allan Shaw Collection*

With the astronauts, Houston, Texas, 1963. *Allan Shaw Collection*

Dave Guard and the Calypsonians, circa 1956. *Allan Shaw Collection*

The Trident Opening, 1966. *Bob Shane Collection*

8

"DO I LOOK LIKE
I'M BREAKING UP?"

The breakup of the original Kingston Trio in August of 1961 came as a shock to the music industry and a deep personal loss to devoted Trio fans worldwide.

Yet to those who knew The Kingston Trio from the inside, it was totally predictable, even inevitable. From the outset the polarity of personalities, primarily between Dave Guard and Bob Shane, virtually guaranteed a short-lived group career. The two were like oil and water, with a complicated rivalry that went back years to when they were kids growing up together in Hawaii.

In the beginning, no matter what their personal differences, music had been their common ground—the one place where they dropped defenses, forgot self-interests, and got close. Music made it all okay, the escape into limbo, where all their problems with each other disappeared the moment they started singing.

Yet regardless of how tight the three were as pals originally, the grind of constantly traveling and working together twenty-four hours a day, for weeks and months at a time, was enough in itself to begin to erode their friendship. During the first couple of years the Trio were doing nearly three hundred concert and club dates a year, plus cranking out an average of three albums a year to meet their Capitol obligations. They were tired—and sometimes sick and tired—of each other.

Guard was a hard worker, driven even, and wanted it note perfect. Nothing was beyond his scrutiny or his criticism if things weren't done to his impeccable standards. Moreover, he wanted to push the envelope to make The Kingston Trio more musically interesting, more avant-garde, and thus help to ensure their longevity. For Nick Reynolds and Bob Shane,

The Kingston Trio were not meant to be overly serious or to depart radically from their established and very successful formula. Spontaneity and personal energy were the biggest part of the Trio's appeal, they reasoned, and neither wanted to tinker with a sure thing. Guard likely recognized this very early on and figured that, ultimately, he would have to work around the other two, replacing them if necessary. Since he was the best planned and organized of the three and was their "acknowledged leader" (a press release phrase that nearly cost Reynolds, Shane, and Werber The Kingston Trio name later on), it was a lot easier for Guard to exert control in certain areas, especially arranging, which they welcomed and for which he was fairly compensated. On the first Kingston Trio album, for example, Reynolds, Shane, and Guard split the writer's royalties on reworked public domain songs 30-30-40, with Guard getting the additional 10 percent for the extra work he did on the arrangements. Other bonus percentages accrued here and there for his extra contributions as a writer and arranger; being the acknowledged leader had its rich rewards, and rightly so. Unfortunately, once money is involved, and particularly where money and control are viewed as being synonymous, trouble is inevitable.

The trouble began with the release of the Trio's album *At Large*, in late spring of 1959. One cut, "Getaway John" (also known as "John Hardy"), is an old public domain song that Guard suggested while the Trio were in New York City during a two-week gig at the Blue Angel. Every afternoon they'd rehearse songs for the new album in the dressing rooms above the club, where Guard first played "Getaway John" for Shane and Reynolds. While it was Guard's idea for the "Getaway . . . getaway . . . poor John" intro, Reynolds said, "We all embellished it, put the harmony on; it was a Trio-arranged song. Dave's idea, Trio-arranged song."[1] The song is tricky, with complex vocal parts, and they were proud upon playback of the final version also recorded in New York. "We listened to the playback, and liked the playback; I remember we were sitting in the studio saying which song should come first and, when it came time for signing the contracts for the writers thing, we weren't around. Dave *was* around and he was taking care of business."[2]

Two months later the Trio were on tour in the Deep South, appearing at the University of Mississippi, when the advance copies of the album caught up with them. This was not unusual; rarely did they stick around for the mixing or "sweetening" or any postrecording details—and in this case it was a big mistake for Reynolds and Shane. Looking over the album for the first time, Reynolds scanned the writer's credits on the label. Guard had taken sole credit for "Getaway John," thus getting his 10 percent extra, despite their agreement that all public domain songs that were arranged by the three would be split equally three ways. "I was furious and confronted him immediately," Nick remembered. "'David, how can this be??!!' I was absolutely aghast. He just looked at me and said, 'Sorry.' And I said, 'So am I. It's really too bad you had to do that.' 'Getaway John' was a flagrant example of just knocking Bobby and I out of the ballgame for a couple of hundred thousand dollars."[3] Guard would later dispute this account, saying that he and Reynolds "pimped" Shane out of the royalties as punishment for Shane's not showing up for rehearsal.

At that moment, Reynolds and Shane made one of the greatest mistakes of their careers. Instead of calling a meeting with Guard and talking things over, including any complaints, grudges, hurt feelings, or resentments—on *both* sides—they did nothing. "We weren't that smart," said Reynolds. "We could have done that, and it could have been aired out, because Dave, although he comes on strong, if you really leveled with him, man, he was a very compassionate cat. I should have said, 'David, I was so hurt over that song, which you know I was at the time, let's not let that happen again. Let's not do anything like that to ourselves again, man, because it's just jeopardizing everybody's future.'"[4]

Guard perhaps never thought that Reynolds and Shane would be angry over his claiming sole authorship, which he felt he was perfectly entitled to do. But nobody spoke up. They rarely did. During the entire Guard era Bobby hardly ever said anything about his feelings, nor did Reynolds or Guard for that matter. "It was very hard," said Reynolds, "especially if Bobby and I had a bitch against Dave because he'd feel we were ganging up on him. Working as close and hard as we were, you know, this intimacy that we had, we knew it was better to just let it ride, man. And he felt real shitty about it, too. But you know, he didn't offer to give us any of the take or anything. I tried, but he said that's the way it was. He said, 'I brought the song in . . . I had the idea for the song.' It was one of the most rehearsed songs we'd ever done, and we changed all this stuff, and he'd written some lyrics. I don't know how much we changed them, but it's still a public domain song even if someone writes the lyrics or comes up with the lyrics; that's part of the thing on the three-way split."[5] But Reynolds never pursued it. "Better left alone than have it stir up the automatic pilot we were on by that time," said Reynolds.[6]

The close friendship that Shane and Reynolds shared only exacerbated the situation. Trios are a strange phenomenon, both musically and socially. Two will always sing in harmony, with the third being stuck with the "joker parts"—filling holes in the vocal arrangement wherever needed. It's the odd man out. Dave may have felt that he was being left out of the music and the camaraderie—*and* being taken advantage of because, in his mind, he was doing most of the work. Nick and Bobby's vocal blend defined The Kingston Trio sound. It was always Nick and Bobby who were the pals, going out to parties after the shows, although Dave was often invited. He was the first in the group to get married, which widened the distance between them as well. The odds are just not stacked evenly in a trio, and it can be easy for one member to feel a creeping paranoia even when there's no reason to feel that way. Shane and Reynolds conceded, too, that they never knew the depth of hurt that Guard might have felt in being left out.

The biggest source of conflict, however, was the huge difference in personality and life view between Dave Guard and Bob Shane. Dave was the thinker, the doer, the organizer; a curious intellectual who was studied in his approach to everything. Those who knew him well described him as a man whose intellect was so deep and ideas so complex that he sometimes had difficulty communicating, which really was his curse. What some people regarded as bossy or distant behavior was often just his frustration in articulating what he already knew and didn't have the patience to explain. "He didn't suffer fools easily," recalls his ex-wife, Gretchen.[7] He also had a sharp tongue. "He could put you down real fast, if he wanted to," Nick Reynolds remembered. "He could make you feel like a real jerk. If I came in with a toothache, for example, he'd say, 'Oh, poor baby.' Then he'd look away and say, 'Can we start now, Nick? Is that okay?' That'd just make you feel shitty; it was an unnecessary kind of bullshit."[8]

Henry Diltz worked with Dave in the studio in the 1970s with The Modern Folk Quartet and said, "The fact that he could be prickly was totally overshadowed to me by the fact that he was so intelligent and funny. I don't care how he was. It was a great pleasure to be in his company and be able to interact with him and listen to him talk and hold forth about different things and just observe him. He could be a little sharp tempered sometimes. He could be hard on you—nothing I ever took personally. But he could throw some zingers at you if you weren't doing it the way he wanted you to do it. But God, he was just so funny! I remember this one part in the song that I was supposed to play on a clarinet. And he'd say, 'No! It's like this,' and then he said, 'Donald is a funny little duck.' It was genius! Immediately, I knew it! He just had a way of doing that and putting words to things. 'Donald is a funny little duck.' I'll never forget that."[9] Guard's quirks notwithstanding, the brilliance and wit and polish of the original Kingston Trio were a reflection of Guard's brilliance and wit and polish. Many regarded him as the indisputable "brains" of the Trio.

Bobby Shane, however, was its heart and voice. Tommy Clancy of the wonderfully raucous Irish Clancy Brothers summed it up perfectly one night when he sidled up to Shane at the bar of the Village Vanguard and shouted, "Aye, Bobby, *you're* the one! It's *you*, lad, you're the one!"[10] Unlike Guard, who was always measured and deliberate, Shane operated on pure instinct. He was naturally gifted, born with a magnificent voice and personal magnetism that could not be studied or learned.

John Stewart, who replaced Guard in the Trio, knew both Guard and Shane very well and understood the radical differences between them and the frictions they created. "Dave wanted to be a real musician and he wanted the Trio to be real musicians," Stewart said, "and that in a way is admirable that the man was into his craft. Music was his thing. He lived and breathed music and he didn't have a sense of it. It was part of the flipside of his thinking. There's an artist who said, 'Get obsessed, be obsessed, stay obsessed,' which is really the engine of art and within your art. You're obsessed with guitars and folk music, which is what you're into. And Dave was thoroughly obsessed and would go off into these obsessions without asking the validity of it. He just *went*. He really did all the work in the Trio—the arrangements that were absolutely brilliant and his playing and his wit and the brilliance of his introductions, and that very strong, edgy voice of his."[11]

Then there's Bobby. "He could walk in hung over from the night before, sing better than anybody in the Trio and have all the chicks fall over him. It gets in everybody's craw; it got in my craw. So you've got that *and* Bobby's really-not-giving-a-damn attitude, and really shoving it in your face that he could do all that. I mean, how could he not be like that when you have that kind of natural power, and Dave was starting to make him feel inadequate because he didn't have the musical knowledge or the abilities that Dave had? Bobby knew that he could just go in and knock you on the floor without even trying. He was the best looking, he had the best voice, he was the sexiest, and he did it no matter how badly he was screwed up or whatever. It was an amazing thing to see. It's like the quarterback in high school who smoked and drank and got drunk the afternoon of the game and just walked through practice and went out and just nailed it. And you had busted your butt to even make it on the team, and the girls loved him and he just walked in the game and won."[12]

Had Guard had his way, Shane would never have become a member of The Kingston Trio in the first place. And vice versa. From the outset, Reynolds was looked upon as the middleman in the group and was perhaps the most brilliant of the three, the "glue" that held it all together musically and personally, including propping Shane up and making sure that he showed up on time, as well as acting as a buffer between Shane and Guard. It's a role usually played by a personal manager, but Frank Werber never had Guard's trust and, in fact, became a major source of Guard's suspicions over management of the Trio's business interests. People outside of the Trio would feed that distrust even more in an attempt to gain control over the group. It was a slow and insidious process, and it started long before the group was worth having control of.

In February of 1958, Frank Werber had secured the Trio's first out-of-town gig at the Holiday Hotel in Reno where they met Jackie Cain and Roy Kral. Jackie and Roy were booked by Associated Booking Corporation, *the* jazz agency owned by Joe Glaser. Within a year, The Kingston Trio was on Associated Booking Corporation's roster as well. It was a natural connection. From the very beginning the Trio was enormously popular with jazz audiences and jazz musicians, so Associated Booking Corporation would book the group in a package with jazz artists. The Trio's first appearance at the 1959 Newport Jazz Festival was arranged by Bert Block via his friend and festival organizer George Wein. It proved to be one of the most successful Trio appearances ever, leading to later appearances at Wein's Storyville clubs in Boston and Cape Cod, as well as the first Newport Folk Festival (an extension of the "Folk in the Afternoon" segment of the 1959 Newport Jazz Festival, which the Trio also played).

Within Associated Booking Corporation, the Trio's business was handled primarily by Block, one of Glaser's top lieutenants, and assisted by Larry Bennett, another Glaser agent and moneyman. The original contract with Associated Booking Corporation was for only one year, a period during which The Kingston Trio became enormously popular and Frank Werber became very friendly with Bert and Larry. Working behind Glaser's back, Block and Bennett approached Werber about starting a new booking agency of their own, ITA (International Talent Associates) with The Kingston Trio as its major act and Frank receiving 10 percent of the take as well as one third of the capital stock. Frank in turn would split his percentage with Nick, Bob, and Dave. Considering that the Trio were quickly becoming the number one concert attraction in the country, a 10 percent gross commission on all bookings (the usual booking agency cut) amounted to a huge sum of money. As far as the Trio were concerned, it would be newfound money and a way that Frank could be compensated more fairly, *and* they'd be getting a cut of the 10 percent as well. Although Werber was an equal partner in Kingston Trio, Inc., the Trio's business corporation, he received none of the writer's royalties from their music. It was a good deal for all concerned, and when the Trio's Associated Booking

Corporation contract expired in April of 1960, they signed with ITA—Bert, Larry, and Frank's new agency.

The only trouble was, it wasn't Frank's agency at all. He never got any money—or ITA stock—from Bert and Larry, and neither did the Trio. Block had talked Werber and the boys into signing the Trio's concert business over to him and Bennett, without so much as a dime of additional income to the Trio in return. Frank had even set up an ITA office in San Francisco, complete with a secretary and a three hundred dollar monthly budget, and Bert and Larry closed the bank account right under his nose. Unfortunately there wasn't a thing Frank or anybody could do about it. Block and Bennett *did* take good care of Trio business while they had it. The Trio always got the best dates at the best terms, but Bert and Larry never split the 10 percent gross commission, and Frank never got a piece of the ITA agency.

"I was promised stock and then they let time pass saying it was being drawn up—hey, I was flat out hustled," Werber said. "The big city boys did me in. I was never that concerned about it originally. I thought I was doing business on terms I usually do business—I'm talking, my word is my bond, and I expect the same thing. What it got down to was that they were trying to off me totally. I was duped by Block and Bennett right up front. They knew how they were going to move."[13]

In 1960, the Trio formed its own concert promotion agency, Sawcon (a derivative of either Shirley Ann Werber, Frank's wife, or Sausalito Concerts—depending on who you ask) under the able direction of Eddie Sarkesian, a Detroit promoter who handled their Midwest dates, whom they respected and trusted. Bert and Larry would later attempt to sue the Trio for back commissions, labeling Sawcon a "corporate shield" to keep ITA from getting its cut. Ironically, Guard viewed the ITA situation as blatant evidence of *Frank's* untrustworthiness. After all, Frank was out to slice himself a bigger piece of the pie. It served him right if Bert and Larry beat him out of the deal.

When it became evident that Frank planned to drop ITA, Bert and Larry immediately began fueling Dave's distrust of Frank. To them, Dave was the chink in the armor, a malcontent who was also in the powerful position of being the Trio's "acknowledged leader." To gain control of Guard was to gain control of The Kingston Trio business, figuring that Nick and Bobby would have to follow Dave or have no group at all. Dave, for his part, saw Bert and Larry as allies in removing Frank, a mutual foe, and for gaining control of the Trio himself. The battle was about to begin, with the biggest ammunition supplied by Artie Mogul, the Trio's publisher.

Mogul was a music business veteran. He'd been around since the early 1940s, cutting his teeth as a road manager for The Tommy Dorsey Band; he later got into publishing with Ray Anthony and then worked for big publishers in New York, including the giant Witmark & Sons. He was also an ex–Capitol Records Artist & Repertoire vice president before striking out on his own to set up and handle the publishing interests for a number of entertainers.

In 1959, the Trio decided to form its own publishing company, Highridge Music. Prior to that, they had been naively dumping all of their public domain tunes into Capitol's publishing company, Beechwood Music, virtually giving away hundreds of thousands of dollars in publishing royalties out of ignorance. Frank had gotten Artie's name from Voyle Gilmore, who had been involved in some publishing matters with Mogul and suggested him as a likely candidate to set up and manage Highridge Music. Soon Werber, Shane, Guard, and Reynolds met at Mogul's New York office to discuss the possibilities. They found him immediately likeable and straightforward.

"I would be delighted to set up your publishing firm and run it for you, and I'll take 10 percent of the gross as my fee," Artie told them with a smile. "But I want to tell you right up front *do not let me handle the money*. Have the checks sent to your accountant, and then send me a check for my commission. Under no circumstances should you let me handle the money; I'm warning you right now."[14] Artie went on to explain that he was a habitual gambler, and in the past had used some of his clients' money on gambling, although he had always paid it back. Even as road manager for The Tommy Dorsey Band he'd gotten in trouble with gambling; seems Artie had been dispatched from Los Angeles to New York to deposit the band's tour receipts, stopping in Vegas along the way and losing it all. He held nothing back from the Trio in that meeting, and they found his candor refreshing and ingenuous. As far as they were concerned, anybody *that* straightforward had to be trustworthy, and anyway, the whole publishing thing was way too complicated for them to figure out. "Go ahead, Artie, you're our boy," they assured Mogul. And they even let him handle the money—just to simplify things.

About a year later, in September of 1960, Guard received one of his periodic royalty checks from Highridge Music in the amount of $15,000— and it *bounced*. With the amount of records the group was selling at the time, Highridge was the funnel for untold hundreds of thousands of dollars in publishing royalties, with $127,000 of it being secretly used to cover Artie Mogul's gambling debts. While Reynolds, Shane, and Werber were shocked, they were not overly concerned; they considered publishing money to be almost "free money," and Artie had already made *tons* of it for them. He'd warned them up front about his gambling, and they never had any doubt that he would pay back every cent—with interest—as he promised (and eventually did). Guard, however, wanted to throw Mogul in jail. And since it was Werber's idea to use him in the first place, Werber could damn well share the cell.

"Well, if you look at it, Dave had a right to be very angry," said Shane. "But what we had decided was to not prosecute the guy and put him in jail, because then he couldn't pay us back. But that set Dave off right there. And of course he felt he was doing all the work. It was just one more thing that got Dave crazy—and it wasn't the first time we'd had a problem with publishing money, either. Another guy, not Artie, was handling international publishing for us in England; took off with money and we never saw him again. But Artie paid it all back as we knew he would, which he couldn't have done from jail."[15]

Dave made sure that going forward his publishing interests would never be put in jeopardy again, forming his own publishing company, Grenada Music, with the help of Freddy Hellerman of The Weavers. "After we got involved with all kinds of bizarre types with the Trio, I went to Freddy and I said, 'God Almighty, is there one honest man in the whole business?'" Guard recalled. "He said, 'Well, Hal Leventhal, my manager, is. He's seen us through thick and thin.' So that's why I went and formed a publishing company with Jane Bowers and Harold and myself, because it was all getting ripped off. So I had to do something about it, and it was a real honor to have Harold as the publisher."[16]

Block and Bennett couldn't have been happier with the Mogul mess. Here was real evidence of Werber's mismanagement and business naiveté, and if Guard was controlling the Trio, who would make better replacements than themselves! Thus began the ugly battle: Guard, Block, and Bennett versus Werber, Reynolds, and Shane, with The Kingston Trio name and franchise as the grand prize to the winners.

That the Trio could continue functioning as an act and a business during those bitter months of late 1960 and early '61 is nothing short of amazing. In the studio they conducted themselves as professionals, producing better records technically with each subsequent album, but emotionally they were on autopilot. And there were occasional flare-ups—Nick chafing under Dave's direction to sing like a black man on "You Don't Knock" for the *Goin' Places* sessions was one—but for the most part, they worked hard and strictly according to their tried-and-true formula.

On the road it was tougher. Besides an occasional dinner together and the forced camaraderie of press conferences and photo sessions, the three rarely hung out together. It was only on stage where the defenses dropped and the music made everything all right, if only for an hour and twenty minutes. Bobby and Nick became even tighter, partly out of mutual defense, not knowing what Dave was planning next. Nick was convinced that each show was their last, and when Frank booked them on an extended tour of Japan, Australia, and New Zealand in January 1961, Nick almost called it quits. "High anxiety is hard enough to deal with in Toledo, let alone being stuck together half way around the world," he said.[17]

Nonetheless, the Trio flew off to Honolulu on the first leg of their tour, bringing along writer Arnold Pearlman and photographer/cinematographer Bert Stern to film *The Kingston Trio on Tour*, which was to be their first TV special. While the group toured Japan, Sid Rudy (their attorney) and Dick Tong (their accountant) flew to New York to inspect Mogul's books and size up the damage. The news wasn't good. Not only was a big chunk of their publishing money missing, Mogul was broke. With that news, Guard became even more reclusive, making it nearly impossible for the group to sing together. Through it all Stern continued to film corny, contrived scenes of the three of them yuking it up together in Japan. ("Here are the boys learning how to use chopsticks!") "God it was *awful*," Reynolds said.[18] After finishing their show commitments in Australia and New Zealand, he and Shane, fed up, flew home.

Once back in the states things moved quickly. Although Artie Mogul had been replaced by René Cardenas, who now handled publishing and some artist management duties for Frank, and a repayment schedule was worked out for Artie, Dave was not to be mollified. From that point on *he* would be in charge of The Kingston Trio's musical and business interests. *Everything* would be subject to his approval—concert and recording contracts, leases, purchases, songs, even the photographs for their programs. Frank's shares in Kingston Trio, Inc., would be redeemed and a new personal and business manager appointed, answering only to Dave.

Guard's leverage in these demands was that he was still the Trio's "acknowledged leader." Guard had even signed concert contracts to that effect. And it was essentially true. "Almost from the start, I kind of regarded Dave as a surrogate father," said Reynolds. "He was a teacher, a guy who knew the structure of a lot of things that I didn't know, and I took just about everything he said as gospel, which it usually was because Dave was rarely wrong."[19]

Naturally, Guard reasoned that without him there couldn't *be* a Kingston Trio. He, Block, and Bennett never imagined that Reynolds and

Shane would end the Trio rather than be coerced into dumping Werber and handing over control of their music and lives. Right or wrong, Frank Werber had been their greatest supporter, defender, and source of wisdom since day one. He'd taken three green kids out of a beer joint and put them on the cover of *Life* magazine, keeping all the business distractions away so that they could do what they did best, "keeping it pure," as Frank called it. Frank was their partner and never kept anything from Nick, Bob, or Dave. If he had used bad judgment in connecting them with Artie Mogul, then they had *all* used bad judgment because they'd all heard the same warning, right from the horse's mouth. And as far as the ITA deal was concerned, they all would have been getting a cut of the action, not just Frank.

Was Dave wrong? Absolutely not. The business *had* suffered occasionally. Frank made mistakes and learned as he went along. But managing The Kingston Trio was not easy with three different personalities, with two continually in contention, and it's to Frank Werber's credit that he did it as well as he did. There should have been greater oversight of Werber, however, as well as Sid Rudy and Dick Tong. Musically, too, Guard's instincts were right on the money. For many people The Kingston Trio represented popular music for "the thinking man," an alternative to the then new and for some intimidating rock and roll, or for the schmaltzy "How Much Is That Doggie in the Window" pop that dominated much of radio in the 1950s. While the Trio never took itself seriously, at least initially, a lot of people did, and Guard rightly felt that the Trio *owed* it to their fans to be more studied, more avant-garde, and committed to even higher levels of art.

"David was ambitious for the Kingston Trio," said Gretchen Guard. "In the beginning he had the idea that a few intelligent young men with some talent and plenty of humor, a head full of songs known since childhood, a dose of bravado, and the grace of God could be successful in the country's emerging interest in folksingers. When this success happened he knew they would have to strive for another level in order to maintain their audience's interest and their own. Although the Beatles were unknown to the American audience at the time, they eventually set the kind of standard for themselves that David wished for The Kingston Trio. The Beatles were always changing, experimenting, reinventing themselves, and surprising their audience with fresh new ideas."[20]

Shane and Reynolds also pointed out that they were working much too hard to consider sitting down and learning how to read music, that so much of what made the Trio successful was its natural energy, that over-analyzing it and experimenting with it would have killed it. They believed that what they "owed" their fans was to continue delivering what the fans had come to know, love, and expect from The Kingston Trio.

Both points of view were valid. In an industry driven by trends, the quickest road to obsolescence is to become complacent and predictable. The Kingston Trio were at the vanguard of the folk revival. They set the standard; the pace position was theirs to keep or lose. The beauty of the Trio's work was its freshness and inventiveness. Every album got technically better and musically more interesting. To expand the genre they had largely reinvented would seem entirely appropriate and worth the effort. But then who knows what Guard had in mind. In the last days of the Trio he was getting into Lydian scales and other avant-garde music theories. He was years ahead of his time, even suggesting the Trio add electric guitars to its folk instrumentation. That same "folk rock" concept would later be "invented" by Bob Dylan in the mid-1960s, but Dave Guard and The Whiskeyhill Singers were among the first to experiment with it in 1962.

It was a difficult dilemma. Certainly, the Trio needed to fulfill their fans' expectations while also raising those expectations by challenging them, much as The Beatles would do in their creative journey. Perhaps what was needed was a *balanced* approach, blending new ideas with the familiar, keeping it fresh and interesting. Years later, Shane was asked if there was something that he wished the Trio had tried musically but didn't, to which he replied, "I would have liked to have tried what Dave wanted us to do at the end. I think we might have stayed on top longer with Dave."[21] The problem, of course, was that by that time Guard was hardly open to other opinions, or collaborations, or any type of balanced approach. "It's strange because he really very badly wanted us to do his ideas," said Shane. "And if he'd had the savvy for being able to talk to people correctly, he could have gotten us to do that probably. But he alienated himself from us. He just got to believing that he was better than anybody else."[22]

It all came to a head on May 10, 1961, in attorney Sid Rudy's office. Nick, Bob, Frank, and Sid Rudy sat on one side of a conference table while Guard sat on the other. Guard finally broke the silence saying, "Well, what's it going to be, boys?" fully expecting his demands to be met. "We're not going to do it, Dave." Guard was incredulous—and angry. "Then, I'm *out*; you'll be hearing from my lawyers," he said, and out the door he went.[23]

"I wasn't surprised by it," said Joan Reynolds, "but I didn't see it coming because they were playing a card game and Dave thought he had the cards and he didn't. Frank called them. Dave lost the card game, Frank trumped him. And Frank didn't try to. I'm just saying it was that. That's when Dave said he could not go on—and then it got nasty, a little bitter.

He thought that Frank was being dishonest and stealing from the company, but he was not. Frank was living very well because he was like a fourth member of the Trio, part of the partnership, and he carried big overhead, more than they did. So Dave called in, I think, Price Waterhouse to audit all the books over the first two or three years—and this is a card game, too—and guess what they found; it was *Dave* that owed the Trio some money! Not much, you know a couple hundred or a thousand, but as far as the books there was nothing on Frank."[24]

The next day, Reynolds, Shane, and Werber received a formal notice from Guard stating that he intended to exchange his shares in Kingston Trio, Inc., by November. But with somebody like Bert Block at Guard's side, they knew it wouldn't be quite so simple. Just a week before the meeting in Rudy's office, Block had sent letters to Reynolds and Shane hoping to enlist their support for Guard and for Werber's ouster, informing them that Werber had been aware of Mogul's situation and the missing funds "for months."

As expected, another letter arrived from Guard instructing everyone to disregard his earlier letter, and that he would provide no written termination notice "until shareholder interests had been determined." What that meant was that Guard was putting nothing in writing until lawyers could determine whether he and Block could take away The Kingston Trio name. Even after the three hundred thousand dollar settlement with Dave had been agreed to and John Stewart had replaced Guard in The Kingston Trio lineup, Reynolds, Shane, and Werber would go before the American Federation of Musicians (AFM) to defend their right to keep the name.

The hearing took place in the AFM office in New York, with Reynolds, Shane, Werber, and their attorney on one side of a large conference table, and Guard, Block, and their attorney on the other. Supposedly, Block had a lot of connections within the AFM, and the suit had been pushed to the union's top echelons. After several preliminary procedures at the union, this was the final hearing. It was all or nothing. They hadn't seen Guard in months, who sat with head bowed, while Block also avoided any eye contact. Essentially, the argument was this: Guard wanted The Kingston Trio name as part of his exit settlement by virtue of being the group's "acknowledged leader." Reynolds, Shane, and Werber maintained that the name was protected under the copyright laws of the state of California as a corporate asset of Kingston Trio, Inc. Ultimately, the question was, is the name Kingston Trio a corporate asset as spelled out in the Articles of Incorporation? Or, is Dave Guard, the signature leader of the group as designated on AFM contracts, entitled to the name?

There was a great deal of verbal testimony, primarily citing similar cases, with Kingston Trio, Inc., supplying all relevant paperwork to support their position. Finally, the litigants were asked to leave the room while the "judges" made their decision. Forty-five minutes later they returned saying, "We find the corporate structure takes precedence over AF of M, and the name shall remain with the corporation and Mr. Guard will have no right to the name Kingston Trio." With that, tears welled up in Dave's eyes and he said, "I want to tell you guys how really sorry I am it had to come to this, and I feel really bad about it. And I think you guys were right."[25]

Years later Guard recalled that he was most surprised and hurt by Reynolds siding with Shane and Werber. Nick said that he'd never seen Dave like that and that Dave finally realized he'd been had by Bert and Larry's influence. Their strategy was simple and effective—divide and conquer, cause internal dissent, take control by feeding David's suspicion and ego. It was a classic business tactic.

Without The Kingston Trio ITA had nothing. The Trio were the locomotive that pulled ITA's "farm team," folk acts that included The Journeymen, The Cumberland Three, and The Brothers Four on the college concert circuit. ("You want The Kingston Trio next month? You gotta take The Journeymen *now!*") When Stewart was selected as Dave's replacement, Block and Bennett threatened to sue Kingston Trio, Inc., because Stewart was a member of The Cumberland Three, one of ITA's acts. It didn't matter that ITA was still booking some Trio dates. They had to slip in a parting shot.

Ironically, Guard may have inadvertently made himself expendable long before dissent had set in. As the group's principal arranger, he most often assigned lead vocals to Shane, with Reynolds singing close harmony behind him. This vocal twosome of Shane and Reynolds came to define the familiar "Kingston Trio sound"; Guard took the tougher yet more transparent "joker parts," sliding in between or below Shane and Reynolds, filling in any empty space. As a result, his vocal presence would be hardly missed to the casual listener. If someone had to go vocally, he was actually the logical choice.

With a group as big as The Kingston Trio, none of their legal or personal quarrels could avoid the press. Less than a month after the meeting in Sid Rudy's office, when negotiations were still tentative and sensitive, *Life* magazine ran a "Spotlight" article in their June 9, 1961, issue entitled, "Kingston Trio's Big Bust Up." It included two photos, one of Guard sitting "forlornly" (as *Life* called it) playing his banjo, and another of Reynolds and Shane kibitzing with each other in the dressing room with the following edited commentary:

> At a one-night stand near Los Angeles, the most famous singing trio in the country made pretty music for the people out front. But backstage there was no harmony. The Kingston Trio was involved in the year's biggest show business bust-up. In one corner, the group's leader, Dave Guard, forlornly strumming his banjo while his two partners, Nick Reynolds and Bob Shane, pointedly yocked [*sic*] it up without him. "A whole gang of differences," said Guard had split them up, so he was pulling out in six months. His defection is likely to cause such an unbrotherly hassle among these old cronies that their most fabled hero, Tom Dooley, would hang his head and cry. Recently Guard has argued with (their manager) Frank Werber over bookings, and another bone of contention is a $127,000 shortage in their jointly owned publishing subsidiary, High Ridge Music. Guard has also been out of tune with Shane and Reynolds. One year, Guard said, "We were 280 days on the road, most of it cooped up in a small aircraft. This is a good cooking pot for any troubles." Helping to make the pot boil over was Guard's demand that the Kingstons begin crooning more authentic music than their brand of psuedo folk songs. He even asked his partners to join him in learning to read music. But Shane and Reynolds refused to alter their successful formula. Nevertheless, Guard's departure is bound to be a bitter loss. He is the group's personality kid, and his personality is their stock and trade, not music.[26]

The final settlement with Guard came in November of 1961, and was as follows: $300,000 ($75,000 in cash and $225,000 in a promissory note) was paid for 245 shares (24.5 percent) of Kingston Trio, Inc., Guard's share of the corporation. It was a lot of money at the time and it would take Reynolds, Shane, and Werber years to finally pay it off. Of the four, Guard probably did the best financially over the years. A divorce would cost him a lot of his assets, but he continued to reap writer and publishing royalties from such songs as "John Hardy" and "Scotch and Soda," and the latter he never really wrote.

The Guard Trio's final performance was at a large outdoor concert on the lawn at Castle Hill, the Crane Estate, in Ipswich, Massachusetts, on August 5, 1961. By this time the pressure was off between the three; they knew the terms of the separation, and there was no animosity. Backstage they relaxed and just had fun kidding around. Everybody in the audience knew that this was their last performance together, so there were a lot of curiosity seekers. One fan approached Dave and said, "I hear you're breaking up," to which Dave laughingly replied, "Do I look like I'm breaking up?"[27] The three cracked up. It was a fun day, and the huge crowd went wild. This last concert could easily have been counted among their very best, except for one incident that quickly brought things back to reality.

Whenever Shane sang and played, he would tap his foot in time with the music. During the last song Guard reached over with his foot and put it on top of Bobby's, as if he were saying, "After all these years, your tempo's for shit my friend, and I'm letting you know that for the last time." Shane, who rarely spoke up to Guard before, just smiled and looked Dave right in the eye and said, "You will *never* do that to me again."[28]

And he never did.

The rancor between Guard and his former associates would linger for years. He would never publicly acknowledge a role in the group's demise, once saying, "I wasn't convinced my associates were doing the best they could," or cease laying the blame on Werber: "Oh there were some big rip-offs going on in the company. And when I squawked, I found out that the people who were ripping us off were going traveling with the people who were supposed to be protecting us. So I couldn't appeal to the people who were protecting us since they seemed to be in the 'same bed' as you say. So I thought, I'm gonna go crazy. So I better leave."[29]

He perhaps came closest to the truth in a 1970s magazine interview when he said, "Nick and Bobby had gotten sick and tired of my trying to shove music down their throats."[30] It was odd, too, that Guard would continue to diminish The Kingston Trio and his own participation in it after leaving, saying that the Trio were a "slick" act, based on stealing songs and on-stage comedy banter stuff from acts playing the hungry i and the Purple Onion, and that they ripped off anything that got a laugh. Even at the 1981 PBS special "The Kingston Trio and Friends Reunion," when he, Shane, and Reynolds had ostensibly laid down their differences, Guard's behavior was quirky. The three had agreed to perform two of their old hits for the show, and to faithfully follow the original arrangements, note for note. At rehearsal, Guard disregarded their agreement, shifting into his own (and drastically different) interpretations instead. Shane was furious, vowing to never again play on the same stage with Guard. Reynolds just shrugged and said, "I was the peacemaker in rehearsals; that was always my job. Dave wanted to do about nineteen chords in 'Tom Dooley'; it's a two-chord song."[31]

In hindsight it is easy to lay blame on one party for the breakup of a group. Dave Guard *did* own a major portion of The Kingston Trio—as they all did—and he had every right to protect his property and its future viability. "Dave was no dummy, understand," Werber would say years later, "nor was he evil or vicious. He gave in here and there sufficiently so Nick and Bobby get it off together. Dave had taste, did research, and was involved in the material."[32] The departure of Guard was an immeasurable loss to The Kingston Trio. Although Stewart was a worthy successor to Guard, helping to sustain the group's longevity and, in many ways, expand its musical scope, it was a *different* Trio, with a different kind of vitality and appeal. The original group was a unique entity, complex and joyous and intellectually stimulating, never to be matched in its brilliance. In a situation where vastly different personalities are thrown together, personally and professionally, clashes are inevitable, and rarely is one person right thus making all others wrong. Dave's reaction to the people and events around him was not the product of a difficult personality; they were perfectly normal feelings—and expected from someone who cared as much as he did and who felt like the odd man out. The old maxim "it takes two to tango" is certainly applicable here, particularly with polar opposites. While Guard and Shane had known each other since high school, they were never outwardly close friends. At some points their friendship was one of convenience and mutual need. Bobby had a guitar; Dave had records from which they learned. According to Gretchen Guard, the more that Shane exhibited a cavalier attitude or what Dave thought to be lack of responsibility, the more Guard dug in and reacted harshly. That clash—and attraction—of opposites really defined the Trio. Perhaps none of them ever grasped the reality that it was those sharp differences between the individual members, studied and freewheeling, that brought them together and made The Kingston Trio unique. It was their "it."

Eventually Guard, Shane, and Reynolds would reconcile their differences, even planning a cross-country reunion tour in 1990, which Shane recounted. "When Dave came to me and apologized for the problems that he had caused me, which is why we had the bad feelings for each other, and also told me that leaving The Kingston Trio was the most stupid thing he'd ever done, that erased all the bad feelings for me. I told him, 'I don't know what happened, but we were good friends in high school. And after we got out of high school, we became friends again to start a group and then slowly but surely it blew away again.' And he took it all back. I never thought he'd do that, but he apologized."[33]

"I think that they all really loved each other and I think that it was too bad they didn't live to be really old, old friends," said Gretchen Guard. "As you know, the pressures of being in the music business and being on the road are almost unbearable after a while, and I think the only groups that really survive are the miraculous groups, like The Manhattan Transfer, and brother groups or family groups, you know? And they're able to overcome all the 'weariness.' It's not that they dislike each other or hate each other or are jealous of each other, it's just that you can't be with the same people all the time unless you're family. The Kingston Trio with David only lasted four years at the most, but if they had been three brothers, they probably could have lasted 20 years."[34]

Near the end of Dave's life, Don McLean got to know him quite well and asked him what caused him to set in motion the events that eventually ended The Kingston Trio. "I was just so tired," Guard replied, and McLean could clearly hear it. "He was completely exhausted," said McLean, who knows well the stress of the road after more than forty years in the music business. "Most people who are civilians out there, who write about music, don't really understand what it's like to make it in show business. But I have been there and it's something that you can't imagine how hard you work for how many years. You never stop. And not only that, but you're making records constantly, and making appearances, and making trips to radio stations—you never, never stop and it goes on for years and years and you do get exhausted in a very profound way, which I understood when he mentioned this to me."[35]

Gretchen Guard added, "I think he was stunned by the way it ended, to tell you the truth, and I think what happened was that you're talking about becoming irrational and issuing ultimatums and I think that's what happened. He didn't talk to me about any of these decisions that he made ahead of time, so I was always catching up and in this case, I gathered that there was a meeting and he was getting really tired of doing most of the heavy lifting. I guess he was the only one who could read music and the only one who could do arrangements and the only one who could write charts and the only one who could change keys and you know, it was—he was doing an awful lot of work and justifiably he wanted the others to take on some of the load. But I think when they got to this point, they apparently had a meeting and he issued an ultimatum and they said, 'well no we don't want to do that so I guess we'll have to find a new guy.' And I think that's not what he expected. I think if he had thought it through or if he had given them a little more wiggle room, it might have turned out differently and I think he regretted the fact that it didn't."[36]

"None of us read music to start with, but Dave taught himself to read music," Shane conceded. "And that's one of the things he wanted me and Nick to do—to learn to read music to further ourselves with that in music. And I agreed with him before he died that I wish I had learned to read music."[37] While the collapse of the first Trio has been laid at Guard's feet, it certainly wasn't solely his doing. Genius has its pitfalls; impatience is often one of them. He wanted it perfect, but The Kingston Trio, by design, was joyfully imperfect. It's what made their music accessible and truly the music of the people. Surprisingly, the combativeness between Dave and Bobby belied a closeness the two shared since they were kids. While Guard's departure came as a relief to all those involved, including Guard himself, it left a personal void with Shane, Reynolds, and even Werber that no one could fill. And anybody who attempted to do so, invited or not, would feel some resentment, as John Stewart learned.

"John had this almost youthful exuberance that was very infectious and very, very neat," Nick Reynolds remarked with affection. "But it almost builds up a resentment, you know, a new face, a new person. It's an intrusion. To Bobby, that never wore off, really. That's how close he and Dave really were, without either one of them ever expressing it, even in a polite manner, much less an honest manner. But we knew the chemistry was right with John from the beginning. There were some rubs between Bobby and John, but a lot of it was this loss of David."[38]

Reynolds felt that loss, as well. Despite the bickering, he and Guard were also close. "He was just a sweet, big, old pussy cat, really, and way too smart to have any kind of sanity in his life at all," Reynolds said. "But God, I loved Dave. You have to be put in David's shoes. I mean, all this talent and energy to be used in a constructive way that he had, and we weren't going along with it, man. We wanted to do what we were doing and not progress too far out, that could have been the life or the death of The Kingston Trio, I don't know. That's for history to tell. Not that we were just resting on our laurels, we did our best. We were like trained dogs, man, we didn't really want to learn a lot of new things. And even then, we knew we'd be taking the stuff farther than just new tricks. Hell, we'd be singing I don't know what—and sort of against our will. So we didn't want to go along with that. But David was blessed with all the great qualities of a person, and his genius just did him in."[39]

Upon hearing the news of Dave's death from lymphoma in 1991, Nick Reynolds reflected on the years when the original Trio were performing with Dave Guard saying, "It was the highlight of our career."

Among the mourners at Dave Guard's memorial service in Portsmouth, New Hampshire, sat his old partner, worthy opponent, and friend to the end—Bobby Shane. In a get-well card to Dave just days before he died, Bobby fielded a final and moving question to Dave above his signature:

"Brothers, ok?"

NOTES

1. Nick Reynolds, interview with the author, Seminole, FL, October 4, 1986.
2. N. Reynolds, interview with the author, October 4, 1986.
3. N. Reynolds, interview with the author, October 4, 1986.
4. N. Reynolds, interview with the author, October 4, 1986.
5. N. Reynolds, interview with the author, October 4, 1986.
6. N. Reynolds, interview with the author, October 4, 1986.
7. Gretchen Guard, interview with the author, Santa Fe, NM, September 3, 2006.
8. Nick Reynolds, interview with the author, Seminole, FL, October 5, 1986.
9. Henry Diltz, interview with the author, Scottsdale, AZ, August 12, 2000.
10. Tommy Clancy, as told to Bob Shane, New York, NY, 1962.
11. John Stewart, interview with the author, Novato, CA, August 1, 2000.
12. Stewart, interview with the author.
13. Frank Werber, interview with Richard Johnston, Albuquerque, NM, 1974, from the Dave Guard and Richard Johnston Kingston Trio collection of materials, 1956–1986, University Manuscript Collections, University of Wisconsin, Milwaukee.
14. N. Reynolds, interview with the author, October 5, 1986.
15. Bob Shane, interview with the author, Phoenix, AZ, July 20, 2001.
16. Dave Guard, interview with the author, Los Altos, CA, November 29, 1983.
17. N. Reynolds, interview with the author, October 5, 1986.
18. N. Reynolds, interview with the author, October 5, 1986.
19. N. Reynolds, interview with the author, October 5, 1986.
20. Gretchen Guard, interview with the author, Santa Fe, NM, January 10, 2010.
21. Shane, interview with the author, July 20, 2001.
22. Shane, interview with the author, July 20, 2001.
23. N. Reynolds, interview with the author, October 5, 1986.
24. Joan Reynolds, interview with the author, Sausalito, CA. August 16, 2010.
25. Dave Guard, as recounted by Nick Reynolds, interview with the author, October 5, 1986.

26. "Kingston Trio's Big Bust-Up," Spotlight, *Life*, June 9, 1961, 126.

27. Dave Guard, interview/conversation with the author, Los Altos, CA, November, 28–30, 1983.

28. Bob Shane, interview with the author, Phoenix, AZ, January 14, 2010.

29. Dave Guard, television (online) interview, "Portrait: Dave Guard," *NH Journal* (New Hampshire).

30. Dave Guard, article, San Francisco *Peninsula* magazine, mid-1970s.

31. Reynolds, interview with the author, October 5, 1986.

32. Werber, interview with Johnston.

33. Bob Shane, phone interview with the author, December 16, 2007; Shane, interview, January 14, 2010.

34. G. Guard, interview with the author, January 10, 2010.

35. Don McLean, interview with the author, Camden, ME, April 23, 2009.

36. G. Guard, interview with the author, January 10, 2010.

37. Shane, interview with the author, January 14, 2010.

38. Nick Reynolds, interview with the author, Seminole, FL, October 7, 1986.

39. N. Reynolds, interview with the author, October 7, 1986.

9

THE NEW BOY

The departure of Dave Guard effectively ended one of the greatest musical groups in the history of popular music, leaving a chasm between fans, family, and music historians. It also created a burden on a multimillion dollar corporation and threatened the stability of a major record label. The Kingston Trio were *very* big business—a musical, social, and economic phenomenon that touched everything. It drove a lot of money, a substantial amount of which flowed through Kingston Trio, Inc., of which Guard owned a big chunk of stock.

Originally formed to help mitigate the Trio's enormous tax liabilities, Kingston Trio, Inc., invested in various enterprises and properties, including an office building in North Beach, an apartment building and spec houses in Sausalito (which they built), a land development company (including seventeen spectacular acres in the hills behind Mill Valley overlooking the Pacific), a waterfront restaurant and lounge (the Trident, also in Sausalito), a concert promotion agency, and a group of music publishing companies. Their most visible corporate asset, and the location of their offices, was Columbus Tower, a magnificent flatiron style building at the corner of Kearney and Jackson streets in North Beach near Chinatown in San Francisco. Originally known as the Sentinel Building, it was under construction during the 1906 earthquake, survived, and was finished in 1907. It remained a venerable San Francisco landmark. The building is rich in history, most notably as the headquarters of Abe Ruef, a corrupt San Francisco politician, lawyer, and union organizer in the early 1900s. The basement was the site of Enrico Banducci's original hungry i, and later Columbus Recording, The Kingston Trio's recording studio. The building was among the Trio's first big investments in 1960.

The majority of Kingston Trio, Inc.'s stock was split evenly between Bob Shane, Nick Reynolds, Dave Guard, and Frank Werber, with a small percentage of shares given to their attorney Sidney Rudy. While Werber shared in the publishing, he received none of the writer's royalties (which later became a sore point). When Guard's intentions to move on became clear and the realization that the corporation was on the hook for at least $225,000 and as much as $300,000 to buy Guard out or lose everything, Shane, Reynolds, and Werber began a search in earnest for his replacement.

Chip Hatelid (aka Douglas), Jim (aka Roger) McGuinn, Mike Settle, Rod McKuen, and a young songwriter from Pomona, California, John Stewart, were given serious consideration. And while Travis Edmondson was rumored to be among those asked to audition, both Shane and Reynolds emphatically said that he was not. But even if they picked the "right" replacement, there was no guarantee that the public would agree. The relief of being free of Guard, or rather being free of the angst and anger the confrontation generated, was quickly replaced with the awful possibility that The Kingston Trio might already be over for good. Once they had agreed that "yes, we're going to go for it," the auditions began.

Roger McGuinn, who later founded The Byrds and was at the forefront of the folk rock era, recalls his audition and the reason he was not chosen: "A friend of mine named Adam Yagodka knew Nick Reynolds and had co-written two songs with him which The Kingston Trio recorded ("Utawena" and "Hangman"). I was visiting from Chicago and staying with Adam and his girlfriend at his uncle's house in Mill Valley. And in that time period, Adam talked to Nick Reynolds because Dave was still with them but they were looking to replace him. So Nick picked me up in this red Ferrari in Mill Valley and took me over to Bob's house where they were having the auditions. He had an Ampex 601 tape recorder in a vinyl suitcase on the floor and a nice Telefunken microphone. So I came over with my banjo and played a couple of songs. I was eighteen so I sounded like a kid and it wasn't right. Oh, I would have been beside myself if The Kingston Trio thing had worked out, but I can understand why it couldn't," Roger reflected. "I think Bob's comment was that my voice wasn't quite mature enough or loud enough. And I was like seven or eight years younger than Dave. I mean it would have been an awkward look."[1]

While McGuinn felt that it was his youthful voice that lost him the gig, it was actually his young age that disqualified him (as well as Chip Douglas, who later cofounded The Modern Folk Quartet and produced The Monkees). Many of the venues the Trio played were clubs where alcohol was sold, and therefore inadmissible to anyone under twenty-one. "Well that didn't stop The Chad Mitchell Trio!" McGuinn said with a laugh. "I had a fake ID, so I played with The Chad Mitchell Trio and I was nineteen at that point. I had a Marine Corps ID that said I was over twenty-one, so yeah! Chicago, you know? You can buy anything!"[2]

Without playing a note, John Stewart had the advantage from the start. He was twenty-one years old, the Trio knew him as a songwriter, they had already recorded two of his compositions, and a year earlier, Werber had helped him and his hastily assembled Cumberland Three secure a recording contract with Roulette Records, which had been shopping for a folk trio to cash in on The Kingston Trio craze. Stewart knew The Kingston Trio's songs and their guitar and banjo licks note for note, and in Frank Werber's mind, he was as close to a perfect clone of Guard as one could imagine. Donnie MacArthur, the Trio's road manager at the time, thought so, too. "When Dave opted out, I thought to myself, well that's the end of this because I didn't think that we would ever find somebody to replace him," MacArthur said. "And then out of nowhere comes John Stewart. And John had been like a disciple of Dave's I guess. He copied Dave from head to toe. His movements, everything on stage, with just a different face—and I think he sang pretty well, they were comparable there, too. He had it down cold. And when he stepped in there, I looked at him and said, 'Shit, we're back in business!' It was just incredible."[3]

John Stewart wasn't so sure. "I was this *kid*, I mean I was scared to death," Stewart recalled. "It was very difficult at first because all of a sudden I was a member of the group that I loved so much. And I knew there were people that were going to be gunning for me and ready to chop me down because I was the number one pick."[4] This self-doubt would follow him, to some degree, throughout his life, fueled in part by ADD (attention deficit disorder), a developmental disorder with a long list of symptoms and potential emotional problems—lack of focus, hyperactivity, depression, mood swings, poor self-image, problems with personal relationships, insensitivity, irresponsible or uncaring behavior, and more. But also, one senses, that Stewart's insecurities were fostered—and continually reinforced—by a strained and distant relationship with his father.

He was born John Coburn Stewart on September 5, 1939, at Mercy Hospital in San Diego, the same hospital where Nick Reynolds was born six years earlier. He was the middle child between two older sisters, Elizabeth (Liz) and Marjorie, and a younger brother, Michael. His father, John Smith Stewart, was a Kentucky native and a well-known horse trainer; his mother, Alice Marston Stewart, was a housewife, born into a prominent and extremely wealthy San Diego family. "Opa" Coburn, John's maternal grandfather, supposedly had been the sheriff of San Diego County.

Stewart's childhood was a normal one, for the most part, although he frequently missed school because of allergies. "But I was very happy on my own," he said. "When I was a little kid I used to play in the dirt, make little cities, little houses, you know. I liked my bike, and loved my electric train." During World War II his father worked at Sperry Gyros installing instruments in bombers, and after the war went back to training horses in Pasadena and Kentucky. "My mom went out to Kentucky to visit him for a few months and left me with my grandmother, and I can still remember being in this great house without my mom, but feeling very at ease, sort of peaceful, by myself. I think that's where I got my loner qualities because I've always really been an independent guy."[5]

From an early age, John demonstrated a highly curious, inventive mind. He was probably the only fifth grader in Pasadena (or anywhere, for that matter) who had an alligator as a pet that he kept in an old refrigerator crate in the backyard. "I'd take him to school when they had an amateur show and had him do tricks. I had a flag that I'd put it in his mouth and he'd shake his head. Then I had a little cannon rigged up with a stick and 'Ollie' would grab the stick and the cannon would fire. The kids went freaking crazy! He grew to be two and a half feet long!"[6]

While the Stewart family was not musically inclined, there was always music in the house. John's older sister Liz played the piano and his mother often played Bing Crosby records, including an album of Bing singing Irish tunes that young Johnny loved. Like Guard, Shane, and Reynolds, Stewart's first instrument was a ukulele, which he strummed along to records by Tex Ritter and Bob Nolan of The Sons of the Pioneers, two huge influences, especially Nolan. Later he took ukulele lessons. "I was really attracted to music. I even got one of those plastic accordions. I did some lip-syncing at a talent show in the 4th grade, one of the few times my dad enjoyed what I did. The song was "Life Gets Teejus, Don't It?" one of Tex Ritter's big hits in 1948."[7]

As a kid Stewart's father put him to work as a racehorse schlepper at the racetrack—shoveling out stalls, cleaning harnesses, and "walking the hots" (walking a racehorse in a circle for two hours to gradually cool the horse down after racing). "*That's* when I heard the music," he recalled fondly, "Hank Williams, Hank Snow, Tex Ritter. I heard some really good music from the radios playing in the stables, not my father's stable mind you, but the other stables right across from his or down the hall, so there was music all the time. It was always on the country stations and then I'd hear pop stations—Patti Page and The Four Lads and of all of that, coming from those tiny radios through their little speakers. It was great!"[8]

Walking the hots for eight hours a day also gave Stewart plenty of time to think, and what he thought about most was music. "I got *real* inside my mind; my imagination was always going. So that's when I started writing songs. I wrote a song for the summer Boy Scout camp, Camp Cherry Valley on Catalina Island, called 'Shrunken Head Boogie.' It was a good song and a huge hit. And I wrote 'The LA Smog Song' in sixth grade—'Oh pitiful for spacious smog'—one of the first politically relevant songs, because no one was writing political songs that I had heard."[9]

He was raised Catholic and attended Catholic schools in kindergarten and second grade. When the family resettled in Pomona where his father trained racehorses at the Los Angeles County Fairgrounds, he went to Pomona Catholic High School, followed by a year at nearby Mount San Antonio Community College in Walnut, California. George Yanok, one of Stewart's lifelong friends, met him at Pomona Catholic when John was a sophomore and George was a junior.

"We were in Sister Wenceslaus's art class together," Yanok remembered, "and it was the only class in school where you have people other than your own grade. So at one point, he came up to me and said, 'You know, you look like Jackie Gleason.' And I said, 'You know, you look like a piece of shit.' He laughed and then we both just started laughing and goofing in art class, and then started hanging out and doing things together." One of the first things they did was form a comedy duo, Yanok and Stewart (or sometimes Stewart and Yanok) with one bit titled "The Handkerchief Brothers," which Yanok admits was a blatant steal from Sid Caesar's TV vocal trio, The Haircuts. Their repertoire was quite eclectic—jokes, skits, and one very unusual musical duet as a closer: Stewart playing "Battle Hymn of the Republic" on harmonica interspersed with Yanok doing "Gene Krupa style" drum solos on an ancient, massive drum set. "It was horrific. Suicidal," said Yanok with a straight face. "That's why they clapped as we were leaving." Impersonations were another crowd pleaser. "John was a *great* mimic. He could do a great Ed Sullivan and would use it to introduce The Handkerchief Brothers. That was our big finale—The Handkerchief Brothers doing 'Battle Hymn of the Republic' with drum solos and harmonica."[10]

Yanok would go on to become an Emmy Award–winning screenwriter, producer, and television comedy writer whose credits include *Welcome Back Kotter*, *Sanford and Son*, *Hee-Haw*, *The Glen Campbell Goodtime Hour*, and others. He also became The Kingston Trio's last road manager and the editor of their farewell album, *Once Upon a Time*.

Like most everyone in America, Stewart first saw Elvis Presley on The Dorsey Brothers' television show on January 28, 1956, singing "Shake, Rattle and Roll." And a year later, on October 28, 1957, he saw Elvis in person at the Pan Pacific Auditorium in Los Angeles and the die was cast. "John latched onto Elvis like this was his destiny and he started doing Elvis. He was not 'Here I am doing Elvis' like Elvis impersonators now; he was like the *alternate* Elvis," said Yanok. "At one point he even put black circles under his eyes so it would make him look a little more like a hillbilly wreck or something. Then he bought his first guitar. We were going to do Elvis as part of our act, and John needed a guitar to complete the Elvis impression so he bought one at a pawn shop for twenty-five cents. It had no strings, which we both agreed was lucky because there was no chance he would try to play it! And I think the first time that we did the Elvis impression onstage was at a Pomona Catholic High School assembly, and a football player, Pat DeCarlo, threw a half dollar at us and put a hole through the guitar! So John was suddenly going into the music thing in earnest. He stopped doing comedy."[11]

"I heard Elvis and it was all over then—I had to have a guitar," Stewart confirmed. "If Elvis played acoustic, I played acoustic. Anything Elvis did was all right with me. Those early Sun Records, the sound—wanging acoustic on 'It's Alright Mama'—I just couldn't believe it. I'd never heard anything like that in my life! *Don't Be Cruel* is still to me the greatest rock and roll record ever recorded. Devastating new sound that was just hypnotic. I played it all day every day for months."[12]

Before long Stewart joined a rock 'n' roll garage band that was being formed by three guys from Pomona—Jack Ward and Gil Marino on guitars, Bob Zeivers on drums, and Stewart as vocalist doing mostly Elvis imitations, sporting a well-oiled pompadour. He also doubled as an ersatz bass player by tuning his guitar down an octave, using heavy strings and adding a DeArmond pickup. As an added touch, the group recruited two Latino friends as backup singers. They called themselves Cobe Stewart and The Furies, which quickly became Johnny Stewart and The Furies, gigging around the Pomona/Chino area doing mostly Elvis Presley, Buddy Holly, Little Richard, and Jerry Lee Lewis covers, plus originals by Stewart. The highlight of the group's short life was playing dances at the Pomona Ebelle Auditorium and the El Monte Legion Stadium, "the Birthplace of West Coast R & B/Rock 'n' Roll," with doo-wop singer Little Julian Herrera. Stewart soon felt the urge to go out on his own as Johnny Stewart, recording his first single, "Rockin' Anna" backed with "Lorraine," on Vita Records, an independent label in Pasadena. The session was paid for by

Ilah Haynes, the woman who wrote "Rockin' Anna," and was arranged by legendary session keyboardist Ernie Freeman, who also played on the session. On the strength of that single, Stewart played a big package show sponsored by a radio station at the Los Angeles County Fair in September of 1958 that featured The Teddy Bears (with Phil Spector), The Champs, Johnny Cash, Ritchie Valens, and according to Stewart, The Kingston Trio. Although there is no documentation of the Trio playing that show, Stewart said that this was where he first met The Kingston Trio. What he remembered most clearly, however, was meeting Ritchie Valens. "I was talking to him backstage," John recalled. "He was the nicest, most unassuming kid who just sang his ass off and wrote those great songs. I mean to still be remembered for three songs, you know? Remarkable. His chops for that age, I mean his "La Bamba" was a *great* version of that song. And "Come on Let's Go"—he was right on the money!"[13]

While "Rockin' Anna" went absolutely nowhere, the experience of recording inspired Stewart to seek a bona fide record deal in earnest. By this time, however, he was no longer interested in being Elvis Presley. He was interested in being one of The Kingston Trio. The discovery of folk music and The Kingston Trio was an epiphany. It was *perfect* for an earnest loner like him. Self-contained. Intelligent. Poetic. Dramatic. You didn't have to dress up like The Hillbilly Cat either, or have Bill and Scotty backing you. And while it wasn't really as simple as the Trio made it seem (talent *was* a factor), it was easy enough for anybody who knew three chords to think they could pull it off, including Stewart. "At that point, I was just in love with them," he laughed. "That's when I had crossed the line. When I heard the first Trio album, and the first song I heard was "Saro Jane," it stopped me dead in my tracks. Bill Cahill, a friend of mine from high school, had gone to school in Santa Clara and the Trio had played at that school. George Yanok had seen them, too, and couldn't believe they were playing those instruments like that. So he bought their album and said 'listen to this': It was 'Saro Jane' and it was like hearing Elvis for the first time. I had never heard anything like that sound and it just froze me. I went out and bought that album and started playing those songs."[14]

Meanwhile, Stewart had been relentlessly promoting himself and pursuing a record deal, getting on a bus every morning in Pomona with a handful of "Rockin' Anna" singles and visiting radio stations and record companies throughout the Los Angeles area. He'd also been busy writing "folk-type songs," including one called "Molly Dee," supposedly based loosely on a popular young country singer Molly Bee (Mollie Gene Beachboard) who'd moved to Pomona from Tennessee and was already on her way to national stardom. Although Stewart went to junior high school with Mollie Beachboard, *the* Molly Bee, he said the idea for "Molly Dee" actually came from Jan and Arnie's rocker "Jennie Lee" (named after an Los Angeles stripper, Jennie "the Bazoom Girl" Lee). Jan Berry, Arnie Ginsberg, and Dean Torrance (who actually sang lead on Jennie Lee) recorded for Arwin records in Beverly Hills. The label was owned by Marty Melcher and his wife, Doris Day. It wasn't long before Stewart approached Melcher about a record deal.

"Marty Melcher was a very nice guy, very thorough businessman," Stewart recalled. "I put on a coat and tie, went in, and I just wouldn't take no for an answer. I played them 'Rockin' Anna' and some of my other songs and they said well, these songs need some work, so I drove right over to my grandmother's house in Beverly Hills, and came back the same day with revisions. Arwin Records!! I finally got signed to a deal!"[15] Melcher wanted to record a song called "The Story of Love," but then Stewart played them some of the folk songs he'd been writing and the label quickly decided he should do a solo folk album—but only if they published Stewart's songs, and he sent them to The Kingston Trio, and the Trio agreed to record some of them. The deal also included Stewart becoming an Arwin staff writer alongside Johnny Otis, a veteran writer, performer, producer, and powerful Los Angeles disc jockey.

Thinking that he somehow "knew" the Trio based on having met them once at the Los Angeles County Fair, and that a recording career with Arwin hung on the remote possibility that The Kingston Trio might actually record one of his songs, Stewart didn't hesitate to approach the group at the Shrine Auditorium in January of 1959. They didn't remember him, of course, but didn't say so and were cordial. "They come in the stage door and there was Dave and his guitar case with this blue canvas cover on it, coat, skinny tie, it was the hippest thing! And I said, 'Dave can I ask you something?' 'Oh, yeah, baby!' Guard replied smoothly. And I told them what Arwin wanted to do, and he says, 'You want them cockin' your songs?!' And I said, 'Well if you guys want to do a song, it will really be a big help.' He says, 'Well come on in and play us a couple.' So I played them 'Johnny Reb' and I can't remember the other song. And Dave says, 'Man, dangerously close!' And Nick said, 'Yeah, they're almost there. Come back when you've got something.'"[16]

It didn't take Stewart long to get back to the Trio with two more songs, "Molly Dee" and "Green Grasses," which he played for them less than four months later during an afternoon rehearsal in the big dining room of the Ambassador Hotel where they were appearing at the Coconut

Grove. But it wasn't quite the reception he was expecting. "I walked in and they were sitting at a table with their instruments and their beers, and Lou Gottlieb was over in the corner playing the piano," Stewart remembered. "And Dave said, 'Oh, here's the local cocksucker.' It was the first time they kind of turned on me. It was a slam, but I weathered the storm because I wanted to play all the songs, and I was very much in awe."[17] Guard could be caustic; they all could. It was a tight-knit club whose members knew each other very well, some from childhood, and they could be merciless with each other without thinking anything of it. Sometimes they felt the need to put some distance between themselves and fans who might act overly familiar, occasionally reminding them that they were not really as "in" as they thought, and "putting them in their place" as Nick called it. Stewart was a nineteen-year-old kid at that time, and an insecure one at that, pitching songs to what was becoming the leading vocal group in the world. So he was fair game.

Reynolds remembered the incident: "In comes this guy with a damn banjo on his back! A tall, geeky looking kid; he sort of creeps in and Donnie intercepts him. So Donnie tells us and asks, 'Do you want to meet this kid? He's got a couple of songs.' Well, we're doing an album, right? And he's got a couple of songs, right? So he comes in and sings two songs for us, 'Molly Dee' and 'Green Grasses.' And you should have seen the flurry of activity! Johnny was great. He was an average banjo player, an amateur player, and a complete fan; he idolized the Trio. So we put him in his place—'Yeah, that's cute' [sounding indifferent]. But we're *really* thinking we've got to sign him up right now! Got any contracts? We weren't out for grabbing any writer's royalties. It had been suggested, but we never took any, except for public domain songs. It was the first time we'd met John, and he was starting to write some songs. And all of a sudden he walks in to the top group in the country, and we said, 'Yeah, those are ballad songs as far as we're concerned. We don't think, you know, there's any hit material here.' But they'd be great album songs, a real neat kind of ballad and a good little shit kicker [sings a verse of "Molly Dee"]—good banjo, guitar, rhythm kind of a thing, which we were looking for all the time. And it just walked in on us."[18]

"I actually played them three songs," Stewart recalled. "I can't remember the other one. So they took the verses from that song and put them into 'Molly Dee' and recorded them a few days later. It was my first year in junior college and I was living at home at the time, and I remember after they recorded 'Green Grasses' I saw Nick and he said, 'Yeah, Dave couldn't get your banjo opening, so we tried to find you so you could come down and play it.' They didn't know where I was."[19] Upon hearing the news, Stewart went down to Capitol, told them he was the writer of "Molly Dee," and was sent up to Artist & Repertoire where someone played him the cut from the session. He would also discover that the album was to be titled *Here We Go Again*, a lyric line from "Molly Dee," and that the Trio had already done the song on a television program. But the biggest surprise would come in the mail six months later—a check for ten thousand dollars in writer's royalties for "Molly Dee." It was just the nudge he needed to quit college.

Despite Stewart's amazing success at selling two songs to a group as enormously popular and influential as The Kingston Trio, and as an amateur songwriter no less, his father was totally unmoved, even dismissive. "My father thought all his kids were absolutely worthless; we never did anything right—yeah, it was one of those relationships," Stewart said. "After I joined the Trio, Mom said that Dad was out at the racetrack and said, 'Yeah, well you know I always tried to help him as much as I could,' and the guys at the racetrack just went 'Oh, give us a break!'" Not only was the elder Stewart not supportive, he forbade his son to play his guitar or banjo in the house. "I had to go outside and play in the car on the street! That's where I wrote 'Molly Dee.' My dad used to speak this Kentucky-eese. When I'd be playing my banjo in the house, he would say, 'Needa mind the wan de bam.' 'Needa mind' is Kentucky-ese for 'never mind,' and a banjo was a wan de bam. Needa mind the wan de bam was his nonmusical angst, jaded perception of what music was."[20] It was not until years later, when his father was on his deathbed, that the two reconciled. A lifetime had gone by without his father's approval, a loss Stewart felt deeply—and resented—adding to his insecurity.

By default, Frank Werber would become an authority figure to John, and not in a particularly benevolent way. Frank was first an astute businessman, and he would say that he always had John in mind as the replacement for Dave. Stewart had proven himself as an able writer, and was already a working musician in a folk duo with John Montgomery, whom he had met in a drama class at Mount San Antonio College. They called themselves John and Monte, playing such clubs as Cosmo Alley in Hollywood, the Kerosene Club in San Jose (opening for the unknown Smothers Brothers), and at the hungry i in San Francisco. In 1960, Morris Levy at Roulette Records called Werber looking for a folk trio, and Frank recommended John Stewart, who immediately formed The Cumberland Three, adding Gil Robbins (his high school choir teacher who had played bass for him and John Montgomery at the hungry i). "Gil had a good voice, he sang with a real legit voice," Stewart recalled. "So I called him and he said 'Yeah let's do it.' He had three children—and one of his kids was [actor] Tim Robbins, who I used to babysit! So Roulette paid for our tickets, we got on an airliner, and we rehearsed for the first time on the airplane in one of those upstairs lounges they used to have on the way to New York." When they arrived, they immediately headed to Gerde's Folk City down in the Village, meeting up with Ronnie Gilbert of The Weavers, Cisco Houston, and Roulette's producer Pete Kameron, former Weavers manager. They auditioned on the spot and passed easily. "I remember Pete Kameron talking that night about The Kingston Trio," Stewart said, "and Ronnie Gilbert saying, "Well, they're the first group that's got the right idea!""[21]

The Cumberland Three was signed to ITA (International Talent Associates), with Bert Block and Larry Bennett handling their booking, giving them a huge advantage over scores of new folk groups spawned by The Kingston Trio's success and the developing national folk craze. Although the group lasted less than two years, they recorded three albums at Bell Sound in New York for Roulette: *Folk Scene. U.S.A.* (with liner notes by Dave Guard), *Civil War Almanac, Vol. 1: Yankees* and *Civil War Almanac, Vol. 2: Rebels*. The Cumberland Three would play the Blue Angel, the hungry i, and other top clubs in the country, as well as tour nationally with comedian Bob Newhart. The group even had a hit in the South with "Johnny Reb" and toured the region promoting it—which is where they got a taste of the *real* record business: "So we go on a station wagon tour of the South," John recounted. "And all of Morris Levy's promo men in Atlanta look like guys from *The Sopranos*, and they put us up in these great hotels. So before I knew it, I was out of money. Finally, we did the round trip and went back to New York—and Morris is pissed that we went through the money!!" The Cumberland Three proved to be an excellent boot camp for Stewart, giving him polish, road and real-world savvy, and experience in the studio. Yet when the end came to the original Kingston Trio, John would still have to audition like anybody else.[22]

By this time John had married Julie Kohler whom he had met at an all-night high school party when he was playing with the Furies. "She was the most gorgeous girl in the whole school, probably the whole county. We went out three times, she got serious, and we ended up getting married. She wanted a way out of Covina, and being the prettiest girl in the county, how could I go wrong?"[23] The day they got married the two flew to New York where The Cumberland Three were playing and got an apartment on East 132nd Street.

Things were not good within The Cumberland Three, which John admitted was mostly his fault. "I was just a real asshole. No patience. Being ADD all my life and not knowing what it was and that it was causing mood swings, it was not pleasant for them, nor me. It was three control freaks in the same group—well, helllooo."[24] By then, John Montgomery had been eased out of the group, and Mike Settle, whom they met in Oklahoma, took his place. The group also recorded two singles for Roulette, "Old Dog Blue" and "You Can Tell the World," but the group's days were numbered.

The Cumberland Three was playing the Blue Angel in New York when Stewart heard the rumor Guard was going to leave the Trio. "It was all over the place," he remembered, "so I called Nick and he said, 'Come on out. We're gonna audition a few people, and let me know when you get here.' Julie and I flew to San Francisco, stayed at the Sausalito Hotel, and called Nick and he said, 'Hang tight.' The next day I went over to Bobby's."[25]

Remarkably, Stewart was the picture of confidence, trading jokes and discussing race cars with Shane and Reynolds as the three went downstairs to Shane's music room. "There were all these gold records on the wall," he said recalling the scene, which added to the pressure. "We sang this song that they hadn't recorded yet, 'Gonna Go Down the River,' and we smoked!" The thing that I brought to it was my rock and roll roots—the way I played the banjo was just more four/four and two/four rather than straight folk strumming. It just locked in more, so we really cooked. I wasn't a good singer, but on some songs I did very well. And then we did one of the Trio songs and that was it." When asked if it dawned on him that he was actually playing with his heroes, Stewart smiled and said, "Oh, it dawned on me."[26]

He had no problems fitting into what they did. "I knew it inside and out. I'm a real good chameleon. In fact, when they were doing 7UP commercials, Frank was suggesting that I write some of the commercials to send to the 7UP people. He said, 'He thinks like the boys think,' which is true. I knew exactly what their thing was. They were doing folk music with the mind-set of rock and roll—*young* folk music with hooks, as opposed to the ethnic stuff I'd heard. So coming from rock and roll, I knew exactly what they were doing immediately. The banjo, the hook line, and the chords had to be simple and had to be repetitive, so it was real easy for me to jump in and start taking over what Dave did there."[27]

Guard's banjo playing had become an integral part of The Kingston Trio sound, and Stewart learned the five-string banjo in exactly the same manner as Guard, from Pete Seeger's *How to Play the 5-String Banjo* paper-back and interminable hours of hunt-and-peck practice, driving everyone within earshot wild. George Yanok remembered the ordeal: "John set out to learn another instrument with strings. The banjo. Not easy. In fact, the closest John ever came to death as a young man was when he was teach-ing himself to play the five-string banjo in a house in San Jose where he was living with me and four of my college roommates. Plink-plink-kaplink . . . all day long with the Pete Seeger book open on his lap. I thought my roommates were going to kill him. And if they didn't I was going to."[28] Like Seeger and Guard, John would play a Seeger Long Neck 5-String Vega, to which he later added Scruggs tuners. He briefly switched to a Gibson long neck banjo during the Trio years, but found that it didn't "cut near as well as the Pete Seeger."

"Bobby and Nick were the most amazing natural players I had ever heard in my life," Stewart remembered. "They didn't know what the chords were called—E was rock and roll, D was Tahitian, and C was cow-boy. But it didn't matter if you called it E or D or Tahitian. They played the hell out of it. Bobby is a great rhythm guitar player. He would break heavy gauge strings a couple of times a set. He played so hard and laid it down; Dave was always so pissed at him that the time would race. It was his excitement! And he would do it and I would just hold back on the banjo, bringing it back. It's like a drummer playing behind the beat and it just gives this tension; I just loved it. That was a great part of the magic of the Trio—it was so natural."[29]

Shane weighed in saying, "Musically, you gotta understand that right from the get-go our show was an *act*. It was all one parcel. You entertained people—that's being funny, being sincere, being off-hand. And John fit right in, picked up on the fact that it wasn't the instrumentation. It's the *singing*. The singing makes it. As long as you play good enough to sing with, that's it. We didn't put in fancy licks and shit. We made it easy for people to play the stuff we do."[30]

But Stewart also recognized, as did Guard before him, that if he had been just like Bob and Nick, the Trio wouldn't have worked. Reynolds and Shane brought spirit and chutzpa. Stewart brought a work ethic. And while Stewart would have to work out the chords and the preliminary ar-rangements and generally walk Shane and Reynolds through the tunes that he had brought in, he would find that they were extremely quick students, having done the drill many times over. And they had plenty to contribute to the entire process, too. Harmony was Reynolds's specialty, and he'd in-tuitively—and creatively—assign who sang what, when, and how. "I'll take a part on top and then you take a part on the bottom," he would say, with Bobby automatically singing lead. Because Stewart was not particularly adept at harmonies, Nick would say, "Why don't you sing *this*"—singing the part till John locked into it. This ability to head arrange was critical to the Trio's success, allowing them to produce an enormous amount of recorded material quickly—and expertly. Some would call it professionalism, but it was really artistry. They understood recording technology and used echo and overdubbing like an artist palette. And Stewart got it right up front. "The method of rehearsing and recording did not change at all for the Trio with me," Stewart said. "That's pretty much what I was doing with my little folk group anyway."[31]

The fact that Stewart wrote folk-type songs was a big plus because it was getting harder to find folk material that hadn't been covered many times over. But what Stewart had going for him the most, apart from his musical abilities, was that Shane and Reynolds loved his dry sense of humor, most of which was entirely off the top of his head. Shane said it created an immediate affinity and liking for John with the audience. At the same time, Stewart felt that while Shane accepted him as a musician, a songwriter, and a comedian, he never accepted him as a singer. The vibrato in his voice was an issue, which Judy Davis helped to minimize, yet it still crept back and Shane would call him on it saying, "You know this vibrato thing of yours, it's not style; it's just you don't know how to sing." But it went deeper. Shane said that John was standoffish in the beginning because he was in awe of being in the Trio, which made it hard to get to know him. "It took me a long time to get to personally like John," Shane admitted, "but then when I did, I *really* liked him, and I think he's a really talented person."[32]

According to Joan Reynolds, what really impressed Nick and Bob was that although John was scared to death, he didn't show it. "He appeared relaxed and warm and funny and humble. He knew all the songs and arrangements so he could sing and play with them, and he was a musician. He could fit in certain places where Bobby and Nick couldn't; he understood that. He had a young bride, but no children, and he brought her to meet everybody. So he was family respectable and they were really kind of impressed."[33]

"He fit in marvelously," said Bob Shane. "John was a completely different personality than Dave—and younger. But he had great humor, and whereas Dave's was more college humor, John's was more universal. John had a different style of playing the banjo, too, which I think was a great asset at the time because we needed something different. When we got John and after rehearsing for a while, we realized, hey, this is just as much fun, probably more fun than it was before. And when we sang with him, right from the start, it felt more melodic to us than it had been with Dave. Oh yeah, we dug him to start with."[34]

Dave Guard would not officially leave the group until August 5, 1961, following a final concert in Ispswich, Massachusetts. In the interim, Stewart was told to keep his bags packed and be ready to jump in when the issue was finally resolved. He'd been well rehearsed and already knew the show. He said he felt like a backup astronaut or a second-string quarterback, always ready to go but not knowing when or where. Even when they'd tell him the next day was it, Guard would decide to go instead. Stewart was "chomping at the bit," as he put it, but still put the time waiting to good use working out tunes for the new Trio album.

"Home" for Stewart, at least temporarily, was a guest bedroom at Frank Werber's sprawling house in Fairfax, and then a spare bedroom at Nick and Joan Reynolds's home up the hill on Santa Rosa Avenue in Sausalito. Every day, he'd take the Reynolds's young son Josh for long walks in his stroller while pondering his less-than-certain future. Eventually, he and Julie found a small apartment in Sausalito. His way of coping with his anxiety was to stuff himself with cheeseburgers. "I looked like a chipmunk," he admitted, puffing out his cheeks, to demonstrate. "They were still with Dave. And I ate like a pig. I was so angst-ridden, you know? I must have gained twenty pounds. I was just twenty-one sitting in this apartment in Sausalito thinking, *what the hell am I doing here?* My voice was not strong; it just wasn't there, to me. So I would sit there and work out new songs for *Close-Up.* And I had my bag packed—any gig I could have gone."[35] Finally, the word came and the Trio with John Stewart played its first official gig, a benefit concert for the Boys Club in Santa Rosa, California, on September 16, 1961, at Santa Rosa Veterans Memorial Hall.

If ever there was a crucible for Stewart it was *this* concert. He had a lot to live up to. He had earlier witnessed the incredible energy of the Guard trio backstage at the Pasadena Civic Auditorium standing in their dressing room as they rehearsed "Remember the Alamo" for that night's show. "I was standing in the middle of this sound and I couldn't believe what I was hearing—that razor voice of Dave's 'one hundred and eighty' and Nick going 'who, oa, oa . . .' I was transfixed." He would experience that same energy, one that nearly knocked him over, literally, in the opening verse of "Darlin' Corey" at Santa Rosa as Shane and Reynolds let loose: "There's a pine log SHAAAAACK!!" Only this time *he* was a part of it. "We walked out on stage, one mike, and we went in to 'Darlin' Corey' and when we sang 'SHACK' it sent a chill up my spine. When they put the juice to it, and I did too, it was terrifying. It was another league. And I'm standing in the middle of it frailing my ass off!"[36]

Such success should have quelled Stewart's fears and reassured him of his worthiness. It didn't. He still harbored doubts about his ability to fit into this phenomenon, replacing someone who had been his hero, and being looked upon as the guy who had to perpetuate it. A lot of people were asking the same question about Stewart's suitability, and for many of them, nobody could ever take Guard's place. The kid who Werber had looked upon as a Dave Guard clone, was in fact no such thing. Not a lesser talent, but a decidedly different one. Stewart would have a difficult time making the transition, continually asking—and annoying—Werber and others with "How am I doing?" and "Am I doing okay?" looking for some shred of reassurance.

Nick Reynolds knew what John was going through and always went out of his way to help him overcome his insecurity. But Reynolds also recognized the need for balance and complete candor in dealing with someone as intelligent as Stewart. "Once Nick was driving me home from rehearsal," Stewart recalled. "And I said I didn't feel well about the rehearsal—and *he* knew the rehearsal didn't go well. I said, 'Jeez, I don't feel right about this, but as long as I know you guys are behind me, as long as I know you guys accept me, I'll be okay.' And Nick said, 'Well, as long as I know that the *people* accept you, we'll be okay.' And I said, 'Yeah, you're right!' Nick was also really tough love. He would rip me unmercifully and I'd laugh, but it was necessary. He knew that I had to get tough or be killed. It was a much faster, much different life than the Cumberland freaking Three. Nick would just go for my weakness and bring it to the surface and make fun of it. I really thanked him for that."[37]

Reynolds remembered Stewart having dinner at the Reynolds home, asking several times "How am I doing?" Nick was straightforward: "I'd say, 'You're doing just fine. It's tough on all of us.' The name was still up in the air, as far as I can remember. I said, 'John, you've got to realize that nothing may ever happen of this. We may never be able to travel as The Kingston Trio, and if we do, God, who knows what kind of acceptance we're going to have after this kind of blow to the Trio? We might not have anybody show up to the shows.' This is how insecure we were."[38]

Part of Stewart's angst could well have been the realization that he was now in a group whose greatest appeal to him had been based on a member who was no longer in the group. It didn't hit him until he went up to Frank's house, put on the striped shirt to have pictures taken of the group, and saw his reflection in the picture window. It was Nick and Bob and *John*, and it didn't feel right. "So there I was, I got to be my hero, but I wasn't my hero," Stewart said. "The group I really wanted to be in would have been with Dave and Nick." In fact, Stewart had wanted to join Dave Guard's Whiskeyhill Singers before he joined The Kingston Trio but Guard said "Naw, man, no baby. We can't have two tall guys that play the banjo and are funny." To which Stewart replied, "Well, you know they want me to join the Trio, and he said, 'No man don't join up with those guys.'"[39]

But Stewart did join up "with those guys," and as Nick and Bob would soon learn, John was his own man, not an imitation of Dave Guard, bringing a freshness and musicality and young spirit to "jaded old Bobby and me," as Nick would say. Stewart said he wasn't consciously imitating Dave, but rather doing an *attitude* that the group had. His instincts were absolutely correct. Attitude was *everything* with The Kingston Trio.

There was another group of concerned observers, however, who weren't so comfortable when Stewart was selected as "the new boy," attitude or not. Capitol had everything to lose if John didn't work out. At the height of their popularity, the Trio accounted for over 20 percent of Capitol's gross sales—and 100 percent of the label's renewed image of hipness and commercial acuity. When the trouble with Guard began, nobody anticipated it would end the way it did, especially Werber. "I don't recall at all ever considering that Guard would split till that thing came down," he confided. "I was in Japan when that happened. It was probably the biggest shock of my entire life that this thing started going sideways. And Dave, rather than say, 'Piss on it, let's go make music,' said 'No, fuck you guys.'"[40] Werber felt that the Trio's popularity was firmly established as a group, that it was bigger than the loss of an individual member. "All I was looking for was somebody that could fill the space. As we were already in orbit, I felt we had a few good years going, and Stewart had sort of been, by divine guidance, standing in the wings." Werber would say that everything about Stewart was carefully considered—musically, psychologically, personality-wise—before picking him to replace Guard. "Without deprecating John in any way, I wanted a bit of a clone. John was a Dave Guard clone. He emulated Dave on the natch, and he was the closest thing really. I believed we would make it. And I instilled in myself and in Nick and Bob the fact the Dave could come and go and we would go on."[41]

Capitol, however, wanted more than Werber's optimistic outlook. They wanted Guard signed to the label as insurance. "When I left, they (Capitol) insisted on signing me," Guard said. "Otherwise, they didn't know which way it was going to go, the Trio or me, what the money thing was gonna be. To pay me off, The Kingston Trio borrowed one hundred thousand dollars from Capitol Records. But how is the Trio gonna pay it back if something funny happened, like if I wound up with the group?"[42] Capitol's president, Alan Livingston, made it clear to Werber that he didn't see The Kingston Trio as being as strong a draw without Guard, and implied that just maybe Capitol would go with Guard instead of Nick, Bob, and Frank. At the time, the Trio was up for renewal of its Capitol contract, and Livingston used it as leverage to get the Trio to re-sign for another year at a lesser rate. "You wanted to sign for another year?" Livingston queried, playing it for all it was worth. "We have an investment, and of course, if we continue with the services of Dave Guard . . . ," letting it hang. "Sign for another year at 5 percent and I'll loan you a chunk for the down payment to Guard."[43]

By this time, Guard had formed a new group, Dave Guard and The Whiskeyhill Singers, that included Guard; Cyrus Faryar, a fellow Punahou School student (class of 1953) and friend of Guard's from Honolulu, where he owned a beat coffeehouse called Greensleeves and would later become a member of The Modern Folk Quartet; David "Buck" Wheat, jazz bassist and Kingston Trio accompanist; and Judy Henske, a folk-blues belter, actress, songwriter, and recording artist. The group would prove to be weaker than its individual members, at least recording-wise.

Guard was bitter, saying that Capitol did absolutely nothing for Dave Guard and The Whiskeyhill Singers. "They didn't want us to come out with anything. We got one pass on the cover, and one pass on the mastering. Nobody ever met us at the airport. There were no ads in the trade papers at all. Somebody passed the word to step on the whole thing. I really liked the people a lot. I liked the tunes. But we got a ton of shit from Capitol on that one." In fairness to Capitol, and as anyone who's ever listened to the *Dave Guard and The Whiskeyhill Singers* album can attest, it's quirky, loose, and overpowered by Judy Henske's vocals. "She a great single, but in a group situation it just didn't fit," Guard conceded. "And I'm sure she felt why would she be in a group at all?" But there were other problems. "The hard part of that group was putting my voice on top," said Guard. "I always used to sing bass in the Trio and now I sing in necktie attire, above the bass voice. So we never did get the brand that we had thought of. We had a lot of smart people that could react very well to each other, but we never had anybody keeping the same movement together in that group. That was the problem there—which was the problem with most groups."[44] Perhaps in an attempt to sound more authentic, or maybe just to thumb their nose at the layered, spatial Capitol sound of The Kingston Trio, the group proudly proclaimed in an ad that they had produced and recorded the album themselves in a studio in Sausalito, sounding flat and without any apparent coloring with echo or overdubbing.

Guard deserved better—and the group *was* better than it sounded on the album. They would go on to record the soundtrack for *How the West Was Won*, which was nominated for Best Original Music Score in the 1963 Academy Awards. A 1962 tape of the group in concert at the Hollywood Bowl singing "Railroad Bill" with Henske replacement Liz Seneff is tight, melodic, and full of energy, a snapshot of what could've been. None of this was lost on Shane, Reynolds and Werber who were uneasy that Guard's new group might upend the Trio. Despite The Whiskeyhill Singers' disastrous first album, they nonetheless had both the Trio's "acknowledged leader" and its renowned bassist David Wheat, who had defected from the Trio after the *College Concert* album.

On August 15, 1961, when the new Trio with Stewart was recording *Close-Up*, their first album together, the control room in Studio B filled up with Capitol executives anxious to see and hear how well Stewart would fit in. After a few bars of "Jesse James," they all shook hands with each other and left. John was in—but he was never *fully* in. From the outset, Stewart was an employee of Kingston Trio, Inc., not a partner or shareholder, a fact that Werber never let him forget. In addition to his salary, he later negotiated a small, sliding scale percentage of the group's net. He also received writer's royalties, but not the publishing, on the many songs that he wrote for the Trio. "I don't remember what the numbers were," Werber said, "but I don't think it was anywhere near unfair to John. Besides, he got a percentage; the more we worked, the more we earned, the more John got. And he made a fortune off those songs he wrote for the Trio. I think John should be intensely grateful, really, because he had a chance to be on board with this unit. It made him. Without that path in his life, I don't think John would have surfaced. The fact that he was a hired hand, well, he was. We didn't ask anybody to join the venture as a partner."[45]

Fact was, Werber and Stewart never liked each other from the beginning. "John felt that Frank did not respect him for the writer that he was and John was shortchanged," said Buffy Stewart, John's wife. "He did not get anything that the rest of the guys got. He didn't even get the publishing on his songs. He was young, he thought, 'Oh I'm in The Kingston Trio, this is great.' All the songs that John wrote, the Trio got the publishing money. He only got the writer's royalties. So he felt that he just got screwed. He was the new guy. He was young, he was excited to be in the Trio."[46]

Werber barely hid his preference for the Guard trio. To him, the Guard trio *was* The Kingston Trio, and Stewart had simply stepped in and filled a void. And while he credits Stewart as doing a good job of standing in for Guard, it was no longer the *real* Kingston Trio, and that they had played a kind of sleight of hand to keep the illusion going. "I think we were all part of that vision, that bit of magic. But the first one was The Kingston Trio, and there was an end to that. And then we called it [the second group] The Kingston Trio, and said now you see them, now you don't. But it's all hindsight anyway. How do I know what would have happened if Dave had stayed?"[47]

There are, of course, many who would take issue with Werber's assessment of which group, Guard or Stewart, was the real Kingston Trio. They were substantially different trios musically, with substantially different audiences years apart in age and viewpoint. One's preference for the Guard or Stewart edition of the group is usually based on which trio the listener was exposed to first, both recordings and personal appearances. Mid-to-late boomers, those who were in high school from 1961 through, say, 1966, were more likely to have heard and/or seen Stewart's version of the Trio; it was younger sounding, too, because Stewart was younger and raised on rock and roll. And what it may have lacked in Guard's precision and intellectual bite, it more than made up for in spirit and musicality.

Stewart first got a taste of Frank's iron-fisted control—and wrath—during the orchestral overdub session of *Something Special*, the Trio's third album with Stewart in April 1962. "We rehearsed and recorded the album as if it were going to be just an ordinary album," Stewart remembered, "and we went back home and didn't hear anything about the strings. So I called Voyle Gilmore and he said, 'Oh yeah, we're doing the strings tomorrow night.' So I said, 'Voyle, I'm coming down,' and I got with [arranger] Jimmy Haskell, who's a very nice guy. And some of the stuff was real movie score stuff; he had a lot of female voices, and I said, 'Jimmy this is really not indicative of what we do, but this new way will work.' He was very cooperative and couldn't be more patient or more inclined to do the right thing. And I flew back to San Francisco and Frank got me on the phone and just raked me over the coals: 'Who do you think you are going down there and being at that session?!' It was the corruption of power, of who the Trio *really* was, of me being the new guy they gave a break to—a consciousness that I would say still exists to a large degree to this day in many of the factions of the Trio. Frank was saying, 'You might make the records, but you aren't in charge.' Little incidents like that were milestones to me saying I'm leaving the group, that's it."[48]

It is entirely understandable that *control* was paramount in Frank's mind and managerial style, given what he, Shane, and Reynolds had gone through to keep control and ownership of The Kingston Trio the year before. No one individual would ever wield that kind of power over the Trio again, no matter how seemingly indispensable their talent. Werber, by nature, was a take-charge executive, used to being the boss and mentor of the group, setting the guidelines and, occasionally, the fines that shaped their ascent to stardom. And while it may seem that Werber's obsession with control was personally directed at Stewart, it was not personal per se. No matter who might have filled Guard's position they would have been "the new boy," constantly reminded that they could have been anyone. Werber wasn't so control oriented, however, that he wouldn't negotiate. He was a master of negotiation as the Trio's lopsided final recording contract with Universal (Decca) would later prove. But he was always determined to win.

After *Close-Up*, *College Concert*, and *New Frontier*, one would assume that Stewart finally would realize how important he had become to the Trio in terms of material, arrangements, and the sound, and that he was in a good position to push back and renegotiate. "Well, I was pretty dumb at that point," he said, "I've never been known as the brightest guy in town. Frank would say, 'You know, John, you don't want to spend money on a lawyer, use Sidney [Rudy, the Trio's lawyer] he's great.' So my lawyer was the Trio's lawyer!!"[49] At one point Stewart decided to leave the Trio to sing with John Phillips and Scott McKenzie in The Journeymen, but that might not have been so easy to do.

While Stewart and John Phillips had earlier been writing partners on several tunes that were recorded by The Kingston Trio, as well as some that were submitted solely under Phillips's name, there is some confusion as to exactly what Phillips's relationship with The Kingston Trio was all about. Ostensibly, Phillips and his group, The Journeymen, had come to the attention of Frank Werber and Rene Cardenas via Bert Block at ITA whom The Journeymen approached in New York looking for a manager on the advice of Dick Weissman, the group's banjo player. Weissman said Phillips was among several people "floated" as a possible replacement for Guard, but that eventually John Stewart was selected.

Yet Phillips said that Werber had already chosen him as the replacement: "Werber's master plan was for me to write songs and join the Kingston Trio, Scott to open for them as a solo act apart from The Journeymen, and Dick to add his instrumental virtuosity to the Trio's mellow sound."[50] Neither Shane, Reynolds, nor Stewart ever mentioned Phillips as being among the few who auditioned to be Dave Guard's replacement. Allan

Shaw surmised that perhaps Werber's "master plan" for John Phillips may have been predicated on John Stewart not being picked and was in fact master plan B (for backup). John Phillips reportedly fell out of favor with Frank Werber, who refused to audition the newly formed Mamas and Papas prior to their signing with Lou Adler. "We tried to get in to see my old buddy Werber," Phillips wrote. "He was too busy for us now. The We Five were breaking big with 'You Were on My Mind' and he made it clear that we were not on his."[51]

In Stewart's ongoing dissatisfaction with Werber and the Trio, he continued to look for different opportunities. He would spend an entire day rehearsing with John Denver in November 1964, while the Trio were playing at the Cherry Hill Arena in New Jersey, to see if the two could sing and write together as a duo. It didn't work out, although they remained friends. What it *did* do, however, was shake up the Trio, and John was able to negotiate a percentage of the net ("minimal at best," he would say), but it created a lot of resentment from Nick and Bob in the process. Despite getting the percentage, Stewart was never a real participating partner. He got none of the big money, had no stake in the Trident restaurant, Columbus Tower, or any of the Trio's real estate properties. "I just wasn't bright enough to know my own strength and the cards I was holding," Stewart admitted, "because at that point I was still a big fan of the Trio with Dave and still played those records and still felt that I was a lesser member. I was very isolated, but it was self-imposed isolation."[52]

The Kingston Trio with Stewart did very well over the next six years. While "the glory days" of automatic gold records, magazine feature spreads, and Trio-mania were waning, the group continued to tour extensively, often playing to sold-out audiences in such prestigious venues as Carnegie Hall, the Hollywood Bowl, Forest Hills, Notre Dame, UCLA and top Ivy League schools, as well as many of the country's best clubs. They also played at the White House and helped open the London Hilton at Conrad Hilton's personal invitation. They were still hit makers, too—"Greenback Dollar," "Where Have All the Flowers Gone," "Reverend Mr. Black," and "Desert Pete" all charted, and some broke the Top 20. But Guard wasn't forgotten. In 1962, Capitol released *The Best of The Kingston Trio* with ten of its twelve cuts from the Guard-era Trio. The album reached number seven on the Billboard charts and remained on the charts for two years. In 1964, it was awarded a RIAA Gold Record Award for sales of over $1 million wholesale, making it the Trio's all-time best-selling album (today the certification is different, requiring sales of $500,000 to qualify for gold). Two more "best of" editions would follow, the second featuring the

Stewart Trio in front of the hungry i on the cover and the third featuring a close-up photo of the Guard Trio. The Stewart Trio were still turning out an average of three albums a year for Capitol, with *New Frontier, #16*, and *Time to Think* easily among The Kingston Trio's finest work.

One of the more fortuitous consequences of the dissolution of the Guard Trio and the resultant exit of bassist David Wheat was the arrival of Dean Edwin Reilly as the Trio's replacement bassist. Like his predecessor, Dean Reilly is an accomplished jazz bassist—as well as a classical, folk, pop, and big band bassist. He has performed and/or recorded with some of the biggest names in jazz and pop, including Frank Sinatra, Ella Fitzgerald, Peggy Lee, Vince Guaraldi, Chet Baker, and Thelonious Monk. Originally a trumpet player, he took up the bass in college, majoring in music at the College of Puget Sound (now University of Puget Sound) near his native Puyallup, Washington. He had long been a fixture on the North Beach jazz scene, and was the house bass player at the Purple Onion as well as the hungry i where he met the Trio in the late 1950s. "We all crossed paths a lot," Reilly said, "so they kind of knew who I was and I got a call to try out. I agreed to do two or three weeks with them to see how we liked each other. My first concert with them was in Seattle and I went onstage cold not knowing anything and just winged it. I figured if I can get through that, I can get through anything."[53] Reilly did fine and went on to Harrah's in Tahoe with the Trio in March of 1962. A month later he was in Capitol's Studio B backing them on *Something Special* and remained their bass player until the group retired in 1967.

When the Trio left Capitol for Decca in the fall of 1964, the group took over its own production by building a studio in the basement of Columbus Tower. Much smaller than Capitol's Studio B, Columbus Recording Studio was nonetheless state of the art for the times, although it took a good deal of time and money to work out technical problems. George Yanok remembered it as being a really good studio, intimate and well equipped. It had redwood paneling and indirect lighting, and a comfortable booth—but it was tiny. While Hank McGill was the studio's resident engineer, Pete Abbott was brought in from Los Angeles to engineer several sessions and hopefully apply some of the old Capitol magic. But Pete couldn't bring Capitol's echo chambers, and the flatness of their first Decca album, *Nick-Bob-John*, made it readily apparent. The echo came back, however, on subsequent releases.

In addition to their own studio, the Trio recorded at Coast Recorders on Bush Street in San Francisco, as well as Coast's sister studio in Las Vegas, United Recording Corporation of Nevada, which they used during a three-week engagement at the Riviera Hotel. While appearing in Houston at the Shamrock Hilton's Cork Club, they recorded at ACA (Audio Corporation of America) Recording Studios, Bill Hollman's legendary Texas R & B and blues citadel (B. B. King, Lightnin' Hopkins, Johnny Winter, Little Richard, Clarence "Gatemouth" Brown).

During the Guard years, the Trio routinely appeared on numerous national television variety shows, with only one "serious" dramatic appearance on Playhouse 90, *Rumors of Evening*, and even that was tied to their music. In the Stewart years, their TV agent, Jimmy Saphier, continued to place the Trio on TV variety shows, as well as negotiate comedic and dramatic roles in *Mrs. G. Goes to College, Convoy*, and a pilot for their own proposed series, *Young Men in a Hurry*. Shane and Stewart recalled a hilarious sequence in *Convoy* where the three are wearing combat helmets during an "air raid on the ship" and couldn't keep a straight face for dozens of takes. "They'd shoot a water machine that was supposed to be the water coming over the hull," said Shane. "And the thing would make a splash and we'd duck at it!" The director was getting madder by the minute, and the harder they'd try not to laugh, the more they would. "Nick and I were trying to be good and not laugh," Stewart said, "but then we'd look over at Bobby with this dumb helmet on and he'd be grinning and we'd just scream."[54]

Young Men in a Hurry was written specifically for the Trio by Dorothy Cooper Foote, produced by Frank Pittman and Andy White and directed by Norman Abbott, whose credits included *The Jack Benny Show, Sanford and Son, Leave It to Beaver, McHale's Navy, Get Smart*, and other top television series. The pilot was shot in 1963 primarily at Paramount Studios in Los Angeles, with exteriors filmed in Phoenix. The storyline involved three young men—a banker (Bob Shane), a real estate salesman (Nick Reynolds), and a lawyer (John Stewart)—who share an apartment at the Martinique (a real place in Scottsdale, Arizona) on Camelback Road and play music together for fun and as a way to make extra money. The cast also included veteran actors Nina Shipman and Ted Knight (*The Mary Tyler Moore Show*), who played Bob's parents. The Trio's acting is surprisingly good, especially Shane's, while Reynolds's and Stewart's hilarious out-of-control washing machine scene is classic Lucy and Ethel. "That was Norman Abbott," said Shane. "He was Jack Benny's producer and he was a comedian also. He walked us through that whole thing, telling us what to do right from the side of the camera and made actors out of us."[55] Off screen, a real uproarious scene was played out in the hotel's restaurant, as Stewart remembered.

"The CBS executives came to Phoenix—Hunt Stromberg, Jr., who was the head guy, and Norman Abbott who was the director, a terrific guy," Stewart recounted. "Norman Abbott had earlier made the mistake of asking Bobby and me if we wanted to see the dailies from the day before. We did, and I just hated myself! And, of course, Bobby loved himself because he looked good. So we're sitting there at the table with Hunt Stromberg and Norm Abbott and Bobby's leaning back in his chair and he made a remark to me to the effect of 'I look great and you look like crap,' so I took my foot and pulled Bobby's chair out from under him and he went over. I jumped on top of him and we went across the restaurant and I was holding Bobby against the wall just about to crack him one and we were separated. Bobby was just laughing, and Frank's like, 'Oh God here we are—in front of the CBS brass!!' We'd had a few drinks at the time."[56]

The proposed series could well have been a hit, but not without consequences. "It would have changed us from what we were to actors," said Shane. "And if it had gone over well, it would've made us a shit pile of money. So we were really torn. But they said we'd have to live twenty-two weeks out of the year in Los Angeles and eight weeks out of the year in Phoenix. We were night people, and we didn't want to get up early to be on the set at 5 a.m. We were San Francisco people, you know?"[57]

The San Francisco part would change for Shane in 1963, when his wife wanted to move the family to Atlanta because, Shane said, the couple was having marital problems. For a while, Bob kept their house in Tiburon and commuted between San Francisco and "Kingston Farm," their Alpharetta, Georgia, horse farm north of Atlanta. Eventually he sold the Tiburon house, making only infrequent trips back to San Francisco for Trio business meetings or flying directly to wherever the start of a tour might be. While this arrangement may have improved domestic harmony, Shane said the distance impacted his relationship with Nick Reynolds and ultimately the quality of their albums. Throughout most of the Trio's history, selecting songs for albums was a fairly democratic process: each member would bring in tunes for consideration that the group would play and assess, then finally arrive at a playlist. If any member didn't like a particular song it would be eliminated from consideration. But after the first few albums finding new material became harder, especially in light of Capitol's overly ambitious recording demands of three albums per year. Stewart's arrival was a godsend; he was a prolific songwriter and a very good one, the source of some of the Trio's most memorable songs, including "One More Town," "Chilly Winds," "Honey, Are You Mad at Your Man," "Molly Dee," "New Frontier," and a catalog of many more. But not every Stewart song was a winner in Shane's book. And John's growing influence on Nick resulted in the Trio recording more and more of John's songs, many of which Bob didn't like.

"It had nothing to do with my not being a friend of Nick's or not liking John or anything like that," Shane said. "It had to do with John writing material every day. He wrote *all* the time. And so any songwriter who writes good songs thinks that everybody should love every song he does. And that's what John was like. He'd say, 'Here's a great song,' and if you didn't like it, he'd get miffed as hell. But because of the fact that I was on the other side of the country and was living there, being there all the time, Nick got tighter and tighter with John and we started doing more of John's songs. And if I didn't like it, it was already sort of written in stone because Nick had already said okay to John. A perfect example is the last album we did, *Children of the Morning*."[58] Eight of the album's twelve songs were Stewart compositions.

Stewart didn't care for the title "The New Boy," a term that followed him throughout his years in the Trio and beyond. But it is used here with utmost respect. Baby boomers felt an affinity with John Stewart for the very reason that he *was* the new boy, just as they were new to the Trio. What's more, he was *their* boy, one of *them* in their favorite group. The Guard Trio was your big brother's or big sister's Kingston Trio—or maybe even your parents' Kingston Trio. But if you were in high school in the early to mid-1960s, the Stewart Trio was *your* Kingston Trio.

Stewart remained a huge fan of Guard even after he joined the Trio, and it is not surprising that he and Guard were friendly over the years. Stewart was a worthy successor to Guard, and one must believe that even Guard might acknowledge it with a "Well done, my Captain" (to borrow one his favorite sayings).

"He just loved to be around Dave," said Buffy Stewart. "Dave was his hero—as a writer, and as a guitar player, as a banjo player; he just wanted to be like Dave Guard. And we would go to Dave's house a lot and this is when Dave was doing the Colour Guitar. He was living up near Palo Alto, and he had all these phrases that were just so far out that John loved! Dave was a totally cerebral guy and into music and strings and colors and notes and just really into the musical aspects of songs. You know tearing the song apart, analyzing it, rather than just the fun of the song—which is what John brought to the Trio. John brought the fun back."[59]

John Stewart certainly did that and much more. But perhaps the most valid—and meaningful—acknowledgment of Stewart's contribution to the Kingston Trio legacy came from Bobby Shane himself:

"Nothing can compare with the original group. And then again, nothing can compare with the Trio with Stewart."[60]

NOTES

1. Roger McGuinn, interview with the author, Windemere, FL, March 2, 2010.

2. McGuinn, interview with the author.

3. Don MacArthur, interview with the author, Novato, CA, February 4, 2010.

4. John Stewart, interview with the author, San Francisco, CA, December 3, 1983.

5. John Stewart, interview with the author, Novato, CA, April 6, 2001.

6. J. Stewart, interview with the author, April 6, 2001.

7. J. Stewart, interview with the author, April 6, 2001.

8. J. Stewart, interview with the author, April 6, 2001.

9. J. Stewart, interview with the author, April 6, 2001.

10. George Yanok, interview with the author, Nashville, TN, October 26, 2003.

11. Yanok, interview with the author.

12. J. Stewart, interview with the author, December 3, 1983.

13. J. Stewart, interview with the author, April 6, 2001.

14. J. Stewart, interview with the author, April 6, 2001.

15. J. Stewart, interview with the author, April 6, 2001.

16. J. Stewart, interview with the author, April 6, 2001.

17. J. Stewart, interview with the author, April 6, 2001.

18. Nick Reynolds, interview with the author, Seminole, FL, October 6, 1986.

19. J. Stewart, interview with the author, April 6, 2001.

20. J. Stewart, interview with the author, April 6, 2001.

21. J. Stewart, interview with the author, April 6, 2001.

22. J. Stewart, interview with the author, April 6, 2001.

23. J. Stewart, interview with the author, April 6, 2001.

24. J. Stewart, interview with the author, April 6, 2001.

25. J. Stewart, interview with the author, April 6, 2001.

26. J. Stewart, interview with the author, April 6, 2001.

27. J. Stewart, interview with the author, April 6, 2001.

28. George Yanok, John Stewart eulogy, Malibu, CA, 2008.

29. J. Stewart, interview with the author, December 3, 1983.

30. Bob Shane, interview with the author, Phoenix, AZ, April 6, 2009.

31. J. Stewart, interview with the author, December 3, 1983.

32. Bob Shane, interview with the author, Phoenix, AZ, July 20, 2001.

33. Joan Reynolds, interview with the author, Sausalito, CA, August 16, 2010.

34. Shane, interview with the author, July 20, 2001. Bob Shane, interview with the author, Phoenix, AZ, April 7, 2009

35. J. Stewart, interview with the author, April 6, 2001.

36. J. Stewart, interview with the author, April 6, 2001.

37. J. Stewart, interview with the author, April 6, 2001.

38. N. Reynolds, interview with the author.

39. J. Stewart, interview with the author, April 6, 2001.

40. Frank Werber, interview with the author, Silver City, NM, April 17, 1984.

41. Werber, interview with the author.

42. Dave Guard, interview with the author, Los Altos, CA, November 29, 1983.

43. Frank Werber, interview with Richard Johnston, January 18, 1974, from the Dave Guard and Richard Johnston Kingston Trio collection of materials, 1956–1986, University Manuscript Collections, University of Wisconsin, Milwaukee.

44. Guard, interview with the author.

45. Werber, interview with the author.

46. Buffy Stewart, interview with the author, San Anselmo, CA, August 17, 2010.

47. Werber, interview with the author.

48. J. Stewart, interview with the author, December 3, 1983.

49. J. Stewart, interview with the author, December 3, 1983.

50. John Phillips with Jim Jerome, *Papa John: A Music Legend's Shattering Journey through Sex, Drugs and Rock 'n' Roll* (New York: Dolphin-Doubleday, 1986), 101.

51. Phillips, *Papa John*, 136.

52. J. Stewart, interview with the author, December 3, 1983.

53. Dean Reilly, interview with the author, San Francisco, CA, September 2, 2007.

54. Bob Shane, interview with the author, Phoenix, AZ, April 7, 2009; J. Stewart, interview with the author, April 6, 2001.

55. Shane, interview with the author, April 7, 2009.

56. J. Stewart, interview with the author, April 6, 2001.

57. Shane, interview with the author, April 7, 2009.

58. Bob Shane, interview with the author, Phoenix, AZ, October 21, 2007.

59. B. Stewart, interview with the author.

60. Shane, interview with the author, October 21, 2007.

10

FOLKIER THAN THOU

Nick Reynolds was once asked what he felt was The Kingston Trio's greatest achievement, its lasting legacy. "We got America up and singing," he answered without hesitation.

Few would disagree, and most would say they haven't stopped singing since. The Kingston Trio's grip on the national psyche was *that* strong. The easy accessibility of their music, just three chords and you're home, empowered legions of Americans to pick up a guitar and sing to their heart's—and conscience's—content.

"They sent more people to banjos and guitars than anything else in the 200 years of this country," said Frank Werber. "They did something musically that broke the barrier down for more people. Perhaps they didn't stimulate your social consciousness or your libido to the extent of Bob Dylan, but maybe they gave you the realization that it wasn't impossible for you to take a guitar, play it, and sing. It gave hope, voice and music to millions."[1]

It wasn't the old "Go Tell Aunt Rhody" type nuggets, either. The Trio offered a wonderfully diverse menu of traditional and ethnic music that many listeners had never heard before—traditional American folk tunes, country, blues, bluegrass, gospel, Appalachian and Scottish ballads, Tahitian and Hawaiian chants, Irish drinking songs, sea chanteys, Mexican folk tunes, English dance hall numbers, Union songs, broadsides, calypso, jazz, Broadway show tunes, even slightly bawdy songs. And while traditionalists would criticize the Trio for bastardizing what they regarded as their sacred folk idiom, it would be tough to deny that The Kingston Trio were one of the greatest catalysts for the discovery, revival, and growth of folk music in America, traditional or otherwise.

Many serious folk music fans may never have investigated and discovered traditional folk music if The Kingston Trio hadn't first piqued their interest. Yet, oddly, once they heard the "real thing," many of these folkies were quick to criticize The Kingston Trio as being phony and commercial, disavowing ever being Kingston Trio fans, let alone acknowledging that the Trio pointed them in the traditional direction.

The Trio never minded honest criticism; they were what they were— three young guys right out of college who made it very big, very quickly. And although they had worked hard to become successful, some critics felt that no real dues had been paid. To go from singing in beer joints around Stanford to being the darlings of San Francisco and New York was an enormous leap. In less than a year, The Kingston Trio had crowds lined up around the block at the hungry i and Blue Angel, while some folk artists gritted it out for years, scuffling to just stay alive, never once compromising themselves or their music.

Moreover, the early 1960s saw the emergence of a number of social protest movements that would steadily grow to national—even global— proportions, addressing serious social issues and problems, accompanied by serious acts of violence and civil disobedience. Yet the music of The Kingston Trio was usually not serious, nor did the Trio intend it to be, unlike some other folk artists who spoke out—and sang out—about such issues and assumed for themselves the mantle of leadership, and relevance, in the folk community.

The first Trio was formed in the late 1950s, seemingly the "happy days" of economic stability and conservative social values. From the outset they were determined to not do any political or controversial material, even though they often appeared with political comedians. They were *entertainers*, not spokesmen or preachers, nor did they see themselves as folk singers, for that matter. They were singers of folk-type material, along with many other genres of music. And while they were heavily influenced by the music of The Weavers and The Gateway Singers and may have been sympathetic to their social and political beliefs, the Trio did not share either group's politics, at least publicly. Professionally they were neither conservative nor liberal. They were neutral. They didn't sing protest songs because they had nothing they wished to protest, and for them to have done so would have gone against their better instincts. Yet without consciously trying, The Kingston Trio created a musical paradigm—a performing model—for the acoustic, urban folk singer–based protest movement of the 1960s. And while they definitely delivered the medium, they did not deliver a message relevant to the changing times.

This does not mean that The Kingston Trio were passé. They were one of the major concert draws in the industry, playing to sold-out venues across the country, from clubs to concert halls to the White House. Although groups such as Peter, Paul and Mary came to present formidable competition to the Trio by the early 1960s, you'd never know it from the Trio's relentless concert schedule.

Some performers synonymous with both traditional and urban folk music would use the stage created by The Kingston Trio to lobby for social change and as a springboard for their own careers. Joan Baez was one of them. According to Nick Reynolds, Baez had sought out the Trio for career advice in 1959 after the first Newport Folk Festival where both had appeared. Following the Festival, the Trio had moved on to Storyville in Harwich, Massachusetts, a Cape Cod jazz nightclub owned by Newport Jazz and Folk Festival founder George Wein. Sitting at one of the front row tables were Baez, her sister Mimi, and their mother. Joan came back stage between sets on two nights asking the Trio for advice: What should she do about a manager? Should she change her style? How should she go about getting a record deal? The boys immediately became experts, each giving their own personal formula for success. One thing they all emphasized though was *don't change a thing*. "Whatever you were doing the other night in Newport, *keep doing it*." Although relatively new in the business themselves, the Trio recognized that the key to their success was that they operated on the "natch." They were true to their own feelings and never let anyone manipulate them or their music to be otherwise. It was sound advice, ratified by their enormous success. Although Baez was totally unknown at the time, she was a star. Bob Shane, Nick Reynolds, and Dave Guard were absolutely mesmerized by this young beauty with the angelic voice. "We knew we were in the company of greatness," Reynolds remembered. She couldn't have been more innocent, completely oblivious to the sensation she had just created. They even gave her their accountant's and lawyer's phone numbers, as well. She thanked them profusely.[2]

Surprisingly, Baez would later deny ever having met The Kingston Trio when Nick Reynolds reintroduced himself to her at a party at Harold Levanthal's uptown apartment several years later. By this time she was a folk music icon. Nick hadn't seen her since their talk at Storyville and went over to say hello. "Hi, Joan, I'm Nick Reynolds of The Kingston Trio? Remember we met at Storyville a few years ago?"[3] According to Reynolds she turned around and said, "I don't believe we've *ever* met," then turned her back and continued talking with her circle of admirers. Reynolds never forgot the incident, and perhaps Joan never forgot it either because to her credit she more than made up for it in her 1987 autobiography, *And a Voice to Sing With: A Memoir.*

"Travelling across the country with my mother and sisters, we heard the commercial songs of the budding folk music boom for the first time, the Kingston Trio's 'Tom Dooley' and 'Scotch and Soda,'" Baez revealed. "Before I turned into a snob and learned to look down upon all commercial folk music as bastardized and unholy, I loved the Kingston Trio. When I became one of the leading practitioners of 'pure folk,' I still loved them, but kept their albums stuffed at the back of the rack."[4]

Over the years many others would also admit that they had actually listened and learned about folk music from The Kingston Trio, including Bob Dylan. "I liked The Kingston Trio," Dylan said in *Chronicles*, volume 1. "Even though their style was polished and collegiate, I liked most of their stuff anyway. Songs like 'Getaway John,' 'Remember the Alamo,' 'Long Black Rifle.' There was always some kind of folk song breaking through."[5] He also admired the believability of the Trio's music. "Folk music, if nothing else, makes a believer out of you. I believed Dave Guard in The Kingston Trio, too. I believed that he would kill or already did kill poor Laura Foster. I believed he'd kill someone else, too. I didn't think he was playing around."[6]

Some performers, such as Doc Watson, were straightforward in their appreciation of The Kingston Trio, telling *Sing Out!* magazine, "I'll tell you who pointed all our noses in the right direction, even the traditional performers. They got us interested in trying to put the good stuff out there—the Kingston Trio. They got me interested in it!"[7]

There were many others who may have shared Doc's opinion, but wouldn't admit it for fear of being viewed as less than an "authentic" or "commercial."

The commercial argument rarely received the close scrutiny it required for validity. Virtually all folk music is commercial and always has been—from the village balladeer in medieval times to New York subway buskers with open guitar cases to Bob Dylan playing in a massive amphitheater; rarely does anybody do it for free, even if it's a benefit.

The problem with The Kingston Trio was that they were perhaps *too* commercial, a function of the enormous economic power they wielded as one of the leading musical groups in the world. The offers from advertisers were continuous, many of which they turned down. But when 7UP approached the group in June of 1959 to do a series of print, radio, and television spots for $255,000, including some with veteran comedic actor

Buster Keaton, they readily accepted. After all, what could be more fun and wholesome and downright American than 7UP?

Writer Ben Blake described some of the radio spots thinly disguised as five-minute "programs":

"Announcer Ken Capenter would introduce the 'program,' the Trio would perform the 7UP jingle ('Nothing does it like 7UP'), Ken would chat with Dave, Nick and Bob on some hopefully humorous topic for about 30 seconds, one of the group's album tracks would play, followed by a 7UP commercial, then the best part—a Trio song newly recorded with augmented lyrics that tied 7UP into the story, lasting anywhere from twenty seconds to one minute—followed by an outro by Ken ('join us next time . . .'), and the Trio's closing theme for 7UP."[8]

"It was a good thing for us," said Bob Shane of the 7UP deal. "It got our name out there on a large scale with a popular soft drink. And the stuff was clever. I thought it was great. It was needed."[9]

Reynolds, however, thought differently. "I think it may have been one of the first major mistakes we made," he said. "It had a lot to do with our loss of credibility to the college audience. To make fools of ourselves in commercials, singing our material—songs we held near and dear—and changing the lyrics ("We're thirsty now but we won't be thirsty long"—to the tune of "Worried Man"), and doing it in a cartoon fashion dressing up in clown suits and space suits and in drag. It turned off a lot of our old fans. Not the purists—I'm talking about the *fans*. I don't care about the purists, you know, that just gives them more fuel for their venom. I've thought a lot about it over the years. Certainly, it was financially an extra bonus over and above the career we had. Big money. We were all thrilled at it. But I don't think we thought about it enough. We sort of disregarded that and put it in the back of our minds. We lost a *lot* of credibility doing that."[10]

Many people incorrectly assumed that the folk music revival, including the protest movement, was totally altruistic. But folk music was also big entertainment business, very well orchestrated and directed by incredibly powerful music publishers, managers, bookers, club owners, record companies, and performers, many of them in New York. The practice of changing authentic folk music to make it more palatable or marketable to the masses was not new. The Weavers did it, The Kingston Trio did it, and there where were plenty of other guilty parties within the folk music revival who did it, some more subtly than others. Call it borrowing or adapting or interpreting or revising, it's all the same thing—*changing*—and the "folk" had been doing it long before the revival.

Change or variation is an inherent part of the "folk process," as Pete Seeger called it. "My father, who was an old musicologist, said, 'Don't bother arguing is it folk music or is it not folk music. It's a waste of time,'" Seeger recalled. "Just know that the folk process has been going on for thousands of years in every field of human endeavor. Cooks rearrange old recipes for new stomachs, lawyers rearrange old laws for new citizens, and musicians have throughout recorded history and probably before then, rearranged old musical ideas for new ears. The actual basic allegory or whatever you want to call it, the poetic thing of 'Where Have All the Flowers Gone,' I now think may be prehistoric because it makes an analogy between flowers and girls and men going to war. Just a year ago, someone sent me a Yiddish song with that exact same plot in it—and it had been collected 150 years ago in the nineteenth century."[11]

The Kingston Trio's intention in changing song lyrics was admittedly financially driven, but they loved the music as well, and they were superb at performing it. But once the "commercial" tag is hung, it's difficult to shake the only-in-it-for-the money onus.

"That's what happens when you're that commercial," said Don McLean. "The Kingston Trio were at the top of their game. They shouldn't have made any bones about it and just rocked on. It was that whole idea in the folk world of whether you were a 'sell-out' or not. I don't know how that whole thing got started. It's an image thing. They all want success."[12]

As for their adapting older songs, even those tunes that the Trio had allegedly stolen, were invariably something somebody else had changed before them. Reynolds laughingly remembered receiving a letter from New York song publisher Howie Richman telling the Trio to pay up on "When the Saints Go Marching In" because they had used too much of The Weavers' arrangement. "We sang a couple of The Weavers' verses by mistake," Reynolds said. "Had we changed a couple of verses or one more verse they would have probably been okay. The technicalities of how many lines or verses or words are 'borrowed' is very specific in copyright law. The Weavers did not write 'When the Saints Go Marching In.' That was their *adaptation*. But the Trio sang enough of their adaptation to where they could lay claim to it—and rightfully so. If you look up 'When the Saints Go Marching In' it's classified as public domain. But you better watch out where you heard it," Reynolds advised, "because the arrangement may already have been changed from the original."[13]

As the Trio's popularity grew, any song they recorded for which they claimed authorship was immediately challenged, especially public domain songs. The bigger the hit song, the bigger the number of challenges. Reynolds said that literally hundreds—even thousands—of people would contest these public domain songs: "They had nothing to lose, and everything to gain."[14] There was huge money at stake when the Trio recorded *any* song, either as a single or on one of their best-selling albums. To protect themselves from costly litigation, they wisely retained the services of Harold Barlow, a New York composer, author, and plagiarism expert who reviewed all prospective Trio tunes to determine whether they were in the public domain or copyrighted. Barlow was recognized as *the* authority in plagiarism, serving as an expert witness in numerous federal trials for over four decades. The Kingston Trio also assigned specific staff members at their publishing companies to check every song before it was released to build a case in the event of a challenge. "That's the name of the game," Reynolds said unapologetically. "They were ready to pounce on us because they knew that's where the pay ticket was."[15]

With the enormous success of the Trio's first few albums, the search for new songs became relentless. Every writer and publisher in the business seemed to be pitching songs to the group—and that was *very* good business for folk music in general. Yet The Kingston Trio were looked down upon by many in the folk community, even resented for helping folk songwriters and musicians by singing their songs. They were viewed as phonies who had no business singing "their" music. But in truth, the Trio never tried to be anything but what they were. They never called themselves protest singers, or even folksingers for that matter. They said they were just entertainers, period. Politically, they steadfastly maintained their neutrality as a group. Individually, they could take any position or espouse any belief they wished.[16]

During the Trio's appearance at the first Newport Folk Festival, Al Grossman, the manager of Chicago's famed Gate of Horn and organizer of the festival with George Wein got into a shoving match with Frank Werber because he didn't feel that The Kingston Trio had any "right" to be there and didn't mind telling him so in the rudest of terms. A few years later, the Trio's publisher received a letter from Grossman imploring the group to record songs written by his new client, Bob Dylan. It was perfectly all right to submit material to The Kingston Trio to record and make you lots of money, but not to acknowledge the group as anything but illegitimate pariahs of folk music. "We'd be sitting in clubs down in the Village," said Reynolds, "and people would sneak up to us and whisper, 'Hey man, would you record this song of mine? I really need the money. Just don't tell anybody I asked you to do it.'"[17]

As for folksinger, author, and radio show host Oscar Brand, while he could be stingingly critical of the Trio, he was essentially positive: "Their songs were copied from records of folk performers, often with the regional accents," Brand wrote in 1962. "Nevertheless, Dave Guard reported, 'When we find something we like, we adapt it. It may not be ethnic when we get through with it, but after all—what is ethnic? Why should we try to imitate Lead Belly's inflections when we have so little in common with his background and experience?' The Trio's use of other singers' material has resulted in many legal tangles, but most observers will agree that they have shown excellent taste in their choices. That their success is not a fly-by-night manifestation has been shown by the continued sale of their records. Hundreds of imitators have appeared and disappeared, proving the original had a very special quality which is not easily copied."[18]

Even the Trio's friend, Newport Jazz and Folk Festival founder organizer George Wein, would say years later that he had been "led astray" by The Kingston Trio, because *he* had booked them to boost attendance in 1959. "I felt that they would give a crucial boost to the fledgling [folk] festival; and they did, drawing more people to Newport than any other group." He also recounted how his Storyville club on the Cape couldn't turn a profit booking such greats as Erroll Garner, Benny Goodman, Louis Armstrong, Duke Ellington, Sarah Vaughn, or Ella Fitzgerald, but "we did make money with The Kingston Trio."[19] Yet in the next breath Wein recounted how much he regretted putting The Kingston Trio on before Earl Scruggs at the first Newport Folk Festival. "I am not particularly contrite about including The Kingston Trio in the Jazz Festival, but I'm very sorry that I put them on before Earl Scruggs. For some folk purists, it would take years for me to achieve redemption. Insulting Scruggs, who could be considered the Louis Armstrong of the banjo, was like insulting 'Pops' himself."[20]

Despite Wein's after-the-fact contrition, The Kingston Trio did exactly what George Wein hoped they'd do—ensure success for the maiden 1959 Newport Folk Festival, delivering a wildly enthusiastic crowd estimated at over fifteen thousand for their performance, as one observer wrote:

"The Kingston Trio mounted the stage like returning war heroes, and proceeded to break nine of the ten rules established by the Committee of Old Folk Farts. They hopped and clowned about, sang joyfully, and generally entertained their fans. With banjoes and guitars a-blazing, and voices sounding out in a reckless abandon, the Trio, like any popular act worth its salt, performed favorites like 'M.T.A.' and 'Three Jolly Coachmen.' Who said that folk singers couldn't put on a helluva show? The only sour note rang out due to the absence of 'Tom Dooley'—the absolutely most favorite of all Kingston Trio songs. It wasn't likely they'd forgotten it, which made one a bit suspicious. Perhaps the boys had made a concession to the song's collector, Frank Warner, who'd performed on the Saturday bill. Even without the monster hit, though, the jubilant set created a frenzy unseen since Elvis had entered the army. It would take M.C. Brand fifteen minutes and a promise to sedate the overly animated teenyboppers. If they'd shut the hell up and let Earl Scruggs play, he'd bring the Kingston Trio back for an encore. They cheerfully agreed. Following the banjo pyrotechnics of Earl Scruggs and an encore by the number one folk group in the land, the crowd—slowly at first—began to fan out of the park. No one knew exactly what had happened over the last few days—they were too tired, hungry, and busy thinking about the jobs and commitments they had to return to on Monday morning. But over time, they'd realize that something special had taken place."[21]

The irony of Wein's angst was that country music performers, including Earl Scruggs with whom the Trio were very friendly, were among the Trio's biggest fans—and vice versa. "I love country and western music," Reynolds said, "and I love every one of those cats, they've been straight and great with us. Everywhere." The Trio played the Grand Ole Opry only once, on October 30, 1966, and it was the only time they'd ever heard a standing ovation for someone in The Kingston Trio doing a banjo solo. Stewart was a good banjo player, not a virtuoso, Reynolds explained, but the audience stood up and cheered after his banjo solo, not just the first song, "Hard, Ain't It Hard," but every solo that he did during the entire show. "Oh my god! The most beautiful kind of an audience! This was *the home of country music*, and we had the proper reverence for sure. I was scared shitless, getting out there on the home turf of some the greatest banjo and guitar players in the world." They later toured Japan at the same time as The Browns, Chet Atkins, Ernest Tubb, three or four other country stars, and stayed at the same hotels. "We had more fun!" Reynolds remembered. "Ernie Tubb getting old and drinking and having a good time and saying that he loved us . . . they were so great."[22]

What's more, "Tom Dooley" received a Grammy for the Best Country and Western Record of 1958 because there was no folk category at the time. Shane recalled that country music was at a standstill in sales, and "Tom Dooley" helped revive country music in a big way. And the only person who ever said anything to the Trio about it was Minnie Pearl, who said, "Thank God for the acceptance of that song! I think you've saved country music."[23]

For the most part, The Kingston Trio's manner of dealing with criticism was to ignore it. The Trio's popularity, however, did not shield them from intense jealousy. They were always considered the renegade group from the West Coast, the golden California boys, spoiled brats moving in on the profits, outside of the Greenwich Village clique and therefore outside of the clique's control. Any deference shown to them was because they were too big to ignore—or because they were the "money pot," the group that could make any songwriter wealthy if they chose to record your song. Shane said he and Nick were amazed at the fact that these people were all very nice to them because "they were smart enough to know that we opened up a whole wide thing for them to make money. It was opened up for everybody."[24]

Eventually, a folk group arose out of New York City that could match The Kingston Trio's record sales and concert draws, carefully handpicked and groomed by Albert Grossman. From the outset, Peter, Paul and Mary were viewed as more *authentic* singers of folk songs than The Kingston Trio and viewed by many to be above the commercialism of the folk revival.

"It's been said that we stole 'Where Have All the Flowers Gone' from Peter, Paul and Mary—which is ridiculous," said Reynolds. "They played the song for us in Boston and we loved it immediately, so Noel said, 'We'll give you the lyrics if you'll teach us 'Lemon Tree' and '500 Miles.' Fair enough. We thought 'Flowers' was public domain. They also played 'Puff the Magic Dragon' but wouldn't give us the lyrics because they wanted to record it themselves. We thanked them for 'Flowers,' called Frank Werber to set up a session in New York to record it, and two weeks later we had it out on the market."[25]

What the Trio didn't realize was that "Where Have All the Flowers Gone" was not a public domain song at all. It was a Pete Seeger song, with verses by Joe Hickerson added later. And when the Trio's single of "Flowers" was released in the fall of 1961, the Trio received a call from Pete himself, as he recounted: "My manager, Harold Leventhal, said, 'Pete didn't you write a song called "Where Have All the Flowers Gone?" I said, 'Yeah, three or four years ago.' And he said, 'Did you ever copyright it?' And I said, 'No, I guess I didn't.' He said, 'Well you ought to—The Kingston Trio just recorded it.' Well, I called up the Trio, and they said, 'Oh, Pete we didn't know it was your song. We thought it was an old folk song. We'll take our name off it right away. So it was very nice of them. They could have not known. I had 'abandoned the copyright.' But they didn't bother about that. They took their name off it, and Harold Leventhal published it in my name and son of a gun, that song pays my taxes each year."[26]

The Kingston Trio liked Peter, Paul and Mary very much. They were rivals but they were friends, too, and over the years the Trio saw a lot of the group, even recording Noel and Peter's song "Come On Betty Home," which was written for Noel's wife. They also became their biggest boosters, telling everybody to listen to this wonderful new group, including Mike Wallace, who put them on his television show on the Trio's recommendation. Enrico Banducci gave them their first West Coast booking at the hungry i thanks in part to The Kingston Trio's urging. Nick, Bob, and John especially loved hanging out with Peter because he always had the most beautiful girlfriends.

Peter, Paul and Mary were often compared to The Kingston Trio, although one senses that they were not entirely comfortable with the parallel. In an interview years after the fact, Paul (Noel) Stookey was asked if he agreed with music author Anthony Scaduto's assessment that Grossman had formed Peter, Paul and Mary to be "The Kingston Trio with sex appeal." Stookey answered, "I would say that we probably were in general terms very similar to the Kingston Trio singing some obscure folk music to the general public, and because there was a girl I guess you'd obviously have to say there was sex appeal. I think in terms of how we played our art, we were really into it more musically than the Kingstons were. I had the feeling from the Kingstons prior, during, and after our emergence that they were having a great time, whereas I didn't feel that was the core of what Peter, Paul and Mary was all about."[27]

The Trio were also impressed with another rising star, Bob Dylan, and the power of his lyrics. But the often caustic, dark facade that the early Dylan presented to the world put off many who were sincerely drawn to his talent. Reynolds recalled a tense run-in with Dylan and his manager Al Grossman at the Dugout, a bar/restaurant in the Village where everybody hung out. It was uncomfortable because at the time Reynolds was dating a girl whom Dylan had been involved with until she broke it off. "I walked in and saw Dylan sitting with Al Grossman in the back," Reynolds recounted, "I looked over and said, 'Hi Al' and Grossman said, 'Hi Nick,' but the only remark from Dylan to me was, 'Uh, I never liked you guys personally or musically, but if you hung out with Susan as long as I heard, and were good to her, I guess you're alright.' He didn't even look up. And Grossman sat there with a warm, approving gaze."[28] Reynolds was neither offended nor surprised knowing Grossman's sentiments toward the Trio and the cliquishness of the Village folk music community. Dylan would later say that The Kingston Trio and Odetta had gotten him interested in folk music in the first place. Funny way to thank them.

Socially and politically, the commitments of Peter, Paul and Mary, Bob Dylan, Joan Baez, and other folk performers to civil rights and abhorrence to racial prejudice was enormously important for America in the early 1960s, bringing awareness to social injustice. Many performers did, in fact, risk their careers—and their lives—in the civil rights movement. But not everybody identified with the struggle was as brave as they may have appeared to be. During the Selma Freedom March, a number of well-known entertainers were hustled out of cars and into the lines just in time to be photographed marching to the courthouse in Montgomery. But John Stewart was among those who really did put their necks on the line in Alabama—manning a makeshift press room set up in a bombed-out black church to get the word out to the national news organizations, being chased by white thugs with baseball bats out for blood, and being threatened by the National Guard rattling their rifles at any protester who walked past. Stewart was a true patriot. He was there as an American, not as a representative of The Kingston Trio. No fanfare, no publicity.

Because much of The Kingston Trio's material was apolitical, some incorrectly assumed that its members were devoid of any social consciousness. Years before the protest movement they were among the first performers, folk or otherwise, to build a clause into their concert contract that prohibited segregation at their shows. Shane and Reynolds had witnessed prejudice in the jazz clubs toward black musicians and were appalled by it. Even the big show rooms in Las Vegas and Tahoe practiced segregation with their audiences *and* performers. While the Trio steered clear of the racial or political controversy that had surrounded groups like The Weavers and The Gateway Singers, and which ultimately sidetracked their careers, they had no intention of meekly standing by and tolerating the persecution of others.

In 1963, ABC Television produced a program called *Hootenanny*, featuring popular folk groups and performers, telecast from college campuses around the country. Pete Seeger and The Weavers had been blacklisted because of a congressional witch-hunt in the early 1950s, and ABC chose to continue the blacklist, enraging the folk community in the process. The plan was to boycott *Hootenanny*, and the Trio were asked by Judy Collins to attend a meeting at the Village Gate to lend support. It seems everybody in the New York folk world was there, including The Kingston Trio. At the time, the Trio were the biggest folk act in the country and were counted on to lend credibility and drawing power to the meeting. Reynolds, Shane, and Stewart were more than happy to sign the boycott petition—and they stuck to it. The irony of it was that some of those who attended the meeting and signed the boycott, including Judy Collins, would later appear on *Hootenanny*. She explained her decision by saying that Harold Leventhal (her manager), Jac Holzman (Elektra Records owner and founder), and Pete Seeger had called a subsequent meeting at Leventhal's office to discuss the boycott. They determined that a boycott, rather than protect the growing folk music movement, would put it in terrible jeopardy. "Then Pete Seeger stood up to speak," Collins recalled, "and told those of us gathered that afternoon that *not* doing the show would hurt the entire movement. Pete said the same thing to everyone who was torn about appearing on *Hootenanny*. Pete was always for the singer and the song. 'Doing the show will be good for the music, like nothing else,' he said."[29] Pete was right as was Judy Collins and all the others who appeared on *Hootenanny*. But neither Pete Seeger—nor The Kingston Trio—were ever invited to appear on the show, or any ABC program for that matter, for many years.

John Stewart said that the hypocrisy and folkier-than-thou attitude of some folk purists toward the Trio didn't really bother them. "We might get a little hot under the collar back in our rooms, but we really took it with a grain of salt. And usually the purists were really good friends and we'd have arguments about it, but there was never really any personal rivalry. We all got along really well. It was more of a saving face, a response to their lack of success. It must have upset them because they could play better, they were more musical, but they didn't have that *thing*, see? They couldn't understand it because it was a totally natural thing for Nick and Bobby."[30]

Bob Shane said, "Almost all of the people we ever met in the Village, we were very friendly with. Really, we were the kind of people who said share the wealth. Share the stardom. There's room for everybody. We're into this kind of music now, have a good time. We're just the ones that made it popular.[31]

"What people didn't realize is that we got along with folk singers wonderfully, they were people we had gotten songs from. Theodore Bikel was a dear friend of ours. And Mary Travers and Dave Van Ronk and all those people that used to hang around in the Village were all people that we met in the early days that were happier than hell that we were getting known because we were giving *them* a chance to make some money, too. And I think the only one that said something disparaging was John Jacob Niles, who said, 'They're not folk singers!' That's great because we never said we were!"[32]

It would be difficult for even the most generous observer or fervent apologist to argue that The Kingston Trio played much of a role in the protest movement. That they established the musical format and venue is plenty important enough. Yet in the final analysis, it can be said that The Kingston Trio, as entertainers, did some very positive things for America.

And they *did* record their share of socially relevant material—"Where Have All the Flowers Gone," "Deportee," "Blowing in the Wind" (The Kingston Trio were the first to record it), "Road to Freedom," "If You Don't Look Around," "Ally, Ally, Oxen Free." As far back as the early hungry i days, the Trio were doing "The Merry Minuet," which at the time was considered the ultimate political satire; every rub was in the song—racial rioting, hunger, nuclear warfare. The Trio sang it with a smile and it made some people very nervous in the late 1950s.

"Tijuana Jail" was another satire and based on a very serious and dangerous problem implicitly sanctioned by the Mexican government. For years American tourists would go down to Tijuana and find themselves being thrown in jail for no apparent reason. It was the most blatant kind of shakedown, and if the unfortunate tourist didn't come up with bail, he or she rotted in their cell. The tune was written by country and western songwriter Denny Thompson and given to the Trio while they were appearing in St. Louis. It's based on a true story about a group of American citizens arrested in a Tijuana gambling club who weren't even gambling yet were thrown in jail for more than a week. The song was meant to be a warning, especially to sailors from nearby San Diego who were favorite targets. The song created such controversy that the Mexican government banned it from Mexican stations and record stores and threatened to block the signal of any radio station in the United States that broadcast it near their borders.

On-stage commentary was really the Trio's forte, accounting for a good portion—and appeal—of their shows. Both Guard and Stewart were skilled satirists, and nobody was safe from their probing observations and caustic remarks. In the beginning, the group used commentary simply as filler between songs as they changed instruments or as a bridge to change the mood from a fast shouter to a slow ballad, a technique they picked up from San Francisco musicologist, comic, and Gateway Singers leader Lou Gottlieb, later of The Limeliters. But as the Trio became more exposed to Mort Sahl and Lenny Bruce (both of whom were friends and fellow hungry i performers), they got into the dynamics of live satire and how to use it to bring an audience around to their point of view. In a concert setting, where hundreds or thousands of people have gathered together because they love a performer's music, a warm and trusting psychological bond is formed. Any joke from the stage is laughed at. Any point of view espoused is embraced (at least for the moment). Because an audience knows, loves, and trusts the performer's music, they are often willing to extend that receptiveness to the performer's personal views. The Trio recognized that they had that power, and they sometimes exploited it. But they also recognized that the audience loved them first as entertainers, and had they taken the commentary beyond entertainment, they would have made no impact whatsoever.

"The minute you preach, you've lost them," said Reynolds. Audience mood, the Trio learned, is a very peculiar phenomenon; one bad vibe from the stage can kill an entire performance, and the Trio developed an almost sixth sense about what was appropriate to sing and say and what wasn't. Once in Washington, D.C., they decided not to sing 'Tom Dooley"; they were burnt out on the song and Guard said, "We're so big now we don't have to sing that damn song every show."[33] When they finished the show without singing "Dooley," the audience became hostile—as if they'd been cheated, and the Trio weren't going to get away with it. A few years later, the Trio performed "Hobo's Lullaby" at a Seattle concert and it deflated the mood of the audience. They never did the song in concert again. This may be a democratic society, but not as far as entertainers are concerned.

The Trio also felt that it was equally beneficial to the country to use their talents to reinforce the good things about America. They saw a lot of those good things with the Kennedy administration and tried to align audiences with the spirit of progress instilled by John and Robert Kennedy. In January 1961, they'd been asked to perform at the Kennedy inauguration, but Guard had vetoed the idea. With Stewart in the group, they became the unofficial Kennedy folk group, mostly through Stewart's friendship with Robert Kennedy. They were great pals, and Stewart would visit Kennedy in the Justice Department whenever the Trio played Washington.

The Kennedys were young, bright, and aggressive, a refreshing change from the old order. With the advent of the Peace Corps and the U.S. space program, there was a palpable enthusiasm surging through America brought out by the Kennedy spirit, and the Trio were thrilled to be a part of it. They felt especially close to the space program and the astronauts. In 1962, the Trio were playing at a club in Houston and several of the astronauts were in the audience. After the show they were invited to Scott Carpenter's house and began a friendship that existed for many years.

The Trio were so moved by the Kennedy spirit and style that they titled one of their albums *New Frontier* and dedicated it to the Peace Corps and NASA. It was one of their very best efforts in the studio, with a rousing Kennedyesque anthem entitled "New Frontier" that seemed to capture the Kennedy spirit. Stewart later presented the first copy to President Kennedy at the White House, where the president commented, "My brother tells me this album is great; it's got a helluva title." The two chatted for half an hour, with the president promising to catch the Trio's show that night if he could. "As you know, John, we've been pretty busy around here lately," the president said with a smile.[34]

The Kingston Trio would never repeat the power of *New Frontier* or equal the feelings of optimism, of wanting to strive for excellence that pulsed through them as they recorded that album in the fall of 1962. But they tried.

In the fall of 1963, the group began rehearsals for an album that would eventually be titled *Time to Think*, one of the most poignant albums to come out the Folk era. The group had wanted to do an album of more serious songs, one that answered the critics' charge that they weren't doing anything "socially relevant." They picked songs that were meaningful to each of them personally, reflective songs that had stuck with them emotionally over the years. It definitely wasn't their familiar upbeat fare. Normally, they would have recorded the album at Capitol Records in Los Angeles, but decided to record it in San Francisco at Sound Recorders where they could take their time and give it a hands-on approach.

"We rehearsed some great songs for that album," Reynolds recalled, "some real ballsy stuff—'Deportees,' 'Coal Tattoo,' 'Ally Ally Oxen Free;' I still get chills when I hear Bobby singing 'Seasons in the Sun' because it's so autobiographical and he doesn't realize it. Or John snarling through 'If You Don't Look Around' which he wrote after he came back from Selma."[35]

Emotionally, *Time to Think* was a difficult album for the group to get through, especially for Shane who had moved to Georgia by this time and whose neighbors may not have shared the group's more liberal politics. The three would get together every day in the downstairs den of Reynolds' Sausalito home, work on the songs, and then troop over to Sound Recorders. Mid-morning on November 22, 1963, just as they'd started to rehearse, the news flashed over the television that President Kennedy had been shot in Dallas. Like everyone else in the country, they sat stunned in front of the set until the official notice flashed that the president was dead. "It was like one of *us* had been killed," Stewart remembered.[36]

Two years later, The Kingston Trio were invited to the White House to sing for Lyndon Johnson's "President's Scholars," celebrating the top high school honor students from across the country. They were joined by Leonard Bernstein, Jose Ferrer, Gerry Mulligan, Sidney Poitier, and others who performed on the South Lawn before LBJ, watching from the second floor balcony overlooking the South Lawn. Vietnam was just beginning to tear the country apart, and when it was the Trio's turn to perform, they sang "Where Have All the Flowers Gone," looking right at LBJ.

He didn't bat an eye.

NOTES

1. Frank Werber, interview with Richard Johnston, Sausalito, CA, January 22, 1974, from the Dave Guard and Richard Johnston Kingston Trio collection of materials, 1956–1986, University Manuscript Collections, University of Wisconsin, Milwaukee.

2. Nick Reynolds, interview with the author, Seminole, FL, October 7, 1986.

3. Reynolds, interview with author, October 7, 1986.

4. Joan Baez, *And a Voice to Sing With: A Memoir* (New York: Simon & Schuster, 1987), 49.

5. Bob Dylan, *Chronicles*, vol. 1 (New York: Simon & Schuster, 2004), 32–33.

6. Bob Dylan, *Dylan on Dylan*, ed. Jonathan Cott (London: Hodder & Stoughton Ltd., 2006).

7. "Doc Watson: An Unbroken Circle," *Sing Out!* 44, no. 22 (Winter 2000): 65.

8. Ben Blake, "The 7UP Commercials," *The Kingston Trio:—The Guard Years*, Bear Family Records, BCD 16160 KK, 1997, 6-CD box set book, 96–99.

9. Bob Shane, interview with the author, Phoenix, AZ, April 7, 2009.

10. Nick Reynolds, interview with the author, Seminole, FL, October 6, 1986.

11. Pete Seeger, interview with the author, Beacon, NY, August 31, 2008.

12. Don McLean, interview with the author, Camden, ME, April 23, 2009.

13. Nick Reynolds, interview with the author, Seminole, FL, October 4, 1986.

14. Reynolds, interview with the author, October 4, 1986.

15. Reynolds, interview with the author, October 4, 1986.

16. Reynolds, interview with the author, October 4, 1986.

17. Reynolds, interview with the author, October 4, 1986.

18. Oscar Brand, *The Ballad Mongers: Rise of the Modern Folk Song* (New York: Funk & Wagnalls, 1962), 148.

19. George Wein, *Myself among Others: A Life in Music* (Cambridge, MA: Da Capo Press, 2003), 315, 128–29.

20. Wein, *Myself among Others*, 316.

21. Ronald D. Lankford Jr., *Folk Music USA: The Changing Voice of Protest* (New York: Schirmer Trade Books, 2005), 49–50.

22. Reynolds, interview with the author, October 6, 1986.

23. Bob Shane, interview with the author, Phoenix, AZ, August 22, 2007.

24. Shane, interview with the author, August 22, 2007.

25. Reynolds, interview with the author, October 7, 1986.

26. Seeger, interview with the author.

27. Paul Stookey, interview with Richard Johnston, Blue Falls Springs, ME, July 7, 2007, from the Dave Guard and Richard Johnston Kingston Trio collection of materials, 1956–1986, University Manuscript Collections, University of Wisconsin, Milwaukee.

28. Reynolds, interview with the author, October 7, 1986.

29. Judy Collins, *Sweet Judy Blue Eyes: My Life in Music* (New York: Crown Archetype, 2011), 150.

30. John Stewart, interview with the author, San Francisco, CA, December 3, 1983.

31. Shane, interview with the author, August 22, 2007.

32. Shane, interview with the author, August 22, 2007.

33. Reynolds, interview with the author, October 7, 1986.

34. John Stewart, interview with the author, Malibu, CA, March 4, 1984.

35. Nick Reynolds, interview with the author, Port Orford, OR, November 11, 1983.

36. John Stewart, interview with the author, Novato, CA, April 4, 2001.

11

1750 NORTH VINE STREET

To aficionados of American pop music, and The Kingston Trio in particular, Capitol Studios in the Capitol Records Tower in Hollywood is Mecca: the most revered 5,598 square feet of hit-making recording space on the planet. The Trio's legacy is literally grounded on the strength of its Capitol albums recorded there from 1958 to 1963.

While the Trio occasionally recorded in studios in New York, Houston, San Francisco, and Las Vegas, and later in their own facilities at Columbus Tower in North Beach, none matched the artistic and technical excellence—and *vibe*—of the Capitol Tower recordings. And it had a lot to do with the company that built it.

Capitol Records offered a perfect synergy of hands-on production and state-of-the-art expertise. Unlike the other major record companies of the 1940s—Victor, Decca, and Columbia—the people who founded and ran Capitol came from within the music industry. They included legendary songwriter Johnny Mercer; Glenn Wallichs, founder of Music City, Los Angeles' largest record store; and Buddy DeSylva, head of production at Paramount Pictures and a noted songwriter. Capitol Records opened in 1942 with twenty-five thousand dollars in seed money from DeSylva, with Wallichs in charge of running the business, and Mercer handling Artist & Repertoire (A&R) duties. It was the first record company based on the West Coast.

Over the next three decades, Capitol's roster would grow to include Frank Sinatra, Dean Martin, Nat King Cole, Peggy Lee, Kay Starr, Stan Kenton, Nelson Riddle, Les Paul and Mary Ford, Tennessee Ernie Ford, Stan Freberg, Ray Anthony, Buck Owens, Merle Haggard, Glen Campbell, The Beach Boys, The Beatles, and The Kingston Trio.

England's EMI (Electric & Musical Industries) Music Publishing acquired Capitol Records in 1955, and quickly drew plans for the Capitol

Tower, the label's combination studio and office building at 1750 North Vine Street in Hollywood. Prior to the tower's 1956 opening, Capitol had used several Los Angeles recording studios starting with the C.P. Mac-Gregor Studio on Western Avenue (off Wilshire) and later Radio Recorders; in 1950 it opened its own studio on Melrose Avenue in Hollywood.

Capitol selected Architect Welton Becket to design the Tower as a striking thirteen-story circular office building, the first of its kind in the world. A separate, rectangular ground floor structure that housed the recording department offices, tape-to-disk dubbing rooms, and three recording studios was joined to the completed tower. With its wide curved awnings and a 90-foot rooftop spire, the building resembled (unintentionally) a stack of 45 records and a turntable spindle. At the time, the 150-foot earthquake-resistant structure was the maximum building height allowed in Los Angeles. It instantly became a Hollywood landmark.

But it was what the public couldn't see, the building's studios, partially bunkered below ground level, that made the Capitol Tower extraordinary. The original configuration consisted of two large studios, A and B, a smaller Studio C (used for small-group sessions, jingles, voice-overs, and commercials), and a series of four underground echo chambers. The studios were designed from the ground up by acoustics expert Michael Rettinger and Capitol's chief electronics engineer, Edward Uecke. Anticipating the popularity of stereo, Capitol had carefully studied it and other developing musical and recording trends. They determined that no existing studio design or present recording technology would accommodate this new direction, and Rettinger and Uecke were assigned specific design objectives to meet an ever-changing recording environment. Capitol wanted its new studios to be spacious and well illuminated, with low noise levels, minimal natural reverberation, and highly controllable acoustics, utilizing reliable and versatile recording equipment. They ordered state of the art, and Rettinger and Uecke more than delivered.

Studios A and B were nearly identical in size and appearance, built back to back, with Studio A proportioned eight feet wider to accommodate big orchestras for live sessions and movie soundtrack scoring, although string sessions were done in Studio B as well. "They both had the same boards and same patch bays," said Jay Ranellucci, Capitol engineer. "The only difference was the actual physical size of the studio itself. A was a little larger and configured just slightly different. But the booths were identical. They were mirror images."[1] Each studio was built as a room within a room, with a one-inch air gap separating the outer studio walls of ten-inch poured concrete from an inner, heavily insulated wall. Thick concrete floor slabs "floated" on layers of cork and rubber. The ceilings were suspended from the roof by wire hangers creating a large air space filled with rock-wool insulation. Ceiling-mounted fluorescent lighting strips, notorious for their hum, had their ballasts mounted outside of the studio to remove any electrical noise. The studios were dead quiet, even in noisy downtown Hollywood with the Hollywood Freeway nearby, yet still acoustically alive.

According to Jim Bayless, then head of Capitol's recording department, the main design objective was to control—and *vary*—the studio acoustics to fit any type of music, "tuning the room" to the artist or recording situation. The first task was to make the studios as acoustically neutral as possible. Accordingly, all inner wall surfaces were curved, built with an irregular, serrated geometry to diffuse sound evenly, preventing echoes, dead spots, and other unwanted acoustical problems. In addition, wall and ceiling splays were angled fifteen degrees to further eliminate any large parallel surfaces.

The second task was to build flexibility. Each wall splay was hinged and movable, consisting of two thick, 10 x 3.5 foot plywood panels veneered with birch on one side and acoustical tile on the other. The main purpose of the splays was to control the amount of total reverberation time in each studio. By simply adjusting the panels, engineers could create a hard, reflective surface (the birch side) for a more "live" sound, or a soft, sound-absorptive surface (the acoustic tile side) for a warmer sound. These wall splays, a Capitol Tower studio visual trademark, are clearly visible on the cover photo of the Trio's *Here We Go Again* album, as well as on album covers and session photos for Frank Sinatra, The Beach Boys, Gene Vincent, and many others.

Capitol's obsession with controlling reverberation also led to one of the tower's greatest recording assets, the legendary Capitol "live" echo chambers. Engineered by guitarist Les Paul, and built fifteen feet under the adjoining parking lot for greater sound isolation from the studios, these four trapezoidal-shaped concrete chambers, all identical, allowed engineers to later "color" the sound with natural (versus electronic) reverb during mixing with amazing results. Capitol would subsequently add four more chambers in the parking lot to meet demand both for Capitol's needs, as well as other labels, such as A&M Records, who used the chambers via phone lines for several years in the 1970s.

All of these design and acoustic elements came together to create a distinctive "presence" in Capitol recordings. "I can recognize a session from Studio A or B immediately," said Bob Norberg, Capitol recording and remix engineer, who later remixed and remastered a number of classic Capitol albums and compilations, including those by Frank Sinatra and The Kingston Trio. "The original Capitol three-track tapes have a sound, they are resonant in a way—I hear the room and it's just a wonderful room sound. It's a warm sound."[2]

Surprisingly, the sound produced at the Capitol Tower studios' inaugural recording session in Studio A on February 22, 1956, was anything but warm and wonderful. It was acoustically *dead*. While the tower studios were designed to duplicate the acoustics of Capitol's revered Melrose Avenue studio, the results were far off the mark. "The sound at Melrose was so good, it took us about a year to work things out [in the Capitol Tower studios] so everyone was happy, including Sinatra," said John Palladino, retired Capitol engineer. "They had immense trouble with those new studios," added bandleader Nelson Riddle who recorded Sinatra at the tower for several years. "Later on, they more or less fixed it, but it wasn't until millions of dollars later that they got it right."[3] Some say they got it even *better* than Melrose.

While the first Kingston Trio album was released in mono, it was by no means a primitive production. Capitol's equipment at the time included state-of-the-art Ampex 300 monaural tape machines and Ampex 350 2-track stereo machines, Neumann U 47 vocal mikes, Sony 37A instrument mikes, RC 44 ribbon mikes for recording bass and brass, and a 10-channel mixing console that facilitated multi-miking as well as overdubbing (which was utilized to some degree on *The Kingston Trio* and its follow-up . . . *from the "Hungry i"*).

Many also assume that because *The Kingston Trio was* released in mono, Capitol did not have stereo capabilities. Not so. The company had been experimenting with stereo for several years in the Melrose Avenue studios. Frank Sinatra's first two stereo albums, *Where Are You?* and *Come Fly with Me*, were recorded in Studio A at the tower studios in late 1957 using stereo machines set up in an edit room on the second floor. Although recorded in stereo, *Come Fly with Me* was released only in mono, which was Capitol's practice at the time; it was not until 1962 that it was released in the original stereo format. In fact, *The Kingston Trio* may have actually been recorded in stereo and mixed down to mono. "Everything was monophonic at Capitol until late 1957, when we began recording most things in stereo, although we were doing some experimental stereo early in the game on Melrose," said John Palladino.[4]

Interestingly, in the late 1950s two-track stereo machines were not necessarily used for creating stereo records, but often as a more convenient or flexible way to produce mono recordings. Even Capitol's three-track machines with left-middle-right channels were designed for flexibility and extra track capacity and could be mixed to mono or to stereo or whatever was needed.

By late 1958 or early 1959, Capitol had added Ampex 351 three-track stereo machines in the Capitol Tower studios as well as their New York City studio at 151 West 46th Street where the Trio recorded *At Large*, its first studio-stereo album. It would take several years for stereo to overtake mono as the most popular phonograph record choice, but the Trio took immediate advantage of the larger recording format to perfect "double-voicing," a recording technique that would further enhance "The Kingston Trio sound."

As the name suggests, double-voicing involves re-recording (or doubling) vocals to give the finished recording a bigger, fuller sound. Beginning with *At Large*, every Kingston Trio album was double-voiced to some degree, including "live" concert albums. Although Voyle Gilmore claimed that he had pioneered the technique on The Four Preps' recording of "26 Miles" and on Four Freshmen recordings, Les Paul was certainly the genesis of the practice, having invented multitrack recording in the 1940s.

The process began by laying down an initial three-track take, using three hanging mikes for vocals and three standing mikes for the instruments. The bass was miked separately. This unmixed "working tape" would contain one voice and one instrument per track, with bass being added to Reynolds's tenor guitar track for greater flexibility in equalization. Always the perfectionist, Dave Guard would sometimes overdub his banjo breaks. On the first take, the voices were recorded softer than the instruments. The tape would then be rewound, the boys would put on earphones to listen to themselves during the playback, and they would simultaneously re-record their identical singing parts, usually just the choruses, on a second tape machine that was also picking up the initial take. When both takes were combined, the vocals would be "fatter" or fuller sounding with each voice distinct and clear.

"They thought we did it with echo," said Bob Shane. "No, it was singing the exact same part over to give it a fullness. It was very easy. Just put on the headphones and sing the exact same part. The main thing was getting it exactly right with the phrasing. Everybody had to be locked in together by eye contact so that we sang exactly at the same time. That's why we did it across from each other, for the eye contact. That way it made it a lot easier to overdub it and stay in the same voice because you know you're all gonna be right together."[5]

While the Trio continued to record vocals and instruments simultaneously, by the third studio album they often found it easier—and cleaner—
to record the instrumental track first on a separate master and feed it to
a second master that recorded vocals and combined both. This way the
volume of the banjo and guitar could be overridden and adjusted to better
blend with the vocals.

If done right, the overdub was almost indistinguishable, an aural
shadow of the initial dry vocal track that gave it more "presence." Sometimes the combined tracks would give the song a six-voice (or more) choral
effect. The process was not easy. Some takes required at least a half-hour to
just set up and record. "Sometimes we'd get it real fast, other times some
songs would take fifty to one hundred takes before we were satisfied," said
Shane.[6]

As the Trio became more adept at double-voicing, including sometimes doubling their instruments in the Stewart years, their arrangements
became more complex. "We'd just keep stacking tracks and adding parts,"
Stewart said with a laugh. "On 'Old Joe Hannah' we stacked *four* choruses
on top of each other. It was wild!"[7] When the "parking lot echo" was
added during the mixing stage, the results could be spectacular. Gilmore
once mused that it took twice as long to mix a Kingston Trio album as it
did to record it.

While Capitol engineers beautifully captured the Trio's vocal harmonies, they deserve equal credit for recording their instruments. Acoustic
guitars, particularly Shane's big Martin D-28 Dreadnaught, require a special
touch in recording. The D-28 is boomy when recorded, requiring rolling
off some of the bottom end. Nick Reynolds's tenor guitar was the opposite,
with a delicate, thinner voice, and higher EQ (equalization)—and Guard's
banjo was anybody's guess. In the mid-1950s, controlling EQ was primarily a function of microphone placement—the closer the instrument to the
mike, the boomier it sounded, and vice versa. It's been said that Voyle
Gilmore and engineer Curly Walter knew little about recording acoustic
instruments when the Trio first walked into Studio B. But from the excellent sound of the recordings, they obviously learned quickly. Condenser
microphones are sensitive to acoustic instruments, so they require skill in
knowing exactly where to place them—the proverbial "sweet spot"—in
relation to the instrument to get optimal sound. It was largely up to the
engineer—and mixer—to shape and color the sound to its optimum. William "Pete" Abbott was highly skilled at it, as was producer Gilmore, who
had a very discerning ear. The clarity, evenness, and distinct separation of
guitar, banjo, and tenor guitar on Trio recordings done at Capitol are ex-

traordinary even by today's standards. And that was no simple feat where Shane's guitar playing was concerned.

Shane was one of the best—and loudest—players of the folk era. He played hard, heavy, and on the backbeat. "It all came from Hawaiians," Shane explained. "Most guitar players play on the first and third beat. They taught me to play 'two four'—the second and fourth beat—which is the backbeat. And they taught me to lay on it, to play it heavy. The rhythm guitar is the drum. It's got to lay the beat. The beat of the song for the whole group is based on what I play."[8] Shane also played a chick-a-boom-type strum, hitting the strings with a heavy pick and muffling the sound with the palm of his hand. "Bobby *attacks* the guitar and absolutely drives it," Stewart once observed. "That's the way it should be," Shane said. "The song should be driven the way you feel it. And that will essentially give you the feeling of The Kingston Trio."[9]

Editing and mixing remained the province of Voyle Gilmore, with assistance from Pete Abbott, as did picking the session takes and the final album selects. "I don't remember having anything to do with editing or mixing until later on when we were using our own studio," said Shane. "That's when I realized that the spontaneity was important—and not going over and over and over till you get it right, That's a pain in the ass. If you can't get it right the first time, you ain't gonna get it right."[10]

Some Trio buffs believe that the group used Studio B exclusively, but session photos taken of both the Guard and Stewart Trios also clearly show Studio A with its telltale projector window used for movie scoring. "They used both," Jay Ranellucci remembered. "I know most of the time I worked with them it was in Studio A."[11] The Capitol Tower studios really became a home away from home for the Trio while recording their contractual three albums a year. All phases of album production were contained within the tower and its studios. Originally, the executive suites were on the thirteenth floor, legal and A&R were on the twelfth floor, publishing was on the third floor, mastering and mixing were on the second floor, and the studios were on the first floor. Capitol even had its own photo studio, under the direction of Ken Veeder, on the ninth floor. Floors 4 through 8 were leased to tenants. The Trio would check into the nearby Sunset Marquis or Sunset Sands, usually during a planned break in touring, to record as much material as possible to fill an album, usually a three-day task.

By all accounts the sessions were fun but very focused, often recording late at night and into the early morning hours to avoid distractions. They also recorded during the day, usually starting mid-afternoon and going until they got all they wanted. "With the Trio sessions, it was kind of go until you drop, unless they had other things to do," Ranellucci recalled. "It wasn't like a regular studio session that was scheduled for three hours and you'd try to do four songs. They just went until they felt that they were happy with it and if not they'd keep going, or they'd come back some other time and finish it."[12]

Often the Trio would arrive at the studio around 3 p.m., do vocal exercises and warm up their voices while microphones were being set up, and begin recording an hour or two later. By late evening, they'd have several tunes in the can, including overdubs. Occasionally, they'd come back for a separate overdub session. Beer was always available, but rarely more than a few were consumed. "We were very serious about what we were doing in there," said John Stewart. "We'd sit side by side with our instruments and concentrate on getting it as good as we possibly could. There'd be three stools in a line, and Bobby or whoever had the melody was in the middle usually. We'd have a music stand for the lyrics and chords sheets and we'd sit there and record. We didn't use earphones, except for the doubling. We just sang it like we did in rehearsal. We worked! Let me tell you! We worked at rehearsals and we worked at recording."[13]

Stewart said that Shane and Reynolds did more than just play chords, doing single note runs, bass, and treble. "That intricate harmonic melody thing at the beginning of 'Coplas'? That's *all* of them!" Stewart said. "And that fast, high-pitched riff on the opening of 'Coal Tatoo?' That's Nick on his tenor. Bobby would do great bass runs, C, B to D, and really lean on it. And then 'Scotch and Soda,' Bobby's playing that as a jazz song! And me, I tuned all the instruments at the gig!"[14]

"The sessions could be long and tedious," said Don MacArthur. "Everybody was pretty much paying attention and being business-like—not a whole lot of screwing around on those things. Voyle Gilmore was the guy that did all the producing when I was with them, and he ran a pretty tight ship. There weren't any excesses. You hear about some of these groups doing a lot of drinking and smoking weed—none of that stuff was going on. Lots of times they'd go in and they didn't have the songs really buttoned down very well. So man they'd really learn the song right there in the studio, and by the time they finished, it was a pretty good product."[15]

"Oh, gosh it was fun," Dean Reilly recalled. "It was upbeat. I liked that part of it. I'm kind of a rhythm player—it was fairly easy for me to follow along; my ear is pretty good. We'd rehearse a little bit in the studio, run down the tune and I'd grab a hold of it there. We looked at each other and nodded and off it went. It was all very natural. They would get together in advance and put the tunes together and the arrangements, and after they got it pretty well down, then I would learn my part. We'd do a tune and then go into the control booth and listen to it and often do it over again. They would change something here or something there and then they would maybe change a key or an ending after hearing it. Usually it took about three days to do an LP, maybe three to six hours a day."[16]

Few outsiders were allowed into the sessions, yet there was always a contingent of publishing agents roaming the halls pitching new songs to the boys. "Mark Twain," from the Trio's *#16* album, was pitched to them in the hallway during a break from the sessions by Harvey Geller, a song plugger who also co-wrote "Oleanna" with Martin Seligson.

Although Frank Werber and Voyle Gilmore were at every session, the Trio were basically self-produced. Officially, Gilmore was the "producer," but he was more of a facilitator than a contributor, concerned primarily with the technical aspects. "He never told us what to do," said Shane. "He let us do what we did and he recorded it extremely well. I used to laugh so much because we would sing a song, especially the ones John Stewart wrote, and he'd say, 'That was really good, but what does it mean?' Voyle was the first one to do double-voicing and he was also the first one to use echo to the effect that he did with real echo chambers at Capitol Tower, big old concrete echo chambers. He was brilliant in the way he produced us. When we tried to make records on our own, it never sounded anything like what he did. The guy was great."[17]

Nick Reynolds added, "Voyle's job was to stay out of our way. He would make sure we were in tune, and if the tempo was off he'd ask us to do it again, but primarily he was behind the glass with Frank and Pete Abbott with the lights out. Pete Abbott was our engineer, and his job was to get what Voyle wanted—and that was important. Later, when we built our own studio in Columbus Tower, Pete came up and worked some sessions with Frank, but it was never the same."[18]

Conceptually, every album was planned and recorded in a "show format" mirroring the type and pacing of material used in live concerts—open with a fast tune, follow with a medium-paced tune, then a comedy number, a Bobby Shane solo, a Nick Reynolds or Guard/Stewart solo, and so on, closing with another rouser.

There was also a Kingston Trio vocal formula, a simple arranging structure that would come to define their signature sound. Typically, the song would start with a unison or solo verse, then shift to two-part harmony, then three-part harmony, a key changeup, then down to a very soft line or verse, a solo, then build in volume singing the final chorus louder and inverting it as a "stinger" for the ending. That was the standard Kingston Trio arrangement, especially for fast openers.

Shane would sing melody, Reynolds would sing harmony, usually a third above Shane, but sometimes higher. Guard or Stewart would sing bass or whatever part was left over on the top or bottom. They'd also sing counter harmonies, with hums worked in behind the solo verses. The vocal assignments were perfectly matched. While all three had fine lead voices, Shane's was the strongest and most distinctive, providing a solid base upon which to build. Reynolds was so adept at harmonization that if Shane sang flat, Reynolds would sing flat harmony with him. In the original Trio, Guard was the most versatile vocalist, and with his uncanny ability to mimic dialects and accents, he could fit seamlessly into any vocal arrangement. Many of the original Trio arrangements were Guard's, with some help, initially, from Lou Gottlieb.

To expedite the recording process, Guard would send Shane and Reynolds a tape of their individual vocal parts to study at home, usually just a simple guitar or piano track done by Erich Schwandt. While all arrangements were finalized in the studio, more began to be worked out from scratch or evolved during the session. "We tried our best to really have the songs down perfect before we went into the studio," said Shane. "But as we got more and more into new stuff, we couldn't rehearse as much because we were traveling a lot. So a lot of times we ended up rehearsing the harder-to-learn songs while we were in the studio doing them. Sometimes we'd put the lyrics on a big sheet of market or 'butchers paper' that butchers wrap meat in, and put it up on the wall with big lettering so we could stand there and read it. On the whole, we had a pretty easy time with it. We didn't have very many songs that required a lot of takes. We'd go in, set up the studio, get all the levels right, have the guys in engineering make sure that every voice was correct. And then we'd start recording. We would make albums so fast you wouldn't believe it."[19]

Shane said that they all had a natural ability to head arrange, which helped move things along in the studio. Harmonization was second nature to Nick Reynolds, which also speeded up the process. "Nick is the greatest natural harmony singer I've ever heard in my life," Shane recalled. "I mean you'd just sing and he'd find the part, just like that. No studying, no going over and over it again. I never had anybody since him that could do that. I've had people that were close, but never like Nick and hitting exactly the right point at the right time."[20]

The charm of The Kingston Trio's music has always been its seeming simplicity, a testament to the ingenuity of the group and the technical expertise of Capitol Records. Their recordings done at the Capitol Tower are still as fresh and powerful as the day they were recorded.

"We've really lost something from back then," said John Stewart, commenting on analog versus digital recording. "Folk music is supposed to be warm and human, and those old tube mikes with the room acoustics at Capitol picked it up better than any studio I've ever heard since."[21]

Physically, the Trio's Capitol studio output still exists and is in very good shape. According to Jay Ranellucci, who remixed all the Guard and Stewart Trios songs on the Bear Family anthologies, Capitol has preserved both the Trio's session tapes and the finished master tapes for all of their albums and singles. "The tapes are mostly Scotch 111 and are in great shape considering their age," said Ranellucci. "Capitol has been very good about keeping everything. We even have most of the old glass and lacquer masters from the early 40s."[22] The tapes were stored at a special storage facility in Dominguez Hills, California, although they may have been moved in recent years to an East Coast location.

In the years since the Trio recorded there, the Capitol Tower studios have undergone at least four major renovations. Both Studios A and B are smaller now to accommodate larger control rooms, which have been switched to opposite sides of the rooms. Studio A is totally unrecognizable from the original Rettinger and Uecke design, with lowered ceilings, wooden slatted walls, indirect lighting, and three vocal isolation booths; large sliding doors also now connect Studio A and B to form one large studio when needed. Studio B, which was Frank Sinatra's favorite and which the Trio used primarily, still retains some semblance to the original room—serrated walls, large reversible wall splays, and in the corner, Nat Cole's shop-worn old grand piano stands sentinel.

There's still an air of excitement and a profound sense of musical history as one walks down the long ramp to the studios. Framed photos of long-ago sessions for Frank and Dino and Peggy line the wall, silent and powerful reminders that this is still very hallowed ground.

NOTES

1. Jay Ranellucci, interview with the author, Hollywood, CA, October 16, 2003.

2. Bob Norberg, interview with the author, Hollywood, CA, October 20, 2003.

3. John Palladino and Nelson Riddle, quoted in Charles L. Granata, *Sessions with Sinatra: Frank Sinatra and the Art of Recording* (Chicago: A Cappella Press, 1999), 115–16.

4. John Palladino, quoted in Granata, *Sessions with Sinatra*, 111.

5. Bob Shane, interview with the author, Phoenix, AZ, April 7, 2009.

6. Bob Shane, interview with the author, Alpharetta, GA, November 23, 1983.

7. John Stewart, interview with the author, Malibu, CA, March 4, 1984.

8. Bob Shane, interview with the author, Phoenix, AZ, July 20, 2001.

9. John Stewart, interview with the author, Novato, CA, April 6, 2001; Shane, interview with the author, July 20, 2001.

10. Shane, interview with the author, April 7, 2009.

11. Ranellucci, interview with the author.

12. Ranellucci, interview with the author.

13. Stewart, interview with the author, April 6, 2001.

14. Stewart, interview with the author, April 6, 2001.

15. Don MacArthur, interview with the author, Novato, CA, February 4, 2010.

16. Dean Reilly, interview with the author, San Francisco, CA, September 2, 2007.

17. Bob Shane, interview with the author, Phoenix, AZ, August 21, 2007.

18. Nick Reynolds, interview with the author, Seminole, FL, October 5, 1986.

19. Shane, interview with the author, July 20, 2001.

20. Shane, interview with the author, July 20, 2001.

21. Stewart, interview with the author, March 4, 1984.

22. Ranellucci, interview with the author.

12

MAKE WAY, BABY!

Bob Shane loved to argue that The Kingston Trio were first and foremost an *act* and that records were just a small part of the total Kingston Trio entertainment package. He's right, of course. The long money and the sustainability of the group came from their numerous concert tours, years removed from the big hits of the past.

But recordings were the *prime* mover that inspired generations of listeners and musicians and singers and songwriters and whole industries to embrace The Kingston Trio and to stick with them for a lifetime.

"Doing as many albums as we did over the first four years—three a year—really helped us solidify The Kingston Trio in doing a lot of different kinds of music," Shane commented. "I mean we were 'world music' before there was a name for it. We just did whatever we liked in whatever language we heard it—Spanish, French, Polynesian, Hawaiian, Tahitian, Maori, Bahamian, West Indies, old timey church type of music. We did a lot of different kinds of stuff. Nobody should have called us folk singers in the first place. We were creating *pop*. I never called myself a folk singer, I never thought of myself as a folk singer. I never thought of myself as The Weavers or The Gateway Singers."[1]

For its time, The Kingston Trio's popularity was a unique phenomenon. While there were other popular folk groups, none had the *participatory* power of The Kingston Trio. Their music was never passive. It was accessible and easy to play and there for anybody who wanted to join in. On any college campus across America, Kingston Trio songs were sung and played religiously, day and night. Wannabe Kingston Trios awaited each new Trio album as if it were the Second Coming, studied it intensely, pondered every lyric nuance, pored over every cover and inset photo, from front to back, over and over again.

For some, it wasn't just fun; it was job training. Henry Diltz, the photographer, musician, and banjo-playing member of The Modern Folk Quartet, described his discovery of The Kingston Trio in Honolulu in the late 1950s: "The Kingston Trio's records were coming out, and to us they were like The Beatles in that you would run down to the record store when a new record was coming out, you'd know about it in advance, and you'd be the first one down there to get it. You'd bring it home and just play it over and over and over. Pick the needle up and put it back, pick it up and put it back, pick it up and put it back. What is he saying there? Is it 'frail father?' or 'frail harder?' And all this offhand stuff they'd say on the records like 'kinda hurts my fingers.' And we'd go, 'Oh, God that's great!' And then we'd learn those songs and play them at Greensleeves, the local coffee house. I met Chip Douglas [Hatelid] there when he was a senior at Punahou School. He also loved The Kingston Trio and he'd gotten two of his classmates and taught them how to play like Nick and Bobby, and they had learned *all* the Trio songs note for note. These kids came into the coffee house one Sunday afternoon, which is when we had hootenannies, and they did all this Kingston Trio stuff, and it had all the excitement of the real Kingston Trio. It was note for note!"[2]

A continent away in Sacramento, California, a young Timothy B. Schmit (now one of the Eagles and a fine solo artist as well) was experiencing the same epiphany upon hearing "Tom Dooley" on the radio. "I was really attracted to that music," Schmit said. "In fact, The Kingston Trio were a huge inspiration to me and a couple of my friends. We pretty much went on to learn from them. We scrimped and saved to get some instruments; I got a copy of a Martin tenor guitar from Harmony through the catalog for fifty dollars." In high school in the early 60s, Schmit and his friends got into the folk craze, listening to the top folk groups and singers—The Limeliters, Josh White, Joan Baez, and Odetta. "But The Kingston Trio struck a chord with me," Schmit recalled. "Something with their music and their harmony really moved us, we just loved it, and we would study it over and over—putting the needle back on the record, saying, 'How are they doing this?' 'What is that?' 'What is that chord?' 'What are they singing there?' We studied them like a bible. I became Nick Reynolds," Schmit continued. "I got the tenor guitar and I was also the shortest guy, so I was perfect. And my other friend played the part of Bob Shane. And then my friend Tom had a five-string banjo so he was Dave Guard. I have a great picture of the three of us trying to look like The Kingston Trio. It's from a rehearsal before the first gig we did when we were fourteen years old. The only thing we didn't have were striped shirts, so we settled on buttoned down white shirts. We called ourselves, "Tim, Tom, and Ron."[3] Folk Era Records author/producer Allan Shaw believes that it was precisely that vicarious enjoyment of Kingston Trio records that encouraged so many performers, folk and otherwise, to follow suit. "When I was listening to The Kingston Trio, I was listening to *me*," said Shaw. "And lots of other people were listening to themselves, imagining themselves in the Trio as well."[4]

Singer-songwriter Don McLean weighed in saying, "Everybody who played acoustic guitar or banjo or anything else, started by hearing The Kingston Trio at the least, or having their records. People don't realize how they dominated everything. Anybody my age, you didn't play acoustic guitar and sing a folk song and not be somehow influenced by The Kingston Trio or by somebody who was influenced by them. The thing about The Kingston Trio is that they were totally natural. It was something that happened and their story made everybody think that it could happen to you. And it was a little bit like kids sitting around harmonizing in the inner cities doing doo wop music, only this was for college kids—white college kids. *People were playing instruments* and that's another thing that The Kingston Trio did. It's very hard to underestimate how exciting they were in that time period in the late '50s to that audience."[5]

There were plenty of lessons to be learned on every Kingston Trio album, starting with the basic ability of discerning quality songs, of picking the best from the rest, especially under the enormous pressure of pumping out product for Capitol. "Those guys all had really, really *good* ears," said McLean, "that's where their real artistic ability was because without the songs, and without the hit records, without those albums—you don't get anywhere."[6] So let's get to this music.

Since the scope of this book focuses only on the Guard and Stewart years, readers may wish to consult *The Kingston Trio on Record* by Benjamin Blake, Jack Rubeck, and Allan Shaw (Kingston Korner, Inc., publisher), which contains a comprehensive discography. They may also want to peruse Bear Family's *The Guard Years* and *The Stewart Years*, hard-bound books that accompany two all-inclusive Kingston Trio ten-CD sets of the same names. Both volumes contain detailed recording information culled largely from Capitol session sheets, as well as extensive song annotation.

My approach in this chapter is primarily anecdotal, based largely on interviews with Dave Guard, Bob Shane, Nick Reynolds, John Stewart, and others who were part of the recording process. It's also *selective*. Not every song on every Kingston Trio album is covered here. I discuss only the songs that may have an interesting story or fact associated with them, or simply due to my own personal preference. With more than four hundred songs recorded between the Guard and Stewart Trios, it is beyond the scope—and space—of this book to cover them all.

The wide variety of songs came from a large variety of sources, old and new. It is important to remember that in studying author credits, the names you read may be far removed from the original source. One of the major criticisms of The Kingston Trio was that they put their names on public domain tunes that were originally written by others. While I am no apologist for The Kingston Trio, it is difficult, if not impossible, to find a folk song in the public domain that is truly pure and untouched. Public domain songs are just that, songs that belong to the public. What can be copyrighted are changed arrangements (called derivatives), adding new verses or changing lyrics of public domain tunes. The trick is to find a totally original public domain song to begin with, because most public domain songs have been changed in some way, numerous times.

Tom Drake, an English teacher and close friend of Bob Shane, worked closely with Shane to research tunes that the Trio could record, including "Blue Eyed Gal," "Blow the Candle Out," "White Snows of Winter," "Mary Mild," "Who's Gonna Hold Her Hand," and "The Escape of Old John Webb." Together, he and Shane rewrote several of these tunes that were considered in the public domain and then claimed copyrights.

"Bobby Shane was a friend and knew of my music/academic background, and he asked me to find him some old songs," Drake recounted. "I spent a couple of days in the library and sent him some tunes. 'John Webb' made it to the top of the pile. None of us understood the content or knew its background. Someone, I think it was Voyle Gilmore, suggested I fill in the gaps so the lyrics made more sense. I wrote the linking verses and changed things around to tell a linear story."[7]

But people learned more than songs from Kingston Trio albums. Martin guitars and Vega banjoes appeared on virtually every Kingston Trio album cover, which was a double bonus for serious Trio fans. Not only could they study Shane's 1958 D-28, they could hear its powerful bass and crisp treble as well. Nick Reynolds's 1929 2-18T and several early 1960s 0-18Ts, also on the covers, revived strong interest in tenor guitars worldwide.

"The Martin guitar thing is definitely a part of me," Don McLean explained, "and was definitely started with The Kingston Trio because of the way they made them sound on those records. I was eleven or twelve, and I never heard anything that sounded like that before. When you line those instruments up—a tenor guitar, and then the D-28 and a bass, and the banjo—you have this incredible, wonderful blend, a very harmonic thing, very natural. It was just a wonderful thing that happened naturally and really took hold of the nation for that time period in a very, very important way."[8]

The Kingston Trio's almost exclusive use of Martin guitars created such enormous demand, that the company was back-ordered for three years and forced to move into a new factory to expand production. Being on the cover of a Kingston Trio album was the best free advertising Martin ever had, because the company did not give away guitars to anybody—not even The Kingston Trio.

THE GUARD YEARS

From February 1958 through January 1961, Dave Guard, Bob Shane, and Nick Reynolds recorded a total of ten albums for Capitol Records, excluding "best of" or other compilations. The first two albums, *The Kingston Trio* and . . . *from the "Hungry i"* are covered in detail in "The Road to Success" chapter, with some additional commentary on song selection here, as well as discussion of *Stereo Concert*.

The Kingston Trio, the Trio's debut album was recorded on February 5, 6, and 7 in Studio B at Capitol Tower studios in Hollywood. It's comprised of twelve cuts that were, essentially, their club set list at the Purple Onion. These songs include "Three Jolly Coachmen," "Bay of Mexico," "Banua," "Tom Dooley," "Fast Freight," "Hard, Ain't It Hard," "Saro Jane" (aka "*Sara* Jane"), "Sloop John B.," "Santo Anno," "Scotch and Soda," "Coplas," and "Little Maggie." Considering that this is one of the biggest and longest-selling Kingston Trio albums (estimated over 3 million copies or higher), every cut is a "classic" among Trio fans, especially "Tom Dooley" and "Scotch and Soda."

Most of these tunes were drawn from the repertoires of the Trio's favorite singers and groups: The Weavers ("Sloop John B," "Bay of Mexico"), The Gateway Singers ("Hard, Ain't It Hard," "Saro Jane"), The Easy Riders/Terry Gilkyson ("Fast Freight"), Odetta ("Santo Anno"). Others, such as "Three Jolly Coachmen" (originally titled "Landlord, Fill the Flowing Bowl"), are labeled "traditional" and are drawn from old songbooks and reworked. In the case of the Trio's version of "Three Jolly Coachmen," Guard said he learned it from a sculptor friend, Nick Brownley, in Palo Alto, although the original dates from the British Isles in the 1600s. "Little Maggie" was picked up from an Obray Ramsey cut on the Riverside LP, *Banjo Songs of the Southern Mountains*.

The Trio's second album, . . . *from the "Hungry i,"* was recorded six months later in mid-August 1958. At least two nights of shows (and maybe more) were recorded in the club's basement showroom and included the following: "Tic, Tic, Tic," "Gue, Gue," "Dorie," "South Coast," "Zombie Jamboree," "Wimoweh," "New York Girls," "They Call the Wind Mariah," "The Merry Minuet," "Shady Grove"/Lonesome Traveler," and "When the Saints Go Marching In."

Again, most tunes are from the Trio's favorite sources: The Weavers ("Wimoweh," "When the Saints Go Marching In"), Burl Ives ("New York Girls" written by Burl Ives but learned from the 1958 *Marilyn Child and Glenn Yarbrough Sing Folk Songs* album), Theodore Bikel ("Dorie," aka "Dodi Li"), and Jean Ritchie/Lee Hays of The Weavers ("Shady Grove"/"Lonesome Traveler").

The album contains only eleven cuts (including a studio recorded "Gue, Gue") plus on-stage dialogue, but Reynolds said that many more tunes were recorded, some of which were included on the *Stereo Concert* album. A photo taken of the Trio on stage at the hungry i in 1958 shows a total of four microphones, a centrally placed Neumann U-47 studio mike in front of Shane, as well as two hanging mikes, one directed toward Guard on the left, and one toward Reynolds on the right. There's also a pencil mike aimed toward Shane's plectrum banjo. Is this a stereo set-up? Probably, but used for better, more inclusive recording in a noisy club setting and mixed down to mono. It does, however, indicate that Capitol had location stereo capability at the time, and thus some of the *hungry i* output was usable for *Stereo Concert*.

Bear Family's *The Guard Years* lists a twenty-eight-song concert on July 13, 1958, as "possibly" being recorded at the Purple Onion, while others assume that it was recorded at the hungry i. But there is another possibility. According to Capitol engineer Jay Ranellucci, The Kingston Trio played and recorded a concert at Chaffey College in Los Angeles sometime in 1958 or 1959, for which he set up vocal and instrument microphones and cables for Capitol's recording engineers. To date, there has been no mention or documentation of the Chaffey College concert or the whereabouts of the concert tapes. The concert tapes that Allan Shaw discovered at Capitol's Dominguez Hills storage facility were not marked and may well be the Chaffey College concert.

Stereo Concert was supposedly recorded on December 15, 1958, in El Paso's Liberty Hall, following a three-week engagement at La Fiesta nightclub in nearby Juarez, Mexico. Yet known dates of their La Fiesta engagement make it more likely that the El Paso concert took place earlier in October of 1958. The concert was recorded by a college student named Lee Morton who worked for a local record store that had just received a new two-track stereo tape recorder. Hearing that The Kingston Trio would soon be appearing in El Paso, the owner of the store suggested that Lee "try out" the new tape recorder by recording the Trio's concert. He was put in touch with Frank Werber who gave his permission—with the caveat that the original tape would go to The Kingston Trio and that the student could make one copy for himself. The tape, which was recorded at 7 1/2 IPS (inches per second) on 1/4 inch tape, was sold to Capitol who released it as *Stereo Concert* with Voyle Gilmore listed as producer. Only ten cuts were released of the fifteen to seventeen songs recorded of the concert. Those original live cuts include "Banua," Three Jolly Coachmen," "South Coast," "Coplas," "They Call the Wind Mariah," "Zombie Jamboree," "Tom Dooley," "The Merry Minuet," "Raspberries, Strawberries," and "When the Saints Go Marching In." Folk Era's enhanced and enlarged version of *Stereo Concert Plus* is covered in "The Post Trio Years" section of this chapter.

At Large

After the first two Kingston Trio albums, *The Kingston Trio* and . . . *from the "Hungry i,"* the Trio settled into an extraordinary recording process of producing very high-quality albums, very quickly, that remained virtually unchanged until the group's retirement in 1967.

It was extraordinary because later it would be impossible to produce a full-length, twelve-cut album, including recording, overdubs, mixing, editing, photography, and trade and retail marketing in such a short period of time. But The Kingston Trio did it because they didn't know they couldn't, and because they were contractually obligated to do so by a determined and very savvy record company that threw all their production resources into making it happen. "We were so fast, you couldn't believe it," said Shane. "I mean nobody ever heard of things like that. The first album we cut in three days. And then we'd go in with all new material and it would take us maybe a week. Today it'd take three years."[9] Shane also gave a tip of the hat to Dave Guard for his ability to sniff out special songs that distinguished all Guard-era Trio albums. "After Dave died, I started thinking about the things he really did for the group," Shane said. "Dave brought in a bunch of wonderful songs, and I never gave it much thought before, but he really did bring in a *lot* of great songs. We all did, but he had songs that were more bodied, had maybe a little more substance to them."[10]

At Large is good example of content and technology coming together, and it truly was extraordinary.

At Large was the Trio's second studio album and the first to be *professionally* recorded in stereo and to utilize overdubbing. It was recorded at Capitol's New York studios at 151 West 46th Street on February 16, 17, and 18, 1959. It was not, however, the first Kingston Trio stereo *release*. In April of 1959, a four-song EP (extended play) was released featuring stereo versions of "Tijuana Jail," its flip side, "Oh Cindy," and *Stereo Concert* versions of "Coplas" and "Tom Dooley." The *At Large* sessions took place after a two-week gig at the Blue Angel, where the Trio rehearsed the album daily in a room above the club. While the New York studio may not have had the pizzazz of its Hollywood counterpart, it was nonetheless an excellent, well-equipped and well-staffed facility. It was certainly convenient, allowing the Trio to take important club dates in New York and throughout the East Coast and still meet its album production obligations. Andy Wiswell was the resident New York "producer," but Voyle Gilmore (and possibly Pete Abbott) was behind the glass, coming east whenever the Trio needed him. In addition to *At Large*, the Trio also recorded *Sold Out* at West 46th Street, as well as several top-selling 45s, including "Tijuana Jail." In November of 1961 they were able to beat Peter, Paul and Mary to the charts by recording "Where Have All the Flowers Gone" in New York just hours after hearing it from them in Boston.

"I liked *At Large*, to tell you the truth," Dave Guard said. "I thought we achieved what we were trying to do in that situation. It was very one pointed. Everybody was super focused and very business-like and we knew we had a lot of good material."[11] Indeed, *At Large* showcased some of the period's best folk and calypso-oriented writers, including Stan Wilson who wrote "Woman with a Rolling Pin," which became Shane's "I Bawled."

"Bobby hung out a lot with Stan Wilson," Guard recalled. "Stan Wilson and The Gateway Singers and Mort Sahl were all at the hungry i in the early days, so I think Bobby patterned his early playing after Stan Wilson for quite a bit of his repertoire. Stan Wilson was a Josh White fan, so all of that sort of came out of the other and came to Bobby." Even the goofy laugh on "I Bawled" got the special treatment on *At Large*. "I think this was the first time we *consciously* recorded in stereo," Guard said, "so we were trying a few tricks and the engineer said, 'Why don't you start the laugh over here and we'll put it over there.'"[12] Stan Wilson was also the source of "A Rollin' Stone" and "Jane, Jane, Jane," both of which he wrote, and "The River Is Wide," "Blow the Candle Out," and "O Ken Karenga," which he arranged but never claimed a copyright. Some of the Trio's best songs were handed to them in New York. Nick recalled sitting with Dave and Bob in the Blue Angel after their show listening to the other acts when they were approached by Irving Burgess (real name Irving Burgee). "He introduced himself as 'Lord Burgess' and said he wrote almost all of Harry Belafonte's calypso albums and that *immediately* gave him credibility with us," Reynolds said. "He'd been around—New York, the West Coast, the Caribbean. We checked that out, and it was true. He said, 'I have some songs I would like to have you consider for recording.' He gave us 'The Seine.'"[13] Burgess was Juilliard-trained, a multilingual vocalist and lyricist whose credits included "El Matador" (which he co-wrote with Jane Bowers), as well as Belafonte's big hits "Jamaica Farewell," "Day-O," and "Island in the Sun."

Not all the songs they were pitched were written with the Trio in mind. Jane Bowers, the Austin, Texas, songwriter, offered "The Alamo," which she wrote for Tex Ritter in 1955, with slightly different lyrics. It, too, was an important song for the Trio, a fan favorite (especially if you're a Texan) and a standout cut on *At Large*. "Later on I tried to get into a situation with her, like a collaboration," Guard said, "because I had heard a lot of good foreign tunes and she was a good lyricist. I thought with these tunes and her lyrics, some good stuff would come out of it."[14] As it turned out, a lot of good material did come from the Bowers-Guard collaboration: "Coast of California," "Senora," "When I Was Young," and "Buddy Better Get on down the Line." The two formed their own publishing company, Granada Music, yet Bowers was not comfortable with their arrangement, feeling that Guard was getting the better of the deal financially. Bowers met the Trio only once, at dinner at her home in Austin with her husband. She did, however, remain an important source of quality songs for the Trio from her own pen, including "San Miguel," "Speckled Roan," "To Be Redeemed," "Sea Fever," and "El Matador" (in collaboration with Lord Burgess).

Lou Gottlieb appears as a songwriter for the Trio for the second time on *At Large*, contributing "Good News," which he got from jazz, blues, and gospel singer Lil Greenwood at the Purple Onion. Gottlieb was well regarded in the San Francisco folk community as a songwriter, co-founder of The Gateway Singers and later The Limeliters, stand-up comedian, and all around erudite folk observer. He knew everyone, including Guard, Shane, and Reynolds, whom he had met at the hungry i before they formed The Kingston Trio.

"They were guys that used to hang out in the dressing room at the hungry i," Gottlieb related. "And then they got together as The Kingston Trio and I worked with them for six months at the Purple Onion. They were the opening act. I was the comic. Maya Angelou was the headliner. I liked them a lot. I liked them personally. They were fun guys to be around and they were sincere singers. And Dave Guard, particularly, I'm very fond of. He's a really, really brilliant man. They cut their records while I was working with them at the Purple Onion, and that's how I got a tune on their first album [*The Kingston Trio*]. It was one of those public domain arranged, published-by-me things. It was 'Rock about My Saro Jane,' which I stole off a Dave Macon record. That was a very fortunate thing because I was in deep trouble financially then. That tune must have made twenty grand for me at least."[15]

When *The Kingston Trio* became a hit album in 1958, it was a huge surprise to everyone, especially Gottlieb. "See, when I started writing for The Kingston Trio, I tried to put that one tune on the album. Then the thing took off. They started needing a lot more tunes." In addition to "Good News" for *At Large*, he later gave them "The Unfortunate Miss Bailey" and a tune he'd gotten from Merlin Hayes called "Round about the Mountain." "In those days if you got a couple of tunes on a Kingston Trio album, you were already somebody in the entertainment industry."[16]

With *At Large*, Voyle Gilmore introduced the group to double-voicing to fatten their vocals, primarily the choruses, as well as some "punching in" of bits and pieces (what Shane called "touching up"). It was also their most polished album up to that time, vocally and instrumentally, which Guard largely attributed to Frank Werber's insistence that the Trio continually rehearse. "We were *forced* to rehearse extra," said Guard. "We were playing Pittsburgh and Buffalo and instead of having any fun by day, our manager just kept us rehearsing basically. So we *had* to do it. There was nothing else to do, so instead of doing anything else we just rehearsed way past our limits more or less. We were super tired all the time."[17]

Throughout 1958 and 1959, they traveled with excellent mentors, playing over two hundred towns with Stan Getz, Thelonious Monk, and other jazz heavyweights. "We heard so much from all of these musicians every night," Guard remembered. "We were playing with *good* musicians. I think the bass player Buckwheat came on the band and that might have had something to do with it, and we realized the Trio would be sort of a well-accepted group. So I think Bobby and Nick got a little more serious with what they were doing, at least for a while."[18]

Guard's banjo playing improved greatly on *At Large*, as evidenced by his competent frailing on "Corey, Corey" and crisp, precise picking on "M.T.A." Part of Guard's genius was his resourcefulness and quick adaptability. In the course of less than two years he went from driving his wife crazy with his plunkety-plunk banjo practicing to being an accomplished and highly inventive player. He was essentially self-taught and instinctively went for what worked best for the song, mixing banjo techniques and styles to fit what he heard in his head. He was no banjo purist, but he became an excellent banjo player.

The big hit to emerge from *At Large* was "M.T.A." The lyrics were written in 1949 to the tune of "Wreck of the Old 97" and "The Ship That Never Returned" by Jacqueline Berman Steiner and Bess Lomax Hawes, sister of folklorist/collector Alan Lomax. Steiner was a Vassar grad, folksinger, songwriter, and activist; Bess Hawes taught guitar and banjo, was a member of the Almanac Singers, and would go on to become a distinguished educator and recipient of the National Medal of Arts. The "The M.T.A. Song" was a spirited campaign/protest song for Walter A. O'Brien Jr., a Progressive Party candidate for mayor of Boston, who used subway fare increases (up to 50 percent more on some lines) by Boston's Metropolitan Transit Authority as a campaign issue. He was later targeted as being a communist sympathizer or socialist because of the leftist bent of the Progressive Party. To avoid any political trouble or controversy, The Kingston Trio changed "Walter" to "Charlie" and went on to record a multimillion seller. Interestingly, the lyrics concerning Charlie's inability to get off of the subway car refer to the fact that not only did the M.T.A. charge ten cents to enter the underground subway stations, but also an additional five cents ("one more nickel") to get *off* the trolley at aboveground stops. And if you were out of change like poor Charlie, you would *never* be able to get off the trolley, thus the "No, he never returned" lyric. Nick Reynolds said that they got "M.T.A." from Maine folksinger Will Holt ("Raspberries, Strawberries," "Lemon Tree") in San Francisco, who had gotten the song from folksinger Richard "Specs" Simmons, and had earlier recorded the song on an album for Coral Records in 1957. Judy Davis, their vocal coach, said *she* was the one who gave them the tune. Take your choice.

After recording "M.T.A." as it was written, it occurred to the Trio that nobody would know what the M.T.A was, and that they needed some kind of announcement to explain it. Thus, the long forty-five-second introduction—"These are the times that try men's souls. In the course of our nation's history, the people of Boston have rallied bravely whenever the rights of men have been threatened. Today, a new crisis has arisen . . ."—was written and dubbed onto the front of the song. They immediately knew they had a hit. Even before they were done with the second take, Artie Mogul and Voyle Gilmore were on the phone to Capitol saying,

"I think we got the next one! The next single! Right here, right now!" And they were right.

Here We Go Again

Here We Go Again, The Kingston Trio's third studio album, found the Trio back in Los Angeles at Capitol's Studio B, where they recorded May 26 and 27 and June 1 and 2, 1959.

With every subsequent Kingston Trio album the group's reserve of ready song material was further depleted. By the time they reached *Here We Go Again*, they had run through many of The Weavers' standards and other folk chestnuts that made up their repertoire. Finding new material would be a perennial problem from then on out, which probably accounts for their willingness to listen to a nineteen-year-old amateur songwriter named John Stewart. As it turns out, Stewart's "Molly Dee" not only fit the Trio's style beautifully, the lyric line from its chorus was a perfect title for the album.

The Trio were also quick to call in Lou Gottlieb, who not only had songs to sell but could arrange them to fit the Trio style—*and* rehearse them with the group in the studio. "The guys called me because their third album was coming up and they had to have something on it, you know, and would I come down and rehearse with them. They were working at the Coconut Grove, and I went down and we rehearsed right in the ballroom. I had a whole bunch of tunes I was trying to give them. And guess who was there—John Stewart! He was about nineteen, and *he* was trying to sell them some tunes, too. In fact, he already had. But the trouble was, I had mine all written out in scores like I usually do, and those guys don't read. So I was really desperate."[19] Gottleib evidently figured something out because "The Unfortunate Miss Bailey" and "Round about the Mountain" made it onto the album.

"The Unfortunate Miss Bailey" is a truly clever piece of theater, highlighted by Guard's extraordinary and perfectly fussy British accent. The genius of Guard, of which there were many facets, was intuitively knowing how to infuse a lyric with just the right inflection, character, or spirit—to "milk it" for all the drama it was worth. "The man with a thousand voices," Reynolds once said admiringly of Guard.

"Haul Away" is another derivative of a traditional, public domain song, in this case a rousing sea chantey, "Haul Away, Joe." The song is credited to Jack Splittard, a droll—and accurate—pseudonym for splitting the copyright and attendant royalties ("jack") three ways between Shane, Guard, and Reynolds.

"Oleanna," credited to Harvey Geller and Martin Seligson, was a public domain song that The Gateway Singers included in their act that the Trio especially liked. "The Gateway Singers just *killed* the song," Reynolds enthused. "So we sang their harmony with the new words and arrangement that Harvey Geller did. He was kind of an old pal from the publishing and writing world. We needed a song, and Harvey would hang out in the hall and say, 'I've got a couple of songs I want you to hear,' so, we'd say, 'Okay,' and he'd say, 'I've got one that might fit in the album, you know!' He's one of the few we let do that."[20] In addition to plugging songs, Geller was a well-known Los Angeles music journalist, columnist, feature writer, publisher, and sales executive for *Variety* and *Billboard*. He later wrote "Mark Twain," one of Shane's favorites, which was included on *The Kingston Trio #16* album in 1963. The Trio also used "Oleanna" in their 7UP commercials.

"E Inu Tatou E" (Let's Drink Together) was a favorite of Shane and Guard from their high school days in Hawaii, and the very first song they sang together on the beach. Written by George "Tautu" Archer and recorded with his band The Pagans in 1945, the song was popular with legions of Honolulu teenagers. Many of the records produced in postwar Hawaii were aimed at the burgeoning tourist trade and were often an amalgam of Hawaiian and hotel lounge music. Tahitian music was a different animal altogether. Guard said that he and Shane were drawn to Tahitian music because they thought it was "wild and exciting," but also as a way of distinguishing themselves from the native Hawaiian groups who had the Hawaiian tunes completely covered. "My prime interest had been Tahitian music, actually," Dave added.

"Goober Peas," credited to Guard, has its origins in the American Civil War and was first published in 1866, purportedly sung by Confederate soldiers bemoaning their miserable living conditions. The tune has been covered by Burl Ives, Tennessee Ernie Ford and, later, Elton John! Guard said he discovered the tune from an eighth grade history book. It's still a favorite cut of many Trio fans for its clean blue-grassy banjo lines and hunt-and-peck guitar accompaniment.

Not all of the tunes on *Here We Go Again* were there by choice, however, as Guard explained. "By this time we were finally running out of material, so some other tunes started to sneak in that we didn't really have much interest in, we just had to fill up the album and they [Capitol] were just starting to want a whole bunch of albums a year."[21]

Guard never specified which tunes were allowed to "sneak in" but the solo numbers are a good bet—"Rollin' Stone," a Stan Wilson tune;

"The Wanderer" by Irving Burgess; and "Senora" by Jane Bowers and
Dave Guard were recorded as individual solos by Shane, Reynolds, and
Guard, respectively. They were easy, simple, and expedient when Capitol
was banging on the door.

Here We Go Again was released on October 19, 1959, reaching number one on the Billboard charts in early December, where it remained for
eight consecutive weeks. The album also generated a Top 20 hit, "A Worried Man" (a derivative of the old Carter Family "Worried Man Blues").

Sold Out

Right behind *At Large* on the album charts was *Sold Out*, the Trio's
fourth studio album, released six months later. The Trio rehearsed the
album in St. Louis at the Chase Hotel where they first met humanitarian
Dr. Thomas A. Dooley, and appeared at a 7UP bottlers convention, November 19–27, 1959. Recorded in New York on September 20 and 28 and
December 7, 8, 9, and 10, 1959, *Sold Out* featured a number of excellent
songs, with outstanding production values thanks, in part, to postproduction at Tower Studios in Los Angeles. While many Trio fans count this
album among their favorites, with Gold Record status that affirms it, Guard
thought differently and panned it. "The material wasn't that interesting to
us on *Sold Out*," he said. "It was all a bunch of things we got out of sheet
music stores and stuff that was just mailed in. It was nothing—I mean in
the early days we were all very unanimous about the way we liked the
tunes and stuff. Later on they [Capitol] just wanted so much material that
everybody would just sort of be responsible for bringing in their four or five
tunes apiece out of which we would work from a slab of fifteen and then
throw away three that just weren't making it on the record. But it was all
just whatever we could get a hold of rather than the early days where we
would all go down to nightclubs and check stuff out and fall in love with it.
But after that, everybody just from sheer fatigue would try to get their own
privacy and go their own way, bring in their own tastes more or less."[22]

There may have been some sour grapes in Guard's evaluation of *Sold
Out*. Among the songs Guard brought in for the album was "Just Once
around the Clock," a melancholy dirge written by Hungarian composer
Sigmund Romberg and lyricist Oscar Hammerstein II. It may have been
that David "Buck" Wheat had a financial interest in the piece and Guard
wanted to record it as a favor to him. "Dave insisted on singing it—and
singing it alone," Reynolds recalled. "He started singing it, and Voyle's
eyes visibly rolled backwards. And it got to the point where they made

take after take, and it was not coming off and not happening. So Voyle said, 'Let's not do any more, let's give it a rest and try it again tomorrow night.' And Dave said, 'No, we've just about got it. And Voyle said, 'Oh, well, we'll do it, but . . .' Dave has a tantrum and walks out of the studio. He thought everybody was against him—and everybody was."[23] Fortunately, Guard returned and work on the album commenced the next day, but "Once around the Clock" remained locked in the Capitol vaults for twenty-seven years until Folk Era released the tune on their *Hidden Treasures* vinyl LP in 1986.

As they did so beautifully on "The Unfortunate Miss Bailey," the Trio's dramatic/comedic sense paid off on "With Her Head Tucked underneath Her Arm," an old (1934) and oft-recorded comedy tune in the English music hall/stage tradition, written by Robert Patrick Weston and Bert Lee. Everybody's had a shot at this tune over the years—from Rudy Vallee to the Clancy Brothers—but nobody does Henry VIII better than Bob Shane. One of the reasons Shane was so revered by fellow singers— including Sinatra—was his ability to put himself emotionally into the song, *any* song. In this song, he *is* Henry VIII, with an amazing sense of drama. "That was taught to me by early guys like Josh White," Shane said. "The most important singers you'll ever hear in your life are the ones who you feel may have lived what they're singing. That's why Sinatra was so special to me because you could follow his escapades with all the people he hung out with, the women he was married to, you could see why he sang certain songs."[24]

"The Mountains o' Mourne" was recorded by Nick Reynolds in *one* take, the first and only such feat by the Trio. Written in 1896 by Irish songwriter Percy French and his partner Dr. W. Houston Collison, "The Mountains o' Mourne" is beloved by the Irish, including this writer's mother who learned it as a child in Belfast, Northern Ireland, and sang it all of her life. The Mountains o' Mourne actually do "sweep down to the sea," gracefully sloping and disappearing into the Irish Sea, south of Belfast.

With "Tanga Tika/Toerau," the first half of the medley, "Tanga Tika," was written by Eddie Lund, "the Father of Modern Tahitian Folk Music" (also known as "the Irving Berlin of the Islands"). The second half, "Toerau," was written by George Archer, who also wrote "E Inu Tatou E." The medley is another throwback to Shane and Guard's high school years in Honolulu. The Trio sounded authentic for white boys, too. "When we sang Tahitian and Hawaiian, Dave and I had a real feel for it, because we knew basically what the words meant, and Nick acquired a perfect feel for it, too."[25]

"Raspberries, Strawberries" is not an old French folk tune. The Trio first heard it from Travis Edmondson, but it was written by Maine native Will Holt, who also wrote "Lemon Tree" which wound up on *Goin' Places*, the Trio's last album with Guard. The Trio recorded "Raspberries, Strawberries" a few months earlier in a Denver studio for release as a single. This version was re-recorded in stereo specifically for *Sold Out*.

"The Hunter," also known as "The Keeper," was published in several English songbooks as early as 1909, with various lyric edits, rewrites, and arrangements over the years. Its "Hey down, hoe down, derry, derry down!" refrain is familiar to generations of English schoolchildren. The Trio's version is taken almost verbatim from The Weavers, yet with enough of a change to warrant a Guard-Shane-Reynolds copyright (or for their close friend Jack Splittard).

"Farewell Adelita" was brought in by Shane, who said he heard it in *Viva Zapata!* a 1952 fictional bio-epic movie directed by Elia Kazan and starring Marlon Brando. This song, perhaps more than any other, demonstrates the amazing adaptability of The Kingston Trio to virtually any genre of music, vocally and instrumentally. It doesn't have to be authentic Mexican, the flavor is close enough. Guard uses a five-string banjo to *approximate,* not replicate, the sound and feel of Mexican music. Shane's phrasing is appropriately formal, sincere, and a touch maudlin.

"El Matador" reached number thirty-two on the charts, but it should have gone higher. Dramatically performed and impeccably recorded, it's a totally believable mini-epic. With lyrics by Jane Bowers and chorus by Lord Burgess, it was a great alliance between two of the leading songwriters of the late 1950s folk revival. There's a certain spatial quality to "El Matador"—and all of the tunes on *Sold Out*—that point to Capitol's legendary echo chambers in Los Angeles. Postproduction of both *At Large* and *Sold Out* were done at Tower Studios in Los Angeles. Echo was rarely recorded live at Capitol, if ever, and added in post.

"Mangwani Mpulele" was learned from an early Theodore Bikel album, *An Actor's Holiday* (Elektra, 1956). The song is derived from an African (Sotho or Zulu) hunting chant. It's possible that the Trio heard it directly from Bikel, with whom they were friendly in San Francisco, Los Angeles, and New York.

"Bimini" was published in John A. and Alan Lomax's 1941 *Our Singing Country: Folk Songs and Ballads,* as was "Round the Bay of Mexico," "Santy Anno" and "Darlin' Corey." The Trio were well familiar with the book, and Guard said it was their source for "Bimini." Odetta, however, was the source for "Santy Anno," and The Weavers were the inspiration for "Bay of Mexico." The Weavers had their own version of "Jack Split-tard," naming their copyright alias "Paul Campbell" a collective pseudonym for Pete Seeger, Fred Hellerman, Ronnie Gilbert, and Lee Hays.

String Along

String Along, the Trio's fifth studio album, was recorded in Los Angeles on April 19, 20, and 21, 1960. It's been referred to as the "Help a Friend Album" because two of the songs, "Bad Man Blunder" and "South Wind," were included to help friends in dire need.

Although the tunes are excellent, the art direction is less than inspired. In place of liner notes there's a photo collage on the back cover—the Trio hanging out of a bus pulling away from the Sunset Marquis Hotel, sitting on the diving board at Frank's house and horsing around in his living room, a rainy night rehearsing in a tent at Newport or Ravinia, the three singing around a mike in Capitol's New York studio, production stills from the Kraft Music Hall television show.

"Bad Man's Blunder" was written by Cisco Houston and Lee Hays and recorded by the Trio at the behest of Fred Hellerman and Pete Seeger of The Weavers to defray Houston's medical expenses, who was terminally ill with stomach cancer. "I never met Cisco Houston," Reynolds said, "but we were being asked by our heroes, people we owe our lives to, to do a song for a friend. They said, 'If you do a song by Cisco, man, it'll really help 'cause there's gonna be one hundred thousand dollars in goddamn hospital bills.' So we said noooo problem."[26] "Bad Man Blunder" was released as a single in May of 1960, and hit number thirty-seven on the *Billboard* charts in August. Not a huge hit, but big enough to pay Cisco's medical bills.

Travis Edmondson, Nick's friend from Tucson who later became half of "Bud and Travis" and was a member of The Gateway Singers, also pitched songs for *String Along*. "You know, Nicky, I've been out of work a long time but I've got a couple of songs, if would you please listen to them," Edmondson asked. "And if you could ever see it in your heart to do your old pal a favor, this would be a real easy way to do it."[27] Nick agreed that indeed it would be, plus the Trio got a great song—"South Wind"— and his friend got back on his feet.

"South Wind" has a curious "tubby" instrumental sound that has long stumped many Trio listeners. The popular belief is that it was BooBams made by David Wheat. They can be played by hand or mallet. Nick used them on "O Ken Karenga." On "South Wind," however, Reynolds said he played a "thumb piano," as he called it, similar to a Kalimba, with a series of tuned tines attached to a box and struck with a small mallet.

"Buddy Better Get on down the Line" is another Uncle Dave Macon tune ("Buddy Won't You Roll down the Line"), but with considerable lyric changes by Jane Bowers and credited to her and Guard. "During the 1960s only a few folksong buffs in the Kingston Trio audience recognized that 'Buddy' derived from a convict-lease blues ballad fashioned on the Cumberland Plateau about 1890," said folk scholar Archie Green on the origins of the tune.[28] It's a standout cut, and much like "The Escape of Old John Webb," powerful by its simplicity and precision. The Trio were very adept at minimalism, emphasizing less to get more. Production values helped—fattening vocals by double voicing and adding spatial presence with natural reverb from Capitol's big concrete echo chambers.

"The Tattooed Lady" was said to have come from Reynolds's cousin Henry Scott, yet Reynolds emphatically denied it, saying that he learned it from his navy captain father, and being in the public domain he shared the credit with Guard and Shane. While the song is long on cleverness, it was short on length, barely clocking in at one minute when recorded. As a result, they simply added a bridge—"What did you say???"—and repeated the song over again.

"Colorado Trail" was written (or more accurately collected) by Carl Sandburg. The Trio heard the song from The Gateway Singers and were smitten by Elmerlee Thomas's magnificent contralto rendition. The Trio would later meet Sandburg, who thanked them profusely for recording both "Colorado Trail" and "This Mornin', This Even', So Soon," another Sandburg tune. "He sent all of us an autographed copy of *The Lincoln Years*," Reynolds recalled. "I think mine says, 'To Nick Reynolds and the Kingston Trio—my appreciation for your wonderful music.'"[29]

"Everglades" was written by Country Songwriter Hall of Famer Harlan Howard ("I Fall to Pieces," "Heartaches by the Number," "Busted"). The Trio had appeared with The Everly Brothers on *The Dinah Shore Chevy Show* in April 1959 and had become friendly with Don and Phil Everly. "We liked the Everly music," said Bob Shane, "and we would run across them here and there. In fact, we told them we were going to put their names in one of our next recordings, and at the end of 'Everglades' we sang 'running through the trees' from the Everlys." The Trio also borrowed the Everlys' opening guitar intro from "Bird Dog" for the opening of "Everglades." Guard said that the original lyric was "running like a mother from The Everly Brothers," but that Capitol wouldn't allow it.[30]

"Tomorrow" is another bit of clever comedic wordplay from the late Chicago-based singer/songwriter, Bob Gibson. At the time the Trio recorded the tune, Gibson was managed by Albert Grossman who brought him and Joan Baez to the first Newport Folk Festival in 1959 which The Kingston Trio were headlining.

String Along would be the last of five consecutive Kingston Trio studio albums to hit number one on the *Billboard* charts. Their live album, *. . . from the "Hungry i,"* stalled at number two, but remained on the charts for years. All groups eventually decline in popularity to a certain degree, some to moderate yet respectable levels, while others disappear entirely. The good ones never forget what got them to number one to begin with, and continually strive to sustain their level of competitive excellence. The Kingston Trio did just that as their next album *Last Month of the Year* so beautifully demonstrated.

Last Month of the Year

Last Month of the Year, released October 3, 1960, may well be the Guard Trio's finest recorded work, although it sold the least. It was the Trio's only Christmas album, but with disappointing sales (initially around twenty thousand) Capitol yanked it. It was re-released a few years later.

"We didn't want to do it as a traditional Christmas album, to sing 'Old Saint Nick' and the usual Christmas carols," Reynolds explained. "That's why we called it 'Last Month of the Year.' It had a real international flair." The album intentionally broke from what was becoming a formulaic Kingston Trio album in which expediency, more often than personal preference, dictated album content. This album would be different. Each member was asked to bring in tunes that were personally satisfying and to focus on the quality of material and arrangements that they expected of themselves. "It was kind of a work of love," said Reynolds, "because we never really concentrated on doing a theme album before. It had always been the same kind of format—some blasters, calypso, maybe a Hawaiian or Tahitian type song, a comedy song, another blaster, a soft ballad, a medium tempo. That was the format we followed most of the time. This album was completely different and it was a real theme album. We worked really hard on it. Really tricky arrangements. Really tricky harmonies. And there's some really beautiful songs on it. Not a real pop album. Not what the general public would go out and buy for their Christmas carol music."[31]

Only the cover made a token reference to the popular concept of Christmas, with Guard, Reynolds, and Shane holding prop Christmas presents at the front door of Shane's house in Tiburon.

The album was recorded at Capitol in the summer of 1960, while the Trio were appearing at the Cocoanut Grove in the Ambassador

Hotel. They all had head colds at the time they were recording, which they felt gave their voices more resonance and a higher pitch. "So we were singing better and in tune on this album than most for recording," Reynolds recalled. They recorded on their days off and after the show at night, usually around 10:30 p.m., recording till 2 or 3 a.m. Then home to bed and sleep all day, work the Cocoanut Grove doing a couple of shows, then go back to the studio. They'd also get up and rehearse in the afternoon. Guard said their voices were shot by singing two sets a night at the hotel, so they recorded only the instrumental tracks at the initial sessions, coming back a month later to lay-in the vocals. Actually, it was only four days later according to Capitol session logs, which have the Trio recording on June 16 and 17, coming back on June 21 and 23, to complete the album with four more tunes. The complexity of the album may have made it seem longer.

"It was a pretty complicated little album, some intricate stuff," Reynolds recalled. "David brought in a lot of the arrangements with stuff like bouzouki instrumentation; Buckwheat played some wonderful gut-string guitar. We really worked hard on that one, working on the harmonies over and over. David was responsible for a lot of that album, but we all brought things in. Musically, it came off very well; it just didn't sell."[32]

The album is composed of traditional carols and adaptations of Christmas legends from Europe and America's Deep South. One tune, and one of the album's standout cuts, is "Go Where I Send Thee" that Shane said isn't a Christmas song at all, but a tune the group heard at a Weavers concert in San Francisco. The liner notes say that the song was originally known as "The Carol of the Twelve Numbers," sung during the Jewish Passover over 1,500 years ago. One thing's for sure, the tune is a rocker as done by the Trio. "It was really a shame that we didn't get it the first couple of takes, because it could've been a *big* song," said Reynolds. "We really killed it on the first few takes, and then they started having us do it over, over, and over again and then it just lost its power."[33] The tune is also known as a traditional African American spiritual collected by Jean Ritchie.

Another standout, and the title track of the album, is "Last Month of the Year," credited to Vera Hall (Adell Hall Ward), an early folk and blues singer from Livingston, Alabama. She shares credit here with Alan Lomax and Ruby Pickens Tartt, a renowned collector of folklore, folk music, and slave narratives in rural Alabama. The Trio got the tune from Alan Lomax and Pete Seeger. And it's a rocker, too.

"Mary Mild" is the story of a young Jesus who uses his divine powers to build a "bridge of sunbeams" to impress neighborhood children, who look down on him as poor, so that they would play ball with him. It's a story that's repeated on every playground in the world every day. And like all mothers, Mary doesn't care if he's the Son of God or not—she doesn't want *her* kid showing off.

Nick brought in two songs, "All through the Night" and "Goodnight My Baby Goodnight," both of which had special meaning to him because of the recent birth of his son, Josh. "I was just knocked out by having a kid." One tune, "A Round about Christmas," stirred up enough trouble to knock Reynolds out of the Christmas spirit and land him in court. "I learned it from Harry Belafonte who learned in from somebody else," Reynolds said. "So Harry and I later in court decided that we *both* owned it. Which is fine, rather than *him* getting the whole thing!"[34]

Make Way

Unlike its predecessor, *Make Way* was a "filler album," as both Shane and Reynolds described it, hastily assembled and recorded October 3, 4, and 5, 1960, in Los Angeles. Such tunes as "Hangman," "Hard Travelin'," "The River Is Wide," and "Blow the Candle Out," while well pedigreed, are vocally boring, as if sung by rote. While others—"Jug of Punch," "Uta-wena," and "Oh, Yes, Oh!" (with a tipsy Nick Reynolds banging on a bass drum with a mallet)—are just plain awful.

At the same time, "Bonny Hielan' Laddie" is one of The Kingston Trio's best efforts. The tune is credited to Guard and Joe Hickerson, but its Scottish derivatives go back centuries. Hickerson originally found the song in an old Burl Ives book of sea chanteys. Guard, however, learned the tune from Pete Seeger. "This was taught to me by someone research-ing the sailors that sailed out of Quebec," said Seeger, "because they sailed up the Saint Lawrence to Quebec in the early days and they sailed up to Montreal, too."[35] "Blue Eyed Gal" is another standout featuring Guard's blazing—and very credible—Scruggs-style picking. The tune is based on a traditional bluegrass favorite, "Fly around My Pretty Little Miss, Fly around My Daisy" and its variations.

"En El Agua," aka "Maria Christina," was written in 1938 by Anto-nio Fernandez for a dual Mexican-American Music Festival in the border town of Nogales, half of which is in Arizona and the other half in Mexico. Shane said he knew the song years before recording it, thought it was public domain, changed the lyrics, and was promptly sued by the Mexican government. Reynolds's "Mexican" warning that "the border is closed to all sailors not wearing raincoats [condoms]" may have hastened the legal proceedings. Earlier, the Trio's recording of "Tijuana Jail" threw the Mexican government into a tizzy, banning airplay of the single in Mexico.

Goin' Places

Goin' Places was the seventh and last studio album done by the Guard Trio, recorded January 14, 15, and 16, 1961, in Los Angeles. It was also the last album period, marking the end of Guard's association with Shane and Reynolds, although formal separation would not take place until August. By the time *Goin' Places* was released on June 5, 1961, it was already common knowledge, thanks to a *Life* magazine article, that the Trio were headed for the rocks. "By this time, things had gotten to the point where Dave was more of an associate, all of the camaraderie of the early days was gone," Reynolds remembered. "It was a click on, click off kind of thing. The music and the audience, but mostly the music, made it all okay."[36]

Guard agreed that while they could still deliver the quality, their togetherness in spirit and single-minded focus was long gone by the time they began production of *Goin' Places*. "Yeah, I think we kind of cracked sky high. The inspiration wasn't so much there, you know? But that was a tradeoff. My analysis is that in the early days we all had the same thought at the same time. We'd see some blond coming down the street and say wow—three minds would click at once. Whatever it was, we reacted the same in almost every instance to stimuli. But over time, the dynamic began to shift. You'd have three different minds with three different thoughts," Guard said.[37]

The album was recorded just before the group departed for Japan and their first Far East tour. Had it been scheduled after the tour it would never have been recorded. Guard barely spoke to Shane and Reynolds during the tour, and only if absolutely necessary. Reynolds and Shane flew "into the sunset" after the tour was cut short, knowing that their dream was over. It was a metaphor for the end, and it was heartbreaking. The sad irony, especially for fans, is that *Goin' Places* is full of great musicianship and promise of wonderful things that could have continued. But the rancor, suspicion, hurt, and jealousy could never be overcome. The title of the album's first cut seemed almost prophetic.

In "You're Gonna Miss Me," The Kingston Trio meets The New Lost City Ramblers. The tune is credited to Mike Seeger, Tom Paley, and John Cohen of the Ramblers and Dave Guard, who met the group through Harold Leventhal, Guard's publisher (what a coincidence). The song is a variation of the Frankie and Johnny tune.

"Pastures of Plenty" was a Woody Guthrie standard written in 1941 describing the plight of migrant workers in the 1930s throughout the West. Guard plays a twelve-string guitar on this tune, a Gibson, which he had custom made. "The twelve-string I got was the first one Gibson ever made," Guard explained. "It's the same one I used in the later albums and I'm using nowadays. We did a show with The Everly Brothers and they were both playing two big black Gibson jumbos. I thought, 'Jesus! I've got to have one of those!' but I wanted a twelve-string, so I ordered one special. They said, 'What do you mean a twelve-string?' So I said just put twelve strings on it. So they sent one with a normal neck on it, so all the strings are equidistant. There was no way to get in and get a string, so they had to remake the whole neck basically. They sent it out, and Harmon Satterlee fixed it up, made it a very wide neck, the widest neck that was possible."[38]

The melody of "Coast of California" was lifted from "Si Me Quieres Escriber" (If You Want to Write Me), a song from the Spanish Civil War in the late 1930s. The tune was recorded by Pete Seeger individually and with The Weavers. Jane Bowers and Dave Guard composed new lyrics. As always, Guard's banjo work is superb, combining frailing and single note picking, evoking the feel of what a plundering pirate epic might be.

"It Was a Very Good Year" was written specifically for Shane by composer/lyricist Ervin Drake in 1961 at the suggestion of Artie Mogul, the Trio's publisher. Drake happened to be in Mogul's office one day and mentioned how much he'd like to write a song for the Trio, to which Mogul responded, "I have a meeting with Bob Shane in about twenty minutes." "Fine," Drake said, "I'll write one now," completing "It Was a Very Good Year" just as Shane walked in. Frank Sinatra covered the song four years after Shane, winning a Grammy for Best Male Vocal Performance in 1966.[39]

"This Land Is Your Land," Woody Guthrie's beloved version of a second national anthem, was written in 1940 and recorded in 1944. It's been covered by virtually everybody in the folk world, from Dylan to The New Christy Minstrels, and adapted by numerous countries with their own set of patriotic travelogue lyrics. Reynolds said that the highest notes he ever attempted were in the chorus of this song.

Six years after recording "Billy Goat Hill," Nick was still talking about "those good old records when you used to stand around one microphone and sing. We used to make some really good records, man," Reynolds enthused. "We did 'Billy Goat Hill' like that, all sat around one microphone with Johnny on the banjo."[40] Well, actually it was Dave on the banjo and it was six microphones. "Billy Goat Hill" really *is* a good old song written by James Day and George Arno (who also wrote The Easy Riders' "Marianne").

"You Don't Knock" was written by Roebuck "Pops" Staples and Wesley Westbrooks. It's a rockin' Staples Singers spiritual, and the Trio did it as good as it gets, but not without locking horns with Guard, who insisted they sing it with a black inflection. Nick Reynolds said, "I remember David insisting, 'This is the way it's going to be done, or we're not doing this other song.' He really pushed his weight on it. 'This is the way you're going to sing it and you have to use this kind of language.'" Reynolds refused, saying, "Jesus Christ, man! Please don't try to make me sing like a black man. We've done spirituals before, we can use rhythms and anything you want to use, but don't make me do impersonations. That's not what I do well."[41]

THE STEWART YEARS

On August 15, 1961, Bob Shane, Nick Reynolds, and John Stewart began to record their first song together as The Kingston Trio in Capitol's Studio B in Hollywood. You can hear the relief—and exhilaration—in their voices. It was a brand new day.

Close-Up

The havoc wreaked on their lives by the breakup with Guard was unimaginable, almost to the point where Nick and Bob questioned whether continuing The Kingston Trio was worth it. There is no such thing as a "good divorce" in any marriage—and The Kingston Trio definitely had been a marriage emotionally, financially, and legally. The same feelings of failure, remorse, anger, and guilt that follow the end of a domestic union were present there.

This first foray into the studio with Stewart was the ultimate test of whether there would continue to be a Kingston Trio. *Close-Up* proved that there could be—but it was a *different* Kingston Trio. Whereas the Guard Trio was predicated on precision with an intellectual bent, this Trio was based more on emotion and musicality. The vocals were on the "natch," as the Trio would say, more spontaneous, energetic, and enthusiastic. There was, however, still one strong musical connection to the Guard Trio in the presence of bassist David "Buck" Wheat. He would also accompany the

Trio on their follow-up album, *College Concert*, his last appearance with the group before joining Dave Guard and The Whiskeyhill Singers.

"We were having fun all of a sudden, which at the end of the other Trio we weren't," said Shane. "If you listen to the very beginning of the original Kingston Trio, the first couple of albums, the overall feel in the beginning was a little more serious than the thing with John. But you know, Nick and I are the kind of people that I honestly don't think we'd have chosen John if we didn't think it would be fun. By the time of *Close-Up*, we had some money, and we were relaxed and we were looking to have more fun." Shane said that since they were breaking from the ways of the old Trio, he and Nick decided to evenly divvy up many of the solos and leads so that everybody had good feelings about the album. "We tried to make it a more democratic way of making records."[42]

"Jesse James" was the first tune to be recorded for *Close-Up*, a satiric ballad about Jesse Woodson James (1847–1882), the murderous Missouri outlaw, bank robber, and gang leader. Stewart had looked forward to recording at Capitol and being part of the "big sound" for which the Trio was renowned. He was in for a big surprise. "When I was recording with The Cumberland Three, it never sounded as full as The Kingston Trio records. So when we recorded 'Jesse James' I said, 'Hey, that sounds good Nick, but it doesn't sound as full.' And he said, 'Watch this—we're gonna sing the chorus again.' And we did it and there was *that sound* and I went 'Holy shit!' We double tracked the chorus on every album after that using a three-track machine, then mixing it down to a two-track and then doubling our voices back on the three-track."[43]

"Coming from the Mountains" was the first cut on side one of *Close-Up*, and the first opportunity for the public to hear the new Kingston Trio, and it's no coincidence that *this* song leads off. It's a travelogue of where the Trio's going—virtually everywhere—"singing a song that *you all know*." The signature Kingston Trio sound had always been Shane and Reynolds singing together, Bobby on lead vocals and Nick shadowing him on harmony. Capitol made sure that the listener heard this lesson up front on *Close-Up* and would come to the obvious conclusion The Kingston Trio sound is alive and well without Dave Guard.

Shane said that "Karu" and "Glorious Kingdom" were given to the Trio in New Zealand by Sir Howard Morrison, a knighted member of the Order of the British Empire and a Maori tribe member. He was also the leader of the hugely popular Howard Morrison Quartet, which opened for the Trio in New Zealand on their last tour with Guard. The Maori people are a Polynesian tribe related to Hawaiian and Tahitian peoples. "Karu" is supposedly an old Maori fishing song, but may actually be Tahitian or from elsewhere in the Cook Islands. "Glorious Kingdom" was another song The Morrison Quartet sang in their lounge show and taught to the Trio. Later, the Trio were sued for copyright infringement of "Karu," and Morrison was added to the credits along with Shane, Reynolds, and Stewart.

"When My Love Was Here" was written by Stewart about his first teenage love at age nineteen while working at a summer resort in the San Bernardino Mountains. "The resort was called Seven Oaks and I was a dishwasher," Stewart recalled. "Her name was Stephanie Butler and her parents lived there for the summer, and she worked as one of the maids. I just had the biggest crush on her, and fell madly in love. I remember dancing with her to 'All I Have to Do Is Dream' and she put her cheek next to mine and it was just one of the great experiences of my life at that time."[44]

"Take Her out of Pity" was brought in by Stewart, who said only that it was "an old, traditional folk song, one of my favorites." Indeed, the tune goes back to the seventeenth century under various titles, including "The Old Maid in the Garret." Most likely, Stewart heard the tune from Peggy Seeger's 1955 Folkways album, *Folk Songs of Courting and Complaint* as "The Old Maid," which is very close to the Trio's version. Nonetheless, the song is credited to Shane, Reynolds, and Stewart.

"The Whistling Gypsy," also known as "The Gypsy Rover," was written by Irish singer, songwriter, and radio host Patrick Leo Maguire. The song was brought in by Nick, who had learned it from The Clancy Brothers. Shane is the whistler on this tune. "He's a damn good whistler," Reynolds said admiringly. "It just surprised the hell out of me!"[45]

Shane said "O Ken Karanga" was given to him by Stan Wilson, whom the Trio gave writing credit. "I don't know if he wrote it; he probably *re-wrote* it," Shane added. "He was a master at taking old songs and rewriting them. It was written as an African type of song, and it was in his show. I was singing it early on, so it was easy to bring that song in."[46] Despite the Trio's largesse with Wilson, "O Ken Karanga" is credited to Massie Patterson, Lionel Belasco, and Maurice Baron. Belasco was well-known for his calypso tunes, and his mother was of Afro-Caribbean descent, so there is some African thread down the line. The tinkling rhythm introduction to "O Ken Karenga" is played by Stewart, who is strumming the strings between the bronze bridge and the tailpiece of a Gibson B-45 twelve-string guitar.

"Reuben James" was written by Woody Guthrie ("The Sinking of the Reuben James") in 1941 to the tune of "Wildwood Flower" and recorded by Guthrie and the Almanac Singers. This *Close-Up* version is one of the Trio's best recordings overall. Subsequent live recordings of "Reuben

James" by the Trio were played faster, with little room for vocal nuance, and as a result the musicality of the tune is diminished. Shane explained, "There were songs that we had to do because people wanted them, but in order to do all the songs that people wanted I think we just naturally speeded them up to get them finished faster. Also, Nick and I did have the desire to play faster than either Dave or John. But the whole rhythm pattern of the thing I wanted to make it a more upbeat thing rather than being dragged down by the same old shit."[47]

College Concert

College concerts were the Trio's favorite venues. Audiences were always appreciative, hip, and tuned-in to the Trio's music and humor. UCLA was especially receptive, not to mention being right in Capitol's backyard.

College Concert was culled from two complete concerts recorded in UCLA's Student Union Grand Ballroom over two nights, December 6 and 7, 1961. It was the first in-person album with Stewart, with new material thoroughly rehearsed by the group and broken-in at the La Fiesta nightclub in Juarez, Mexico, from November 22 to December 3. "It was one of the biggest things we did with John," said Reynolds. "We got close to four hours of material. The kids were fantastic. My God! Our adrenalin started pumping—you could hear it on 'O Ken Karanga.' I never played that kind of drumbeat before—or since. I just kind of created it on the spot! The audience couldn't have been better, man, at any college show we'd ever done."[48]

It's widely believed among Trio fans that only half of *College Concert* is "real" and that six tunes—"Chilly Winds," "Oh, Miss Mary," "Roddy McCorley," "Five Hundred Miles," "Where Have All the Flowers Gone," and "Goin' Away for to Leave You"—were recorded in the studio as replacements for the live versions with canned audience applause added. Shane, Reynolds, and Stewart, however, have all said that was not entirely true. "They weren't so much *done* in the studio as they were *enhanced* in the studio," said Shane. "They came from the concert tapes, but we beefed them up with voiceovers in the studio, singing over the parts to make it sound fuller."[49] "Not on every song, but on some of the songs," Reynolds added. "We wouldn't change or add any new parts, but just to fill it out, because recording live is pretty raw stuff. We did some overdubbing, just lightly where it was terribly out of tune. I could be real flat on the damn high note or an ending or something like that, or run out of wind. But overdubbing would just sail you through that shit, and make it stop and end right on time. We were enhancing everything at that time. Just touching up the tunes! Nothing more boring than perfection. Voyle had a reputation to live up to, man. He didn't want any horror songs."[50]

Stewart said that *College Concert* was a totally effortless album to do. "We just breezed through it." But what he remembered most about *College Concert* were the acoustics of the Grand Ballroom at UCLA and how they enhanced the quality of their performance: "The hall was very live and we could hear ourselves very well. It had real reverb to it because of the live-ness of the hall that I think really added to the performance. It was exciting. It was like playing in a bathroom, which I think made that album sound like it does and we were totally at ease with it. If we had been in a dead hall acoustically, it wouldn't have been as inspiring as playing in that hall at UCLA."[51]

The concert starts off with "This Little Light," an old gospel song purportedly written by a student at the Moody Bible Institute in Chicago in the early 1920s. While labeled a "children's song" with simple call and response lyrics, it became a civil rights anthem of sorts in the 1950s and '60s. The song was first collected by John Lomax at a Texas prison in 1939.

"Chilly Winds" and "Oh, Miss Mary" were written by John Stewart and John Phillips—partly in a rowboat in the Sausalito harbor and partly in all-night writing sessions. The two had known each other from New York during The Cumberland Three and Journeymen days in the Village. By 1961, Phillips had moved to California and caught up with Stewart who was living in Sausalito. "It was a real up time in my life," Stewart said. "John [Phillips] and I had written 'Chilly Winds,' but it was really John's song and we sat up one night and wrote about fifty verses to it. 'Oh, Miss Mary' was my song, and Phillips came in and we worked on it together and a really terrific friendship developed. Being with the Trio, and the energy of that first album being a success, really carried me along."[52]

While "Laredo" ("Streets of Laredo") was originally taught to Stewart by Frank Zappa, the Trio pinched a version from The Smothers Brothers. "We got big laughs with things like 'Laredo,' which we'd stolen from The Smothers Brothers," Reynolds recalled. "And I think The Smothers Brothers came to see the show and said, 'We want to thank you very much for stealing our shit.' They were pissed off, and I don't blame them. It was one of their good bits. Downright thievery!"[53]

This concert version of "O Ken Karanga" is highlighted by a spectacular drum solo by Reynolds on BooBams. John introduces the song by saying it was "written by Chubby Checker and the Congolese Army Band," and suggesting that the audience "dance down the aisles tearing off bits of clothing, shrieking filthy words." Shane is still tickled by it. "The minute John realized that he could use his humor and people would pay attention to it and respond to it, he started using it on stage," said Shane. "He was funny and most of the time it was just off the top of his head. And I just loved his humor."[54]

"Roddy McCorley" was a real Irish political rebel, executed in 1800 in the town of Toomebridge in County Antrim near Belfast in Northern Ireland. The lyrics are based on a poem by Ethna Carberry (Anna Johnston). The song came to the Trio via The Clancy Brothers and Tommy Makem, their source on all things Irish. The "drum" sound was actually Shane turning the A string over the bass E string of his guitar, holding them with his fingers and drumming them with his fingers.

"Ballad of the Shape Things" was written by Broadway and comedic lyricist Sheldon Harnick, who also wrote "The Merry Minuet" from the Trio's . . . *from the "Hungry i"* album. The "Shape of Things" became a permanent addition to their concert repertoire, with Nick and Bob singing side by side, and Bob pointing to the top of Reynolds's head when the words "golden fruit" were sung. They were accompanied by Stewart on guitar.

"Goin' Away for to Leave You" is one of three John Phillips songs on *College Concert* that he either co-wrote with Stewart or wrote by himself. Ironically, when Phillips was forming The Mamas and Papas, he came to Werber and was flatly ignored. No one knew why Werber had developed an intense dislike for Phillips, but he was forbidden to enter the Trio offices again.

"I really liked that album," Shane said fondly of *College Concert*. "Nick was experimenting with the BooBams, and the humor was up, and the whole thing was up. It was just an enjoyable gig to play—and it was a *great* feeling record."[55]

Something Special

Released July 30, 1962, *Something Special* lived up to its title, both good and bad. Shane said it was one of his favorite albums, and there's plenty to justify his praise. Reynolds called it "sort of a bullshit album," also with some justification.

The concept was to record The Kingston Trio accompanied by a full orchestra—strings, brass, woodwinds, percussion, and backup singers— doing their usual folk-oriented repertoire. Such out-of-the-norm albums are often indicative of the artist having trouble coming up with something new and fresh, or of waning interest on the part of the record-buying public. Shane said it was neither. "Voyle Gilmore came up with that idea because those kind of albums were popular at that time. Also we were looking to play Vegas more and the orchestra thing might have fit in well playing those big showrooms."[56] Putting full orchestras behind folk groups was not new. The Weavers recorded numerous songs for Decca backed by The Gordon Jenkins Orchestra, as well as others.

The album was time-consuming and expensive to produce, requiring four sessions to record the Trio alone (March 15 and April 23, 24, and 25, 1962) and three orchestral overdub sessions (May 18 and 21 and April 25, 1962). Veteran Los Angeles composer, conductor, and arranger (including Ricky Nelson's early Imperial hits) Jimmie Haskell scored the charts and led the orchestra for *Something Special.*

The criticism has been that some of Haskell's arrangements were heavy-handed or otherwise inappropriate for some of the songs, particularly those with the female background voices. "He had these singers that were just too much freakin' frosting," Stewart said, "so I worked with him on that and I did more pruning than anything."[57] Yet some of Haskell's arrangements are perfectly suited to the songs. "Away Rio" is beautifully scored and expertly interpreted, with just the right blend of French horn, flute, banjo, and soaring strings that give it the grandeur of a movie epic soundtrack. The song is an old sea chantey, long in the public domain, and refers to the Rio Grande do Sul of Brazil, not Mexico's Rio Grande. Stewart brought the song in, and wrote the bridge, "One more day, Johnny, One more day" sung in a minor key. Stewart remembered "Away Rio" as one the best songs he ever did with the Trio.

"Pullin' Away," also known as "The Wagoner's Lad," is another exceptional orchestra cut with understated strings, allowing Reynolds's tenor guitar to be heard accenting the rhythm. Stewart wrote Nick's solo bridge, "Long is the road, dark is the night, look over your shoulder, he's waving goodbye."

Reynolds said of the album, "Frank and Voyle would get together and say, 'Geez, we're putting out the same kind of stuff you know; let's try something with some background.' A lot of people were doing it. I loved some of the songs. The original tracks were good; we left a little bit out of the stuff instrumentally that they said would be covered with the orchestra. Jimmy Haskell came in and watched us record it. And we talked to him. There were some good songs on it. 'One More Town' was on it, and a whole bunch of things. But we didn't hear it until after we got back from Hawaii. But it was different, and once again, the wrong thing to do—like the 7UP commercials. It probably didn't hurt our image. It didn't really make much difference at that time. Our records had leveled off. We were selling a good number, but nothing like before."[58]

"One More Town" is the standout tune on *Something Special*, one of two songs of which John Stewart felt most proud (the other being "Honey, Are You Mad at Your Man"). It was issued as a single backed with "She Was Too Good to Me" (Capitol 4842) in September 1962. While *Something Special* charted at number seven on *Billboard*'s album chart, "One More Town" only reached number ninety-seven as a single, only four notches below "Jane, Jane, Jane," which was also culled as a single from the album. Reynolds once mused that "She Was Too Good to Me" could have been another "Scotch and Soda" for Shane if he had pushed just a little harder emotionally. "It was almost there." The female backup singers didn't help much either. Bear Family's *The Stewart Years* has both the album version with strings and the version without; the latter is a killer.

The strangest cut of all, "Strange Day," was originally a joke that Stewart and his friend George Yanok knew and decided to turn into a song. The writer's royalties were no joke. Yanok laughed all the way to the car dealership where he bought his first new car in years.

New Frontier

In many ways, *New Frontier* was a defining album for The Kingston Trio—a document of their art, creative use of the studio technology, and, above all, their enormous individual and collective talents. Anybody who heard it, including their competition within the increasing folk ranks, had to have realized that The Kingston Trio was still in a league of its own.

Despite its title, *New Frontier* is not a theme album. Only one song, "New Frontier," makes any connection to the Kennedy administration and spirit. Stewart *did* dedicate the album to the Peace Corps, enough of a link to warrant a private meeting between JFK and Stewart at the White House in July of 1963, when the Trio were appearing at the Carter Barron Amphitheater in Rock Creek Park. The Kingston Trio were a favorite of the Kennedys beginning back in the Guard years, but they loved the Stewart Trio, too, and John would become close to Robert Kennedy and his family. Whenever the Trio would play or travel through the Washington area, John would make it a point to stop and visit Robert Kennedy at the Justice Department, bringing with him the latest Kingston Trio album. And so it was with *New Frontier*. It was Robert Kennedy who suggested that

Stewart personally present the album to President Kennedy and arranged their meeting at the White House. John recalled the experience:

"I went to the White House and gave President Kennedy a copy of *New Frontier*, and I remember standing in the Cabinet room looking at this big sailfish on the wall. I knew when he had walked in the room. I could *feel* that he had walked into the room and I turned around and there he was, tanned and smiling. I handed him the album and he said, 'Oh yeah, how's "Greenback Dollar" doing?' I said, 'Mr. President how would you have heard "Greenback Dollar"?' He said, 'Oh I heard it driving to work one morning!' So we laughed—he said, '*New Frontier*, yeah I've heard that; it's very good, John.' I said, 'You've heard it?' He said, 'Yeah, I think Bobby played it for me. You're over at the Carter Barron? I'm going to try to make it over. We're a little busy around here lately.' And that was it. I was such a Kennedy fan and he just made politics something heroic to me."[59]

Stewart also became friendly with the astronauts during this time and was later approached by NASA to do a film on the moonshot that traced the program from the Revolutionary War, showing its historical place. "I got to be friends with Scott Carpenter and hung out with him in Seabrook, Texas. John Glenn was his next-door neighbor! It was just an incredibly heady time for me and I got to know Bobby Kennedy, so it was really the pinnacle point of my life being the middle of all this."[60]

The Trio viewed *New Frontier* as somewhat of a personal mission, an implicit challenge to groups such as Peter, Paul and Mary, who were becoming hugely popular and eclipsing the Trio's record sales. "We rehearsed *New Frontier* very hard at Bobby's house in Tiburon," John Stewart said, "and Jerry Walter from The Gateway Singers worked with us on harmonies. It was like having a trainer when Jerry was there because it was someone to bounce things off. It wasn't just the three of us. He gave us new energy, and the fact that he was there made us work harder on that album than any album since *Close-Up* or *College Concert*."[61]

"There were tricky arrangements on *New Frontier*—trickier and more complicated," said Nick Reynolds. "We called for help because we didn't have the speed and facility within ourselves now that David was gone to really 'arrange' something other than just a three chords, three guys, three verses, and three melody thing. We wanted to get it a little more interesting. Jerry was very good. He didn't work the whole album, but there were maybe five or six songs on the album that he helped us line out and arrange, like Lou Gottlieb did on the early ones, too. Jerry was a real musician and could figure it out and knew what to do."[62]

Stewart said that *New Frontier* was the first album that gave him a feeling of what the studio was really all about, how different it was compared to live shows, and how it could be used as a highly creative medium. Indeed, the power of *New Frontier is* the studio, using overdubbing and Capitol's echo chambers to create a dramatic spatial grandeur or "bigness" to the songs that could never be replicated on the stage.

New Frontier is a collection of standouts, led by the Trio's 1963 hit, "Greenback Dollar," written by singer/songwriter/actor Hoyt Axton and Ken Ramsey. It reached number twenty-one on the *Billboard* charts, jumpstarting their popularity at a time when their competition from other folk artists was at its fiercest. "Greenback Dollar" is a great cut made even more powerful and dramatic by Capitol's echo chambers.

"Honey, Are You Mad at Your Man" is credited to John Stewart, who drew heavily from two songs, "Skillet Good and Greasy," a traditional tune recorded by Woody Guthrie, Uncle Dave Macon, Bob Gibson, and many others, and "Ruby (Are You Mad at Your Man)," a bluegrass classic recorded by The Osborne Brothers. Stewart and Reynolds partly sang as a duo on this cut, joined intermittently by Shane who added the lead. The engineer used echo to "color" the track, putting Stewart and Reynolds in deep echo and bringing Shane in with drier echo, layering the overall sound. Instrumentally, the tune is driven by a droning banjo lick, played by Stewart, over moving chords. Clever.

While Shane and Stewart were not bluegrass musicians, "Poor Ellen Smith" and "Genny Glenn" were certainly skilled facsimiles. Stewart said that he was listening all the time to Earl Scruggs and Doug Dillard and Eric Weisberg and people like that, and "having my mind blown," but could never really get three-finger picking down like they could.

Reynolds added, "I remember rehearsing 'Poor Ellen Smith' in Chicago at a hotel out by the airport, and boy we just loved that song! We'd do that for the folkies in Old Town. They couldn't believe what they were hearing! They would be at our hotel or downtown, I don't remember performing it on a stage, but boy it was a hot arrangement! I don't think it ever got recorded properly, because it was just too dynamic."[63] Shane's guitar playing, too, was as solid and right on the beat as any seasoned bluegrass rhythm guitarist. By the way, "Poor Ellen Smith" is based on the real murder of an Ellen Smith in 1892 by Peter DeGraff in Winston-Salem, North Carolina. Stewart said he got the tune from an Alan Lomax album, although it's been recorded by numerous sources over the years.

"The First Time (Ever I Saw Your Face)," written by English singer, songwriter, actor, and activist Ewan McColl, is perhaps one of the most beautiful love songs ever written, and one of Shane's very best vocals. It was composed for Peggy Seeger, McColl's wife. Shane brings to the song all the emotion and honesty McColl intended to convey to Peggy, the young woman he loved—and wed—who was twenty years his junior. Roberta Flack would later record "The First Time (Ever I Saw Your Face)," which became the biggest hit of 1972.

"Long Black Veil" was a country hit in 1959 for Lefty Frizzell, one of Shane's favorite singers. Shane had been listening and playing Frizzell songs since he first heard him on the jukebox at Fort DeRussy as a teenager. He later included Frizzell's country tunes, right down to imitating Lefty's twang, in his solo gigs at the Pearl City Tavern after leaving Menlo. *New Frontier* was perhaps the most eclectic Trio album of all—country, bluegrass, gospel, cowboy, English and Mexican love ballads, satire, patriotic anthems. And somehow it all fit together. It was a hit maker and game changer. It was also one of the Trio's personal favorites, both musically and emotionally.[64]

The Kingston Trio #16

The artistic and technical lessons learned on *New Frontier* carried over to *The Kingston Trio #16*, recorded four months later on January 16, 17, 21, 23, 27, and 28, 1963. This, too, is an exceptional album, with a diverse mix of quality material and high production values. Even Ken Veeder's stark black-and-white cover photography is a classy departure from the ordinary.

This album marks the first appearance of Glen Campbell on banjo, guitar, and background vocals. At the time Campbell was a top Los Angeles session musician and a member of the elite "Wrecking Crew" that played on virtually every major hit coming out of Southern California in the early to mid-1960s. It was also the first time that a Billy Edd Wheeler song appeared on a Kingston Trio album. In addition to "Reverend Mr. Black" for #16, the West Virginia native would supply "Desert Pete" (*Sunny Side!*), "Jackson" (*Sunny Side!*), "Ann" (*Back in Town*), and "Coal Tattoo" (*Time to Think*). The Trio was in good company; Billy Edd Wheeler tunes would sell over 57 million copies for more than ninety top artists, including Elvis, Johnny Cash, Neil Young, and Kenny Rogers.

"Reverend Mr. Black" would become the Trio's second major hit in less than a year, reaching number eight on the *Billboard* charts in May 1963. Stewart sang and spoke the solo recitation on this cut, with a background chorus that included Shane, Reynolds, Donnie MacArthur, and Glen Campbell, whom Stewart said sang the melody an octave higher. The chorus, incidentally, is a derivative of the African American spiritual

"Lonesome Valley." Shane recalled that during the rundown of the song, Campbell suddenly stopped playing and said, "Wait a minute! I know what this song needs!" He ran out of the studio and down the block to Music City on the corner of Sunset and Vine and bought a six-string banjo that he then played on "Reverend Mr. Black" and several other cuts. Surprisingly, John Stewart did not like "Reverend Mr. Black" and did not want to record it, but Voyle Gilmore talked him into it. The song later became one of the Trio's signature tunes, and Stewart had to learn how to perform it in concert. Since Campbell played it on a six-string banjo and Stewart played a five-string banjo, John cleverly improvised the key change before the final verse by sliding his capo up two frets while dampening the fifth string with his thumb. That's why it always sounded so different in live performance. "Revered Mr. Black" was the second highest charting Kingston Trio single, its number eight *Billboard* position second only to "Tom Dooley," which reached number one.

John Stewart remembered "Old Joe Hannah" as one of the most over-dubbed songs in Kingston Trio history. "We overdubbed the vocal on that four times! There was more tape hiss than there was a vocal because we couldn't get it to work, and it just got to be this hodgepodge."[65]

The Trio's first real political statement (not counting "Merry Minuet" and "Where Have All the Flowers Gone") may well have been "Road to Freedom," which was written by Stewart, who continually urged the Trio to be politically relevant, but often with little success. "Nick was with me in spirit but Bobby really didn't want to do that," Stewart said. "I pushed it hard—I was going to the Selma March when Bobby was living in the South and it could have been a lot more intense than it was. It got a little testy but it never got full-blown, but I could feel the political climate going that way and Bobby and Nick and Frank to a great degree wanted to keep the Trio doing what the Trio did, and there's really no right or wrong in that situation."[66] *Time* magazine later ran an article, "Folk Singers Hootenanny under Fire" (January 8, 1965), and used the lyrics of that chorus of "Road to Freedom" as the opener.

Don MacArthur, the Trio's long-time road manager, also got into the act on #16 as the writer of "River Run Down," one of Nick's solos. "I was just messing around one day and wrote these lyrics," MacArthur said, "and I showed them to John and he said, 'Hey, those look pretty good.' So he wrote the music and I wrote lyrics." "I don't know how he did it," Stewart marveled, "and I don't know if he ever did it again, but he hit it!"[67]

MacArthur said that he and Glen Campbell did a lot of overdubbing on #16 and that it was not unusual for him and anybody else that might happen to be in the studio to be enlisted to sing. "Voyle Gilmore would just say, 'You know what? Let's get some more voices on there, and let's just jump in and blast away!' You couldn't really tell if it was my voice specifically," MacArthur said, "but we'd just fill up the background with it. My voice is in there a whole bunch of places. In all of the chorus overdubbing, I was right in there wailing away. Me and Glen Campbell."[68]

Like its predecessor, #16 had no weak cuts or fillers, and such tunes as "Run the Ridges," with its intricate guitar lines and soaring, choir-like chorus remained spectacular and instructive nearly fifty years later. (Interestingly, Stewart borrowed, and duly paid for, a phrase from the lyrics of a song his friend George Yanok had written in 1963—"running the ridges of my greenland, Tennessee.") Even the old Mexican folk tune "La Bamba," picked for the album as a last resort because they had run out of material, is given new life and drive, especially with Nick's Mariachi yelps and John's repeating banjo line.

Sunny Side!

By the summer of 1963 the stress of churning out three albums a year was catching up with the Trio, and Stewart said that *Sunny Side!* did not match the level of effort that went into *New Frontier* or *#16*. With the incredible grind of playing so many days on the road, of doing the same thing, the excitement had worn off—and they were doing three albums a year. "That's a lot of albums to do. And trying to find new things to do, and other groups coming along and just sort of taking the wind out of our sails."[69]

While *Sunny Side!* wasn't their best album, it still had its high points, starting with Glen Campbell's single-note guitar runs on "Jackson" playing opposite Shane's D-28 and Stewart's twelve-string driving acoustic rhythm. As a guitar track alone it's the best cut on the album. Terrific harmony between Shane and Reynolds, and Stewart's Johnny Cash imitation is, well, interesting. "Desert Pete" also features some fine six-string banjo flatpicking by Campbell. The song, written by Billy Edd Wheeler, was released as a single and charted at number thirty-three in September 1963. It was the last Kingston Trio single to break into the Top 40.

Bob Dylan makes his first appearance as a writer on a Kingston Trio record with "Blowin' in the Wind." The song was recorded almost simultaneously with that of Peter, Paul and Mary. But unlike their version, which became a major hit, the Trio's failed to even chart. The melody to "Blowin' in the Wind" is possibly a derivative of the Negro spiritual, "No More Auction Block."

The most interesting tune on *Sunny Side!* is "Ballad of the Thresher," a song about the USS *Thresher,* a nuclear-powered attack submarine that sank in April 1963 with the loss of all 129 men on board. It was written by a Dallas attorney who brought the lyrics to Stewart and asked him if he would write a melody to it. Stewart said yes, and the attorney paid for the Trio's recording session. "I hate my vocal on that, but I really love the song," Stewart remarked. "It was one of the better Trio songs."[70]

"Marcelle Vahine" was written by Augie Goupil, a Tahitian drummer, singer, bandleader (The Royal Tahitians), and dancer who was the rage in both the United States and the islands in the 1930s and '40s. This tune is one of his best known and was sung by Guard and Shane as kids in Hawaii. Reynolds, too, was an Augie Goupil fan in high school, and he and Shane sing it here as a duo. Stewart added, "It's one of the great Hawaiian songs that Bobby and Nick can just nail. They were so good at those songs—it's Bobby's heritage, and Nick would just jump in. I didn't even sing on that."[71]

Shane has been singing "Those Brown Eyes" to legions of beautiful women since his college days at Menlo. Many of these women believed that Bob composed it just for them. Actually, Woody Guthrie wrote the song with later adaptations by The Tarriers—Alan Arkin, Bob Carey, and Erik Darling—in the mid-1950s.

Sunny Side! contains only eleven cuts, one short of the usual twelve found on most albums in the 1960s. Originally the album contained one more cut, "Woody's Song" (aka "The Folksinger's Song"), written by Mike Settle, but deleted by Capitol for fear of a lawsuit because they felt the lyrics insinuated that a well-known folk collector was making deals with a prison guard to record an inmate and take credit for his songs. The album had already been released, with two thousand promotional copies in circulation, when Capitol pulled it and quickly reissued it without the offending cut. Nobody knows why they didn't replace the cut; they had plenty of backups.

Time to Think

For Trio aficionados, including the Trio members themselves, *Time to Think* was their finest hour. Recording began on September 11, 1963, at Capitol studios in Los Angeles with "Ally Ally Oxen Free." All the other songs were recorded in San Francisco at Coast Recorders, with Voyle Gilmore and Pete Abbott present, on November 19, 20, 25, and 26 and December 2, 1963, literally in the middle of the country's darkest hour, the assassination of President John F. Kennedy.

On November 22, the day of the assassination, the Trio were rehearsing *Time to Think* at Reynolds's house in Sausalito. John's friendship with the Kennedys and his recent meeting with JFK made it all the more painful. "I can't believe we did that album," Stewart said as if it were yesterday, "it was tough."[72] Nonetheless, he gathered the strength to write "Song for a Friend" as a tribute to the president, and recorded it four days after the assassination. His grief and despair are unmistakable in his voice.

Despite the calamitous events around them, *Time to Think* was carefully planned and performed. From the outset it was never intended to preach or protest or make a political statement of any kind. "*Time to Think* was basically songs that were meaningful to us as a group and personally, based on where we were in life at that time," Shane explained. "And I think that it was one of my favorite albums because it had more meaningful things. It wasn't political. Politics, you know, I always tried to explain to people that we're an entertainment act. And politics is not entertaining in any sense of the word. We're not on stage or records to politic at all. This album was from the heart."[73]

"The Patriot Game" is not about the Easter Rising of 1916 or the civil war in Northern Ireland, but a later IRA (Irish Republican Army) skirmish, the Border Campaign in the mid-1950s. It was written by Dominic Behan, a Dublin songwriter-novelist, Irish Republican activist, and brother of Brendan Behan. It's long been a favorite IRA rallying song; the Trio learned it from The Clancy Brothers. "Bobby has always wanted to be Irish," Nick once quipped, and he certainly got his wish with his rendition of "The Patriot Game."

"Hobo's Lullaby" was written by Texas singer-songwriter and bona fide hobo Goebel Reeves in the 1930s. Reynolds said he learned it from Fred Hellerman of The Weavers. It's been recorded by Woody Guthrie, Arlo Guthrie, Pete Seeger, Emmylou Harris, and Ramblin' Jack Elliott. But to Kingston Trio fans, Reynolds's version is the only one that counts. Despite its popularity among fans, the Trio sang it only once in concert. "It totally bummed out the audience," Reynolds recalled. "Maybe it was too sad, but it turned them off immediately and we never sang it again."[74]

John Stewart wrote "If You Don't Look Around" upon his return from the Selma march and said that he had a hard time getting Bobby to sing it. But Bobby *did* sing it, which shows that their give-and-take attitude, a key factor in the longevity of their professional and personal relationship, was still intact regardless of politics.

The personal introspection that Shane alluded to as part of *Time to Think* is best evidenced in two of his lead vocals, "Turn Around" and "Seasons in the Sun." Shane is the proud father of five children, three of whom are girls. And he was definitely the black sheep ("Papa, please pray for me, I was the black sheep of the family"), albeit a beloved and extremely gifted black sheep. Reynolds saw the connection saying, "Yeah, the 'too much wine and too much song, wonder how I got along' part. That's Bobby."[75]

While some of the tunes on the album speak of horrific acts of injustice and prejudice, *Time to Think* is essentially an album of hope. "These Seven Men," written by Michael Stewart, John's brother, salutes the original seven astronauts, pioneers of the U.S. space program. "Ally Ally Oxen Free" had its gentle exhortation "Time to make our minds up if the world at last will be, ally ally ally oxen free." And, fittingly, the last song on side two, "Last Night I Had the Strangest Dream," voices the greatest hope of all, "I dreamed the world had all agreed to put an end to war." Stewart agreed, saying quietly, "It just killed Nick and I. We couldn't hardly sing it without crying."[76]

Back in Town

According to musicians union session sheets, *Back in Town* was recorded on April 1, 2, 3, and 4, 1964, at the hungry i in San Francisco, on the last four days of a two-week engagement. Yet documents found at Capitol indicate that the recording dates may actually have been January 1 and 4, March 4, and April 2 and 3 of 1964.

Regardless, the bottom line was the same: it was The Kingston Trio's final album for Capitol—and it should have been stronger. This is an expedient album. According to Stewart, one of the tunes, "Walkin' on This Road to My Town," was worked up during the sound check!

In fairness, The Kingston Trio in a nightclub setting was not The Kingston Trio in Studio B at Capitol, nor was it supposed to be. Audiences know the difference between a perfect studio cut and a live "floor number," and a reasonable facsimile will do just fine. They've come to see their heroes in person, with humor, personality, and spontaneity. And there are several cuts on *Back in Town* that rise to the Trio's usual high standards.

The old folk and blues standard "Salty Dog" ("Salty Dog Blues") is funny, tight, and enthusiastic, boosted by Glen Campbell's terrific twelve-string backing. Shane said that Dick Rosmini, the folk era's virtuoso twelve-string guitarist, also played on *Back in Town*, albeit briefly and not credited.

"Farewell Captain," written by Michael Stewart, is energetic and obviously well rehearsed. The song is about a cowardly Confederate dropout and features Nick on lead vocal (whom Stewart drolly announced was picked because he "fit the part best").

Mason Williams makes his first appearance as a songwriter on a Trio album with "Them Poems," short comedic music rhymes sung by Bob Shane ("Them Lunch Toters," "Them Stamp Lickers," "Them Hors d'oeuvres"). Two years earlier Williams recorded a live album entitled *Them Poems*, which contained the preceding short tunes and a dozen more of "them" others, as well as a not-so-funny-today song entitled "Sweet Someone" sung with a lisp.

The quality of song material on *Back in Town* was exceptional, including new songs by Billy Edd Wheeler ("Ann"); Al Shackman, jazz guitarist and Nina Simone's long-time musical director ("Walkin' on This Road to My Town"); Rod McKuen ("The World I Used to Know" and "Isle in the Water"); and Dino Valenti, also known as Chet Powers ("Let's Get Together"). The set was opened by "Georgia Stockade," a rework of the old 1920s classic "Columbus Stockade Blues."

Overall, *Back in Town* is not a bad album, but it's not a particularly memorable one either. Given that the Trio's contract with Capitol had already expired by that time and not yet been renewed, one would think that the Trio would endeavor to make an album that Capitol, and more importantly, the public, would not easily forget.

THE DECCA YEARS

As early as the *Something Special* sessions in 1962, Shane said that the Trio had some concern that Capitol might not keep them on the label. Although they would deliver a Top 10 hit and two Top 30 hits in 1963, the arrival of the Beatles was reason for real concern. Capitol Records was a subsidiary of EMI (Electric & Musical Industries), a diversified British company that had signed The Beatles to Parlophone, one of the company's London-based labels. Initially, Vee-Jay Records produced The Beatles albums and singles in the United States until EMI sued and Capitol took over U.S. distribution and marketing. In short, EMI was potential trouble for any Capitol artist who wasn't a consistent best seller.

There is some sad irony that a group that at one time was the most popular and influential musical group in America, if not the world, could be dumped by the company to which it gave new life and untold millions of dollars over a seven-year period. But that is the mercurial nature of the music business.

"Memories are short in show business," Reynolds said philosophically. "And I can't really blame Capitol for putting all their money and effort into The Beatles, and they did a beautiful job—as they did for us—with record distribution and promotions that we'd never get again. When you're hot, you're hot. When you're not, you're not."[77]

Technically, Capitol didn't cut The Kingston Trio loose. Gilmore said that it was Werber's doing that the Trio didn't re-sign with Capitol, that he was asking "an arm and a leg" because he wanted to be a viewed as "the world's greatest manager," and that Capitol did "everything possible to keep them."[78] Reynolds disagreed, saying that Capitol offered no more than a 1 percent increase as an incentive. "You see, they had this group called the Beatles that was selling *millions* of records a week, so it was kinda like, 'Oh, gee, sorry you're not re-signing, bye-bye.'"[79] But Werber more than made up for it when he negotiated a whopping contract with Decca in October of 1964. The deal, worth between $750,000 and $1 million for a term of five years, with provisions for extensions, was for "services of the group both as recording artists and producers." Trouble was, the Trio's albums weren't selling anywhere near the volume that would justify Decca's spending that kind of money—and Werber knew it from the start.

"For me, after the Decca deal for $750,000, it just seemed like a good long day's work," Werber mused. "I'm a card player. I groove on the peaks and valleys of a deal while it's in the works. We did a lot of mind fucking on *that* deal. Nothing illegal, just playing cards, and they lost. It's like *Let's Make a Deal*. They got the box, looked inside, and there's four loser albums." At the same time, Werber also intimated that somehow Decca didn't work hard enough with the Trio: "They didn't keep it alive, they didn't protect their investment, a dumb company. That's why I was hoping to get them on the hook for that much, trying to hand them some motivation. But I can't say that's why we failed. The thing was dead by then album-wise."[80] John was at the signing of the Decca deal with Nick, Bob, and Frank in the office of Milt Rackmil, Decca's president. "It was the worst day of my life," Stewart remembered years later with a touch of rancor. At that time, as with the Capitol albums, Stewart shared in none of the Decca royalties. He was still the hired hand.

The Trio would record four albums for Decca before the contract was terminated. And while few would disagree that these albums do not match the quality of their best Capitol albums, several of them come surprisingly close. But it wasn't the same, as Stewart pointed out: "Just the recording aspect—once we lost Pete Abbott, once we lost Voyle Gilmore and those great echo chambers at Capitol and really good engineers, I don't know,

I just wasn't bright enough or ballsy enough to say this is not cutting it; we've got to go back to where we were. Frank had the Tower and he had the studio built and it was pretty much a situation where the die was cast. It just got to be too much of an in-house project." Producing—or rather lack of a producer—was one of those classic "in-house" issues. Frank Werber is listed as the producer on all four albums, but as Stewart put it, "Define the role of producer. Frank was in the booth—that's about it."[81] Frank had a great ear and knew the Trio's capabilities, but he was one of *them.*

With the Decca deal the Trio had the opportunity—and the money— to bring in the best outside producers in the industry, people with the savvy, the songwriting, the studio and musician sources, and, above all, the objectivity to assess the Trio's individual and group strengths and take them in a new direction. Werber's veiled assertion that Decca didn't work hard enough for the Trio is preposterous. It was *Werber* who didn't work hard enough for the Trio at that critical point—the major domo who didn't *insist* that an outside firebrand be brought in to reinvigorate the Trio and marshal the enormous individual talents of its members. Instead, they took the elevator to the basement.

The Kingston Trio: Nick-Bob-John

The most obvious difference from the Capitol albums in this first Decca outing is the absence of Capitol's echo chambers that had always been a part of the Trio's signature sound. "It sounds like shit," was Stewart's professional assessment, although "flat" would be a more accurate description.

Supposedly, the album was recorded at Columbus Recording in only two days, October 9 and November 21, 1964, with ten of the twelve songs having been done in only one day. That's impossible, of course, and is indicative of poor or no detailed session record keeping. What's more, contrary to what was shown by those "session sheets," at least three songs were recorded elsewhere: "Love's Been Good To Me" and "Little Play Soldiers" were both recorded at Coast Recorders in San Francisco on July 2 and 3, 1964, and "Love Comes a Trickling Down" at United Recording Studios of Nevada, Las Vegas, on August 24, 1964, when the Trio were playing at the Riviera Hotel.

Whatever its flaws, including total lack of creative art direction, this album is filled with excellent tunes and excellent musicianship. In its way, the album is a refreshing change and an accurate snapshot of what the Trio really sounded like live, which could be terrific.

"Midnight Special" is a traditional folk-blues "prison tune" from the early 1900s and has long been in the public domain, even though it was incorrectly credited to Lead Belly (Huddie Ledbetter) by John and Alan Lomax, who recorded Lead Belly's version at the Angola Prison in 1934. The Trio undoubtedly heard it performed by The Weavers, who featured the song in their act and recordings.

Fred Hellerman of The Weavers and Frances "Fran" Minikoff (composer of "Come Away Melinda") collaborated on "Poverty Hill." Ironically, the lead is sung by Reynolds who came from a wealthy family. Hellerman had earlier arranged the "Ruby Red" single for the Trio, the song that was on the flip side of "Tom Dooley." He was offered a percentage of the royalties on the record, which ultimately sold over 3 million copies, but chose instead to take a hundred dollar flat fee.

According to Nick, Fred Geis was a hobo, songwriter, folksinger, and adventurer. One of his alleged compositions was "I'm Going Home," which the Trio recorded and duly paid him, only to discover that Fred had borrowed the melody from "The Land of Milk and Honey" from "Hello, Dolly." The Trio was sued and Fred traveled on. Years later, Geis showed up at Reynolds's ranch in Port Orford, Oregon. "He pulled up in a Cadillac," Reynolds recalled with a laugh, "so we visited for a while, and right before he left, he said, 'I want to borrow a dollar.' Which is a hobo tradition or something like that. So I gave him a dollar and I never saw him again."[82] Reynolds never saw his dollar again, either.

The Kingston Trio had long admired Tom Paxton's work, and vice versa since Tom's student days at the University of Oklahoma. The Trio would record four of Paxton's songs, "Where I'm Bound," "Last Thing on My Mind," "Bottle of Wine," and "My Ramblin' Boy," the latter included on *Nick-Bob-John*. Shane sings the lead on the tune for which he is perfectly suited on several levels. An uninspired "Farewell" ("Fare Thee Well My Own True Love") is sung by an uninspired duo of Stewart and Reynolds. So many Dylan tunes from which to choose and they picked this one? When asked to comment on "Love Comes a Trickling Down," John Stewart looked directly at this writer and with a straight face said, "An unfortunate title."

Stay Awhile

After the Trio moved from Capitol to Decca, Stewart bemoaned not having engineer Pete Abbott and Capitol's echo chambers, yet he got them both back, albeit briefly, on *Stay Awhile* and possibly its follow-up, *Somethin' Else*.

Stay Awhile was allegedly recorded at Columbus Recording, January–March, 1965. The time period may be accurate, but this sounds like a Capitol album—bathed in echo, with precision mixing, editing, and mastering. It's "The Kingston Trio sound," which strongly suggests a freelancing Pete Abbott, Coast Recorders (where *Time to Think* was recorded a year earlier), and postproduction-for-hire at Capitol. Abbott was instrumental in *that* sound. Stewart concurred, saying they were really "into" *Stay Awhile*, and that Abbott was definitely involved. He also it said that it was not until after *Stay Awhile* that they went to Columbus Tower.

"Stories of Old" was recorded at Coast Recorders in San Francisco on July 2, 1964, and an alternate take of "If I Had a Ship" was recorded at ACA Recording Studios in Houston, Texas, on January 25, 1965, while the Trio was appearing at the Cork Club. Both of these tend to support the belief that *Stay Awhile* was not in fact recorded at Columbus Recording.

Regardless of where it was recorded, *Stay Awhile* is filled with quality material and quality players. "Hanna Lee" features the outstanding harmonica blues riffs of Billy Roberts, whom Shane knew and brought in for the sessions. Roberts, a native of South Carolina, had kicked around Greenwich Village in the early 1960s, moved to San Francisco, and was playing in numerous clubs, as well as opening for The Steve Miller Band and Santana. Roberts was also an excellent songwriter and the composer of "Hey Joe," which was recorded by The Jimi Hendrix Experience. Shane said Billy lived in New Orleans for a while and learned blues harp from the top black blues harp players there. He was renting a basement apartment at Shane's home in Tiburon at the time of the *Stay Awhile* sessions.

The Trio had known "Gonna Go Down the River" for years but never recorded it before *Stay Awhile*. It was the tune Shane and Reynolds used to audition Stewart back in 1961. It was written by Nashville songwriters Buddy Mize and Dallas ("Elvira," "Alley Oop") Frazier.

Mason Williams quickly became a ready source of good songs for the Trio, and three are featured on this album—"Three Song," "Yes I Can Feel It," and the pull-out-all-stops rocker "If I Had a Ship." Williams also wrote the liner notes to *Stay Awhile*, which included a special "Them Poem"—"How bout them Kingston Trio, ain't they honeys, singing my songs makin' me money!"

Tom Paxton contributed two classics, "Bottle of Wine," the anthem of all college fraternities, and "Where I'm Bound," a favorite of everyone who sang in the folk era and everyone who listened to them, from Dion to The Chad Mitchell Trio. "Rusting in the Rain," written by Rod McKuen, is perhaps the best song on the album.

Lack of response to *Stay Awhile*, in sales and airplay, was because it was simply irrelevant for the times. The number one song on *Billboard*'s Year-End Hot 100 chart for 1965 was "Wooly Bully" by Sam the Sham and the Pharoahs; the number one hundred song was "How Sweet It Is (To Be Loved by You)" by Marvin Gaye. There was no room in the middle for The Kingston Trio—or Peter, Paul and Mary, for that matter. Seemingly over-night, popular folk music had become passé. Dylan had gone electric in 1965. "Folk rock" had replaced folk music. And few performers of the folk era were equipped to make the transition. But The Kingston Trio certainly tried.

Somethin' Else

Despite being dismissed by critics and largely ignored by the public, *Somethin' Else*, the Trio's answer to folk rock, is a highly credible album—and a well-produced one. Released in November 1965 and (supposedly) recorded at Columbus Recording in San Francisco, it too has the Pete Abbott/Capitol sound.

In addition to acoustic guitar, banjo, and stand-up bass, the Trio is backed by a four-piece electric rock band consisting of Randy Cierley (aka Sterling) on nine and twelve-string guitars, jazz drummer Jerry Granelli (Vince Guaraldi Trio, Ornette Coleman, Sly Stone, We Five), jazz/rock drummer John Chambers (We Five, Big Mama Thornton, Joe Turner, Elvin Bishop), organist Andrew Belling, and Rex Larson on electric bass. Randy Cierly is also credited with co-writing and "special arrangements" of several tunes.

Numerous songs have been written about Parchman Farm, the Missis-sippi State Penitentiary, including those by blues legends Bukka White and Son House, both of whom were inmates at Parchman. The Trio's version is lifted directly from native Mississippian Mose Allison's "Parchman Farm," which is different from the others. Although the Trio's version (which is incorrectly spelled "Parchment Farm") doesn't have Allison's boogie-woogie piano beat, it still rocks. "Red River Shore" is an old cowboy song collected by John Lomax in 1937. His son Alan later adapted, arranged, and recorded the tune for his *Texas Folk Songs* album. The tune has been recorded by various groups, including The New Christy Minstrels and The Norman Luboff Choir.

Stewart's melodies have always been one of his strongest suits, and "Where Are You Going Little Boy" and "Dancing the Distance" are two of his most beautiful. The lyrics, too, are eloquent and moving. Mason Wil-liams co-wrote "Dancing Distance," as well as three others by himself on this album—"Long Time Blues," "They Are Gone," and "Interchangeable

Love," which is less than a minute long. One of Canada's favorite sons, Gordon Lightfoot, contributed "Early Morning Rain" to the album, fitting nicely in the folk-electric groove.

Not everything on *Somethin' Else* lives up to the album title. One tune, "Verandah of Millium August," credited to Stewart and Randy Cierley, is just somethin' weird, a really bad imitation of Dylanesque nonsense.

Children of the Morning

The best thing about *Children of the Morning*, The Kingston Trio's eighteenth—and last—studio album, was the cover. It was shot in a beautiful wooded area of Marin County, with the Trio posed on a rustic footbridge over a creek, singing with guitars and banjo, while five very disinterested little boys stare off into nowhere. Great photo. Not so great album.

By the time *Children of the Morning* was recorded at Columbus Recording Studio in February, March, and April 1966, The Kingston Trio was effectively finished as a viable recording act. The album is unapologetically expedient, driven by a contractual obligation to Decca. Of the twelve songs, eight are conveniently written by Stewart. The rest are anything that the group could quickly grab and sing with minimal effort—"Less of Me," "A Taste of Honey," "Lei Pakalana," and The Beatles' "Norwegian Wood."

Reynolds and Stewart considered *Children of the Morning* one of their best albums, but felt it was "ruined" by poor mixing, which they only discovered upon returning from a long tour after the album had been released. Shane, on the other hand, disliked the album, saying he was back in Georgia when Nick approved all of Stewart's songs, most of which he didn't care for. Fact is, Shane's not being present *was* a problem, with critical decisions being made for him in absentia. And if he wasn't there to voice his opinion, he got what somebody else thought was right. It explains, too, why so many songs on the album are duets with Nick and John, missing Bob's voice—the definitive voice of The Kingston Trio. As for Nick and John, they said that Shane was not open to doing new songs, no matter how hard they tried to convince him otherwise. Perhaps they were the ones that didn't get it.

Once Upon a Time

But they weren't quite finished yet. And for three weeks in the summer of 1966, Nick, Bob, and John were in complete sync with each other, and the main showroom of the Sahara Tahoe literally rocked. *Once Upon a Time* was a two-record "live" album recorded by the Trio over a three-week engagement, July 1–22, at the hotel in Lake Tahoe, Nevada. Included are six previously unrecorded tunes, "Tomorrow Is a Long Time," "Rovin' Gambler/This Train," "One Too Many Mornings," "Colours," "Goodnight Irene," and "Babe, You've Been on My Mind." Most of the rest of the songs, including several from the Guard era, had only been released on studio albums and not as live concert recordings.

The rest of the playlist includes "Hard Travelin'," "Early Morning Rain," "M.T.A.," "Police Brutality" (comedy), "A Day in Our Room" (comedy), "Wimoweh," "Tom Dooley," "Hard, Ain't It Hard," "Getaway John," "The Ballad of the Shape of Things," "Greenback Dollar," "Tijuana Jail," "Silicone Bust" (comedy), "I'm Going Home," "Where Have All the Flowers Gone?" "Scotch and Soda," "Blind Date" (comedy), and "When the Saints Go Marching In."

The two-album set was finally released in 1969 by Bill Cosby's and Roy Silver's Tetragrammaton Records after being rejected by both Capitol and Decca. According to Voyle Gilmore, Werber wanted twenty-five thousand dollars cash, up front, for an album that Decca had already declined and that he "just couldn't see it." Perhaps it was the stiff advance that helped put Tetragrammaton out of business in 1972.

"It was sort of my last labor of love," Werber said of *Once Upon a Time*. "I can't tell you how many hours of tiny little cuts there are in there, because I wanted to present what to me is the Trio. I included a balance of everything that I believed was what they were all about at that time, what was reflective of their state of the art. We had like two shows a night for two weeks. Nobody had ever recorded in that room, it was the first time. We set up all our own gear, came up with Hank McGill [Columbus Recording's staff engineer], and I think we did a hell of a nice job. I think the finished package is really a definitive presentation of the Trio as it was when it said goodbye—when it was at its peak of doing its thing."[83]

George Yanok was the Trio's road manager by this time, having replaced Joe Gannon, and he was asked to get involved with production of *Once Upon a Time*, beginning with scouting the Sahara Tahoe showroom with Werber. Six weeks later he found himself in the basement of Columbus Recording mixing *Once Upon a Time*, mostly by himself, as he recalled.

"You know what happened? It sat there. John was going to mix it and then John got in a fight with Frank and he didn't mix it. Frank was gonna mix it and Frank was too busy building an empire. And it sort of fell to me by default. It wasn't that anybody came to me and said, 'Now we want you to mix this album.' Frank said go down to the studio and make sure the thing works. And so I spent I don't know how long down there, maybe three nights down in the studio, the only thing I could think to do was take the UCLA album [*College Concert*], which was the closest ambiance I could think of to whatever was already on the record, and see if I could make it sound like that."[84]

Once Upon a Time was an interesting album, one of the few documents of the Trio's last year together that exhibited the total phenomenon that was The Kingston Trio. As Shane has said many times, The Kingston Trio was primarily a *live act*, it's where they made the most money—and had the most fun. The records were just gravy.

Over the course of ten years, the Trio easily played over one thousand concerts, in all kinds of venues, all over the country, all over the world. In 1959 alone, the first year of the Trio's national popularity, Guard estimated that they were on the road 328 days. "You'd be tired all the time, but you know, it's a great way to see America!" he often quipped.

The closeness of traveling and playing together nose-to-nose every night often implodes groups. Yet the obvious camaraderie of Shane, Reynolds, and Stewart is abundantly evident throughout *Once Upon a Time*. Although their time together professionally would be over in less than a year, the three remained lifelong friends.

THE POST TRIO YEARS

Following the release and disappointedly short shelf life of *Once Upon a Time* in June of 1969, Kingston Trio recordings became a thing of the past. With the exception of a few "best of" compilations, very little Kingston Trio product was available. True, Bob Shane had formed and was touring with The New Kingston Trio and would later release recordings from this group, but no rare or unreleased material surfaced from the "glory years" from the Capitol and Decca vaults. And in Capitol's case, Capitol engineer and remix editor Jay Ranellucci confirmed that Capitol still kept *everything*—from the finished master tapes to the recording session tapes themselves, including all unedited takes and studio chatter, from start to finish. Their historical and collectable value notwithstanding, outtakes, alternates, rehearsal tapes, and B-side songs are often mediocre, deemed inferior to a better take or a better song altogether. Serious collectors and die-hard fans cherish them, of course, but some artists deeply resent what they consider private rehearsals or work-in-progress being made public.

John Stewart was furious that a previously unreleased "Softly, as I Leave You" appeared on the Bear Family anthology *The Stewart Years*, considering it unfit for release *ever*. To my ears, the tune was beautifully done by the Trio, especially Stewart's solo, and certainly was worthy of release—and serious promotion—when it was recorded at Capitol Tower in early 1963. But I'm not John Stewart.

On the other hand, without these remnants fans would have heard nothing "new" from the Trio for almost two decades. It was not until 1985 that Allan Shaw and then business partner Steve Fiott released an album of obscure Capitol B sides and previously unissued Trio masters on their Folk Era label. The album, entitled *Rediscover The Kingston Trio*, contained six cuts from the Guard Trio and six from the Stewart Trio.

Guard Trio cuts include three unreleased tunes from the *Goin' Places* sessions—"Adieu to My Island," "Golden Spike," and "The Wines of Madeira." From the *Make Way* sessions, two unreleased tunes—"Oh Mary" (later reprised with John Stewart on *Close-Up*) and "Sea Fever." The final Guard Trio cut, "Blue Tattoo," was recorded on March 4, 1958, and intended as a single but never released due to the tune being covered by the Four Lads.

The Stewart Trio cuts include "Allentown Jail," recorded in 1962 as the B side to "C'mon Betty Home"; "Folksinger's Song" (aka "Woody's" song), removed from *Sunny Side!* for fear of a defamation lawsuit; "Old Kentucky Land" and "Rocky," recorded in late 1961—in *German*—for release as a 45 single in Germany. Reynolds remembered the Trio laughing their way through the session as they read the German lyrics phonetically. Their German vocal coach, however, was not amused. "Green Grasses" was written and sung solo by John Stewart on this cut, although it had previously been recorded as a single by the Guard Trio; and "Love Has Gone" was recorded in 1963 during *The Kingston Trio #16* sessions.

Treasure Chest, released in 1986, is a Folk Era compilation CD of Guard Trio songs drawn from their *Rediscover The Kingston Trio* and *Hidden Treasures* vinyl LPs, as well as several B sides. Most of these tunes have already been covered earlier in this chapter, with the exception of the select following.

"Sally (Don't You Grieve)," a Woody Guthrie tune, was recorded by the Guard Trio to be the B side of "Blue Tattoo," which was also recorded at the same session. Neither of these original cuts were released, although "Sally" was later re-recorded as the B side for another single; "Ruby Red" was the B side of "Tom Dooley," arranged by Fred Hellerman of the Weavers; "World's Last Authentic Playboys" was an exceptional find, recorded by the Trio in the New York *Sold Out* sessions in 1959. Written by the Trio's bassist David Wheat and Bill Loughborough, it was later re-recorded for Dave Guard and The Whiskeyhill Singers' first album.

In 1994, Vanguard Records released *The Kingston Trio Live at Newport* CD, recorded in July of 1959 before a crowd of fifteen thousand at the first Newport Folk Festival, at which The Kingston Trio were the headliners. "They [The Kingston Trio] were incredibly successful, which in purist folk music circles in those days was not always the politically correct thing to be," said Mary Katherine Aldin, well-known American traditional music proponent, speaker, *LA Weekly* columnist, writer, radio show host, and the producer of *Live at Newport.* "However, it was obvious to George Wein and the rest of the folks who were putting together the talent lineup for the 1959 Newport Folk Festival that booking this group was a must." Despite the outcry from folk purists and critics, The Kingston Trio were the Festival's indisputable top crowd pleaser, as evidenced in part by the deafening applause on this CD. "When the Trio took the stage, the audience response was wildly enthusiastic, but when they tried to leave the stage at the end of their scheduled set there was nearly a riot," Aldin recounted.[85] The Trio live set included "Saro Jane," "M.T.A.," "All My Sorrows," "Remember the Alamo," "E Inu Takou E," "Hard, Ain't It Hard," "Merry Minuet," "When the Saints Go Marching In," "Three Jolly Coachmen," "South Coast," "Scotch and Soda," and "Zombie Jamboree."

Over the years, both Folk Era Records and Collector's Choice Music have been excellent sources of Kingston Trio CD reissues and rare previously unreleased Trio recordings. In fact, Folk Era issued the very first Kingston Trio CD, *Stereo Concert Plus* in 1986, an enhanced and expanded reissue of the Trio's original *Stereo Concert* album. The original album included "Banua," "Three Jolly Coachmen," "South Coast," "Coplas," "They Call the Wind Mariah," "Zombie Jamboree," Tom Dooley," "The Merry Minuet," "Raspberries, Strawberries," and "When the Saints Go Marching In." Folk Era's *Plus!* version includes eight additional cuts: "Saro Jane," "I Bawled," "Santy Anno," "Ruby Red," "Pay Me My Money Down," "Watsha," "Little Maggie," "Shady Grove/Lonesome Traveler," and "Lei Pakalana."

Folk Era has also reissued virtually all of the Trio's Decca albums—*Nick-Bob-John, Stay Awhile,* and *Children of the Morning*—with most songs from the *Somethin' Else* album spread among the three CDs as bonus tracks.

Among the rarest Kingston Trio CDs from Folk Era are two previously unreleased college concerts, *Flashback! 1963*, recorded on October 3, 1963, at the University of Kentucky in Lexington, and *Snapshot*, recorded in November 1965 at Murray State University in Murray, Kentucky. Each is approximately ninety minutes long, on two-CD sets. Soundwise, these are not professionally recorded concerts, both taken from either house PAs or other stationary positions within the concert location. In addition to the standard Kingston Trio repertoire hits, *Flashback* includes "Little Light," "The Wagoner Lad," "Big Ball in Boston," "One More Town," "Two Ten, Six Eighteen," and "Ballad of the Quiet Fighter." *Snapshot* also includes standard Kingston Trio hits plus "Where I'm Bound," "They Call the Wind Mariah," "Last Thing on My Mind," "Parchment Farm Blues," "Hanna Lee," and "I'm Going Home." These two concerts make for fascinating listening, each a different "snapshot" of the Stewart Trio on the road playing to their favorite fans of all, college students.

Likewise, *Collectors' Choice Music* has released numerous Kingston Trio CDs, including "two-fer" reissues of all the Guard and Stewart Trios' Capitol albums, plus *The Kingston Trio Live at the Santa Monica Civic Auditorium, The Final Concert, The Lost 1967 Kingston Trio Album: Rarities Volume 1* and *Turning Like Forever: Rarities Volume 2.*

Released in 2007, *The Kingston Trio Live at the Santa Monica Civic Auditorium* was The Kingston Trio's last *recorded* concert with Dave Guard on April 21, 1961, but certainly not their last hurrah, which would come on August 5, 1961, with their last concert with Guard at the Castle estate in Ipswich, Massachusetts. The Santa Monica concert was a good one, and one of the few where the concert versions of their songs are very faithful to the record. And despite the fact that less than a month after the Santa Monica concert, Guard would send notice of his intention to leave The Kingston Trio, there is no discernible coolness or rancor or pathos evident in their stage patter and interaction with each other. It sounds like they're having fun, especially when Pat Boone makes a "surprise" appearance from the audience, joining the Trio in singing "You're Gonna Miss Me." There's also a video included with the CD of the Trio and Pat singing the same song on *The Pat Boone TV Show*. The only negative with this CD is the recording itself—flat, poorly equalized with almost no audible bass; it was probably taped directly from the auditorium PA system. The playlist includes "Run Molly, Run," "Bad Man Blunder," "Come All You Fair and Tender Ladies," "Bonny Hielan' Laddie," "Zombie Jamboree," "Colorado Trail," "You're Gonna Miss Me," "The Merry Minuet," "Go Where I Send Thee," "Coplas," "Guardo El Lobo," "You Don't Knock," "They Call the Wind Mariah," and "When the Saints Go Marching In."

In 2008, Collector's Choice Music released a second CD of The Kingston Trio's 1966 Sahara Tahoe concerts entitled *Twice Upon a Time,* consisting of alternate takes and nine concert tunes not included on *Once Upon a Time*. While the camaraderie and performance levels are high, it's obvious these are leftovers, unevenly mixed and rougher in spots than *Once Upon a Time*. This CD includes thirty-three tracks, with a total playing time of seventy-six minutes. The nine previously unreleased concert tunes include "Where I'm Bound," "They Call the Wind Mariah," "The Merry Minuet," "Hanna Lee," "Thirsty Boots," "Reuben James," "Hit and Run," "Little Maggie," and "The Spinning of the World." There's also a bonus video of the Trio singing "Tomorrow Is a Long Time."

The Final Concert, released forty years after the Trio's last performance at the hungry i on June 17, 1967, is a fitting end piece to their wonderful career, recorded at the club that helped start it all a decade earlier. For many years, Frank Werber sporadically shopped the tape of this performance to interested parties at a rather stiff price, but with no takers. This writer first heard the tape at Nick Reynolds's ranch in Oregon in 1986. It was fun watching Nick relive the concert, adding hilarious commentary as it progressed, especially with John "Mr. Rude" Stewart's greetings from the stage to hapless guests in the audience. Before I left Nick's house, he gave me the cassette of the performance we'd been listening to. I still listen to it and it's still funny. The tracks include "Hard, Ain't It Hard," "Early Morning Rain," "M.T.A," "Tomorrow Is A Long Time," "Reverend Mr. Black" (a new arrangement), "Ballad of the Shape of Things," "Thirsty Boots" (a first-time recording), "Colours," "One Too Many Mornings" (another new arrangement), "Tom Dooley," "Wimoweh," "Where Have All the Flowers Gone," and "Scotch and Soda." Sad, enthusiastic, tired, relieved. You'll hear it all on this CD.

Also released in 2007, *The Lost 1967 Kingston Trio Album: Rarities Volume 1* is a collection of false starts, song fragments, rehearsals of new songs, and studio chatter that includes a bonus track entitled "Fun with the Trio in the Studio." Supposedly, Nick Reynolds took strong issue with Collector's Choice for releasing this CD, saying that it was a private rehearsal tape where the Trio were simply trying out different songs, and that in the future no such recordings could be released without his explicit approval. Not surprisingly, and perhaps at Bob Shane's insistence, the Trio focused strictly on songs from the top songwriters of the day—Paul Simon, Fred Neil, Donovan, Bob Lind, John Sebastian, Steve Gillette, Tom Campbell, Tim Hardin—*and* John Stewart. These songs include "Love Me Not Tomorrow," "Homeward Bound," "The Other Side of This Life," "The Dolphins," "Try for the Sun," "Elusive Butterfly," "Nashville Cats,"

"Darcy Farrow," "Don't Make Promises," "Running out of Tomorrows," "Catch the Wind," and "Reason to Believe."

Turning Like Forever: Rarities Volume 2, released a year later, is composed primarily of alternate or practice takes of songs from the Trio's four Decca albums including, "Love's Been Good to Me," "Stories of Old" (instrumental backing track), "Little Play Soldiers," "Love Comes a Trickling Down," "Go Tell Roger," "If I Had a Ship," "When You've Been Away for a Long Time," and "Children of the Morning." The remaining vocal cuts include tunes by Mason Williams, Rod McKuen, Donovan, and John Stewart—"Road Song," "Love Poem #1," "Love Poem #2," "January Summer," "The Summer's Long," "To Try for the Sun," and "Adieu Foulard." The CD playlist is rounded out by a 1963 radio interview with Bruce Hayes on "Hootenanny for Saturday" on KHJ Los Angeles, and a series of 12 eight- to seventeen-second radio promos for Bill Terry at KCPX Salt Lake City in 1964.

In 2010, Bob Shane himself released a thirteen-track CD entitled *Above the Purple Onion* taken from an old reel-to-reel tape of 1957 rehearsal sessions of Shane, Guard, and Reynolds in manager Frank Werber's office loft above the Purple Onion, as well as downstairs on stage during some of their earliest shows. Shane has also written comprehensive liner notes on the tunes and times of which they were recorded. In all, it's a fascinating historical document of The Kingston Trio's most critical formative period. Tracks include "Run Joe," "Three Jolly Coachmen," "Shenandoah," "Tanga Tika Toerau," "Marcelle Vahine," "Minoi," "Leipakalana," "Fox Went out on a Chilly Night," "I Bawled," "Go Where I Send Thee," "Venga Jaleo," "Truly Fair," and "Pay Me My Money Down." It's available only through The Kingston Trio Store (www.kingstontrio.com).

But the ultimate Kingston Trio compilations are Bear Family's *The Kingston Trio: The Guard Years* and *The Kingston Trio: The Stewart Years*, ten-CD boxed sets released in August 1997 and April 2000, respectively. Not only do these box sets contain *every* known Kingston Trio recording (at the time of release)—early demos, studio, club, concert, and rehearsal outtakes, alternates, jingles—but each also has a hard-bound book with comprehensive discographies, studio logs, song annotations, group biographies (by this writer), and numerous photographs, ads, and memorabilia. These box sets are a must for fans, historians, and keepers of the flame. If you've got these box sets, you've got it *all*.

And that's a lot.

NOTES

1. Bob Shane, interview with the author, Phoenix, AZ, April 6, 2009.

2. Henry Diltz, interview with the author, Scottsdale, AZ, August 12, 2000.

3. Timothy B. Schmit, interview with the author, Los Angeles, CA, September 16, 2010.

4. Allan Shaw, interview with the author, Scottsdale, AZ, August 5, 2009.

5. Don McLean, interview with author, Camden, ME, April 23, 2009.

6. McLean, interview with the author.

7. Tom Drake, "Kingston Place Forum," February 5, 2005, www.kingstontrioplace.com.

8. McLean, interview with the author.

9. Shane, interview with the author, April 6, 2009.

10. Bob Shane, interview with the author, Phoenix, AZ, January 15, 2010.

11. Dave Guard interview with Elizabeth Wilson, *The Kingston Trio on Record: The Dave Interview* (Naperville, IL: Kingston Korner, Inc.. 1986), 55.

12. Dave Guard, interview with the author, Los Altos, CA, November 28, 1983.

13. Nick Reynolds, interview with the author, Seminole, FL, October 4, 1986.

14. Guard, interview with the author, November 28, 1983.

15. Lou Gottlieb, interview with Ronald D. Cohen, San Francisco, CA, July 19, 1955.

16. Gottlieb, interview with Cohen.

17. Guard, interview with the author, November 28, 1983.

18. Guard, interview with the author, November 28, 1983.

19. Gottlieb, interview with Cohen.

20. Nick Reynolds, interview with the author, Seminole, FL, October 6, 1986.

21. Guard, interview with the author, November 28, 1983.

22. Guard, interview with the author, November 28, 1983.

23. Reynolds, interview with the author, October 6, 1986.

24. Bob Shane, phone interview with the author, October 21, 2007.

25. Bob Shane, interview with the author, Phoenix, AZ, April 9, 2009.

26. Reynolds, interview with the author, October 6, 1986.

27. Reynolds, interview with the author, October 6, 1986.

28. Archie Green, *Only A Miner: Studies in Recorded Coal-Mining Songs* (Urbana: University of Illinois Press, 1972), 234.

29. Reynolds, interview with the author, October 6, 1986.

30. Shane, interview with the author, April 7, 2009.

31. Nick Reynolds, interview with the author, Seminole, FL, October 7, 1986.

32. Nick Reynolds, interview with the author, Port Orford, OR, November 11, 1983.

33. Reynolds, interview with the author, October 7, 1986.

34. Reynolds, interview with the author, October 7, 1986.

35. Pete Seeger, interview with the author, Beacon, NY, August 31, 2008.

36. Nick Reynolds, interview with the author, Seminole, FL, October 5, 1986.

37. Dave Guard, interview with the author, Los Altos, CA, November 29, 1983.

38. Guard, interview with the author, November 28, 1983.

39. Bob Shane, conversation with the author, fall 2007.

40. Nick Reynolds, "Fun with the Trio in the Studio," *The Lost 1967 Kingston Trio Album: Rarities Volume 1*, Collectors' Choice Music, 2007.

41. Reynolds, interview with the author, October 5, 1986.

42. Shane, interview with the author, October 21, 2007.

43. John Stewart, interview with the author, Malibu, CA, March 4, 2004.

44. John Stewart, interview with the author, Novato, CA, April 6, 2001.

45. Nick Reynolds, interview with the author, Seminole, FL, October 8, 1986.

46. Shane, interview with the author, April 6, 2009.

47. Shane, interview with the author, October 21, 2007.

48. Nick Reynolds, interview with the author, Seminole, FL, October 8, 1986.

49. Shane, interview with the author, October 21, 2007.

50. Reynolds, interview with the author, October 8, 1986.

51. Stewart, interview with the author, March 4, 1984.

52. Stewart, interview with the author, March 4, 1984.

53. Reynolds, interview with the author, October 8, 1986.

54. Shane, interview with the author, April 6, 2009.

55. Shane, interview with the author, April 6, 2009.

56. Shane, interview with the author, April 6, 2009.

57. John Stewart, interview with the author, Novato, CA, April 7, 2001.

58. Reynolds, interview with the author, October 8, 1986.

59. Stewart, interview with the author, March 4, 1984.

60. Stewart, interview with the author, March 4, 1984.

61. Stewart, interview with the author, April 6, 2001.

62. Reynolds, interview with the author, October 5, 1986.

63. Reynolds, interview with the author, October 8, 1986.

64. Shane, interview with the author, October 21, 2007.

65. Stewart, interview with the author, March 4, 1984.

66. Stewart, interview with the author, March 4, 1984.

67. Don MacArthur, interview with the author, Novato, CA, February 12, 2010; Stewart, interview with the author, April 7, 2001.

68. MacArthur, interview with the author.

69. Stewart, interview with the author, March 4, 1984.

70. Stewart, interview with the author, April 7, 2001.

71. Stewart, interview with the author, March 4, 1984.

72. Stewart, interview with the author, March 4, 1984.

73. Shane, interview with the author, April 7, 2009.

74. Reynolds, interview with the author, November 11, 1983.

75. Nick Reynolds, conversation with author, Port Orford, OR, 1983.

76. Stewart, interview with the author, April 7, 2001.

77. Reynolds, interview with the author, October 7, 1986.

78. Voyle Gilmore, interview with Richard Johnston, Ethel Island, CA, January 26, 1973, from the Dave Guard and Richard Johnston Kingston Trio collection of materials, 1956–1986, University Manuscript Collections, University of Wisconsin, Milwaukee.

79. Reynolds, interview with the author, November 11, 1983.

80. Frank Werber, interviews with Richard Johnston, Sausalito, CA, January 17 and 23, 1974, from the Dave Guard and Richard Johnston Kingston Trio collection of materials, 1956–1986, University Manuscript Collections, University of Wisconsin, Milwaukee.

81. Stewart, interview with the author, March 4, 1984.

82. Reynolds, interview with the author, November 11, 1983.

83. Frank Werber, interview with the author, Silver City, NM, April 17, 1984.

84. George Yanok, interview with the author, Nashville, TN, October 26, 2003.

85. Mary Katherine Aldin, *The Kingston Trio, Live at Newport*, Liner Notes (Vanguard Records Newport Folk Festival Classics, October, 1994).

13

STILL AT LARGE

"We never wanted to be the Mills Brothers of folk music," Nick Reynolds said when asked why The Kingston Trio were calling it quits after ten years, a thousand plus concerts and millions of records sold. Their final appearance was on June 17, 1967, on the very stage that helped launch it all, the hungry i in San Francisco.[1]

It had been an exhilarating ride. They had changed not only the course of popular music, but the course of people's thinking and doing and looking and listening. There was probably not an area of American pop culture that was not touched in some way, directly or otherwise, by The Kingston Trio. With the addition of John Stewart in 1961, the Trio survived the loss of Dave Guard, and for six more years they prevailed—and in some years prospered greatly—before complacency and changing musical tastes eroded their edge.

"Peter, Paul and Mary came along and became politically relevant, and Dylan came along and of course, The Beatles," Stewart recalled. "I said, 'Holy shit! This thing is changing!' And I started working harder than ever. And the harder I worked, the more resistance I got to the point of saying, 'Don't you see? We've got to make a change here. We've got to do something.' I really wanted to be a part of that. I was writing protest songs and I went to the Selma march and the country was changing and I was changing and the group wasn't. And I think the way that Bob and Nick reacted to other groups taking over was to do other things, like auto racing and skeet shooting, rather than attack the problem. That was the beginning of the end. I said, 'I've got to get out of here. I've got to leave.' Gave them a year's notice and at that point Nick said, 'Well I've been doing this ten years, I wanna go, too'—he knew about Oregon and had been up there and he just wanted to go and be a person again."[2]

By this time, Frank Werber had diversified Trident Productions, managing and producing the We Five, who in 1965 had a huge hit with Sylvia Tyson's "You Were on My Mind," as well as The Sons of Champlin and a few other early San Francisco counter-culture rock groups. Werber had also created and managed the Trident Restaurant on the Sausalito waterfront, one of the country's original "fern bars" and the Bay Area's best avant-garde jazz venue. As far as Werber was concerned, the Trio had been on automatic pilot for some time and finally the end was inevitable. In April of 1966, Shane, Reynolds, Stewart, and Werber met at Columbus Tower and mutually agreed to disband The Kingston Trio in one year, milking as much money from "farewell" concerts and club dates as possible.

Shane was supposedly the one dissenting vote to disband the Trio, a point he flatly denies, saying that he too was ready to move on, preferring that the Trio disband on its own terms rather than being edged out by a changing market. "We saw it coming with The Beatles," he said, "and we all agreed it was time."[3] He would remain in the music business, first as a single, then in a duo, and finally forming another trio. Shane was first and foremost an *entertainer*. He would sing and play as long and as passionately to ten people for free as he would to a packed stadium for fifty thousand dollars. He couldn't have cared less if Peter, Paul and Mary or Bob Dylan were becoming more relevant than The Kingston Trio. The Trio would always be relevant to *him*—and to a sizable portion of the public, as he correctly reasoned.

When the Trio disbanded in June 1967, Shane stayed at Decca as a solo artist, recording two singles for the label in Nashville. One song, "Honey," was written and produced specifically for him by Bobby Russell and released as a single in two test markets. But it went no further, and Decca elected not to release it nationally. He was also offered "Little Green Apples," another song written by Russell, but Shane declined to record it. Both songs became monster hits for Bobby Goldsboro and O. C. Smith, respectively. Shane didn't like working as a solo and had not done so since playing clubs in Hawaii in 1957, preferring to sing as a duo or a trio instead. For a short period he teamed up with Travis Edmondson as Shane and Travis, playing the hungry i and a few other clubs. He then decided to re-form The Kingston Trio with new members, which required approval from Werber and Reynolds, his partners in Kingston Trio, Inc. But it wouldn't be without considerable cost.

Werber had no desire to manage another Kingston Trio, and Reynolds had no intention of going back on the road, so the two agreed to lease the name to Shane providing his group was "worthy to bear the title."

What's more, the word *New* was to be added to the name *Kingston Trio* so that there would be a clear delineation between the old and new groups and, more pointedly, assure that The New Kingston Trio would not be mistaken as either the Guard or the Stewart version of The Kingston Trio. To many long-time fans of The Kingston Trio it was a critical distinction that could impact attendance. Earlier, Shane had formed a trio with banjoist Mike Heard and guitarist Dave Peel that he called The Shane Gang. Heard was replaced by banjoist/songwriter Jim Connor ("Grandma's Feather Bed"), and Peel by guitarist/vocalist Pat Horine in a group with Shane, which in 1968 became The New Kingston Trio.

Connor and Horine were talented, versatile musicians and vocalists, and blended well with Shane. Of the early "after groups," this was perhaps one of the best, although none really had the pure acoustic sound since Shane added drums (Frank Sanchez) and electric bass (Frank Passantino and Stan Kaess) backing. The group briefly recorded for Capitol Records, which issued only one 45, but not the album the Trio had anticipated. After Capitol declined to release an album, Shane negotiated a deal with the Longines Symphonette Society to release an excellent ten-song album by The New Kingston Trio entitled *The World Needs a Melody*. This was used by Longines as a promotional inducement for a ten-LP, sixty-four-song boxed set of Kingston Trio recordings from Capitol entitled *American Gold*. Shane had issues with Connor and Horine, and in 1973 replaced them with two "new folk"—North Carolinian Roger Gambill and Bill Zorn from Phoenix, Arizona. Both were experienced in the folk genre, Gambill with his own duo, Gambill and Moore, and Zorn fresh out of The New Christy Minstrels. Zorn, who played banjo in the Trio, remained with the group until 1976 when he moved to England, where he worked with his brother in various musical enterprises for the next twenty years. He was succeeded by George Grove, a veteran Nashville session player, Opryland musician, and studio manager, then based in Newport News, Virginia.

Also in 1976, Shane finally became the sole owner of The Kingston Trio name—and it too didn't come cheap. In addition to swapping his Kingston Trio, Inc., stock, he gave up all future record royalties from The Kingston Trio's substantial catalog of albums and singles, on most of which he sang lead vocals. Shane has never disclosed the price, but whatever it was, it was apparently worth it. Attendance picked up immediately. Roger Gambill was a fine guitarist, a wonderful and versatile vocalist, and a consummate comedian, different from but very much on par with Dave Guard and John Stewart. Sadly, Gambill died of a heart attack in 1985 at the age of forty-five, and Bob Haworth of The Brothers Four took his place in the Trio. Three years later, Haworth left the Trio to pursue other musical interests and something truly unexpected happened—Nick Reynolds re-joined The Kingston Trio after a twenty-two-year absence.

At the time Reynolds was semiretired and had moved back to Coronado, California, his hometown. Shane and Grove were determined to bring Nick back into the fold, and he quickly accepted the offer. Reynolds said that over the years he had missed the camaraderie of the Trio and had occasionally performed as a duo with John Stewart, even recording an album together, *Revenge of the Budgie*, in 1983. "It took me about fifteen minutes to feel comfortable singing with the Trio again," Reynolds said.[4]

As far as Shane was concerned, Reynolds's return was absolutely no different than when Stewart had replaced Guard. The Trio now had two of its founding members, with the third, George Grove, the second-longest tenured member of The Kingston Trio next to Shane. And for the next ten years it really was like the good old days until Nick retired for the second and final time in 1999 and Bobby Haworth rejoined the group for five years. Then, in March 2004, Shane suffered a heart attack, and though he recovered, his performing days were over. Bill Zorn then stepped back into the group, joined a year later by Rick Dougherty, formerly of The Limeliters, who replaced Haworth. This group—Grove, Zorn, and Dougherty—continued as The Kingston Trio and today perform to enthusiastic audiences nightly. Bob Shane is their mentor and manager, and occasionally makes guest appearances with them whenever they perform in reasonable proximity to his home.

There are many long-time Kingston Trio fans who still consider only the Guard era Trio or the Stewart era Trio as the *real* Kingston Trio, with any other configuration nothing more than a "tribute group." But the Grove, Zorn, Dougherty Trio is different, technically and historically.

Both Zorn and Grove were members of the group when it included Bob Shane, one of the founding members of The Kingston Trio and the Trio's lead singer at that. What's more, George Grove was in the group when Nick Reynolds, also a founding member of the Trio, rejoined Shane as The Kingston Trio and sang with Bob and George for ten years. In total, Grove has spent over thirty-six years as a member of The Kingston Trio, and he was a huge fan of the group long before that.

As ex-Journeymen Dick Weissman put it, "The group slogs on without any of the original members, although banjoist George Grove has been a replacement so long he is practically an original."[5]

Moreover, this Kingston Trio is more faithful, instrumentally, to the original. With the exception of Paul Gabrielson's electric stand-up bass, it's all acoustic—Martin dreadnoughts and tenor guitars and long neck banjos.

Vocally, it's the same division: Bill Zorn sings lead, Rick Dougherty sings tenor, and George takes "the magic notes" or, as Dave Guard used to call them, "the joker parts"—whatever's left on the top, bottom, or in-between. "We are three very different voices," said Grove, "and we had to find our own way."[6]

George Grove is a classically trained orchestral musician, a graduate of Wake Forest University, and holds a master of music degree in jazz composition from the University of Las Vegas. He writes music and arranges Trio songs for performing with various symphony orchestras.

Bill Zorn has been a professional singer, songwriter, musician, actor, comedian, voice-over talent, producer, and member of The New Christy Minstrels, The Kingston Trio, and The Limeliters. He has toured extensively throughout the United States, the United Kingdom, Europe, and the Far East. In 1979, he and his brother had a top ten hit, "Car 67."

Rick Dougherty has toured throughout the United States as a solo folk singer and guitarist as well as a member of The Limeliters, The Kingston Trio, and The Folk Reunion. He holds a degree in music and is an accomplished opera stage director, including directing forty operas for small opera companies.

Considering Zorn's history with Bob Shane and Grove's with Shane and Reynolds, today's group is a proper *evolution* of The Kingston Trio. "We're the ones that continue to keep the lights burning," said Grove.[7] John Stewart was charged with the same daunting task, and years later remembered it with amazement.

"A few weeks ago, I sat down and watched all The Kingston Trio TV appearances on shows from 1959 up to the last Andy Williams Show," Stewart said. "And I watched the transition from Dave, and all of a sudden I was looking at a clip of the Trio on the Bell Telephone Hour—and *I* was in the group. I was just twenty-one and I was scared to death. I was gawky and my ears were sticking out, and you know, this is strange to admit, but it's the first time it really hit me: 'My God! I was one of The Kingston Trio!'"[8]

❦

Donald David Guard passed away on March 22, 1991, at his home in Rollingsford, New Hampshire, from lymphatic cancer. He was fifty-seven years old.

Nicholas Welles Reynolds died on October 1, 2008, of acute respiratory disease at Sharp Memorial Hospital in San Diego, California. He was seventy-five years old.

John Coburn Stewart died on January 19, 2008, at Mercy Hospital in San Diego, California, after suffering a brain aneurism. It was the same hospital in which both he and Nick Reynolds were born. He was sixty-eight years old.

Frank Nicholas Werber died of heart failure in Silver City, New Mexico, on May 19, 2008. He was seventy-nine years old. He was buried on his ranch.

David "Buck" Wheat died in his sleep in Los Angeles, California, in 1985. He was sixty-three.

Voyle Gilmore passed away on December 19, 1979. He was sixty-seven.

NOTES

1. Nick Reynolds, interview with author, Port Orford, OR, November 11, 1986.

2. John Stewart, interview with the author, San Francisco, CA, December 3, 1983.

3. Bob Shane, interview with the author, Phoenix, AZ, April 15, 2012.

4. Nick Reynolds, press release upon rejoining The Kingston Trio, 1989.

5. Dick Weissman, *Which Side Are You On? An Inside History of the Folk Music Revival in America* (New York: Continuum, 2005), 263.

6. George Grove, interview with the author, Las Vegas, NV, April 2012.

7. George Grove, phone interview with the author, April 2012.

8. John Stewart, interview with the author, Malibu, CA, March 4, 1984.

BIBLIOGRAPHY

Baez, Joan. *And a Voice to Sing With: A Memoir.* New York: Simon & Schuster, 1986.

Bayless, James W. "Innovations in Studio Design and Construction in the Capitol Tower Recording Studios." *Journal of the Audio Engineering Society*, April 1957.

Blake, Benjamin, Jack Rubec, and Allan Shaw. *The Kingston Trio on Record.* Naperville, IL: Kingston Korner, 1986.

Brand, Oscar. *The Ballad Mongers: Rise of the Modern Folk Song.* New York: Funk & Wagnalls, 1962.

Cohen, Ronald D. *Rainbow Quest: The Folk Music Revival and American Society, 1940–1970.* Amherst: University of Massachusetts Press, 2002.

Collins, Judy. *Sweet Judy Blue Eyes: My Life in Music.* New York: Crown Archetype, 2011.

Dylan, Bob. *Chronicles.* Vol. 1. New York: Simon & Schuster, 2004.

Dylan, Bob. *Dylan on Dylan.* Edited by Jonathan Cott. London: Hodder & Stoughton, 2006.

Gahr, David. *The Face of Folk Music.* Photographs by David Gahr. Text by Robert Shelton. New York: Citadel Press, 1968.

Granata, Charles L. *Sessions with Sinatra: Frank Sinatra and the Art of Recording.* Chicago: A Cappella Press, 1999.

Green, Archie. *Only a Miner: Studies in Recorded Coal-Mining Songs.* Urbana: University of Illinois Press, 1972.

Green, Paul. *Capitol Records Fiftieth Anniversary, 1942–1992.* Hollywood, CA: Capitol Records, 1992.

Hood, Phil, ed. *Artists of American Folk Music: The Legends of Traditional Folk, the Stars of the Sixties, the Virtuosi of New Acoustic Music.* New York: William Morrow, 1986.

Lankford, Ronald D., Jr. *Folk Music USA: The Changing Voice of Protest.* New York: Schirmer Trade Books, 2005.

Phillips, John. *Papa John: A Music Legend's Shattering Journey through Sex, Drugs, and Rock 'n' Roll.* Garden City, NY: Dolphin-Doubleday, 1986.

Pollock, Bruce. "Dave Guard: The Kingston Trio." In *When Rock Was Young*, 131–43. New York: Holt, Rinehart and Winston, 1981.

Wein, George. *Myself among Others: A Life in Music.* Cambridge, MA: Da Capo Press, 2003.

Weissman, Dick. *Which Side Are You On? An Inside History of the Folk Music Revival in America.* New York: Continuum, 2005.

Whitburn, Joel. *The Billboard Book of Top 40 Hits: 1955–2009.* New York: Billboard Books/Crown Publishing, 2010.

INDEX

Note: "KT" refers to The Kingston Trio; "PS" refers to the photospread.

Kaess, Stan, 257

Kameron, Pete, 151

"Karu," 223–24

Kazan, Elia, 214

Keaton, Buster, 173

"The Keeper," 214

Kennedy, John F., 115, 183–84, 229–30, 235–36

Kennedy, Robert, 183, 229

Kent, Edward, 23

Kenton, Stan, 6, 187

Kerouac, Jack, 51

Kingsley, Al, 99, 101

Kingston Quartet, 46, 59, 63

Kingston Trio, *PS*; appeal of, xiii, xv, 56–57, 69, 102, 129–30, 173, 196–97, 199; appearance of, xiii, xv, 45, 60, 84, 111–12; awards and honors received by, xiii–xiv, 162; breakup of, 119–37, 159–62, 220; commercial ventures of, 172–74; comparison of versions of, 160, 162–63, 166, 222, 258–59; criticisms of, xv, 5, 60, 108, 170, 175–78, 181, 202, 243; current version of, 256–59; earnings of, 66, 90, 98, 112–13, 120–21; final performance of original, 133–34; impact of, xiii–xv, xvii, 60, 169–72, 181–82, 199–201, 255; interpersonal dynamics of, xii–xiii, xvi, 30–31, 54–55, 69, 91, 114, 119–38, 149, 154, 165–66, 220, 246; musical influences on, 5–7, 28–29, 60–62, 70, 170; musicianship in, xvi–xvii, 70–72; name of, xv, 59, 120, 131, 156, 256–57; on-stage banter/commentary of, 60, 134, 182–83; origins of, xi, 39, 41–42, 56, 170; and politics, 11, 60, 170, 180–84, 209, 233, 236; popularity of, 72, 92, 98, 102, 113, 174, 243, 248;

recording sessions of, 75–78; record sales of, xiii–xiv, 162; rehearsals of, 58–59, 85, 208, 251; repertoire of, xvi, 5, 165, 169, 175–76, 195, 202, 205, 207, 210–12, 250; song arrangements for, xvi, xvii, 7, 120, 132, 153–54, 192, 195–96, 218, 230, 259; Stewart and, before becoming a member, 147–50

The Kingston Trio (T996) (album), 76–77, 87, 90, 97, 190, 203, 208

Kingston Trio, Inc., 57, 124, 128, 131–33, 141–42, 159, 256–57

The Kingston Trio: Nick-Bob-John (album), 240–41, 248

"The Kingston Trio and Friends Reunion" (television special), 134

The Kingston Trio Live at Newport (album), 248

The Kingston Trio Live at the Santa Monica Civic Auditorium (album), 249

The Kingston Trio #16 (album), 163, 211, 232–34, 247

The Kingston Trio on Record (discography), 201

The Kingston Trio on Tour (television special), 128

Kitt, Eartha, 84

Knight, Ted, 164

Kohler, Julie, 151–52, 155

Kraft Music Hall (television show), 99

Kral, Roy, 77, 124

Lambert, Hendricks and Ross (vocalese trio), 82

"The Land of Milk and Honey," 241

"Laredo," 226

Larson, Rex, 243

Last Month of the Year, 217–19

"Last Month of the Year," 218

"Last Night I Had the Strangest Dream," 237

ABOUT THE AUTHOR

William J. Bush is a music journalist whose articles have appeared in *Acoustic Guitar, Guitar Player, Frets, Flatpicking Guitar, Pennsylvania Heritage, The Sounding Board* (Martin Guitar Company newsletter), *The Guitar Player Book,* and *Artists of American Folk Music.* He has also written for EMI/Capitol Records, Folk Era Records, Bear Family Records, and Shout! Factory (Sony). In 2006, he appeared in the PBS documentary *The Kingston Trio: Wherever We May Go.*